D0427061

BRITISH FOREIGN SECRETARIES
1807–1916

BRITISH FOREIGN SECRETARIES

1807-1916

STUDIES IN PERSONALITY AND POLICY

BY

ALGERNON CECIL

KENNIKAT PRESS
Port Washington, N. Y./London

BRITISH FOREIGN SECRETARIES

First published in 1927
Reissued in 1971 by Kennikat Press
Library of Congress Catalog Card No: 70-118463
ISBN 0-8046-1212-9

Manufactured by Taylor Publishing Company   Dailas, Texas

PREFACE

SOME years ago I tried to sketch the development of the organisation and administration of the Foreign Office in the concluding chapter of the *Cambridge History of British Foreign Policy*. The present volume is an attempt to visualise the leading characters in Foreign Office history—to see what manner of men they were, and what they made of the Foreign Secretariat. The book, if I have done my work properly, should serve as a modest introduction to the study of British diplomacy in recent times, for the story is carried forward from one figure to the next with as much continuity as the biographical treatment permits of. It is open, indeed, to the reader to complain that there are gaps among the figures as also inevitably in the narrative of events. Certain Foreign Secretaries, such as Wellesley and Iddesleigh, receive no notice; others like Malmesbury almost no notice; and one at any rate—Lord Lansdowne—very inadequate notice. To such charges I must plead guilty, only observing that art does not grow less long for all the toil of scholars and students, nor life seem less short for all the skill of doctors and surgeons.

Even apart from the omissions confessed, these studies do not succeed in covering the whole administrative history of the Foreign Office from its inception in 1782. They start, roughly speaking, where the seeds of the Grand Alliance against Napoleon were sown, and they end before the fruits of the Great War of 1914 were gathered. For this late beginning, as for the date of the conclusion, a reason, distinct from the obvious biographical one suggested by the careers of Canning, Castlereagh, and Lord Grey, can be given. During almost the whole of the first twenty-five years of his constitutional existence the individuality of the Secretary of State for Foreign Affairs, and therefore of the Foreign Office, was overshadowed by that of the Prime Minister. This was due to three circumstances in particular—that none of the earlier Foreign Secretaries, with the exception of Fox, were, as such, men of much account; that Grenville, who was perhaps the ablest of them, was mostly in power during a war which attracted the best energies of the Prime Minister into the sphere of foreign affairs; and, last but not least, that the Prime Minister himself was, except for a short interval, none other than William Pitt. This book might, therefore, be said, with no more than trivial inaccuracy, to take its start as the Foreign Office emerges from the shadow cast by Pitt's greatness and to take its leave as the Foreign Office disappears again into the whirlpool of Mr Lloyd George's versatility.

Had it deserved a device, I should like to think that *"tout comprendre c'est tout pardonner"* would have been appropriate. True up to a point even in domestic relationships both public and private, the aphorism seems to me so much the more true in the international sphere that foreign affairs are immeasurably more complicated and that the conflict of opposing or apparently opposing interests has a patriotic rather than a personal or party character. *"Tout comprendre,"* perhaps we might say, *"c'est beaucoup pardonner."* I hope, at any rate, that I have succeeded, so far as in me lies, in writing *sine ira et studio* about the recent as well as the distant past, even though I have not understood this to signify, any more than Tacitus did, uncertainty of standpoint or tepidity of opinion. I should be sorry, indeed, if anyone supposed that I thought that the old notion of a balance of power was of equal worth with that of "Areopagus," or that the dashing diplomacy of Palmerston compared favourably in value with the goodwill pregnant with sympathy, the quietness engendering confidence, the patience consummated in peace that distinguished the diplomatic work of Aberdeen. But of these things enough is said further forward.

For the rest, I have especially to thank my old and, if I may say so, very distinguished friend, Dr G. P. Gooch, for much friendly interest, generous aid, and invaluable advice, and Mr Kenneth Bell, Fellow of Balliol College, Oxford, for most kindly reading through and criticising the proof-sheets. I have incurred other debts which I am as little able to repay. I take, however, this opportunity of thanking certain friends and kinsfolk for their help—Lord Stanmore for the loan of certain papers relating to his grandfather, Lord Aberdeen; Mr Herbert Fisher, Warden of New College, Lord Cecil of Chelwood and Lady Gwendolen Cecil for some valuable suggestions and criticisms; and, last but not least, my wife for her help with the final revise. It is probably unnecessary to add that none of the above must be held to be responsible for any opinions that I have expressed.

I should like to add a word of very sincere thanks to the publishers of the book for their invariable courtesy, helpfulness, and consideration.

January 1927.

CONTENTS

ix

CONTENTS

I

CASTLEREAGH

[ROBERT STEWART, VISCOUNT CASTLEREAGH.—Born 1769.
Foreign Secretary, 1812–1822. Succeeded his father as 2nd
Marquis of Londonderry, 1821. Died 1822.]

CASTLEREAGH

In the drama of individual life two elements combine to make the play—the elements, as we are accustomed to call them, of character and circumstance. Political drama duplicates the first of these and shows us on the stage of domestic politics three forces in interaction—personal character, national character, and the opportunities afforded to or limitations imposed upon their development by time and place. Another factor has to be reckoned with in any just appreciation of foreign policy. The scholar needs to perceive, the historian to show, not as if it were merely part and parcel of the environment, but as a larger manifestation of human will and solidarity, the complex entity of international civilisation. This elusive, indeterminate force, compounded as it is of many national constituents, imperfectly assimilated the one to the other, makes of the treatment of foreign affairs in some respects the most difficult of literary enterprises. Here for the research student is a maze more intricate than any other; a jig-saw puzzle where the pieces perpetually fail to fit; a forest where the wood is for ever vanishing behind the trees. Here for the historian is a stage wide as the world itself: here, if he can but once raise the drab curtain of parchment and protocol, lie the elements of drama on the grandest scale: here he can see the forces of wisdom and destiny locked in a large embrace, and here experience the rarefied, intoxicating atmosphere of courts and kings : here, too, the players seem more brilliant and more subtle, the play more momentous, more pregnant with good and evil, than in the provincial theatre of home affairs. What statesman of high imagination has not wished to cut a figure upon these footboards? Would not even Disraeli's career have seemed wanting in dramatic climax without that last display of rant and posture at Berlin? Or what Foreign Minister has ever coveted another office? Even Aberdeen, sad old Scotsman as he was, dispassionate and other-worldly to the last point compatible with taking any interest at all in the business of the State, is no exception to this rule. "He is just like Palmerston (and I suppose everyone else who has been Foreign Minister)," observes Clarendon, himself no eager candidate for office, "in caring about foreign affairs more than anything else." [1]

Let this be as it may, the primacy of the Foreign Department over all other departments, in spite of the fact that the Home Secretary ranks as senior to the Foreign Secretary, emerges, like an article of the Constitution, in the doctrine that foreign business is in some peculiar sense the concern of the Cabinet as a whole, and in the idea, so inconsiderately pressed by Lord John Russell and in a kind of way reasserted by the appointment as Foreign Secretary of Mr Balfour in 1916,[2] that the Foreign Office is the only departmental position really compatible with the dignity of an ex-Prime Minister. Another consideration seems to vindicate this view of its prestige. To a degree not to be matched, except in the case of Prime Ministers, or possibly in that of Lord Chancellors, British Foreign Secretaries enjoy the reward of remembrance. Home Secretaries, War Secretaries, Colonial Secretaries, Irish Secretaries, Indian Secretaries, Presidents of the Boards of Trade and Education—how many of these are remembered? One here, another there! A Cardwell, a Chamberlain, a Macaulay, or a Morley—in each office one of its chiefs in half a century or more, and that rather for sheer force of personality than for discharge of business! But at the Foreign Office so many Secretaries have been remembered that the Premiership itself hardly seems able to give its holders a better title to be praised amongst famous men. We may see this not obscurely as we examine the careers whose course is traced in the pages of this book. Castlereagh is never Prime Minister, yet stands out upon the frieze of time a larger man than Liverpool. Canning becomes the head of an administration but only for a fleeting moment: his Premiership enshrines his tragedy, his

---

[1] Maxwell, *Life of the Fourth Earl of Clarendon*, ii. 151.

[2] He had been, it is true, First Lord of the Admiralty in the Asquith Coalition Government, but the point is that, as soon as the retirement of Lord Grey had created a vacancy, the ex-Prime Minister gravitated to the Foreign Office. The Lord Presidency of the Council and the office of Lord Privy Seal cannot be treated as departmental in the ordinary sense of the word and do not therefore come into consideration.

Foreign Secretaryship makes his reputation. Aberdeen's name also is inscribed on the roll of Prime Ministers, but all his merit is due to his diplomatic record. Palmerston's prestige is based for the most part upon his connection with foreign affairs and his famous defence of his proceedings as Foreign Minister. And, if Clarendon and Granville incontestably look slight beside so famous a chief as Gladstone, it is by virtue of the efficiency of his work as Foreign Secretary that Lord Rosebery escapes the reproach of being great in word but not in power, and for the dexterity of his foreign administration that Salisbury stands out a head and shoulders above his fellows. The last study in this book offers perhaps the finest illustration of the thesis under consideration. No one can doubt the greater range and measure of Lord Oxford's political talent in comparison with Lord Grey's, yet, when it comes to an estimate of the influence of the one man and of the other in bringing Great Britain into the greatest war in history it may well be that Lord Grey will seem to have filled the more important rôle.

The Foreign Office is, at least, the equal in opportunity of any post that an Englishman can hold, and of the Foreign Secretary it may truthfully be said that the world is his occasion. If rhetoric and alliteration were more in vogue, we might say that he holds the happiness of forty million—or perhaps more truly of four hundred million—people within the hollow of his hand; can take, as chance decrees, from one his life, from another his child, from a third all the vigour of his manhood, from a fourth his fortune, from a fifth his career, almost, as Providence does, in the twinkling of an eye, just by the composition of an ill-conceived despatch, by some show of weakness here or of obstinacy there, by a misreading of the signs of the times, by lack of policy or from neglect of diplomacy. The Foreign Office must, in short, be reckoned the most anxious appointment that a Prime Minister has to make; and it is no great wonder that Salisbury, whether or not he really made the characteristic remark attributed to him that there were only two offices in the Empire beyond the power of good average ability adequately to fill, solved the difficulty of selection by taking both the offices in question into his own hands and combining the Foreign Department with the Premiership. The wonder is rather that no Prime Minister had done this before and that only one Prime Minister has done it since. Not, however, that such pluralism is necessarily good, or even in close harmony with the system of checks and balances inherent in the Constitution, but that there is no post where more certainly than at the Foreign Office an unskilful minister can quickly bring about a world of woe.

For the rest the Foreign Secretary stands in a special relationship to the Crown and to the Country. The political influence of the Sovereign lasted in foreign affairs, as may be seen from Queen Victoria's Letters, far longer than it lasted elsewhere, and might perhaps still retain a certain importance if the war had not brought to the ground the great despotic monarchies of Europe. Even yet any British King can, at will, become, not indeed his own foreign minister, but the first and best diplomatist in the nation's service. A more subtle understanding connects the Foreign Secretary with the Country. The custom of the Constitution long prescribed, if it does not still prescribe, that, an outgoing minister should give his successor all the information and assistance in his power. A continuity of policy in the administration of foreign affairs, without parallel in other departments, is thus established; and the Foreign Secretary is under a very special obligation to appear as the trustee of the nation as a whole. For this reason his credentials are of unusual importance. In no contemptible sense he must be able to face both ways, to look inwards into England, so that he may show his countrymen that he is a man like-minded with, if also larger-minded than themselves, and then outwards over Europe, and again towards America, envisaging all questions without partiality or hypocrisy, in the grand manner of one to whom the first and last end of diplomacy is peace and to whom all the friends of peace are by virtue of that name alone the friends of England.

Not every Foreign Secretary has been able to do even the latter of these things; and not all have attempted to do the former. Castlereagh was the first to make a remembered effort to do them both. Yet, though the Foreign Office was but thirty years old when he took it over in 1812, there had been two men of greater brilliancy there before him. There had been Fox, who was Foreign Secretary only just long enough to show how efficient he might have proved if time and opportunity had been given him. And there had been Canning. But Canning's triumphs are to be found not in the two years' administration which eventuated in his duel with Castlereagh, but in the period after Castlereagh him-self had passed away and Castlereagh's policy had fallen, not much to its advantage, into his keeping,   It was, however, from neither of these that Castlereagh learned diplomacy.   Another and a loftier spirit formed his model.   Pitt, though he neither called the Foreign Office into being, nor held its seals, stands in the background of its story, casting the magic of his mantle for the next fifty years and more over its representative men.   Castle-reagh, Canning, and Aberdeen all knew him personally—gradu-ated, so to speak, in his school, and took from him, each of them, such things as the lesser may borrow from the larger mind.   At a later date Lord Rosebery, an artist in search of a hero and an actor in love with a part, saw him with the halo of history round his head, painted him in the fresh colours of a vivid style, and, himself still young, showed him to us who were younger, not as a party leader nor simply as a patriot soul, but as the pure spirit of England walking the floor at Westminster, as Nelson walked the deck of the *Victory* and Wellington the field of Waterloo.   We might think that a dream, or a canonisation cunningly effected in the absence of the devil's advocate, if Scott had not been before-hand with it and, in four lines of eternal beauty, coined a con-temporary epitaph that makes every other epitaph sound poor and all the promise of posterity seem small.

> " Now is the stately column broke,
>   The beacon-light is quenched in smoke,
>   The trumpet's silver sound is still,
>   The warder silent on the hill."

It was from beneath that broken column, with the smoking beacon and the stillness behind him, that Castlereagh started to work through failure, anxiety, disappointment, amidst good report and evil report, by labour, by courage, by patriotism un-feigned if inarticulate, towards the goal that Pitt had indicated and, so far as the times allowed, pursued.   His own personality suggested none of those symbols that had risen to the poet's imagination at the thought of Pitt.   He was no lofty pillar, no winged fire passing from hill to hill, no clarion rousing an echo in every vale.   But in this lay his greatness, that the things which Pitt's eyes had desired to behold and had not beheld, after long years he accomplished and at the date that Pitt had appointed

for their fulfilment. The disciple is not above his master; yet
to have done with five talents a work well worthy of those
possessed of ten, is not undeserving of high praise.

It was upon men of something less than the highest talent that
Great Britain had to rely in the crisis of the struggle with Napoleon. Pitt left her in 1805, Fox, her earliest Foreign Secretary,
properly so-called, in 1806. As the famous prelude, already
cited, reminds us, it was as if demi-gods had been taken away in
the hour of sorest need. For

" . . . ne'er held marble in its trust
Of two such wondrous men the dust.
With more than mortal powers endowed
How high they soared above the crowd !

Theirs was no common party race,
Jostling by dark intrigue for place ;
Like fabled Gods, their mighty war
Shook realms and nations in its jar ;
Beneath each banner proud to stand,
Look'd up the noblest of the land,
Till through the British world were known
The names of Pitt and Fox alone."

In the year in which those words were written Castlereagh
launched the enterprise of the Peninsular War and discovered
the genius of Wellington. In the same year the Emperor of the
French, with all the Continent paying him court, touched at
Erfurt the summit of his career. Five years later Castlereagh
had welded together the coalition that drove Napoleon back
into France; six years later he had made him an exile in Elba;
seven years later he had shut him up for ever within the prison
of St Helena. No British Foreign Secretary has ever initiated,
carried on, and completed so great a work. Yet, though it was
the greatest achievement in Castlereagh's career, it was but one
side of his endeavour. He restored peace in his time but
planned a new temple of peace for posterity.

Castlereagh derived something from each of the three ill-
assorted islands that have combined somehow to give us our
empire. On his father's side he was a Stewart, a race not invariably unlucky. The wisest fool in Europe gave lands in Ireland
to these kinsmen of his about the date of his accession to the
throne of England; and in Ireland they prospered, rising gradu-

ally in wealth and consequence, until in the year of the outbreak of the French Revolution, Robert Stewart, a landowner in
Donegal, was made Lord Londonderry. His son, another Robert
and the subject of this study, was then just twenty, having been
born in 1769—in the same year, as some who know how com-
plementary to one another the two men's careers were to prove
may observe with curiosity, as Wellington, and actually on the
very day of June that was nearly a half century later to bear
the impress of Waterloo. On his mother's side, Castlereagh
inherited the blood of the Seymours, and with the blood that
"lofty presence" which Scott noticed as a product of the graceful
Seymour stock.[1] His home at Mount Stewart in Strangford
Lough thus completed the threefold cord that bound him to the
British Isles. It was one of those delicious spots where wood and
water and wild life blended together in dissolving dreams of
beauty. In the study of a life from which poetry is mostly
crowded out and where an imperturbable common sense so generally takes hold of one's attention, we may reasonably pause to
catch a passing glimpse of such clouds of glory—clouds that,
when the child has grown into a man, fade indeed from his path
but yet sometimes gather again, so that we may fancy them, if
we choose, just, so to speak, resting on the horizon beyond that
cottage in a garden at North Cray, with its adjoining menagerie
of birds and beasts, where the weary Minister used to seek refuge
from affairs of State and gratify his great love of flowers.

At Mount Stewart, then, Castlereagh may be said to have
stretched his wings for flight. It was a time when youth was
soon astir and early on its way to fame. With Pitt, Prime
Minister of England at twenty-three, it was no great matter,
perhaps, that Castlereagh was sitting in the Parliament of Ireland
at twenty-one, Keeper of the Privy Seal at twenty-seven, to all
intents and purposes Secretary to the Lord Lieutenant at twenty-
eight, and actually so at twenty-nine. This last post had
attained a great importance by reason of the appalling menace of
the political situation.

Ireland in 1798 had reached one of the major crossways in its
chequered history. Republicanism had slipped across the seas
from France and invasion was following in its wake. The
Presbyterians in the north liked the new revolutionary ideas well

---

[1] *The Journal of Sir Walter Scott* (Douglas, 1890), i. 291.

enough, for these were the logical complement of their religious creed and no bad expression of their thoughts on freedom. Not so the Catholics; though their grievances were clamant, since Catholic Emancipation in Ireland had gone half-way, and just so far as to give the more ignorant of them votes and refuse to the more educated of them the right to stand for Parliament. Wolfe Tone, meanwhile, with his Society of United Irishmen, was hard at work bringing into unholy alliance all who might make an end of the English domination—the French with their eternal hatred of Albion; the Ulstermen with their new-found faith in democracy; and the Catholics with their innocent desire to be treated like decent citizens instead of like suspects, false in faith, and foes to King and Country. Of these enemies of England the last were at once the most important and the most tractable. Concessions such as they later received, if boldly given them then, might have made them good subjects of the House of Hanover; and Fitzwilliam, who was lord-lieutenant for a few hopeful weeks in the beginning of 1795, knew it well. But Pitt and Portland had long halted between two opinions, and when at length they came to a decision it was the worst imaginable. Fitzwilliam, who had better, in the circumstances, have never been appointed, was recalled; and, with his fall, there fell also the hopes of Catholic Emancipation that he had been permitted to excite.

The road was now open for Wolfe Tone; and he struck for national freedom and an Irish republic almost at the moment when Castlereagh took over the work of the Irish Secretaryship from Pelham, who though resident in England still maintained for a year or two longer a nominal control. It was no impossible matter to put the rebellion down, since the Catholic magnates, both lay and spiritual, stood for the most part by the Government; but it was a different matter altogether to blend anew in any tolerable combination the distracted and contending forces in the Island. Castlereagh saw the problem clearly and rested his solution of it upon two considerations—the impossibility of refusing to the Catholics parliamentary representation, and the imprudence of giving it to them in such a way as to give them also a majority. Only the project of a union between the Kingdoms of Great Britain and Ireland met both these points; and to the carrying of an act of union Castlereagh devoted all his powers. No scruple, no sentiment, no fear of a nemesis did he allow to stand in his way. His was the hand that, without recoil or tremor, carried through the vast business of corruption by means of which a bridge, ill-built on bribes and titles, was thrown across the Irish Channel and two peoples were affirmed to be at one who were, in fact, as different as they could be. His was the cynicism that allowed the Irish Catholics to barter the solid reality of a separate legislature against the covert suggestion of a fuller and fairer citizenship. And his, too, was the policy, so passionately denounced when it turned again and rent its promoters, of bringing the priests into politics to assure the passage of the Act of Union.[1] We can say, if we will, in his defence, that, had the Irish only seen their advantage where we see it, and had George III. only suffered Catholic Emancipation to be carried in 1801 instead of leaving it to his son to swallow in 1829, the end might have justified the means; but we may not say that the things he did were but part and parcel of the times and not deserving of reprobation, for Cornwallis, his official chief, was frankly disgusted at them. Sin boldly, says the proverb, if you sin at all. Castlereagh was, after all, perhaps, the better man of the two. He made no pretence of washing his hands, knowing that he was, at least, personally disinterested; and the calmness of his demeanour and the confidence of his speeches showed all the courage of decision and were a great factor in his success. For all that, his methods were unworthy of his large and noble nature.

The truth is that upon the threshold of his career Castlereagh had stumbled against the genius of the coming century without recognising its strength or feeling its appeal. Though in the first flush of manhood he is said to have drunk a toast in honour of the sovereignty of the people and the downfall of the Bastille,[2] he cared nothing for the thought of democracy and never rated the notion of nationality high. To be well-governed was, as he saw things, of much more consequence than political representation, and a wider unit always to be preferred as a guarantee of peace and order to a state circumscribed by natural frontiers or racial sentiments. He thought imperially long before to do so became

---

[1] Lecky, *Hist. of Ireland*, v. (c. xiii.) 328. " In the strange irony of Irish history, few things are more curious than the fact that it was the English Government which persuaded the Catholic priests to take an active part in Irish politics, and to take part in them for the purpose of carrying the legislative union."

[2] Hassall, *Castlereagh*, p. 12.

the fashion, and laboured to make Europe a homogeneous whole when the League of Nations was still a distant dream; but a United Ireland and a United Italy never entered into his philosophy. Thus, in suppressing the Rebellion of 1798, he wished nothing better than to do the work with English troops and to make the need of English domination plain.   All his hope for Ireland was that she might take her part in the prospect of Empire that was spread before his eyes.   "There can be little doubt," he wrote to Sir Lawrence Parsons, whose high-minded and eloquent defence of the Irish Parliament still preserves the best reason of its supporters, "that a Union on fair and liberal principles, effected with the goodwill of both Kingdoms, would strengthen the Empire." [1]   Whether, if the Irish had then received what they had been led to expect in the way of political emancipation, they would have some day entered into the British conception of *imperium et libertas* no one can now pretend to say, for the pitch was queered from the first by the obstinacy of the King.   He had been left by Pitt in an unpardonable ignorance of the vital issue. "What is it this young Lord has brought over, which they are going to throw at my head?" he observed to Dundas with reference to Castlereagh and Catholic Emancipation; "The most Jacobinical thing I ever heard of!" [2]   This was in the beginning of January 1801.   A month later Pitt, conceiving that his honour was involved in the introduction of a measure so nearly promised and so eagerly anticipated, resigned office, and Addington for three years reigned—a *roi fainéant*, if ever there was one—in his stead.

The passage of the Act of Union gave Castlereagh to the British Parliament.   His services had been such that he might, had he wished it, have entered there as an English peer; and, though Pitt and Portland approved his resolution not to press his own or his father's claims, it was conveyed to him that an English peerage lay at his disposal or that of his father or his descendants at any time at which they might desire it.   But, as things turned out, he remained himself till the last year of his life a member of the House of Commons; and it is by the courtesy title which he bore there that he is known to history.   His leader-ship of the Lower House was indeed no mean feature of his career,

---

[1] Castlereagh, *Mems. and Corresp.*, ii. 32.
[2] Hassall, *Castlereagh*, p. 49.

and gave him a prominence as much greater than Liverpool's in the Government as his character and abilities were more remarkable than the Prime Minister's. He spoke without magic of phrase or pride of diction, but in the way that Englishmen have confidence in; with much clumsiness, that is, and mixture of metaphor, as a man will who is feeling his way towards the truth of things and whose eloquence is not in word but in purpose.

For some months after he arrived in England, Castlereagh pressed upon the Addington Administration the desirability of tranquillising three-fourths of the Irish people by enabling Catholics to enter Parliament, paying Catholic priests out of public funds, and relieving the Catholic ratepayers of direct payment of tithes to the parson by making these chargeable to the landlord. Then, apparently realising that little or nothing could be effected in this direction whilst George III. was King, he accepted Addington's offer of a seat in the Cabinet and the Presidency of the Board of Control. The development was not unimportant in his history. It made him familiar with the name of Wellesley. The elder Wellesley and his more famous younger brother [1] were at this time engaged in consolidating British rule in India by suppressing French intrigue. Behind that intrigue lay the mind of the Corsican soldier who knew England already for the strong enemy of his ambition and fought it with the same spirit that his compatriots display in their vendettas. We regard Napoleon now with a generous interest, taking him for a prince of gamblers who lost his throw, and finding in his story the stuff of high romance. To our forefathers, who saw him at closer quarters, he appeared, rather, like some fabled monster that grew ever larger as they gazed. They fought him as a pestilent fellow, as the enemy of good faith and freedom, as an adventurer, a bully, a braggart, a liar, a man who played merely for his own hand; the negation of all they stood for, swore by, and understood. There is a world of meaning in Wellington's terse and caustic comment when in his own old age Napoleon's name was mentioned to him—"Wasn't a gentleman!" Just that; nothing more needing in fact to be added, since this was the damnedst thing that one man might say about another. Larger generalisations govern our conception of that struggle with France—Reac-

---

[1] I have for convenience referred to them from this point onwards as Wellesley and Wellington, though the latter was not so created until 1809.

tion as against Progress, Free Institutions as against Militarism, the Family as against the State; these and others like them. But we may get nearer to the standpoint of our forefathers if we think of it as a straight fight between English gentlemen and a low-class blackguard. A certain decency in the conduct of life was of the essence of their creed; and "Boney" outraged it at every turn. So when in the end they had thrashed him well, they thought of shooting him like a common felon, and refused the very name of Emperor to one whose Empire had stretched from the Ebro to the Niemen. It fell to Castlereagh to do as much as any man of his time to bring about the downfall of this human prodigy. The consolidation of that last and greatest European Coalition which marched victorious into Paris was especially his work. But, long before he forged the arms, he had found the man for his purpose. Assaye was won by Wellington during his presidency of the Board of Control, and formed in fact the outstanding feature of his Indian administration. In this manner there began his association with one who was, politically speaking, his other self. Irishmen, Tories cast neither quite in the mould of Eldon nor yet in that of Peel, lovers of freedom and of peace, in sentiment aristocratic, in temperament moderate, in habit of mind practical, in purpose plain, the two men were admirably fitted to co-operate with one another. And Castlereagh seems quickly to have become sensible of the affinity. It was by his advice that Wellington entered Parliament, in his wake and with his ideas that Wellington became Chief-Secretary for Ireland, on his nomination that Wellington took command of the army in Portugal in 1808 and returned there again in 1809, and through his support that Wellington was maintained behind the lines of Torres Vedras. We shall not greatly err if we think of them as brothers in age, in political opinion, in diplomatic method, and, after a manner, in arms. They were, in truth, the great Twin Brethren under whose guidance the Revolution, incarnate in Napoleon, was fought and foiled.

The last months of Pitt's last administration first saw Castlereagh at the War Office; and he returned there under Portland between 1807 and 1809 after the fall of the Ministry of All the Talents. His real, if modest, merits, his noticeable, if not altogether undeserved ill-luck whilst he held this post, were such as to provoke Salisbury's memorable observation that "a War

Minister must find his reward in his conscience or his salary." [1]
Military success is readily put to the soldier's credit; failure as
quickly laid on a civilian's back. Castlereagh, as a matter of fact,
in his capacity as Secretary of State for War, was immediately
responsible for two military decisions as pregnant with victory
as any that the British Government took in the whole struggle
with France—the decision to support the Spanish rising of 1808
and the decision to place Wellington in command of the British
forces sent to Spain. The place, the hour, the man—he had
found them all; and when men remember that it was in the
Peninsula in 1809 and by Wellington's hand that the first faint
warning of defeat was traced along the towering walls of the
Napoleonic fortress, they should spare a thought for the
minister who backed the Spanish rising and selected the British
general.

In other respects, no doubt, Castlereagh did less well. Though
in the adoption of a policy of large, in place of little strategic
blows he showed a superiority of strategy above that of his
predecessor, his administration was clouded by reproach and
failure. The bombardment of Copenhagen, where a military
force under Wellington co-operated effectively in the seizure of
the Danish fleet, brought neither to his Department nor to
Canning's any special credit, for moralists shook their heads
even then over that violation of neutrality as they have done
ever since. And the other incidents with which he was connected at this time—all of them well known beyond their deserts
—tend to strengthen a cumulative impression of bad management.
The fatal rhyme about the Earl of Chatham and Sir Richard
Strachan, which no history book can remember to forget and
no memory forget to remember, has immortalised the Walcheren
expedition—the "Gallipoli" adventure of that time; as well-
conceived and as carelessly executed. Here, doubtless, Castlereagh had himself to thank for a bad commander. But in the
business of the Convention of Cintra, where his selection of
Wellington had been over-ridden by the Cabinet, he had to bear
the sins of others. His duel with Canning, which concludes this
lap of his career, has sealed the impression of his ill-success as
Secretary for War. For Canning, the brilliant Canning, if we are
to believe the accepted, though not quite assured story of this

[1] *Essays, Biographical,* p. 10.

affair, evidently thought him incapable. The work of the Foreign Office and of the War Office, lay, as it always must in time of war, near together; and Canning is said to have informed the Prime Minister that either he himself or Castlereagh must leave the Government. Portland appears to have accepted the latter alternative, but to have stipulated that the fall of Castlereagh should be deferred till a more convenient season. For months, therefore, before he knew of it, Castlereagh was doomed, and, when he got word of the intrigue, he demanded satisfaction from the intriguer. It would have been more just to challenge the procrastinating intermediary. The Ministers fought, but neither fell upon the field, though both from power.

For two critical years, therefore, of English history Castlereagh, for five critical years Canning wasted ability by disuse; and yet they were, as far as we can tell, of all Englishmen living the most competent to direct foreign affairs. And it was actually no more than a generous piece of pique that brought Castlereagh to the Foreign Office in 1812, and an ungenerous one that kept him there until his death in 1822. Wellesley, ambitious, clever, and casual, could hardly have been expected to throw up so high a prize, as in fact he did, because his brother was not well supported in the Peninsula; nor could Canning have been credited with such immeasurable self-esteem as to refuse to enter the Government unless Castlereagh would offer to surrender to him, not the Foreign Office only, but the leadership of the House also. Yet to these circumstances Castlereagh owed his tenure of the Foreign Department for ten momentous years.

Perceval, best remembered by his melancholy fate, appointed him in February 1812, and Liverpool continued him in the post after Perceval's assassination. Lord Liverpool had a good proportion of the qualities that we now associate with the name of Mr Baldwin. He was industrious, unassuming, considerate, honest, a man of good ability and much tact, the obvious cornerstone of a well-built house. Among his colleagues only Eldon and Castlereagh were remarkable men; the rest being of mediocre or even less than mediocre capacity. That an Administration so composed should have proved the longest of the century and carried the Country successfully through the most critical of its wars and the most uneasy of its post-war periods, is a comfortable fact, showing that well-fitting parts are a more important consideration in Cabinet workmanship than intellectual beauty. Given the nature of the times, the two chief posts in the Government were filled to perfection. The Country needed above all things to steer a steady course; and no pilots could have been steadier or more experienced than Liverpool and Castlereagh. Pitt would have been more inspiring, Canning more brilliant. But towards the end of a long war, tenacity is more congenial than inspiration, and character more important than cleverness.

And in fact both inspiration and cleverness were already well provided with representatives in the counsels of Europe. Alexander of Russia, whatever else he may have been, was the high dreamer of his age; dreaming with the aid of the greatest of all powers terrestrial as he talked to Napoleon on the raft at Tilsit; dreaming with the aid of powers celestial at the supreme hour of his inward illumination, whilst Moscow lay burning at his feet; dreaming with Madame de Krudener in her salon in Paris; dreaming with the Allied Monarchs of Eastern Europe, who themselves only feigned to dream but inwardly marvelled, of a Holy Alliance and a heavenly peace through all the world.

If Alexander represented the inspired visionary, Metternich gave a fine rendering of the character of a clever man of the world. To begin with, he had, as Professor Webster tells us,[1] " a keen appreciation of facts, showed moderation, had the faculty of compromise"—qualities that, as the same high authority avers, were Castlereagh's own, and that brought the two men readily into touch. But also Metternich was a past-master in the methods of what we call, with more self-righteousness than altogether befits us, the ' old diplomacy,'—of putting his trust, that is, in dexterity and secrecy rather than plain dealing. Not that he deserved to be condemned as false by the greatest liar of the age! "Il ment trop," Napoleon is reported to have said of him. "On peut mentir quelquefois, mais toujours c'est trop."[2]   All that the epigram really proves to us is that the epigrammatist had met his match.

After the sun of Austerlitz had blinded the Austrian Eagle, after Wagram had clipped its wings and caused its offspring to be caught and caged, Metternich, first at Paris as Austrian Ambassador and then in Vienna as Chancellor, waited and

---

[1] *Foreign Policy of Castlereagh*, p. 100.
[2] Quoted in the *Diary* of Frances, Lady Shelley, i. p. 74.

dissembled. No country, perhaps, has ever occupied a situation more critical than his during the last years of Napoleon's domination; nor any minister been called upon to take a more momentous decision than he in 1813. If he moved too soon, the Habsburgs must be lost and Austria dismembered; unless he moved soon enough, Europe must miss her last opportunity of deliverance. He timed his blow to a nicety. It was in the summer of 1813 that the Fates, so long complacent, had definitely brought the abhorred shears within reach of the career of Napoleon. In the north Alexander and Frederick William, in the south Wellington, were as blades closing to cut, and only greater force seemed wanting to bring them together. Still, the risk for Austria was immense. By a master-stroke of diplomacy Metternich at this juncture assumed, to the annoyance of both parties, the rôle of mediator, and, while he waited, armed. Then at length, decided perhaps by Wellington's victory at Vittoria and Castlereagh's promised subsidies, he took on 7th August the decision which ranged Austria with the avengers of an outraged Continent. And forthwith the penultimate act of the Napoleonic drama began.

The Allies moved forward—a motley crowd of emperors and kings, of statesmen and diplomatists and soldiers, fearful of Napoleon's military genius, of one another's territorial greed, of the making of peace before the time, and the continuance of war longer than was necessary; a company distracted by dreams and schemes, dynasties and disputes, and united only in the wish to push Napoleon across the Rhine. They had accomplished just so much, when Castlereagh met them at Basel about the middle of January 1814. He had come out rather at the wish of the Cabinet than his own; and his arrival was cordially welcomed by a young man whom we shall meet again and who, up to the time of his coming, had had charge of British interests at the now perambulating Court of Austria. "With relation to the enemy," Aberdeen told him, "our situation is as good as possible—among ourselves it is quite the reverse. Everything which has been so long smothered is now bursting forth. Your presence is absolutely providential. If you come without partiality and prejudice, as I make no doubt you do, in spite of all the pains taken to prevent it, you will be able to perform everything; and no words are sufficient to express the service you will render." [1] This diagnosis was correct. Castlereagh's influence became quickly apparent. The Grand Alliance drew together and passed insensibly from being a temporary expedient for war into a lasting agency for peace. It is here that we first touch the great idea upon which, not only the rest of Castlereagh's career but the whole international history of Europe from his day to ours forms a commentary. He came out, not merely in the hope of settling conclusions with Napoleon, but of welding Europe into such a homogeneous whole that no new Napoleon should be possible. Some such notion had already haunted statesmanlike minds, and not long before. Pitt, on a Russian initiative, had given the matter consideration in the year before his death, affirming in a Note addressed to the Russian envoy, Novossiltzoff, in January 1805, his approval of a plan for establishing a league of nations to enforce a public law. The conception, however, lacked as yet all thoroughness of thought. It was not distinguished from, but rather identified with that of the balance of power, which is as if one were to identify the cause of even justice with that of equal strength. And it remained obscure in what philosophy of international ethics the foundations of the new public law were to be laid—whether in the evangelical mysticism of Alexander or in the practical good-sense and honesty conceived as the best policy, characteristic of Pitt and his countrymen, or in some deeper, more universal principle, if such existed, that might reconcile by transcending these two ill-assorted points of view.

Castlereagh's mind was rather strong than subtle; and he had, besides, still to learn to know and understand the men with whom he had to deal. He was sanguine enough to suppose, before ever Leipzig had been fought, that the progress of the great idea could be sufficiently advanced by his subordinates at the Allied head-quarters as to be fit for parliamentary discussion some six weeks afterwards; and he was ignorant enough, a little before he came out and met him, to picture Metternich, who was no more than forty and some years younger than himself, as a man well advanced in age.[2] It needed his presence at the centre of events to clear his vision and to give his judgment and character full play.

---

[1] Castlereagh, *Mems. and Corresp.*, xi. 142.
[2] Stanmore, *The Earl of Aberdeen*, p. 35.

Another question, as he found, took precedence of that relating
to the permanent constitution of a league. The Allies had got
to make up their mind what precisely they were fighting for.
Except Prussia, which desired vengeance—and had much reason
to do so—they were remarkably free from the wish to serve
France as she had served them. But their standpoints were
curiously different. Alexander, the idealist, fancying himself a
Liberal, wanted above all things to march triumphantly into Paris,
as Napoleon had done into Moscow, and then, with such a *beau geste*
as the French talk of but never make, to heap coals of fire upon his
former adversaries. Metternich, the man of the world, was consumed by the fear that in the event of complete success, Russia
might swallow Poland whole, and Prussia Saxony in part; and
his attitude was determined by these considerations. Finally
Castlereagh, the wisest and most disinterested of the three,
looked to no other end than the reduction of France to its
proper size and the resumption by Europe of its peaceful habits.
But, from whatever ulterior motive, all these three men alike
desired to bring France to reason rather than to judgment, and
to leave her sane instead of frantic. With a statesmanship the
example of which was lost upon a later age, they put the past
behind them and looked only to the future, took into account
the susceptibilities of those they were about to conquer, and in
the end called their foes into counsel. A moderation, not at
times altogether unallied with fear, marked every step of their
advance, and, though they never paused, they twice agreed to
parley. At Frankfort they offered Napoleon the frontier of the
Rhine, and at Châtillon the boundaries of 1792. In making these
offers Austria and England lead the way. Castlereagh, even from
home, had seen that the line of Austrian policy ran nearest to his
own; and his advice to Aberdeen comprised an instruction to
keep well with Metternich. On his arrival he found in the
Austrian Chancellor, not indeed a congenial spirit, but a mind
which often met his own. It was otherwise with Alexander,
whose attempt to challenge the fullness of his power to represent
the British Government caused him extreme annoyance.

The Russian Emperor, like some other idealists, had but little
notion of throwing his brains into the common stock, and so intent had he become at the moment of Castlereagh's arrival, upon
dethroning Napoleon in style, that to all appearance the Grand

Alliance would have been shattered but for Castlereagh's admirable diplomacy. It was he who brought Metternich and Alexander once more into line, persuading the one to keep the Austrian forces in motion and the other to reopen negotiations with the failing but not yet fallen foe. With armies always on the march and diplomatists always in the camp, the diplomatic dispositions of both parties were, however, too quickly affected by the military situation for an agreement to be possible. Napoleon would have accepted the terms of Frankfort when the Allies were at Châtillon; and the Allies might have given all and more than all the terms of Châtillon when for a moment and for the last time Napoleon's hand regained its cunning and the Allied armies were forced back across the Marne.

In the hour of panic, while Alexander quailed, it was again Castlereagh who saved the position. He had the power to give and the power to withhold the captured colonies of France, and without the colonies in their pocket the Continental Powers were likely to bargain with Napoleon in vain. So the Châtillon terms were not amended in the enemy's favour, and Napoleon, finding them insufficient, merely played with them until all was lost. Meanwhile Castlereagh took advantage of the chastened sentiments of the Allies to weld them into a strong defensive alliance. He would have liked, as is known, to have made it an alliance against all offenders, but this was beyond his strength. He managed, however, to unite the great Powers of the Coalition in a bond of mutual defence against French aggression for twenty years to come, and to engage them severally to put sixty thousand men into the field whenever occasion required. This was that provision of the Treaty of Chaumont which initiated the idea of the Concert of Europe, and established under the guise of a Quadruple Alliance the formal, recognised ascendancy of the stronger over the weaker states of the Continent which we accept almost as part and parcel of the nature of political things, and which has kept a tenacious hold even upon the high-flying constitution of the League of Nations.

The importance of Castlereagh's success at the moment of its achievement was totally obscured by the more urgent undertaking of the four Allies to keep a hundred and fifty thousand men in the field until they could bring the war to a conclusion. Napoleon had delayed too long to agree with his adversaries whiles he was in the way with them.   By that 9th of March of 1814 when the Treaty of Chaumont was signed he had almost spent his strength and all but exhausted his ingenuity; and the military end, as Caulaincourt perceived, was evidently near. What the diplomatic end was to be no one clearly saw.   Castlereagh had from the first set his face against the petty pretenders to a throne which had held both St Louis and Napoleon—against Bernadotte, whom Alexander was thought to favour, as well as against a regency under Marie Louise, which Austria might naturally prefer.   His good sense doubtless warned him that there is nothing a country needs more in the hour of defeat than a firm and stable Government.   The competitors in his view were two and two only—the chiefs of the House of Bourbon and Bonaparte; and to this view he brought Metternich.   He himself preferred the older line, but he was for a long while ready to treat with the younger.   For he made peace the first consideration, provided only that it was accompanied by adequate safeguards. Napoleon, however, fought the battle of the Bourbons more certainly than the warmest of their friends; and his last brilliant feat of arms finally turned the scales in favour of the stout, scholarly old gentleman whose appearance and attainments seemed big with the promise of peace.

Nothing, however, had been actually determined when the Sovereigns of Russia and Prussia rode into Paris; and neither the Emperor Francis nor the ministers of England and Austria were present to detract from the splendour of the decisive and arresting part that Alexander had so long desired to play.   Francis and Metternich had their own reasons for absenting themselves from the last, or what seemed to be the last, scene of the Napoleonic drama; and Castlereagh left the Russian Emperor to take the leading rôle with the more confidence perhaps that the ablest diplomatist in Europe was waiting in the capital to press the solution that he himself preferred.   Talleyrand, as soon as Alexander was arrived, took him to his house and presented the argument for the restoration of the Bourbons in a shape acceptable to the mind of an ideologue.   "We can do everything," he said, "with a principle.   I propose to accept the principle of legitimacy which recalls the Bourbons to the throne."   Alexander prolonged the pleasures of deliberation for a day or two, discussed the matter in turn with soldiers and statesmen, and then in the end took Talleyrand's advice. In point of fact, that astute personage had only recommended the line of least resistance in circumstances where every other line would have meant an angry storm. Romance played for a moment round the figure of the Comte d'Artois, who acted in his brother's absence as the king's representative, but by the time the fat, old King and the sour Princess, who, if the settlement had held, would in due course have presented a startling contrast to her mother as Queen of France, were come, the nation was probably alive to the fact that all Alexander had bestowed upon them was the benefit of a *pis aller*.

It remained—and it was no small remainder—to clear up the mess left behind by twenty years of magnificent misrule, to give back to France her sanity and to Europe its equilibrium. The Allies, on Metternich's recommendation, dealt with the French situation at Paris, but reserved the European settlement for a Congress that was to meet at Vienna. The former issue presented no great difficulty. The frontier of 1792—the terms of Châtillon —held good for the Bourbons as they might have held good, if he had only consented in time, for Napoleon. To give the new French Government every chance of popularity no indemnity was allowed even to Prussia for all that she had suffered. A wise dispassionateness, moreover, enabled France to recover the most part of her captured colonies, though the charge against Castle-reagh of neglecting British imperial interests is sufficiently answered by the fact that he held back the Cape and Mauritius —stations on the route to India and the former destined to become the nucleus of a vast dominion. A last touch of Quixotic generosity crowned these benefactions, and the French were actually permitted to keep the art-treasures they had stolen in the course of their conquests. No defeated nation was ever treated more handsomely or with more studied consideration; and of that astonishing restraint the British Foreign Secretary was the life and soul.

Castlereagh's conduct brought him the highest distinction an English statesman can look to, for the House of Commons rose to its feet at his entry. But there were, of course, complaints and criticisms particularly amongst the smarter members of the softer sex. "No murders, no torture, no conflagration—how ill the pretty women of London bear it!" writes Samuel Whitbread in the *Creevey Papers*.[1]   A hundred years later, with Democracy installed and women enfranchised, British ministers had shaken themselves free from that 'mildness and indulgence even to the offending states' of which Castlereagh had spoken to his colleagues as the right principle of action.[2]   Mr Lloyd George himself trod a measure with the daughters of Vengeance who demanded impossible indemnities and the Kaiser's head upon a charger.   So, as cynics observe, do we progress towards perfection!

Such things, then, the Powers determined at Paris during the April and May of 1814.   In June Castlereagh was back in London. In September he left for Vienna, and until January of the next year remained there in conference with the leading statesmen of Europe.   The choice of this capital for the Congress was one of the master-strokes of Metternich's genius.   It gave him an indeterminate but real control over the proceedings, and to Austria for the next thirty years a diplomatic position altogether beyond her deserts.   Castlereagh, however, had no reason to object, for Metternich was at this juncture and for some while after, his best friend in Europe.   There were two reasons for this. One was a common dislike; the other and greater a common object.   Both men were out of sympathy with Alexander and both men wanted to make Austria stronger, Metternich because it was his country, Castlereagh because he was still sufficiently under the spell of the old idea of a balance of power to feel that France and Russia were too powerful, Austria and Prussia too weak to maintain an equilibrium.   It was his fear of the two exterior Powers that made him wish to increase the weight in Europe of the Central Powers.[3]   His policy ought in itself to have made Prussia as valuable an ally as Austria, but in the case of Prussia he was handicapped by the personal relations already established between the Prussian King and the Russian Emperor —relations in themselves worthy of all respect, since they were founded on the rarest of qualities, political gratitude.

The conclusion of the war had left three prizes in suspense— Poland, Saxony, and the domination of Italy.   Russia wanted the first, Prussia the second, and Austria the third; and each of these Powers had the object of its ambition well within its

---

[1] i. 191.
[2] *Camb. Hist. of British Foreign Policy*, i. 472.
[3] Alison, *Lives of Castlereagh and Stewart*, ii. 633.

grip. It was not, indeed, without reason that, as the tension grew, both Alexander and Frederick William took occasion to point out that, did they but choose, they could acquire what they sought by merely holding on to it. Castlereagh was wise enough not to make any attempt to deny that possession is nine points of the law or to threaten measures which he might have no power to execute, and merely contented himself with observing that a title to property without any treaty-right behind it was too insecure to be satisfying. The Powers assembled must in truth have cut a wretched figure if the Congress, which aimed at giving a new public law to Europe, failed to come to an agreement about matters so eminently negotiable.

Yet, but for Castlereagh's presence at Vienna, the European Congress, like the Grand Alliance before it, bade fair to split into its component parts. At no moment of his career was he greater than during this time of acute and perilous tension, for he stood to a peculiar degree alone. From home warnings reached him that the Government was in no mood to be dragged into war over the affairs of Poland and Saxony; and the only definite instruction that the Cabinet sent him was to this effect. But he was not to be turned aside from a course that he saw to be imperative by the timidity or ignorance of colleagues far removed from the scene of action. In taking his own line he took a greater risk than any Foreign Secretary had had cause to take before, or could, in these days of quick communication, be permitted to take again. Time and circumstance had thrust a rare opportunity of independence upon him; and his character and ability proved equal to the occasion.

Not that the end was either easily or immediately attained! Castlereagh's first scheme of a settlement miscarried completely. Willing to satisfy Prussia with the gift of Saxony and unwilling to grant Russia her way in Poland, he conceived the plan of playing off the gratification of the one against the disappointment of the other. Prussia was to be permitted to swallow the Saxon Kingdom whole on condition that she supported the British and Austrian representations to Alexander against any similar self-indulgence on Russia's part in Poland. Castlereagh dragged an assent to this plan both out of the reluctant Metternich and the embarrassed Hardenberg. But the Monarchs proved less pliable than the Ministers. Alexander altogether refused

to hear of abandoning his Polish project, and Frederick
William with no less resolution refused to hear of abandoning
his ally.

The failure of this negotiation threw Castlereagh completely
into the arms of Metternich, and from that moment he refused
to countenance the absorption of Saxony by the Hohenzollerns.
Things had reached a deadlock, and might have remained there
if the Great Powers of Europe had been only four in number,
for the Allies were now equally divided. But there was another
great, if defeated Power in existence, and one to which the fate
of Saxony appeared of primary interest. Talleyrand, with the
credit of France in his keeping, was hanging about the skirts
of the Congress. To him, at this critical juncture, Castlereagh
turned, and not in vain. The French Plenipotentiary made it
clear that, subject to one condition, France would stand by
England and Austria in resisting the Prussian claims. The
Powers opposed to Russia and Prussia were therefore no longer
two but three.

It was, however, not till after Christmas that Castlereagh
played the decisive card which lay ready in his hand. He would,
if he could, have preferred to settle matters otherwise than by
cutting across the old understanding between the Allies. But
the Prussians were unyielding and left him no alternative. He
insisted therefore upon the admission of the French Envoy to a
formal conference about Poland and Saxony and, when Hardenberg refused in menacing terms, he replied by concluding with
Metternich and Talleyrand a secret treaty, binding their three
countries, if attacked, to make common cause against Prussia,
with armies of 150,000 men apiece. He protected himself, it is
true, from the charge of any real change of front by requiring
France as part of the agreement to adhere in any event to the
terms of the Treaty of Paris; but he had, nevertheless, done
violence to the opinion of the British Cabinet, so far as he knew
it at the time, though, in fact, a letter from the Prime Minister
approving the idea of an alliance with France was actually on its
way. His resolution brought immediate fruit. Alexander, to
whom Frederick William's ambitions were no consuming interest,
was already wavering when the discovery of the secret treaty
decided his doubts. The Prussian claim on Saxony was reduced
to less than half of the whole; the loss of Leipzig, upon the

acquisition of which the Prussians had set their heart, compensated by Russia with the cession of Thorn.

Castlereagh had precisely realised his object in the West. Prussia was made stronger but yet not too strong. In the East he was less successful. Russia took the duchy of Warsaw, subject to an undertaking to grant the Poles home-rule. This fell short both of his private aim, which was to partition Poland between the three Powers interested on more even lines, and of his disingenuous, public declaration, intended only for the consumption of the House of Commons, in favour of Polish independence. Neither here nor in Italy, any more than in his early days in Ireland, did he manifest interest in the principle of nationality or faith in the virtue of liberal constitutions. The main matter, as he saw clearly, was to get Europe back to peaceful habits, and, the *status quo ante* the shortest road to that consummation. The time, besides, was so little ripe for Italian unity that the Venetians saw with regret the extinction of their famous Republic. The actual choice lay between the domination of the Italian peninsula by France or by Austria; and from the point of view of British sea-power there was every objection to the first and none to the second. The fate of Naples alone caused much searching of heart. Its restoration to its Bourbon sovereign was the condition, already alluded to, that Talleyrand had attached to his support of England and Austria at the Congress. From another side there was pressure to the same purpose. Castlereagh cannot have been indifferent to the opinion of Wellington, who urged in the strongest terms that Murat's presence in Naples, with Bonaparte close at hand in Elba, constituted a standing menace to Europe in general and to France in particular.[1] But for Metternich, and also to a less degree for Castlereagh, the deposition of King Joachim involved a case of conscience. Austria, in the crisis of the struggle with Napoleon a year before, had bought his support with a guarantee of his kingdom; and England, though not formally committed, was consenting to the deed. Castlereagh took the view that Murat had failed to fulfil the terms of this compact, but his anxiety to secure some further evidence of treachery from the archives at Paris shows that the case was not as fully made out as it might have been. The event no doubt did all that any event could have done to put Murat

[1] Castlereagh, *Mems. and Corresp.*, x. 227.

in the wrong, but double-dyed traitor though he was, it must
be said in his defence that no one can reasonably be expected to
play fair if his associates are preparing to drop him overboard.
This was Murat's situation, and it is not to be wondered at that
the dashing trooper, whose sword, like some fairy wand, had converted him from an innkeeper into a king, came hopelessly to
grief in the narrow ways of diplomacy.   His Kingdom lay almost
literally between the deep sea and the devil, with the British
Fleet riding triumphant on the surrounding waters and the
Corsican tempter biding his time at Elba and preparing to come
back in great wrath even if only for a short time.

Napoleon's return was in truth for Murat a temptation all the
more irresistible that other hope was wellnigh gone.   He rose,
calling upon Italy to follow, and rushed impetuously into the
field at the head of that Neapolitan army of which a well-qualified
critic had said that, clothe its units as one might, in blue or green
or red, the result was always the same, and that result that they
took to their heels.   He would have done more wisely to wait.
In Napoleon's judgment his action was the immediate cause of
the counter-intervention of Austria.

Though Murat was the first to move, the dawning of the
Hundred Days soon set all Europe in motion.   Even diplomacy
quickened its march.   "The Congress is dissolved," Napoleon
is supposed to have declared the moment that he set foot in
France.   He was completely mistaken.   The Congress closed up
its ranks, stiffened its back, and pursued its way with a business-
like fortitude, even whilst his star shot up once more, menacing
and brilliant, into the sky, and hung suspended above their
labours.   Great Britain was less concerned in the detail of these
concluding negotiations than she had been in the more general
lines of the settlement.   Castlereagh, indeed, at the urgent
instance of his colleagues, who were none too sure of their
capacity to make head against the Opposition in the House of
Commons, had left Vienna some few days before Napoleon slipped
across to France from Elba, bearing with him a prize more grateful to some of his countrymen than any other that he could have
brought—a declaration that the slave-trade violated the laws of
humanity, with some definite prospect of its early, complete
abolition.   And Wellington, who took his old friend's place at
the Congress, had not much more than time to see the Allies

renew those solemn pledges by which Castlereagh had bound them to mutual support, a year earlier, at Chaumont, before his services were required for the campaign of Waterloo.

The Allied Governments were thoroughly at one in the desire to dethrone Napoleon, but they were not equally unanimous in desiring to enthrone again the infirm old man whom the faithful revered as Louis Dix-Huit and the wags, with at least as much exactitude, denominated Louis des Huîtres. The penultimate King of France had never much appealed to the feelings of Alexander, and did so the less that Napoleon had made him acquainted with the text of the secret treaty concluded at Vienna between England, France, and Austria, and unfortunately preserved among the archives at Paris. It was, however, a cardinal feature of British foreign policy at the moment— actually 'the keystone,' so Liverpool declares in a letter of this date to Castlereagh, of the whole [1]—to restore the legitimate sovereign; and Castlereagh and Wellington managed it between them. Louis was first associated with the Four Powers in the new edition of the Treaty of Chaumont and then, after Waterloo was won, advised to follow close upon the heels of Wellington's victorious army. It was a hard business to give the elder line of the Bourbons a second chance of popularity. France had sinned again, and sinned outrageously, and, in days like our own, it might have been cogently argued that mercy and moderation were lost upon her. But though they could not save her a second time from the infliction of indemnities nor grant her precisely the same favourable frontier that she obtained before, nor confirm her in the possession of the treasures of which she had despoiled the art-collections of the Continent, some of her conquerors still strove, and not in vain, to leave her powerful enough to take her proper place among the great nations of Europe.

Statecraft is of many kinds. It is not possible with tape and plummet to measure the comparative contributions of different men, but, if to pursue, unmoved by criticism and undeterred by accident, a line of policy once well thought out and presently to be vindicated by the event be the high test of public talent, then in Castlereagh and Wellington we may recognise men cast in the finest mould of political wisdom. Our own times do, in fact, afford

[1] Wellington, *Suppl. Desp.*, ix. 573, 20th February 1815.

us some means of estimating their achievement.   For Germany
read France; in place of four years' warfare set down twenty; to
one proved conviction subjoin another consecutive offence—
and the courage and sagacity of the two British statesmen will
then be plain.   Theirs was no easy task.   The feeling of the
Prussians against the French was such as the French in our day
have returned, in full measure and running over, to the Germans.
A niece of Castlereagh's who accompanied him to Paris during
the negotiations in 1815 relates a story which was current in
the circles in which she moved.   A young Prussian officer, it was
said, after the Allies entered Paris, had been quartered upon an
old French couple.   They did their best to make him comfortable,
and he appeared to be well satisfied with his reception.   But in
the very hour of his departure he destroyed or damaged all the
furniture of his apartment and brought them in to see it.   They
asked him in amazement why he had used them so ill.   Had they
not used him kindly; of what did he complain?   He replied that
no one could have treated him better; but that he had asked
purposely to be quartered upon them in order that he might so
do to one of their rooms as their son had done to every room in
his father's house in Berlin.[1]

Between the punitive sentiments of Prussia and the protective
and pecuniary considerations that weighed with Austria, Castlereagh, during the negotiation of the second Treaty of Paris,
found himself for perhaps the only time in his career the close ally
of Alexander.   They were both of them essentially generous,
though the generosity of the Briton was always cool and
measured, and that of the Russian impulsive and ill-considered,
and they managed between them to fix the indemnity to be
exacted at the moderate figure of 700,000,000 francs, as well as
to save for France the provinces which Louis XIV. had filched
long enough ago to make their restoration rather a misfortune
than a benefit to the inhabitants.   A crucial issue was the
question whether the frontier-fortresses, of which the Allies were
to be put in occupation, should be ceded for a time or in per-
petuity.   Here the immense weight of Wellington's authority,
which was all the while exerted, contrary to the usual habit of
soldiers, on the side of moderation, was of especial value.   No-

[1] Emma Sophia, Lady Brownlow, *Slight Reminiscences of a Septuagenarian*,
pp. 172-3.

thing that could rankle, nothing that could instigate France to initiate another war, ought in his view to be imposed upon her. His opinion prevailed, but the French returned him hatred for his good-will.

It was in the course of these negotiations that Castlereagh penned a characteristic sentence which has been already quoted and is become famous. "It is not our business," he wrote, "to collect trophies, but to bring back the world to peaceful habits." [1] The context dealt, not with the intransigence of other Governments, but with the effect of the treaty upon British public opinion. About this he had no illusions. "In extorting the permanent cession of one or two fortresses of great name," he observed, "our labours would carry with them an *éclat* which is not likely to attend them according to the course we recommend." The Cabinet were well aware of it, and had themselves in the beginning favoured a more rigorous policy. But his high wisdom had converted them; and they faced the risks involved with an equanimity very different to what our times have seen. "You cannot expect our peace to be popular," wrote Bathurst, a week later, "although I am persuaded its policy will be hereafter approved, if it shall succeed in what we, I think, wisely proposed as its main object—the re-establishment of the legitimate monarchy in France." [2] At the distance of a century, a generation that has witnessed the Peace of Versailles is in a position to do justice to the character and conduct of these Conservative magnates whose minds were open so wide to reason and whose eyes were shut so close against party profit.

On the same day on which the Second Peace of Paris was concluded, there was signed anew—and for the third time—the Treaty once styled of Chaumont. As during that deadly peril in 1814, as again after Napoleon's flight from Elba, so now, when peace was finally assured, the four victorious Powers pledged themselves once more to resist any attempt on the part of France to disturb the concord of Europe. The Treaty was so framed as plainly to bring the restoration of Napoleon or his family into the category of such an attempt; and in this respect the third edition of the compact went beyond the first and deprived France of the complete management of her own affairs. In another and more

---

[1] Castlereagh, *Mems. and Corresp.*, x. 486.
[2] *Ibid.*, p. 501.

important way it varied the previous agreement. On Castle-reagh's initiative the High Contracting Powers agreed to renew their meetings, not merely (as Alexander had suggested) to see that the provisions of the Treaty of Paris were carried out, but to consult 'at fixed periods' about their 'common interests' and 'for the consideration of the measures which at each of these periods should be considered the most salutary for the repose and prosperity of Nations and for the maintenance of the Peace of Europe.'

The British Foreign Secretary had thus gone some way towards establishing a permanent league of the Great Powers of Europe. The famous sixth clause of the treaty that he had framed to give effect to his idea was in one sense the complement and in another the contradiction of the project of the Holy Alliance which Alexander had sprung upon the world some two months earlier. The Irishman and the Russian were working at the same problem, but their points of departure were as widely remote as their places of origin. They had both seen that Europe was without coherence, but the one looked to a common religion and the other to a common interest to provide a remedy. The Holy Alliance was designed to unite all the Governments of Europe in a league whose members were to base their conduct upon the principles of the Christian Gospel. What Alexander precisely expected of his conception is difficult to divine, for his mind was never at rest with itself, and, though at one moment he regarded Liberal constitutions as the practical outcome of his plan, it proved in the event to be a strong bulwark of Legitimist Monarchy. But what Castlereagh thought of it is on the other hand almost too well known to repeat. It was, he said, "a piece of sublime mysticism and nonsense." And Metternich echoed Castlereagh's sentiment by calling it "a loud-sounding nothing."

Alexander might, as Castlereagh in fact supposed,[1] be wrong in the head, but he was too powerful a person to be treated as a crank or a dreamer. All the rulers of Europe made themselves parties to the Alliance, except the Pope and the Sultan, who were deemed unfit to belong to it, and the Prince Regent who got off with a personal letter of sympathy on the ground that formal signature would not be in keeping with the British Constitution. We may presume that they shared Metternich's opinion; or else

[1] Wellington, *Suppl. Desp.*, xi. 175.

they might have assented less lightly to a scheme whose possibilities of interpretation were formidable enough.

The Holy Alliance, though, like some other institutions to which their founders have been so rash as to attach that perilous adjective, it lent itself to ridicule, was not so foolish an affair as its critics thought it. There was in it an element wanting to the Treaty of Chaumont but not absent from the conception of a perfect society. Castlereagh, with his strong common sense but limited imagination, had been content to lay the foundation of the European concert at which he aimed in the obvious interest that the Powers had, at the conclusion of twenty years of warfare, in the preservation of peace and in the equal obligation that they lay under to maintain the Treaty of Vienna. But a defensive alliance to maintain a territorial settlement no more satisfies the idea of a Society of Nations than the policing of property satisfies the idea of the State. A soul as well as a body is necessary to every institution which men call into being to give their humanity fuller or richer life—a kernel of faith and feeling, as we might say, at the back of the protective shell. It was this that Alexander saw, but he saw it all in mist, as dreamers see things in Russia. He took the Gospels for a common creed and offered their precepts as a manual of statecraft, but he never showed how Christianity was to become an organic structure or its doctrines to be applied to the political conditions of the time. He was, therefore, immediately at the mercy of Castlereagh's criticisms and Metternich's cunning.

So much it is not difficult to see; but to understand the full significance of this period of Congresses and Conferences we have to remind ourselves that Europe stood in urgent need of public law and political science. Only a few years before the vain shadow of the Holy Roman Empire had been chased from its last retreat by the artificial sunlight of Napoleon, and the dying idea of a common civilisation and of spiritual coherence which, in spite of a thousand surface agitations, had been inherent in the political system of Europe in the Middle Age, deprived of even the symbol of existence. International ethics, as Consalvi perceived, had something still to lose in this development of international politics. From the doctrine of the Canonists who had tempered the legacy of the Roman jurists with Christian principles and caused Christendom to rise out of the ashes of old Rome, the world, after suffering the ideas of Grotius, was slipping, actually in Castlereagh's life-time, under the influence of Bentham—Bentham who made every nation a law unto itself and found no binding sanctions of public morality outside the parchment of a treaty. His specious doctrines were countenanced either consciously or unconsciously by the conclusions reached at Vienna. The dissolution of the Holy Roman Empire was formally accepted, and, in place of that exhausted yet still memorable symbol of organic European unity, there was set up nothing more arresting than the inevitably mutable and temporary provisions of a compact.

It was this misfortune that Castlereagh and Alexander in their different degrees attempted to obviate. They had, however, as might have been expected, separate remedies, and in the interaction of those remedies is to be found the key to the history of the years that followed the Vienna Congress.

Alexander, casting his eyes to heaven and his net to catch all the Christian Powers of the Continent, both small and great, except the Pope alone, desired to see such things as perhaps we see, even if only through a glass darkly, and to know such things as perhaps we know, even if but in part. His was the poet's dream—a parliament of Man, a federation of the World—though in that parliament kings were alone to speak and from that federation all but true believers were to be repelled. But Castlereagh held his eyes to earth. He was determined that England should pull her weight in Europe, and he knew that she would never consent to commit herself beyond the defensive principles of the Alliance that he had first formed at Chaumont. He had therefore no place in his project for any but the Greater Powers, being concerned rather with force than opinion and perceiving that those Powers in combination would give him all the strength he needed to carry his purpose through. He failed to see, however, that the diplomatic machinery which he created for his purpose in the shape of periodical congresses and conferences would with difficulty be restricted to the business that he had in mind, and might, in a world distracted by new ideas, give an inconveniently generous interpretation to its prescribed duty of taking salutary measures for the repose and prosperity of nations. As Professor Alison Phillips very well expresses it, he did not "realise the import of his attitude." [1] It was to be brought home to him, however, before he died.

The seven years that passed between the downfall of Napoleon and the death of Castlereagh have at first sight all the look of an anti-climax—just a series of tedious conferences standing in broad contrast to the diplomatic and military pageants that had preceded them.   Something might be gained in the comprehension of this period if we were to conceive it pictorially: in the front of the picture the figures of Metternich, Alexander, and Castlereagh; in the middle distance a family group, ensconced upon unsteady thrones—the Bourbon kings of France and Spain and Naples; on the far horizon a rock, and standing out upon that rock the figure of Napoleon, dim, gigantic, projecting himself into the future, creating his legend, which was a legend indeed, and awaiting the appointed time of his apotheosis.

Somewhat so might the European situation have been depicted in the latter days of Castlereagh.   It was Metternich who turned it to immediate account.   He knew, as Talleyrand knew, that a principle was necessary to hold the fabric of society together, and he chose, as Talleyrand had chosen, the principle of Legitimism.   We may condemn his choice; we shall not be wise to condemn his statecraft.   Only our own jealously-guarded insularity and our own cameleon of a Constitution enable us to profess that strong variants of government can live in peace and comfort side by side.   They do no such thing.   They view one another with the utmost jealousy and the most vigilant alarm, and sooner or later they come into conflict.   Democracy, it has been wisely said, is rather a form of civilisation than a form of government.   So it is with monarchy, aristocracy, theocracy, and their modifications.   They cannot live in peace, for at heart they are at war.   Have we not seen it with our own eyes and can we not testify to it?   The Boer oligarchy was an offence to the Democratic Imperialist; the Russian and German despotisms to the Liberal; the Dual Monarchy, with its many races and languages, to the Nationalist.   Such systems appeared petty, or tyrannical, or out-of-date because they were judged, not as instruments of government but as organs of civilisation.   The Englishman who cannot work when he wants to, because his trade union puts a spoke in the wheel; the American who cannot

[1] *Camb. Mod. Hist.*, x. 12.

get at alcohol except by bribery and corruption, because the
State forbids him; the Frenchman who but a little while ago
was unable to associate with others of a like mind in a religious
community, because the powers that were held secular opinions,
might equally have all of them seemed to Metternich the
victims of social injustice acting through bad institutions and
upon mischievous theories. We know, of course, or, at least,
if we do not know, it is not for want of being told, that he was
mistaken and that the society which he upheld, compared to
that which we enjoy, was harsh as the words of Mercury were
harsh beside the songs of Apollo. But we must recognise, nevertheless, that he went about what he took to be his business with
an energy and ability worthy of a better cause. Evil communications corrupt good manners. To Metternich the communications of the Revolution were evil and the manners of the
Ancien Régime were good. He set before him the object of
rolling back the advancing tide of democracy; and he rolled it
back, with tremendous consequences for the next generation,
for over thirty years. In this purpose of his, both Castlereagh's
Concert of Europe and Alexander's Holy Alliance afforded
valuable assistance; and his diplomatic adroitness enabled him
to make the most of them. Castlereagh had arranged for a
meeting of conferences at rare periods for specific purposes;
Metternich assembled them with inconvenient frequency for
general discussions. Alexander had imagined that his mystical
philosophy would hatch a grand charter of humanity; under
Metternich's incubation it brought forth a manual of high prerogative and a bill of pains and penalties.

Three European Conferences were held in Castlereagh's life-
time—those of Aix-la-Chapelle, of Troppau, and of Laibach—
and it is an aid to the memory if we associate each with the
affairs of one or other of the three Bourbon States and recollect
that chronology and geography are kind enough to correspond
and that the hand of the chronometer progresses as the finger
on the map passes through France, then round from France to
Spain, and finally from Spain to Naples.

The main business at Aix, whither Castlereagh journeyed in
company with Wellington in the early autumn of 1818, was
to deal with French affairs. The Duc de Richelieu, a wiser
and a greater man than his namesake the Cardinal—if peace,

that is, and not strife, be the foundation of government—was now in power. He had gained the regard of the British statesmen, and they in turn gave him their support. With the assistance of Wellington, who had the great house of Baring at his back, the French indemnity of seven hundred million francs was liquidated; and with Wellington's concurrence the French reparations, estimated on one assessment at twelve hundred million francs or more, were compounded for the fifth part of that sum. The settlement reflected the customary easiness of the British and closeness of the French people in all matters of finance,[1] and illustrated the unflinching manner in which Wellington, regardless of ingratitude and even attempted assassination, pursued his policy of setting France upon her legs. The Conference of Aix-la-Chapelle sealed this generous endeavour. The financial pressure was lightened, the military occupation removed. The Allies had made a handsome contribution towards 'royalising France and nationalising the Monarchy.' It remained with the Bourbons and the *émigrés*, if they had it in them, to do the rest.

France, until lately little ·better than a convict on ticket-of-leave, was now once more free. Was she to be admitted, as Richelieu pleaded, to share in the counsels of the Greater Powers, and if so upon what basis? The question, to all appearance innocent enough, opened, as by a side door, a much larger issue. For France had been the focus of revolutionary movement and was interesting to her neighbours principally on that account. Alexander saw the opportunity for the Holy Alliance, and proposed the creation of a mutual guarantee amongst the States of Europe for the preservation, not only of their territories, but of their form of government. All internal anti-monarchical revolution was, in fact, to be suppressed by exterior international force. Austria and Prussia found the Russian plan congenial. But Castlereagh had no authority to approve it if he would, nor any wish to approve it if he could. He joined issue at once, and ultimately arranged that the Quadruple Alliance of Chaumont should be renewed, but that France should be admitted to the conferences foreshadowed in the additional sixth article of that Treaty as redrafted in 1815. This diplomatic achievement was

---

[1] "The French Government," Wellington wrote to Clancarty, "have behaved most shamefully in this question (of reparations)," *Suppl. Desp.*, xii. 492, 23rd April 1818.

veiled by fine phrases, designed to please Alexander, and by
sarcastic comments, calculated to reassure his Cabinet colleagues at home. "The benign principles of the Alliance of the
26th September 1815 (the Holy Alliance)," Castlereagh wrote,
"may be considered as constituting the European system in
matters of political conscience. It would, however, be deroga-
tory to the solemn act of the sovereigns to mix its discussions
with the ordinary diplomatic obligations which bind state to
state and which are to be looked for alone in the treaties which
have been concluded in the accustomed form." [1] " The Concert
with France is confined within the limits of the most restricted
interpretation which can be given to Article VI. of the Treaty of
Alliance of November 20, 1815, viz. it is confined to the maintenance of the Peace as established and consolidated by the
Treaties therein enumerated." [2]

Thus for the moment Castlereagh had won all along the line.
He had reasserted his great idea of diplomacy by periodic
conference—"a new discovery," so he told Liverpool with more
optimism than was wise, "in the European Government, at
once extinguishing the cobwebs with which diplomacy obscures
the horizon, bringing the whole bearing of the system into its
true light, and giving to the counsels of the Great Powers the
efficiency and almost the simplicity of a single State." [3] He
had drawn France out of her isolation and added her to the
Concert, thus forestalling that alliance between France and
Russia which of all such diplomatic possibilities was the only
one that he held to be really formidable to the liberties of Europe.[4]
He had obtained from Alexander in personal intercourse a re-
pudiation of his supposed intrigues with the French, and he had
given him in return a practical dissertation on the character of
the English and their constitutional inability to deal with political
questions except as urgent issues. He had discovered an
ambiguous formula which solved in his own mind the difficulty,
more subtle than he saw, of deciding in what circumstances
Europe was entitled to prune its rotten branches. "The only

---

[1] " Memorandum on the Treaties of 1814 and 1815 " (printed in Webster's
Congress of Vienna, App. viii. p. 166).
[2] " Castlereagh to the Cabinet " (quoted from Webster's *Foreign Policy of
Castlereagh*, p. 159).
[3] Webster, *Foreign Policy of Castlereagh*, p. 153.
[4] *Ibid.*, p. 152.

safe principle," he wrote, "is that of the law of nations: that no
State has a right to endanger its neighbours by its internal
proceedings, and that, if it does, provided they exercise a sound
discretion, their right of interference is clear." [1]   And, finally,
he had provided for another reunion of the Greater Powers
at the next convenient opportunity, without permitting their
conferences to 'degenerate' (his own compromising fateful
word) into congresses by the admission of the smaller nations,
or their assemblies to grow into an 'areopagus' by the inclusion
of general matter in their agenda, or their guarantee of existing
apportionment of territory to be enlarged into a guarantee of
existing forms of government.

No diplomatist in fact had more nearly attained his ends;
and yet, except for Wellington, he stood alone in his ideas.   He
had gone a little further than was acceptable to his colleagues at
home and had fallen a good way short of what was wanted by
his coadjutors abroad.   The Cabinet, with Canning well ahead
of them, and the Country well behind them, desired to be quit of
Continental conferences; the rulers of Austria and Russia and
Prussia to make the Continent safe from revolution.   Neither
group had got their way, for Castlereagh had proved a match for
them all.   It followed inevitably—and this was its real disadvantage—that his policy became rooted in his personality and
not in the circumstances of the time.   His aloofness was felt
both at home and abroad.   He inspired confidence but not conviction.   Only Wellington and Liverpool, perhaps, amongst his
countrymen saw things at all as he did; and amongst the foreign
statesmen with whom he mixed there was probably none that
shared his standpoint.

We ought also, if we are fair, to recognise something more.
Castlereagh's work for mankind, disinterested though it was, was
also half-hearted.   To the jealous eyes of Europe, British humani-
tarianism, in his hands as in those of some of his successors, doubtless seemed in an irritating sort of way to stop just short of any
sacrifice of vital British interests.   There was nothing that the
Country had more at heart than the abolition of the slave trade;
there were few things that other nations complained of more than
the British right of search.   Yet when Alexander proposed to

[1] " Memorandum on Treaties of 1814, 1815 " (Webster, *Congress of Vienna*,
p. 170).

accommodate the two standpoints by appointing an international
board of naval control with an international fleet under its orders
off the West Coast of Africa, Castlereagh made heavy weather.
There was in him, as there has been in almost all his countrymen
before and since, the feeling that the prerogative of Britannia
is of divine right and not subject to alien limitation.

Metternich was in a better position to throw his mind into the
common stock.   A natural genius for diplomacy, coupled with
a clear perception of the character of the State that he had to
govern, with its central situation and its straggling provinces,
tempted him along a different path.   Austria could never enjoy,
like England, the splendour of an isolation built upon sea-power,
or, like Russia, the prestige of an endless army of willing slaves, or,
like France, the enthusiasm of a people head over ears in love with
soil and soldiers.   A brilliant diplomacy alone could make her
great.   Metternich perceived this and gave his country for a whole
generation the hegemony in Europe.   Close students of his
career point to these years between 1818 and 1822 as those in
which he touched the summit of his skill.   Never, at any rate,
did he work more untiringly, with greater zest or greater appearance of achievement.   Circumstances played into his hands.
Even whilst the Powers terrestrial sat calming the wind at Aix,
the Powers celestial were suffering the whirlwind to rise throughout the length and breadth of thinking Europe.

Not only the Bourbons seemed to shake upon their thrones.   In
England, Liverpool's Government looked like falling; and Peter-
loo discovered a yawning abyss beneath their feet to those who
were upon the watch to find one.   In Germany the assassination
of Kotzebue, a Conservative publicist at one time in close touch
with the Russian Emperor, by a student of the name of Sand,
revealed the everlasting, inevitable peril of letting young men
drink deep of the strong wine of new ideas; and the crime was
not rendered the less alarming by the fact of its palliation by men
of light and standing.   This was in 1819.   The next year opened
with a revolution in Spain, which brought its worthless sovereign
to his knees and the concession of a constitution.   Six months
later his namesake, relative, and compeer in tyranny and
treachery, Ferdinand of Naples, suffered a similar fate and
subscribed to an identical document.   Meanwhile in England the
Cato Street Conspiracy, which proposed to sweep the whole

Cabinet out of existence at a single swoop, showed what sort of spirit was abroad; and the now forgotten Bonnymuir riot outside Glasgow confirmed the dark impression. Such manifestations may have been as little dangerous as Liberals would have us believe; but it was useless to expect a generation that could look back upon the blood and havoc of the Revolution in France to treat them lightly. Even Brougham and Mackintosh, devout Liberals as they were, were constrained to pronounce the crisis grave. But of all the enlightened spirits of the time the most affected was the Emperor Alexander. His faith in human nature steadily lost ground, and a final dramatic horror—the murder of the Duc de Berry, a prince in the immediate line of succession to the throne of France—coming as it did after the murder of Kotzebue and coinciding nearly with the Cato Street plot, changed him from an apostle of Liberalism to an advocate of repression. The daggers of Sand and Louvel had indeed cut the Gordian knot of his tangled theories, and at Troppau, where in the autumn of 1820 he talked with Metternich over the tea-cups, he made his confession and professed his discipleship to the high-priest of the *ancien régime*.

The negotiations which led up to the assembly of the Troppau Conference are of supreme consequence in the life of Castlereagh. To those, who recognised, as he had done, the solidarity of Europe, the revolution in Spain could not be a matter of indifference, but to those, who, like Alexander, regarded Europe in the light of a moral civilisation, it had the effect of a call to arms. The Russian Emperor offered indeed, forthwith, as the mandatory of Europe, to send a hundred thousand men to put things straight in the Peninsula. A Russian army marching across Central Europe was no agreeable idea either to France or Austria. But only Castlereagh opposed the notion on principle, for he alone really disapproved the idea of the Holy or, as Dr Temperley would have us call it in this latter phase, Neo-Holy Alliance with its now well-defined object of maintaining everywhere a monarchical form of government. His desire to keep in being a council of the Greater Powers had always had its dangers; and in the year 1820 his creation became at last too strong for its creator.

It was in these circumstances that Castlereagh drew up that famous state-paper, which subsequently received the approval of Canning, and which supplies, more perfectly perhaps than any other document we have, the key to his mind and to the mind of others who have followed him. The memorandum of May 5, 1820, which can now be read without suppressions,[1] takes its start from the standpoint that, while the Allied Powers could not be indifferent to the Spanish situation, any appearance of offence to Spain by calling a conference to debate Spanish domestic business should be studiously avoided. Military intervention, Castlereagh goes on to argue with all the weight of Wellington's authority behind him, would, even if it were proper, be impolitic in the case of a proud and obstinate people. For the same reason political representations, if made at all, should be made, not by the Powers corporately but individually, corporate action being calculated to offend and not persuade. Thus gradually Castlereagh approaches his central contention. The Great Alliance, he declares, "was an union for the reconquest and liberation of a great proportion of the Continent of Europe from the military dominion of France; and, having subdued the Conqueror, it took the state of possession as established by the Peace under the protection of the Alliance. It never was, however, intended as an Union for the Government of the World, or for the superintendence of the internal affairs of other States."

Doubtless the Alliance so far interfered with the domestic concerns of France as to ban the family of Bonaparte and stigmatise the idea of Revolution, but these apparent exceptions to the general rule of non-interference were directed not so much against Democracy as against Militarism. For the rest the Great Powers of Europe and Russia in particular appeared to be well able to protect themselves by reason of their larger military establishments from any danger threatening them from Spain. For all that, Castlereagh did not attempt to deny that cases might arise—cases involving, as he said, "always a question of the greatest possible moral as well as political delicacy "—where one state might have cause to interfere in the internal concerns of another. These he did not attempt to discuss, though we know that he held that the guiding principle by which they were to be determined was that of self-defence. As regards Great Britain, at any rate, it seemed clear that, with her representative institutions and national sentiments, interference in the domestic affairs of other states must always be distasteful except in

[1] *Camb. Hist. British Foreign Policy*, ii., App. A.

response to some urgent and tangible peril; and he took occasion to point out that the attempt to extend the sphere of the Quadruple Alliance beyond the preservation of the Treaty of Vienna would drive a wedge between the despotic and constitutional members of the Alliance itself. " . . . We are a Power," he concluded grandly, "that must take our principle of action and our scale of acting, not merely from the expediency of the case, but from those maxims which a system of government, strongly popular and national in its character, has irresistibly imposed upon us. We shall be found in our place when actual danger menaces the system of Europe; but this country cannot, and will not, act upon abstract and speculative principles of precaution."

There, then, enunciated in terms which left no room for misunderstanding, were the ideas to which, not Castlereagh's school only, but Canning's school also were content to subscribe, at any rate with their lips. For the next century they formed the theoretical basis of that boasted continuity in British foreign policy of which we speak, as they were also the practical source of many of its difficulties as well as of much of its strength. Their nature and origin is writ large upon them, and no one can study them long without perceiving it. They were laid deep in that sensible, unimaginative, tolerant view of things which is an Englishman's, or at least an educated Englishman's portion; they were conditioned by an insular security which is fast disappearing and a constitutional growth where contradictory ideas have long flourished in an amity almost or quite unattainable amongst more logical races; and they were drafted by the hand of an aristocrat, to whom Democracy was perhaps an even less acceptable notion than Absolute Monarchy. A great patience is apparent in every line—the patience of one who can afford to bide his time and is resolved to see his road spreading out clear before him.

To Metternich, differently constituted, differently educated, differently situated, there seemed to be a more excellent way of dealing with the European situation. Whilst he was at one with Castlereagh in wishing to keep the Russians out of Spain, he became urgent as the year wore on to get the Austrians into Naples. And for this a price had to be paid to Alexander, since the Russian Emperor would not agree to let the Austrian armies operate except in the capacity of the outstretched, avenging arm of Europe. The situation, therefore, necessitated another Congress where the Powers might sit in conclave over Neapolitan affairs. Metternich might well have feared that this would give occasion for conversations about Spain also. He ran the risk, and triumphed gloriously.

The Eastern Powers of Europe were represented at Troppau in all their strength, but Castlereagh did not come, and was only with difficulty persuaded to allow his brother—at that time ambassador at Vienna—to attend there for the sake of appearances and in the character, more or less, of an observer and emphatically not of a plenipotentiary. France followed the English lead and sent persons of little consequence to represent her halting opinions. Thus for the first time in that century the three autocratic Powers of Europe stood ranged together against the two constitutional Countries of the West. It was the precise development which Castlereagh had anxiously foreshadowed in his state-paper—a new *motif*, as one might say, if the metaphor be not too ambitious, in the diplomatic symphony of the coming period, of which we shall catch the refrain again from time to time and whose final and loudest variation is to be found in the misnamed Dreikaiserbündnis, or League of the Three Emperors of 1872.[1] Out of the tangled politics of the time Alexander had at last contrived to drag the form and methods of a super-state, and Metternich an organised defence of monarchy against revolution, whilst Castlereagh, the first begetter of these systematic assemblies of Europe—or of what counted for most in Europe—in council, was left high and dry, his plan perverted, his much-sought countenance of the proceedings cruelly abused. To the astonished and dissentient ears of the British Ambassador, the Monarchs and Ministers assembled —regardless, as Castlereagh complained, of the fall of the House of Stuart and the rise of the House of Hanover—sounded forth in their famous *Protocole préliminaire* the theme of Legitimist Monarchy in all its superb intransigence. States, should they permit a revolutionary change of government, "the results of which threaten other states," were to be placed upon probation outside the pale of the Alliance or even, if circumstances seemed

---

[1] It was strictly a Dreikaiserverhältnis (there being no written agreement). See the *Camb. Mod. Hist.*, xii. 139.

to require, to be compelled under pressure, pacific or military as the case might be, to return to its bosom, but presumably after expiating their fault by the loss of their new institutions.

Castlereagh, it need scarcely be said, was not prepared for this. He had no easy faith in the value of constitutions. He knew, from A'Court's despatches, that Naples was being decently governed, before a minority made the revolution, that a constitution of English make had just proved a failure in Sicily, and that a constitution of Spanish make was not likely to prove a success in the sister-kingdom. He knew that developments in the south of Italy could hardly fail to affect Austrian administration in the north of the peninsula. Also he knew that Austria enjoyed under the terms of a secret treaty the right to object to any change in the old Neapolitan constitution; and he was content, and even glad, to see this right enforced. But he was totally opposed, on grounds already sufficiently defined, to the consolidation of Europe under one supreme authority, and to the imposition with a high, repressive hand of new forms of government upon independent nations, whether small or great. Stewart represented his brother's objections, and, after the conference at Troppau had dissolved into a new conference at Laibach, recorded his brother's protest. But Metternich had all the strength that he needed with Russia at his back. Austria was commissioned to take action in Naples; and the Neapolitan army, in spite of the popular idea that the love of freedom furnishes the power to secure it, collapsed at Rieti in the most ignominious manner possible before the Imperial forces. We must not suppose that Castlereagh greatly minded; he was more in sympathy with Metternich's repressive measures than he always cared that the House of Commons should know.

In the very month of March 1821 which saw the collapse both of the Neapolitan and Piedmontese revolts, a more formidable bid for constitutional freedom on the part of the Greeks brought Castlereagh and Metternich once more together. It was essential to keep Alexander quiet, for neither England nor Austria wanted to see Turkey dismembered nor Russia at the Narrows; and the two Ministers met in Hanover and agreed upon a common, though not a precisely identical, policy. Between them they held the Emperor in play for the best part of a year, Castlereagh by the boldness of his front, Metternich by the apparent pliancy of his purpose. A new congress in the autumn of 1822 had been arranged for, and to that congress everything could conveniently be referred.

Meanwhile Castlereagh did not hesitate to convey to the Emperor in some sentences which have justly brought his consistency into question, that in his view the existing form of government in the Turkish Empire was secured by the settlement at Vienna and the protective alliance of the Powers concerned in it. It is important where words are ambiguous to quote them exactly. "The nature of the Turkish power," he said, "was fully understood when the existing state of Europe, including that of Turkey, was placed under the provident care and anxious protection of the General Alliance." The best that can be said in defence of this utterance is that in the Turkish problem the territorial and the constitutional issue could not be divided—that Turkey was not made for a constitution and that no constitution could be made for Turkey. The essence of the Eastern question lay in the fact that every gain of political freedom by the Greeks, or for the matter of that any of the Turkish subject-races, involved a corresponding loss of territorial sovereignty to the Turks, and that each surrendered slip of Turkish soil was calculated, so far as anyone could see, to bring Russian influence, though not perhaps the Russian Empire, nearer to Constantinople, nearer to the magnet that had drawn Russian seamen and Russian steel ever since the days of Rurik. Neither by Castlereagh nor by any other English minister for many years to come was a solution of this vexed and complex issue to be found, and, when it came at last, it was something wholly different from what anyone had in his time dreamed of. He, with his usual good sense, was, indeed, well content to leave the conclusion of the whole matter to the wise hands of Time; and to these he desired and advised the Greeks to commit their cause. His main position is plain enough. He held that, so far as Europe was concerned, Peace was the supreme consideration, Revolution a more urgent peril than Oppression, and Turkey "a necessary evil" incidental to the maintenance of the European system.

Even as he argued, a new outburst of revolutionary activity in Spain began to attract the eyes of Alexander away from the troubles of the Christian population of the Turkish Empire; and it became plain that the Spanish question must have a great place at the coming congress. For that Congress, as well as for the preliminary Conference at Vienna, Castlereagh was bound in the August of 1822; and the curious may like to speculate whether in the event his presence there would have added to or diminished his fame. On the one hand his relations with Metternich were once again close; his prestige, dimmed by the results of Laibach, had recovered; and his faith in non-interference was unimpaired. On the other side it may be urged that France under Villèle's guidance had passed over from the constitutional to the autocratic school, and was now hand-in-glove with Russia, and resolved to intervene in Spain; that Prussia stood behind them; that Metternich was always an uncertain factor; that Castlereagh was likely in the end to stand alone, as in fact befell Wellington, who took his place. Let all this be as it may, one thing at least is clear. Castlereagh, had he gone to Verona, would have grappled with his difficulties, unassisted by that calm energy of mind and body which had carried him so far. He had become an ineffably tired man, worn down by a strain that included the largest responsibility as well in domestic as foreign affairs; perplexed by the strained relations that had arisen between the King and Liverpool and between the King's mistress and his own rather lovable and very respectable frump of a wife; and pursued by abuse, of which Shelley's effusion, written in 1819, serves still to perpetuate the character. Old Addington, whom we mostly recall as the Paddington of the famous simile, is here coupled with Castlereagh; and together they appear to the vision of the frenzied bard as

> " . . . two vultures sick for battle,
>   Two scorpions under one wet stone,
> Two bloodless wolves whose dry throats rattle,
> Two crows perched on the murrained cattle,
>   Two vipers tangled into one." [1]

The poem was published only in 1832, but appropriately in the month of August.

Castlereagh had now completed ten full momentous years of office without a break; and he was under no illusion as to his own exhaustion. "The session had to end, or I should end," he told Chateaubriand, as the Parliamentary recess drew near.

[1] Similes for two political characters of 1819.

But the burden of leadership in the Commons was no sooner lifted than it was replaced by that of diplomacy; and to one who expressed a hope that a trip abroad and the society of many old friends presented a pleasant prospect, he replied, holding his hand upon his forehead: "At any other time I should like it very much, but I am quite worn out here." The country home to which he had betaken himself failed to bring him its customary balm. He had in truth run his race, and his mind was losing its balance. Not the doctor, but his old colleague and friend was the first to perceive how matters stood with him. With a bold simplicity, Wellington told him, which was perhaps after all the wisest course, that his fears for his safety and wild imaginations of persecution showed a brain disordered. He knew the sanity of the Duke's own judgment too well to doubt the truth of the warning. "Since you say so," he replied, "it must be so." In modern conditions he might, perhaps, with rest have gradually recovered. In the days in which his lot was cast, bleeding was still the panacea of physicians. Weakened still further in body, his mind was even yet a match for his attendants. They removed his razors; but he remembered a pen-knife, and with one fatal stroke achieved his end. Sudden death as often as not has to pay a tribute to scandal as well as a tribute to sensation ; and Castlereagh had by his actual delusions given the gossips their cue. It was suggested, not only that he feared, but that he had cause to fear, the disclosure of some hideous episode in his private history, and that he took his life in consequence. Such things have been. But in Castlereagh's case only an extreme capacity for believing in obscenities, or an extreme incapacity for sifting evidence, should provide a defence for those who countenance and continue the story; for it rests, as Professor Webster points out,[1] upon the idlest gossip, and it relates to one whose record should place his reputation above reproach.

Good character can, however, in sensational circumstances arouse suspicion almost as easily as ill-fame. Castlereagh's apparently blameless life; his devoted attachment to a wife who appeared to others only a figure of fun; his habitual aloofness, untiring industry, cold exterior and lack of demonstrative enthusiasm, all tended to invest his personality with enough

[1] Webster, *Foreign Policy of Castlereagh*, p. 486.

strangeness to make any dreadful improbability seem plausible. Some of us can remember how, in our time, the sudden death from purely natural causes of one whose character, though far more subtle, was not without curious points of likeness to that of Castlereagh, was immediately attributed by the feverish sensationalism of comparatively sane human beings to the results of a duel with its usual romantic accompaniment. Others, older, can afford to be amused at the supposition that in the suicide during an attack of fever of a great English peer the world had beheld the self-inflicted execution, under pain of exposure, of Jack the Ripper. The stories about Castlereagh may be classed with these. He was in his time, and after his time, a man, by reason of his detachment, greatly misunderstood. If Professor Webster is right, he had only two strong affections; and the subjects of those affections—his brother and his wife—were not gifted with sufficient understanding to meet him on equal ground. Wellington alone perhaps really entered into his thoughts and gauged to the full his wisdom. But Wellington wasted no time on biographical studies. It was not, therefore, altogether surprising that only in 1862, after Stewart and Alison had tried and failed, was someone found with the requisite qualifications to paint Castlereagh's literary portrait. Then, at length, the work was done with a sureness of touch and a breadth of sympathy which left little room for other biographers.

Salisbury had close affinities with the subject of his brilliant essay—the conservatism void of sentiment and broad-based upon reason; the detachment at times wisely, at others unwisely disdainful of opinion around; the absence of enthusiasm, of faith in causes, of fondness for catchwords; the belief in caustic commonsense, in resolute government, in the freedom that is felt as against the liberties that are boasted about; above all an overmastering interest and supreme ability in the conduct of foreign affairs. In a memorable passage, which discovered much of his own philosophy, this judicious admirer observed that, "Lord Castlereagh's was not a mind in which excited feelings had destroyed the proportion between different objects of desire." "He knew," Salisbury continued, "the very different values of the boons for which men indiscriminately clamoured. The graduation in his mind seems to have stood thus: he cared for nationality not at all; for the theoretic perfection of political institutions very little;

for the realities of freedom a great deal; and for the peace and
social order and freedom from the manifold curses of disturbance,
which can alone give to the humbler masses of mankind any
chance of tasting their scanty share of human joys—for the sake
of this, he was quite ready to forgo all the rest." [1]   This searching analysis best discovers the hidden beauty and distinction of
character latent in one in appearance, as it happened, beautiful
and distinguished beyond the ordinary.   For the loftiest bene-
volence does its work by stealth, without noise of words, without
the acclamations of the multitude, without "the roaring" and
without "the wreaths."   Castlereagh, as one or two trifling
incidents recorded of him suggest, had this truly aristocratic
ideal before his eyes.   And it was perhaps this very aristocracy
of soul that secured for him the last honour of the Christian.   He
was monstrously misrepresented and vilely abused by men who
were so little fit to govern kingdoms that they had not yet
learned to rule their own lives or establishments.   Political
ineptitude, speaking through the mouth of Shelley, told how,
as it walked amongst "visions of poesy" it had "met Murder
on its way" and how Murder "had a mask like Castlereagh."
Political malice, spitting mud through Byron's brazen lips,
styled him "an intellectual eunuch," a "cold-blooded, smooth-
faced, placid miscreant," "the vulgarest tool that tyranny could
want," "a tinkering slave-maker, who mends old chains"; [2] as
a minister, "the most despotic in intention and the weakest in
intellect that ever tyrannised over a country"; [3] and, finally,
with a last discharge of nauseating venom, "carotid-artery-
cutting Castlereagh." [4]   Nor were there even wanting some to
execrate the tired body as it passed to its last resting-place within
the Abbey.

There Castlereagh lay, but little considered, for close upon a
century.   Then, amidst the diplomatic muddles of our time,
the diplomatic merits of his once disparaged policy began to
appear.   One of the ablest and most diligent of our living
historians [5] in a series of studies, large in learning, examined and
displayed his work.   His figure grew in size and splendour.   He

---

[1] Salisbury's *Biographical Essays*, p. 62.
[2] *Don Juan*, Dedication, xi.-xiv.
[3] *Ibid.*, Preface to Canto VI.
[4] *Ibid.*, x. 159.
[5] Professor Webster.

became recognised as one of the best friends of Europe and of peace. At length, when the Treaty of Locarno was ratified in London, his portrait was placed above the heads of those who set their names to that pacific pact, as if he were the appropriate patron-saint of their endeavours. Thus, after a life closed in fitful fever, after the long eclipse of reputation that overtakes for a time even the greatest when they have been a little while dead, and after foul-mouthed poets and the coarser kind of critics have done their worst, he fares well.

II

CANNING

[GEORGE CANNING.—Born 1770. *Foreign Secretary*, 1807–1809, and 1822–1827 (April). Prime Minister, 1827 (April). Died 1827.]

CANNING

In the course of that large training in humanity which comes of the study of character there is, as Plutarch long ago perceived, a particular education to be derived from the juxtaposition of two personalities whose genius is similar, whose careers compare, whose ideas meet only to part, and part only to meet again, but who are nevertheless impassably divided by the great gulf fixed by nature between each man of talent and his compeers. For an exercise in this kind it would be hard to find a better subject than is suggested by the names of Castlereagh and Canning. The mention of the one almost invariably evokes that of the other. They were contemporaries; they were of Ulster origin; they were engaging in appearance and endowed with charm; they were Tories, though both had had early adventures in Whiggery or worse; they were alike schooled and inspired by Pitt; they made their mark in the same office, where in fact the one succeeded the other without any open breach of policy; they both sustained the same Prime Minister, who, but for their support, would probably have fallen; they both acquired a great mastery over the House of Commons; and they both died, as at any rate men see things, before their time.

And yet everything was as different as it well could be. Castlereagh started with the, at that time apparent, and even in the present time not altogether negligible, advantage of a title, with a recognised position in society, an assured income, and a reputation for political ability not derived from smart talk or boys' debating societies but from early contact across the Irish Channel with the most obstinate of British political problems. Canning, the son of a penniless barrister whose widow had taken for a living to the provincial stage, depended upon the chance of an Eton education, which an uncle had given him in a fortunate hour, and for the rest upon his wits. They were, as the sequence showed, wits indeed, and afforded all the contrast imaginable to Castlereagh's patient ability and lack of solid education.[1] For Canning had penetrated to the recesses of a liberal education, was a master of the humanities and a student of history and economics, a dialectician, satirist, essayist, orator, even in some measure a poet. His wit and charm in conversation are noted by Scott, who knew him well and liked him, not less than his lash of a tongue in debate which "fetched away both skin and flesh and would have penetrated the hide of a rhinoceros."[2] He shone, little as he showed himself after his marriage, high above the firmament in a society which had listened to Pitt and been taught by Burke; which had Sheridan for its playwright, Scott for its novelist, Keats and Shelley to sing it songs, and Sidney Smith to make it merry. No man, perhaps, of parts more brilliant ever held the first places in the State.

And in all this Canning presented a contrast to Castlereagh, who never dazzled for all his brains, who left no witticisms behind him like the old hit about Pitt and Addington, London and Paddington; nor household words, like the "Friend of Humanity" which children love before they penetrate its meaning; nor famous phrases, like the memorable boast that the New World had been called into existence to redress the balance of the Old. At every point except one, indeed, Canning appears, and is, the better man of the two—quicker, clearer, smarter, cleverer, beyond discussion more talented. But in one quality he was indisputably Castlereagh's inferior: and its possession in larger measure, at the crisis when their careers crossed, gave to his rival an advantage so complete and decisive that never, whilst Castlereagh was alive, did the two come again into competition. The lesser man intellectually was the stronger man morally. Castlereagh possessed what we call character. His patriotism had in it as little self-seeking as is ordinarily possible; he placed his abilities unreservedly at the disposal of his country and set no price upon them. It was otherwise with Canning. It was not enough for him, at the critical juncture in 1812 when Liverpool asked him to join the Administration, that Castlereagh should offer to vacate the Foreign Office in his favour. He wanted to get full value for his talents and to deprive a man, whom he took

---

[1] Temperley, *Life of Canning*, p. 129. Cf. *The Journal of Sir Walter Scott*, i. 291.   [2] *The Journal of Sir Walter Scott*, ii. p. 20.

for his inferior, of the leadership of the House of Commons also. Greedy of all, he got in the end nothing, lost the great prize of a commanding voice in the counsels of Europe at the great assize of Vienna, and spent ten years either in the administration of an inferior office or without any office at all. The incident showed him to be what some of the best men of his party always took him for—an *arriviste*. Yet he was no unprincipled adventurer. He stood faithful, at the risk of unpopularity and at the cost of some tangible disadvantage, to the cause of Catholic Emancipation, in which he profoundly believed, and whence, unless some pontifical quality in his conversation is responsible for it, he presumably derived the nickname of "the Pope"; [1] and he remained loyal to Queen Caroline, whose friend he had been and whose little Court he had once frequented. Only he seemed to his contemporaries to lack that supreme gift of disinterestedness which men desire most of all things in a leader, and the absence of which they are quick to detect. He seemed to want all too much, as we should say, to 'scintillate' and to 'score,' all too little to convince. Erskine put the whole matter in a nutshell. Castlereagh, he declared, never made a speech without making a friend, nor Canning without making an enemy. And that though Canning's speeches are monuments of style and Castlereagh's beacon-fires of mixed metaphor!

There was one thing more that insensibly drew the men apart in policy. Canning, a firm believer in the political merit of the middle class and the representative of a great industrial constituency,[2] adopted, perhaps unconsciously, the competitive standpoint of the merchant—its exaggerated individualism and vigorous faith in competition both within and without the State. Castlereagh had another philosophy latent in his bones—a larger international generosity and a better use for co-operation. He knew, as Canning never knew, the statesmen of other countries; and he wished rather to persuade than to outwit them. His policy had its reward partly in peace, but much in promise; Canning's in spectacular triumphs, commercial gains, and the jealousy of less successful rivals.

The points of agreement and difference between the two men are, indeed naturally enough, most obvious in the sphere of foreign affairs. Claiming to continue the policy of his predecessor,

[1] See the *Letters of Lord Granville Leveson-Gower, passim.*   [2] Liverpool.

and, in fact, adopting both the general principles outlined in
Castlereagh's famous memorandum of May 5, 1820, and the
particular instructions drafted by him a little before his death
in view of the coming Congress at Verona, Canning immediately discovered a distinct and even conflicting disposition.
He was aware of this himself. "You know my politics well
enough," he wrote to Bagot, in the year in which he resumed
the direction of the Foreign Office, "to know what I mean when
I say that for *Europe* I shall be desirous *now* and *then* to read
England." [1] It was in truth as an Englishman unaffected or but
little affected by the larger thought of Europe that he approached
the problems of his department; and it is the growth and development of the national or imperial, as it is in Castlereagh the growth
and development and disappointment of the cosmopolitan or
continental outlook, that affords the key to his diplomacy.

Canning was born in 1770, a year later than Castlereagh.
Under circumstances already alluded to, he went to Eton, where
he made as much mark as a boy may do, and then to Oxford,
where he made so much more mark than other young men that
Portland offered him a seat in Parliament.[2] As the offer showed,
he was still a Whig, but he declined it, for already his mind was
turning. Pitt had fixed his gaze, and a few months later had
fixed his politics. They were and they remained the politics of
a man who had seen what Democracy can be when it falls under
the power of revolutionaries; but they were also the politics of
one for whom the old Tory faith had no meaning. Canning's
political creed was the creed of most sensible men—a creed the
tenets of which sensible men, in a world constituted like our
own, are more and more likely never to tell. He believed a
little in most organs of government but in none overmuch. He
wanted a king but not a despot; a peerage but not a caste; a
House of Commons but one in which selection had a voice as well
as popular election; a free Press but not one able to smother or
shout down the men in power. He wanted, in fact, the British
Constitution very much as he found it; and his reforms were not
in the direction of fundamental change but of increased efficiency.
If he had a political passion it was for nationality; and his
political system reached no further, dissolving, in fact, if the

---

[1] Quoted by Temperley, *Life of Canning*, p. 125.
[2] Temperley, *Life of Canning*, p. 31.

truth be told, just at this point into a theology as obscure as Alexander's:—Every nation for itself and God for them all.

For the rest, the French Revolution was for him, as for Burke who was his best philosopher, the dominant fact of the time. Only his broad, all-penetrating humour seized not upon its sublime but its comic aspects; and he had the genius to treat it as a joke. His opportunity was admirable. Equality as a political sentiment was not then the stale shibboleth that we expect to find in the mouth of every candidate for Parliament, constantly impeding by its crude mendacity the intelligent treatment of social and economic problems, but an active principle in which people were innocent enough seriously to believe. Canning was the first to master its immense, unconscious humour, and ridiculed it in the *Anti-Jacobin* beyond repair. Friends of Humanity meet us still on exalted platforms and needy Knife-Grinders at the corners of the streets, but we have no excuse if we take them for anything but what they are, or forget that they represent the two eternal types of political ineptitude, between whom wiser men have somehow to force their way along.

France and the friends of France offered in the years of Canning's political apprenticeship as good a target as humourist could desire and as profitable a text as Conservatism could look for. The tale was, of course, the same as Russia has told in our time—real grievances, well-meant efforts at reform, fine words, fine promises; in due course, a house swept and garnished; then a thousand devils let loose upon it, murder, rapine, anarchy, and a bold general propaganda in their favour, the whole business concluding in a constitution less representative than the *ancien régime* and a tyranny more emphatic than that of the king. There were two schools of thought amongst the British foes of the Revolution—the two schools that we so constantly encounter in the study of foreign policy—the continental and the insular—but the event made them one. Burke was fighting the Revolution as a European, Pitt at first only as an Englishman because English interests were attacked. The French satisfied the requirements of all their critics. They declared for a general rising against constituted authority and they attacked England in particular—for England thus early knew that she must reckon this the equivalent of an attack upon herself—by invading Belgium.

Canning's mind in respect of the question of peace or war with

France is not perfectly clear, and is not rendered clearer by the fact that between 1796 and 1799, when he was Under-Secretary for Foreign Affairs, he accomplished, to all appearance with considerable success, the reputedly impossible task of serving two if not three masters. The poetry or verse of the *Anti-Jacobin*, to which Canning, to our certain knowledge,[1] contributed, with some casual assistance from Frere, "The Friend of Humanity," "Mrs Brownrigg the Prenticecide," "The Song of Rogero," and parts of "The Progress of Man," belongs in its entirety to some few months in the winter and spring of 1797–98 and is conceived in the spirit of Burke and under the influence of his famous *Reflections*. But at the Foreign Office Canning is at once the confidant of Pitt, who was earnestly soliciting peace in a manner very repugnant to the author of the *Letters on a Regicide Peace*, and the spokesman of Grenville, his immediate departmental chief, who was all for fighting to the finish—so much the spokesman in fact that the speech of 11th December 1798, which made his name as an orator, is a determined plea for Grenville's point of view. He was, however, only an under-secretary, and nobody has ever been at the pains to lay down as a matter of constitutional doctrine that an under-secretary is entitled to a mind of his own. In any event, Canning's first connection with the Foreign Office was probably of more influence in forming his opinion about the interior organisation of the Department than about its exterior policy. He stands out in the domestic history of the Office as one of its great reformers, a severe but also playful pedagogue, castigating ambassadors like the unfortunate Strangford with no light nor easy hand, confusing dignified officials like Hammond by ringing for them just when they were posed in pomp before foreign representatives, and perplexing old friends like Bagot with a rhyming despatch that has become a household word in diplomatic history.[2]

[1] Temperley, *Life of Canning*, p. 44.

[2]   Foreign Office, *January* 31, 1826.

Sir,

    In matters of commerce the fault of the Dutch
    Is offering too little and asking too much.
    The French are with equal advantage content,
    So we clap on Dutch bottoms just 20 per cent.
        (*Chorus*) 20 per cent., 20 per cent.

(*Chorus of English Customs House Officers and French Douaniers.*)
    (*English*) We clap on Dutch bottoms just 20 per cent.
    (*French*) Vous frapperez Falck avec 20 per cent.

This, however, is to anticipate later developments by a good deal. Only, before we pass on to the study of his foreign policy, it is as well to notice how much more care Canning paid to the departmental machine than many men think worth while, and how great power he drew from that admixture of praise and blame which, playing judiciously upon the motives of hope and fear, extracts from most men, as from all, or almost all boys the best that is in them.

Canning left the Foreign Office in 1799 to become a member of the Board of Control, to which appointment he added one or two others of minor consequence. In this manner began that connection of his with India which acted throughout his life as a kind of second string to his bow, but which has been almost eclipsed by the Indian celebrity of his son.[1] An exceptional circumstance, as it happened, tended on three separate occasions to cut short his activities in this direction. In 1801 it was Catholic Emancipation which provoked Pitt's resignation and his own in Pitt's wake. Retirement from office brought with it the unfortunate temptation to let his wit play around Addington. The new Prime Minister was no worse fool than many of the respectable persons who provide the staple, indispensable furniture of Cabinets, whether of Conservative, Liberal or Labour manufacture; but he looked irresistibly comical when he was preferred to Pitt, opposed to Napoleon, and presented as the son of Chatham's apothecary. Canning had his fun about "the doctor" and "the Villa Medici"; and "happy Britain's guardian gander" was neatly trussed. But smart jokes in the Lobby cost a long price in the House, and that strong section of Tories, whom Addington adequately represented, did their best to see that Canning paid his debts. He was indeed a man just too witty to be wise.

Addington's administration came to an end with the Peace, and, with Pitt again in power, Canning recovered office. His post was not of much consequence; nor did he hold it long. The times were pregnant with chance and change. Pitt's death drove him once more into opposition, and Fox's death brought him back once more to power. At the age of thirty-seven he became Foreign Secretary in Portland's Government. His administration is remembered, not so much for its energy as for two incidents, neither of which told to the advantage of the Country, causing

[1] Lord Canning.

it, as they did, a loss of reputation abroad and the loss of a good servant at home.

The seizure of the Danish Fleet and the duel with Castlereagh are still rather mysterious affairs; and it does not appear, as regards the former, that the Canning Papers, so long withheld by the late Lord Clanricarde, are going to provide light in obscurity. But if the historian still goes hungry for want of knowing for certain upon whose information Canning acted, the moral philosopher at least remains well-filled. For the case of conscience involved is as pretty a morsel as ever British casuist was set to cook. Canning, as the reader may remember, in the belief that Napoleon and Alexander had agreed on the raft at Tilsit to compel Denmark to use the Danish Fleet against Great Britain, anticipated their expected action by seizing the Danish Fleet himself. His proceedings involved the violation of Danish neutrality and the bombardment of the Danish capital. His defence was that the safety of the State is itself the highest law. The plea at best is perilous enough, for it can be urged by any Power that chooses to think its security endangered and twisted to justify anything from the murder of the Duc d'Enghien in 1804 to the German invasion of Belgium in 1914. But whatever the plea is worth, the pleader ought at the very least to be able to prove to posterity that it rested upon facts and not upon fears. Unfortunately for Canning, this is just what he and his advocates have failed to do. Not only is the source of his information about what passed between the two Emperors on the raft still obscure, but the information itself, we have reason to believe, was incorrect. If it came "direct from Tilsit," from Mackenzie or some Russian officer, the informer was betrayed into that too intelligent anticipation of events which is the bane of all seekers after secrets, whether they be spies or journalists; if it came from Talleyrand, as some suppose, he may have wanted to deceive; if it was derived from the Prince Regent of Portugal, as Malmesbury—a contemporary authority in a good position to know since not only was he the doyen amongst the English diplomatists of the day but his son actually at the time Under-Secretary of State for Foreign Affairs and deeply implicated in the transaction—asserts, then the Prince Regent must have said a great deal too much. For—to borrow Professor J. H. Rose's words—"the plan of coercion was conditional" whilst

"Canning believed it to be absolute and immediate."[1] The coercion of Denmark, that is, was conditional upon Great Britain's refusing a Russian offer to mediate between herself and France. And there was no certainty even that Great Britain must refuse. Talleyrand at this very time was commenting to Napoleon on the relatively pacific character of the British despatches.[2]

It is unlucky if you are fighting an immoral or non-moral tyrant to give a general impression that you are indifferent to public law and a believer in *force majeure*. It is still more unlucky if the opinions of a powerful idealist are still hanging at all in the balance. Yet into both these blunders Canning by his precipitancy fell. Naval and military critics may be left to make his excuses. More detached persons will be content to say that the two years of his foreign administration were the most difficult of the war, and that, with Napoleon threatening to raise a fleet numerically the equal of our own by the amalgamation of the Continental navies, a Foreign Secretary must not be judged too severely for shortness of thought. Yet the psychologist will hardly take it to be a chance that one who all his life failed to appreciate the value of European solidarity and thought in terms of nations, should have caused his country to commit the most unsocial act in all her history.

Of the duel with Castlereagh—of its cause, significance and effect—enough has been said elsewhere. For those who were serving with him, it must have emphasised Canning's other great and kindred defect—his want of *esprit-de-corps*. As he had a difficulty in understanding the value of a code amongst nations, so he had also a difficulty in understanding the obligations of a code amongst men. He was a good man to serve under but not as good a man to work with on a parity.

The duel, for the rest, was the outcome of departmental differences, upon which the native antipathy of the two men all too readily fixed. We know that they opposed one another over the Walcheren business, over the best method of aiding the Spanish rising, over the appointment of Wellington to the command in Portugal, and apparently also over the respective merits of Moore's and Frere's work in Spain; and we may judge from what we know about these affairs that there was something to be said on

[1] *Camb. Mod. Hist.*, xi. 298.
[2] *Ibid.*, p. 299.

Canning's side but more on Castlereagh's. The less brilliant man, as often happens, was the better statesman; but it took Canning some years more to recognise Castlereagh as even so much as his equal, and in those years the flood-tide of his opportunity was lost.

But for his reckless gibes, his tactless suggestions and his inordinate self-esteem, Canning might have entered the Governments either of Perceval or of Liverpool. But neither could Sidmouth, who was one and the same as the Addington of his jests, nor Eldon, whom he had been planning to deprive of the Lord Chancellorship so that Perceval might take the great seal and he himself secure the Premiership,[1] nor yet Castlereagh whom he required to vacate, not only the Foreign Office, but also the Leadership of the House of Commons in his favour, be expected to welcome him as a colleague. Thus, through his own ambition, he was left to wander for some while in the wilderness, and for some while more outside his proper orbit. For a couple of years and under exceptional circumstances he became British Ambassador at Lisbon, but the appointment brought him more trouble than reputation. Then, in 1816, he was offered the Presidency of the Board of Control—a post corresponding, so far as the then constitution of India allowed, to that of Indian Secretary—and was wise enough to accept it. The accession of George IV. in 1820 threw him once more out of power, for he was unwilling, in face of his old friendship with her, to act with the Ministry against Queen Caroline. Two years later a new and magnificent prospect opened before him—a prospect all the more grateful that he had much reduced the not inconsiderable fortune which his wife had brought him, and that there was no appointment in those days like an Indian one for increasing one's income. Just, however, as he was about to sail for India, over which he had been nominated Governor-General, there came in his career a sudden, dramatic, wholly incalculable turn of the wheel of Fortune. Castlereagh killed himself; and, immediately, Canning became the obvious man to place at the Foreign Office.[2] The obvious man, but, not for that, the popular nominee amongst those who would have to serve with him and under him! For we have to remember that there were two offices to be filled—

[1] Temperley, *Life of Canning*, p. 110.
[2] Temperley, *Foreign Policy of Canning*, p. 29.

the Leadership of the House as well as the Foreign Office. Canning resolved at once that he would have both or neither; and he let it be known. With India in his pocket and no equal in debate, with a declining interest in domestic politics and a feeling that in regard to foreign policy the plums had been already plucked, he could afford to wait the issue with equanimity. For five weeks, Liverpool, his best friend in the Cabinet, was in no position to surrender to his terms. Then, at length, under Wellington's constraining influence, King and Cabinet came in to heel, and on 15th September 1822 he received 'the whole heritage,' as he named it, of Castlereagh.

It was a fine heritage, but, as he knew well enough, neither at home nor abroad the heritage it once had been. The Tory Government was very old, and men had long been expecting, though, as it proved, prematurely, the inevitable swing of the tireless pendulum of opinion. Abroad, as it seemed, the great decisions had already been taken, the new grouping of the Powers effected, and the hands of Time's clock pushed back by the supple fingers of Metternich. Canning had arrived at last, but, as he thought at the moment, too late upon the field to realise his ambition. His exact feelings are on record: "As to foreign politics, what is there remaining but the husk without the kernel?" [1] So one might reasonably argue, and so in the case of a less brilliant personality it might have proved! But, as it was, within a lustrum and without any formal breach with the work of his predecessor, Canning stamped the impress of his mind upon the Foreign Office, started another school of diplomacy, brought into sight a new, a far horizon, caused an old chapter of history to be closed and a fresh one to be opened. It was small wonder that Acton acclaimed him as the greatest of all our foreign ministers.[2] He is at least very great—the embodiment of the centrifugal, as Castlereagh is the embodiment of the centripetal, force in our European policy.

We have now to pick up the main skein of the story at the point where the Fates, snapping the thread of Castlereagh's life, caused us to drop it. The weeks in which the dead Minister had intended to complete his plans and strengthen his under-

---

[1] Temperley, *Foreign Policy of Canning*, p. 29.
[2] " No Foreign Secretary has equalled Canning " (quoted in Temperley's *Life of Canning*, p. 268).

standing with Metternich had slipped by in idle hesitations; and Canning, when he took his place at the Foreign Office in the middle of September (1822), found the Congress actually upon him. He was no lover of conferences, and he had been strongly of opinion that Castlereagh had countenanced them too freely at Aix, yet he made no hostile gesture such as might seem to imply disagreement with his predecessor's views. Wellington, Castlereagh's best friend in public policy, went off to Verona with Castlereagh's instructions in his bag. Only, before the British Representative reached his destination, Canning had found occasion to throw the question of Spain definitely into the foreground of British, as it was now also of Continental policy, and to emphasise Castlereagh's clear admonition to observe 'a rigid abstinence from any interference in the internal affairs' of that country by a vigorous instruction 'frankly and peremptorily to declare,' if occasion offered, that, come what might, the King of England—for that was still the phrase—would be no party to any interference in Spain either by force or menace. The tone of the despatch showed at once that a man, energetic and high-handed, had replaced a man tired and tactful.

The diplomatic situation at Verona was curious but clear. The Great European Autocracies, their mutual sympathy no longer distracted by the time-honoured tie between Castlereagh and Metternich, had drawn together again and were bent upon intervention in Spain, where disorder was continually gaining ground. France, as Villèle, her royalist Prime Minister, made plain to Wellington when he passed through Paris, was of the same mind, but not for the same method. She favoured intervention; but it was to be her own intervention and to take place at her own time, for she desired to have for herself all the honour and glory that was to be had out of the affair. She had good cards to play. She was the Power in the closest touch both diplomatically and geographically with the King of Spain, and she played her hand with great skill. Wellington was left to make his ineffective protest against any intervention at all, and, having made it, to pass for all practical purposes off the stage. From the other three Powers represented at Verona more was to be obtained; and France obtained it. They were invited to state whether, in the event of a rupture of relations with the Spanish Government, they would give the French a diplomatic backing, and also, what moral and material support they would accord in the event of hostilities.

Alexander placed himself at once at the French disposal; Metternich and Frederick William concurred but with reserves. France, however, had got all she needed to make her safe from revolution at home, should she want to slip her armies, already on a spurious pretext aligned along her south-western frontier, actually across the Pyrenees. There was nothing wanting to make her completely mistress of the situation but that the Eastern Powers should withdraw their Representatives from Spain before she did so herself. This would give her both the prestige of independent action in Europe and the last word at Madrid. Montmorency, who, as Foreign Minister, had carried through the European side of the negotiation at Verona, was therefore dropped at Christmas, and Chateaubriand—the great Chateaubriand— substituted in his stead. But the reins of French policy remained in the hands of the King and Villèle. Whilst the Eastern Autocracies were threatening to withdraw their representatives in Spain, a despatch from Paris, drawn up on Christmas Day and inserted in the *Moniteur* a day or so later, breathed pious aspirations that the Spanish Government might be able to reform itself, vague promises of friendship if it did so, vague threats of interference if it did not. Then at the end of January, after the ambassadors of the Eastern Powers had been withdrawn, Louis XVIII. came out into the open in his speech to Parliament. A hundred thousand Frenchmen, he told his subjects, were ready to march to the help of his cousin in Spain, so that Ferdinand might be free 'to give to his people the institutions they could not hold but for him.'

The words contained the frankest declaration of Legitimism that had yet come from the head of the restored monarchy of France. On the principle of no interference with the domestic business of other States, Castlereagh would probably have left King Louis to express what sentiments he liked to his subjects, leaving it to them to dethrone him if they disagreed. But Canning had not so learnt diplomacy. The words seemed to him a challenge to the political system in which he believed; and he represented to the French Government that they contained doctrine which struck at the roots of the British Constitution and could not therefore, with the countenance of Great Britain, be applied to Spain.   Not content with this he spoke at Harwich, adumbrating the possibility of war.   His blood was up; he had, or thought he had, the opinion of his countrymen at his back, and he believed that with bluff and bluster—for he seems to have had no real intention of going to war—he would be able to stay the outstretched hand of France.   His calculations as regards France, had all England been behind him, were possibly, though not probably, correct.   But he was, in fact, reckoning without George IV. and the more Tory members of the Government.   To them at least, if to no one else, there was nothing disagreeable in the idea of the suppression of the Spanish revolutionaries; and they spoke their thoughts out where the French might hear them.   Canning's protest, even though he absurdly maintained for his own satisfaction that Great Britain never condescended to employ a menace not meant to be put into force, was seen to be what it was, and the French went upon their way unheeding.   February slipped on into March, and then, since the Spanish Revolutionary Government would not bend, it was quickly broken by Angoulême's army.   Liberty—if liberty it was—proved, in spite of all that its prophets are fond of maintaining, just as helpless in Spain as it had done in Naples; and Ferdinand, in spite of the remonstrances of his foreign friends, re-established his reign of horror.

One weapon remained in Canning's hands; and it was a weapon of great range and strength.   The Spanish Colonies in South America, ever since the Mother-Country under the influence, first of Napoleon and then of the Liberal Constitutionalists, had fallen into division and disorder, had been loosening themselves from a tie that had lost all prestige or merit.   In their struggle to get free they could not but gain from the recognition of their independence by the Anglo-Saxon Powers, the one already the leading state in the Western Hemisphere; the other the mistress wherever she chose to be, of the ocean highways of the world. Castlereagh had moved in the matter with his usual cautious deliberation.   It was no part of his political philosophy to countenance republics where monarchies were possible, or to wish to shear his old Allies of the Peninsula of their famed inheritance in the Indies.   Nevertheless, he had asserted firmly, so soon as the Napoleonic Wars were over, that same principle which was the governing rule in all his dealings with other countries—the principle of no military interference; and from this principle no

offer of special advantages for trade could move him. He had
remained neutral, yet for a long while willing to mediate, if
mediation were any good, between the Spanish Government,
still proud and unbending in all its helplessness, and the Spanish
Colonies, invincible so long as no stronger forces came to the
aid of the Mother-Country and yet just hesitating to break clean
away from all their past. He had refused to commit England
in all this business to the opinion of either of those two gigantic
Powers of the world whose organic principles, as Tocqueville supposed would ultimately dispute the field of political development,
and may even yet, though not precisely in the manner he supposed, actually do so.[1] The great, if still but half-formed,
Democracy of North America was pressing on towards a full
recognition of kindred institutions in neighbouring States; the
iron Autocracy of Russia, actually at that time through the
possession of Alaska an American power, was as urgent for the
suppression of ideas pregnant with danger to established things.
Castlereagh's mind, whatever its real bias, showed in this case
an even poise. He distrusted Liberal institutions, and, so far
at least as South America was concerned, with only too much
reason; equally he would have nothing to do with an arbitration
backed by force. He waited upon events, and events in the
end made his course clear to him.

To a nation of shopkeepers, such as we were then and must
hope to be some day again, commerce is a more important concern
than constitutions. The trade that had grown up between
England and South America during the war with Napoleon was
now a vital interest to British merchants and, as long as the status
of the South American peoples remained unsettled, British
merchantmen and British goods were liable to seizure. Castlereagh, in truth, desired no commercial monopoly in those parts
for his country. Had the Spanish Government been willing to
accept his mediation, he would have made it a condition that
trade, modified only by a fair preference in the Spanish favour,[2]
should be free with all the world. But, as things worked out, he
could only take the shortest way to meet the requirements of his
fellow-citizens. The South American Colonies were therefore
admitted to the benefit of that relaxation of the Navigation Act

[1] Tocqueville, *Democracy in America* (Engl. tr., 1875), i. 445.
[2] Webster, *Foreign Policy of Castlereagh*, p. 413.

which up to this time had kept the British colonial trade in leading-strings; and by this curious back-door they entered the comity of nations.

The matter could not be left there; and in the months before his death Castlereagh, but only after the delivery of one last hopeless invitation to the Spanish Government to agree with its Colonies quickly while there was yet time, had been preparing to raise, at Verona, the issue of a *de facto* recognition of the revolted States. What we know of his general standpoint, and what memorials we have of his specific utterances on the subject, alike lead us to suppose that he would have tried to resettle the lost possessions of Spain under forms of monarchical government—a solution more likely to approve itself to the Powers of the Holy Alliance than any other.

At this point, however, as we have seen, the British Foreign Office changed hands and French foreign policy became militant and aggressive. Canning, worsted in the diplomatic struggle over Spain, gave at once to Castlereagh's policy of recognition the twist that might have been expected of him. Out of a shield he quickly forged a sword; and during the memorable situation that ensued it was plain that Great Britain, after long halting between two opinions, had been definitely attracted out of the orbit of the Holy Alliance into that of the American Republics. A magnificent or, as some would say, magniloquent phrase subsequently celebrated this new venture of policy. "I called the New World into existence," said Canning,[1] "to redress the balance of the Old"; and he did not go so much beyond the truth. It would be too speculative to say that he had changed the course of history, but he had most assuredly made a gesture of unending significance—a gesture showing that Great Britain, at least, was willing to forget old colonial resentments, to take the Americas at their own valuation, and to invite their influence to bear upon the affairs of Europe.

To Canning, as Dr Temperley has lately made plain, the famous doctrine associated with the name of President Monroe is really owing. He originated it and would have fought for it; and Monroe neither did the one, nor would at that time have done the other. It was Great Britain, and not the United States, which made the South American Colonies safe from European

[1] Speech, 12th December 1826 (Affairs of Portugal).

attacks during the last phases of their struggle for deliverance. The capture of Cadiz by the French, in the end of September 1823, had resolved the last of the Foreign Secretary's hesitations. From Cadiz a Spanish army, shipped by France and blessed by Russia, might have set forth, in emulation of ancient and more glorious exploits in Spanish history, to recover for Spain the lost wealth of the Indies. It was essential, therefore, to make a counter-move, and to make it quickly. Early in October Canning completed the commercial recognition of the revolted Colonies by the appointment of British Consuls to various posts in South America, and during the same month he secured the political independence of the still inchoate States by a diplomatic conversation with the French Ambassador. It is improbable that Polignac, who filled that office, understood the full importance of a transaction which Canning was careful to register as a memorandum, but, however that may be, the effect of it was to knock the bottom out of any plans of French interference across the Atlantic. Confronted by Canning with a series of direct questions on French policy, Polignac explicitly declared that France abjured any design of acting against the Spanish Colonies by arms. On his side the British Foreign Secretary made it plain that Great Britain would suffer no restrictions to be placed upon her South American trade, nor enter into any conference on the subject of the Spanish Colonies, except in the event of the United States being also invited, and then only on the understanding that Great Britain was recognised to have a predominant interest in the question beyond that of the other Powers of Europe. To the substance of these opinions Polignac, good, easy man, assented. They were forthwith embodied in a memorandum which bears his name and which went the round of the Cabinets of Europe. The British Navy, without lifting anchor or hoisting sail, had paid off in New Spain the French score in the Peninsula.

Canning did not forget to return thanks where thanks were due. In the best remembered passage in all his speeches, and in language which places him among the great masters of classic prose, he drew the comparison between England herself and the slumbering power of her Fleet.

" Our present repose," he told the sea-faring folk of Plymouth, at the end of that critical October of 1823, "is no more a proof of

inability to act than the state of inertness and inactivity in which I
have seen those mighty masses that float in the waters above your
town is a proof they are devoid of strength and incapable of being
fitted out for action.   You well know how soon one of those stupendous
masses, now reposing on their shadows in perfect stillness—how soon,
upon any call of patriotism, or of necessity, it would assume the likeness of an animated thing, instinct with life and motion—how soon
it would ruffle, as it were, its swelling plumage—how quickly it would
collect all its beauty and its bravery, collect its scattered elements
of strength and awaken its dormant thunder.   Such as is one of these
magnificent machines when springing from inaction into a display
of its might—such is England herself : while apparently passive and
motionless, she silently concentrates the power to be put forth on an
adequate occasion."

Canning had spoken, as if in a general manner and without
particular intent, yet so as to set England thinking by his eloquence and to rally to his standard that force of public opinion,
which perhaps only Chatham before him had known how to
evoke.   A month later another voice, speaking the same tongue
as his three thousand miles away, repeated in more emphatic
tones the substance and more than the substance of his policy.
Monroe's message has eclipsed the Polignac Memorandum,
but Monroe, or, more accurately, Adams, might never have
ventured to put it forward, had not Canning already in the
preceding August conveyed to Rush, the American Ambassador
in England, his wish for a joint declaration on the part of the
Anglo-Saxon Powers to the effect that they neither wished themselves to annex any portion of the Spanish Colonies nor would
allow any other Power to do so.   The proposal was refused, but
only because Great Britain was not ready to give the new republics immediate political recognition, that matter being in
Canning's eyes "one of time and circumstances."   Monroe,
therefore, put forward the American veto upon European interference in the Western Hemisphere in the form of a message to
Congress, with the knowledge that England at least, if not also
the United States, would fight to make it effective, or at least any
part of it likely to be assailed.   In the same comfortable assurance
Monroe went on to distinguish the system of the Americas from
that of Europe under the Holy Alliance, and to warn the world
that, whilst it neither was nor would be any part of their policy
to interfere with the existing colonies or dependencies in America

of any European Power, they would brook no interference on the part of such Powers with American Governments which had declared and maintained their independence.

No one can read the Monroe message without perceiving that it is in its way almost as formal an assertion of republican as the Troppau Protocol of monarchical theory. The Western World had thus produced a strong counterpoise of political ideas to those associated with the name of the Holy Alliance—too strong, indeed, for Canning who still remained in sentiment a monarchist. Foreign policy, as has already been said, does not go unaffected by political theory. Canning by his frank recognition of the power of the States and of their place in the world had in fact established an opposition of mind as well as of material forces. The greater Powers of the Holy Alliance had a sufficiently plausible case against Liberalism as it showed itself in Europe with revolution as its pioneer. It was otherwise with the Liberalism of America, which expressed itself naturally in republican institutions and pacific principles. The argument from Robespierre and Napoleon was obviated by the argument from George Washington and President Monroe; and the follies of Jacobin and militarist France answered by the unaggressive nationalism and half-Quakerish ideals of the Federated States of North America.

This was not all. Canning's recognition in his conversations with Rush of the United States as the foremost Power in America, coupled with his demand for their inclusion in any international conference upon American affairs raised them both in their own esteem and in the esteem of others; and we, who at the distance of a century can take stock of his policy, may see in it the first beginning of those things of which we ourselves have seen the end. The appeal to America to throw its weight into the scales of a Europe divided upon the issue of self-determination had to wait for an answer until President Wilson sat in the seat of President Monroe; but the answer, when it came, lacked nothing in decision. To Canning himself, dexterously used as he was by Adams to furnish a kind of shelter behind which American ideas might grow without European interference to maturity, his own work might well seem in the light of time—to borrow the figure of a story just then lately published—to bear a likeness to that of Frankenstein, and the States to be no better than a Frankenstein's monster. He had not intended that the lost Colonies of England should exercise a sort of hegemony over the Western Hemisphere and by virtue of it exclude the nations of Europe from the unallotted territories of America; nor did he fancy the institution of a universal, undiluted Republicanism throughout the South American continent.[1] Such consequences, however, were latent in his policy and represented the price that had to be paid for the great diplomatic defeat which he proceeded to inflict upon the European monarchies.

Confident of sufficient strength to complete his purpose, resolute not to enter a European conference, and hopeless, after a final, rejected offer of mediation, of bringing the Spanish Government to face realities, Canning during the critical twelve-month of 1824 waited only upon circumstance, upon occasion, and upon his colleagues to cross the Rubicon of his policy. The fear that the United States, whose recognition of certain of the insurgent Republics dated from 1822, might under the double effect of this act and Monroe's message consolidate their influence in South America, before Great Britain was in a position to play an even game, drove him forward; the angry opposition of the King, who very possibly supposed himself a legitimist monarch as he certainly supposed himself a combatant at Waterloo, and of the Cabinet, where a majority of the members cordially disliked any revolutionary proposal, held him back. His ways were, indeed, sufficiently opposed to the old conciliatory ways of Castlereagh to irritate those who had been familiar with his predecessor. Though he was at one with Castlereagh in discountenancing all direct interference with forms of government, and was no more of the school of Adams than he was of Alexander, he had been at issue with him for years in regard to diplomacy by conference. Conferences, he said very plainly, were either useless or dangerous; useless if the parties were already agreed; dangerous if they differed; and he declared that he had no place in his system for ' Areopagus and the like of that.' Wellington, Castlereagh's second self in all matters of diplomacy, disliked both the man and his methods, and led a stout opposition to his proposals; yet it was Wellington, with his soldier's high sense of reality, who in the end saw that resistance must give way and persuaded the King to it.

[1] Temperley, *Foreign Policy of Canning*, p. 127.

The Country was, in fact, behind the Foreign Secretary. British merchants, above all, had reason to be tired of a state of things which left them open to all manner of impositions; and City princes backed their clamour. It is significant that Canning forced the Cabinet to the first stage of political recognition upon a trader's pretext. During the summer they agreed to empower the British Consul at Buenos Aires to negotiate a commercial treaty, the conclusion of which would carry by implication the point at issue. Franker action came with the winter; and the continued presence of the French armies in Spain helped to further it. In a memorandum to the Cabinet Canning played upon the old fear of a family-compact between the two branches of the House of Bourbon, arguing that the possibility of union between the resources of France and Spain was best met by the recognition of the revolted Spanish Colonies as independent states. This was, it need scarcely be said, no serious danger so long as the Polignac Memorandum held good. No compact between France and Spain, except a compact to use force, would restore to the latter her lost dominions; and, if Canning held, as was apparently the case,[1] that the French occupation of Spain constituted the primary reason for British action, it can only have been because he wished to have what his most distinguished pupil described as a "tit for tat" with France.

The French Government, indeed, had got even better than it gave. The time came when the French forces withdrew from Spain; but the time never came when the Spanish Colonies of South America returned to their old allegiance. On the last day of the year 1824 Canning completed that famous despatch which on his instructions was subsequently read—and it can have been no agreeable task—by the British Ambassador at Madrid to the Spanish Minister of Foreign Affairs. No kindly phrases softened the hard premises of his argument—premises in which he reflected with unsparing directness upon the failure and folly of the Spanish, the patience and solicitude of the British Government—nor was any effort made to sweeten the hard consequences of the conclusion that the sands had run out altogether in the case of some of the Colonies, and were fast running out in the rest. In every case British policy must, he argued,

[1] Temperley, *Foreign Policy of Canning*, p. 151.

be governed by the realities of the situation. The independence of Mexico, of Colombia, and of the Argentine would therefore be recognised at once; that of Chile might wait until fresh information removed all doubt that the end had come; that of Peru for so long as a last hope of reconquest lingered.

Thus then matters ended, and Spain fell from her great estate into the rank of a second-rate Power. So complete was her decline that, when she crosses the path of international policy in 1846 or 1870 or 1898, it is only because she has a queen to be wedded, a crown to be snatched, or an island to be taken away. Her weight in the counsels of Europe has become as nothing, and her Empire, like her energy, is gone.

Canning had scarcely finished officiating at the obsequies of the Spanish before his presence was required at those of the Portuguese Empire. He attended with the more alacrity that there seemed a good hope of converting Brazil into an independent monarchy instead of an independent republic. The Royal House of Braganza, which had taken refuge in its transatlantic dominions during the struggle with Napoleon, had had the wisdom to recognise that it must divide to reign. The King had returned reluctantly to Lisbon, but the heir to the throne remained at Rio with the title of Regent to his name and complete independence within his reach. The understanding was that he should rule as his father's deputy so long as he could, but that, if this arrangement proved unacceptable to the Brazilians, he should agree to a project of separation. In the course of the following year he found cause to exercise his powers, and invested himself with the purple and the country with a constitution. His action, if it had not exceeded his instructions or the necessities of the case, had nevertheless outstripped his father's goodwill. King John was jealous of his son's superior rank, and angry at his subjects' formal separation. More intelligent, however, than the King of Spain, he realised his impotence and invited British mediation. Canning was interested in the question, not only because trade with Brazil was an important British interest, but because it touched the wider question of the relations between the divergent ideals of the two Hemispheres, which, as he conceived, would break completely away from one another in thought and sentiment unless the British Government could build a bridge between them. In this belief he did his best to bring the

Portuguese and their revolted Colony to an amicable understanding; and under his pressure an agreement was made in London in the summer of 1825 between the Portuguese and Brazilian Governments, which, though conceding to Dom Pedro both the style and authority of Emperor of Brazil, nevertheless added to King John's list of dignities an imperial title.

The matter was hardly worth the trouble which it had given to everybody concerned. Within a year or less, king and emperor though he was, His Most Faithful Majesty—for so diplomatic usage was accustomed to describe the sovereigns of Portugal—had joined the majority of mankind, leaving behind him the memory of a vacillating, inept, toothlessly-mumbling old man, plagued by the blood of a mad mother, the tantrums of a termagant wife, and the ambitions of a pair of sons, of whom the elder had deprived him of the greater part of his dominions and the younger had conspired to deprive him of all authority over the rest. As soon as he was gone, Portugal fell into a worse confusion. Dom Pedro, still in default of any other settlement the heir to the throne, was more concerned about the prospects of his seven-year-old daughter than the welfare of his ancestral country, and more interested in the experiments of political science than attentive to the practical conditions of political liberty. He consequently renounced his title in favour of his child, and, not content with presenting the Portuguese with a girl-Queen, gave them also the unwelcome and untimely gift of a constitution. Canning, though he was by no means in love with Dom Pedro's proceedings, could not resist making merry at the Austrian expense over this cuckoo's egg which a Legitimist Sovereign, who happened incidentally to be the Emperor of Austria's son-in-law, had thus incontinently hatched. An uncontrollable sense of humour had been a grave defect in his politics, and it was a characteristic weakness in his diplomacy.

Round Queen Maria da Gloria, then, emerging from her nursery to contend for a throne, such Liberalism as Portugal contained began forthwith to revolve. Tory Democracy, on the other hand—the Nobility, the Clergy and the Populace—looked to the Emperor's brother, Dom Miguel, to give them what they really wanted and what he had it in his power to confer—an absolute monarchy embodied in a popular king.

Canning had a double interest in Portugal—the political interest attaching to an old ally and a personal interest arising from his having for a short time held the post of British Minister at Lisbon at the close of the Napoleonic Wars. It was the only country of Europe about which he could claim to have had an opportunity of acquiring intimate knowledge; but his conception of the Portuguese was romantically, or at least rhetorically incorrect. "I could not contemplate those holy ruins," he assured his own countrymen in speaking of the Lines of Torres Vedras, ". . . without rendering a just homage to the character of the nation which, by all that it has done, and more by all that it has endured, has raised itself to a pitch of moral eminence so far beyond the proportion of its territory, population, or power."[1] This faith of the year 1816 in the ethical attainments of the subjects of King John must have suffered loss in 1823 when there came a demand from Palmella for British help to keep them in order. Canning had firmly refused the Portuguese Minister's request for military assistance; Great Britain did not on principle, he conveyed, interfere in the domestic affairs of other countries. Holding, however, apparently, that ships and sailors lay in a different category to soldiers and field-guns, he had sent a naval squadron to lie off the Tagus. It proved of the greatest help in sustaining King John and his Liberal supporters against the political intrigues of Dom Miguel, but, from the point of view of the Holy Alliance, its presence must have appeared indistinguishable from military intervention, and may explain, if it does not excuse, the puzzled policy of Sir Edward Thornton, the British Minister, whom Canning reprimanded and recalled for mixing himself up, to King John's complete satisfaction, in the internal government of the country and countenancing a fresh request for British troops.

All this was past history by 1826, but it has its place in the formation of any estimate of Canning's policy. Before that year was out he was to find, what others had found already, that circumstances have an inexorable logic of their own, before which the best-considered principles have a way of breaking down. The very proposal that he had so much blamed Thornton for transmitting, was that which he was himself presently compelled to adopt; and British troops were shipped off to compose the

[1] 2nd April 1816 (quoted from Temperley's *Life of Canning*, p. 115).

quarrels of the Portuguese. The thing came about in this way. Saldanha, a Liberal and one of the few effective personalities in the country, declared for the new Queen and the new Constitution; and his action was for the moment decisive. Dom Miguel was in Vienna, and the Absolutists were for the time nonplussed. Some intransigent soldiery, however, took refuge in Spain, where they could count on the sympathy of the Government. Safe across the border, they carried out a policy of raids and made ready for more extensive operations, the Spaniards helping them with material. The Portuguese Government, too feeble to deal with the matter themselves and reasonably fearful of getting involved in a war with Spain, appealed once more for British aid; and Canning, after some hesitation, came to the conclusion that the situation contemplated in the Anglo-Portuguese treaty of defence had now occurred. His was an arguable case, but nothing more. For the Spaniards, though they were supplying arms and ammunition to the Portuguese revolutionists, were not themselves attacking Portugal; and the Portuguese revolutionists were only formidable because their own country was in sympathy with them, and, as the event ultimately proved, greatly preferred Dom Miguel to Dona Maria. Had it been a question of sustaining an absolute sovereign against a constitutionalist revolution, who can doubt that the British people would have held it no business of theirs to intervene? Canning, for all his claim to limit interference to defence, when he spoke of planting the standard of England on the well-known heights of Lisbon as a pledge that foreign dominion should not come there, or boasted—for it was in this same speech that the famous boast was made—of calling the New World into being to redress the balance of the Old, was appealing to a sentiment which reached behind the immediate issue to a larger principle of constitutional liberty, and was with him, as it had not been with Castlereagh but was to be with Palmerston, no mere private opinion, but an authoritative dogma officially professed. The first, red-hot version of his speech shows this clearly enough:

"I fear," he said, "that the next war to be kindled in Europe, if it spread beyond the narrow limits of Spain and Portugal, will be a war of most tremendous character—a war not merely of conflicting armies, but of conflicting opinions. I know that, if into that war this country enters . . . she will see under her banners, arrayed for the contest, all the discontented and rest-less spirits of the age, all those who—whether justly or unjustly —are dissatisfied with the present state of their own countries." [1]

He would have been quite correct if only he had said that the war of opinion was already joined and England already a party to it. To the annoyance of Metternich, but amidst enthusiasm in England, five thousand British bayonets were dispatched to fortify the Portuguese charter and maintain Queen Maria upon her throne. They came, were seen, conquered, and remained. A twelvemonth later Dom Miguel, having sworn to the Constitu-tion though with some reservation in favour of his own Legitimist rights, arrived upon the scene. He was hailed by cries of "Viva Dom Miguel I., rei absoluto!"; and so he became within a month or two of his landing. For the Constitution dissolved at his approach, no man desiring or at least daring to support it, and Canning being no longer alive to back it up. Wellington, who had become Prime Minister and understood the mentality of the people of the Peninsula far better than his deceased colleague, promptly withdrew the British forces; and the occasion of a speech that has never been forgotten faded into a diplomatic incident, an English score in Portugal to set off against a French score in Spain, a 'tit for tat' between Canning and Villèle. Long before this, however, British public opinion had found another vent for its constitutional enthusiasm.

The Greeks, as we see them now, no longer afford any agree-able illusions, the last remnant of the old magic attaching to their country and their name having been lost in the tragedy of Venizelos. A fickle, foolish people, incapable of standing by the man they had found, or of understanding the hour of their visitation, they can hardly again excite enthusiasm or again attract the sympathy of Europe. It was very different in Canning's time. It was possible then to let fancy play around them, and all the more tempting that the burning thoughts and burning questions of the Greeks of old time still formed the source and centre of every liberal education. Gladstone, who had turned a child's eyes upon Canning beneath his father's roof, caught, while still an Eton boy, as so often on a larger stage at a later day, the passion of a people struggling to be free, raised it to

[1] See Temperley, *Foreign Policy of Canning*, App., pp. 580-1.

a higher power of nobility than it, in this case at least, deserved, and, always insensible to the pricks of humour, attended Eton Montem, clad in the kilt of a Greek mountaineer. A greater than Gladstone had, however, made the cause his own. Byron, that dweller in marble halls and amidst all the exotic imaginations of the East, that harper chanting the tale of sea-girt islands, gilded with eternal summer and blest with everlasting names, had seized upon the cause of Greece, half-doubting what he did,[1] yet perhaps in good assurance that, at the least, his genius, shamed by darkest scandal, would sink at death into a sea of glory. Had he not lived, had he not died, Canning might never have been moved to change the policy of maintaining the *status quo* in the Levant which Castlereagh had bequeathed to him. As it was, a rising tide of public opinion in favour of interference enabled him, in face of strong opposition in the Cabinet, to cut British policy adrift from its ancient moorings and to trust it boldly to the fortune of events. Neither scholarship nor sentiment, however, led him by the nose. He knew the modern Greeks for what they were—"a most rascally set"[2]—and it was from no false identification of them with the ancient inhabitants of the soil that he acted as he did, but upon other and more solid grounds.

The problem of the fate of Turkey—the Eastern Question— was destined to take rank as the greatest of all the diplomatic problems of the nineteenth century. It interested the four Great Powers of Canning's time, and was to interest Germany and Italy also when they grew to self-consciousness. England was interested as in everything that bore immediately upon the problems of the Mediterranean or remotely upon the problems of India. France was interested because of her ancient protectorate over the Latin Christians of the Levant and her traditional influence at the Sublime Porte. Russia was interested in the fortunes of the Orthodox subjects of the Sultan, whose liberation promised to add so many provinces to her Empire; in the fate of the Straits, which confined her southern warships to an inland sea; and in the future of Constantinople, toward which, since the time of Catherine the Great, her longing eyes

---

[1] "I believed myself on a fool's errand from the outset," Byron to Napier (quoted in " Nicolson's *Byron : The Last Journey*, p. 158).

[2] Temperley, *Foreign Policy of Canning*, p. 329.

were turned. And Austria was interested in any aggrandisement of Russia, for that would mean a corresponding reduction
in her own importance and security. The grouping of the
Powers, as the Greek insurrection proceeded and the Eastern
Question gained precedence of other issues, was at first the same
as had obtained at the Congress of Vienna. England and
Austria, with France beside them, drew to one side, Russia with
her henchman Prussia, to the other. It was Canning in conjunction with the Princesse de Lieven—the wife of the Russian
Ambassador to the Court of St James's—who made a change of
partners in the same.

The diplomatic revolution of 1826 came about in this way.
Castlereagh and Metternich had intended to hold in check
Alexander's desire to interfere in Turkey on the plea, always
peculiarly grateful to the Emperor's ears, that intervention
must come from a Europe united. And Metternich, after Castlereagh was gone, pursued the same policy, allowing the representatives of the Holy Alliance to assemble at Petersburg in 1825,
not in order to reach an agreement, but to prolong a procrastina-
tion. When the Conference met, Alexander, therefore, was
dexterously impaled upon the horns of a well-considered dilemma.
Greece, Metternich declared, if she were not to submit, would have
to be made completely independent; because the Emperor was
all for the liberation of the subject-races of Christian Turkey,
and yet also all against rebellion against constituted authority,
and these things were contrary the one to the other. The
proposal did its work, for Alexander dissented, and the Conference
dissolved. But it did also more than its work, for it left Alexander
in a mood to break away from the tutelage of the Austrian
Chancellor.

Canning, after his manner, had kept clear of the Petersburg
Conference, and with the better will that he foresaw its issue
correctly. But, though he still professed to the Greeks, as he
had done the year before, that England must not be asked to
do anything inconsistent with neutrality, an event had just
occurred which was to induce him to shift his standpoint.
Ibrahim Pasha, in command of an Egyptian army, had landed
in the Morea, giving thereby a superiority to the Turks both by
land and sea. His soldiers were good; his talents were great;
his cruelties or severities promised to do the rest. Unless the

Great Powers intervened, the Greeks were doomed—doomed, so Lieven declared, actually to be transported to Egypt and to have Egyptians planted in the Morea in their stead. England was not prepared to hear that Byron had given his life for such an end as this; and Canning knew it.

Upon such a framework during the summer of 1825 Princess Lieven wove her webs, slipping across to Russia, whispering in the ear of Alexander, dragging admissions out of Nesselrode, returning with an undertaking in her pocket that, if England were to move in the Greek matter, Russia would raise no opposition. It was no misfortune to her that Alexander perished in the middle period of her activities. In his place there came to the throne the man who, until "General Février" turned traitor thirty years afterwards, was to occupy a position of immense consequence in the counsels of Europe. Nicholas I. did not break with the ideas or policy of Alexander, but pursued them with a sterner and a stronger purpose. In him there is apparent the same sense of the solidarity of European Governments, the same dislike of rebellion against constituted authority, the same regard for Christianity as the ultimate foundation of peace and progress, and even the same inclination, when it suited his purpose, to flirt with Liberalism abroad though never at home. The English statesman whose political temperament was best calculated to suit that of Nicholas was also, as it happened, the English statesman whose political influence was to oppose itself to that of Canning in the Cabinet. The despatch of Wellington on a special mission to Petersburg, designed to bring about an Anglo-Russian understanding as to the affairs of Greece, was therefore a clever stroke of domestic as well as foreign diplomacy. The Protocol, which resulted, has been made a subject of reproach to the Duke, though not with justice nor by Canning.[1] It gave effect to the ideas that the parties to the negotiation held in common; but it did not, and could not in the nature of things, give them a common standpoint or outlook. Great Britain and Russia were agreed in desiring to recommend British mediation to the belligerents, and agreed too that the settlement ought to give Greece autonomy but not independence; but they were not agreed as to the course

---

[1] Unless, that is, his objection to one article as ' not very artistically drawn,' be reckoned a reproach. See Temperley, *Foreign Policy of Canning*, p. 391.

to be followed, if the Turks refused to go to arbitration. Only in one event—the actual transplantation of a Greek population from Greece—was Canning prepared for war; whereas, before Alexander's death, war had apparently been resolved upon by Russia, if the Turks did not give way. The new understanding was in truth embarrassed by the fact that each party to it had an *arrière pensée*. Russia had no real intention of bringing the non-Greek part of her quarrel with Turkey within the scope of the diplomatic understanding; and the British Government was rather concerned to prevent the intervention, or, at any rate, the single-handed intervention, of Russia in Turkish affairs, than to bring the business of Greece to a quick conclusion by compelling the Porte to swallow the terms agreed upon.

The Protocol was signed in April 1826, yet matters dragged on for more than a year before anything decisive seemed likely to be done. Russia, indeed, settled her special quarrel with Turkey in the course of the summer in the only manner which the Turks understood—by the threat of war if her demands were not conceded. But Canning was in no position to use such methods, with half his colleagues opposed to him, and Austria and Prussia holding back. Diplomacy dawdled, although delays were obviously dangerous, since the power of Ibrahim was growing and the resistance of the Greeks beginning to fail. At last, in the July of 1827, after Canning had become Prime Minister and Dudley taken his place at the Foreign Office, those three Powers, which for our generation at least will always seem to enjoy a prescriptive right to be called the *Entente* Powers, came to an understanding. The Treaty of London gave general effect to the provisions of the Protocol, with the condition added that, in the event of recalcitrance, the belligerents should be compelled by force to accept an armistice, whilst matters were arranged by England, France, and Russia on the lines proposed. It was secretly agreed that pressure, if it came to that, should take the form of naval action calculated to cut off Ibrahim and his army in the Morea from their base in Egypt. Canning, however, still hoped for a pacific collapse on the part of the Turks, and did his best to bring it about by advising the Pasha to cut his fortunes loose from those of the Sultan. This negotiation failed; and there was nothing for it but to give instructions to the Allied admirals to make a demonstration. Before they had time to take action, Canning was dead.

The end of his career came hardly less suddenly, hardly less dramatically, than that of his predecessor. He was not, as we reckon age now, an old man, but he was a tired man and a man who in the months immediately before his death had suffered an unusual and in some respects cruel strain. He was divided from the most part of his colleagues, not only by the development of his Eastern policy, but by the far more acute issue of Catholic Emancipation, of which he had long been an advocate and which could actually boast a majority in the Commons in its favour in 1825. Another and perhaps a deeper gulf— a gulf whose depths at all events we can no longer successfully probe—divided him from men like Wellington. They did not credit him, not to put too fine a point upon it, with being quite a gentleman, and distrusted him accordingly. His relations with the Whigs, who approved both his foreign and Catholic policy, with the Press and with the populace—all of them in those days calculated to surprise—added strength to their dislike. The great world—*ce beau monde qui gouverne le monde*—likewise found him wanting. Princess Lieven professes to discover that "He had very gauche manners, and sinned against the etiquette of elegant society." [1] Liverpool's illness, which threw the Premiership into competition, brought matters to a head. Had George IV. possessed character or judgment, the crisis would have been quickly over. As it was, it dragged on for six weeks. The King appears to have enjoyed the exceptional importance and occasions of petty malice that the situation afforded him. There was a kind of fun in playing off Canning, whom he described as an old woman, against Wellington, who had so often made him sensible that the King's Government was a better man than the King—a kind of fun in making two human beings, whose temperaments and trainings jarred, hate each other rather more than they did before. George was a poor creature at his best, but never poorer than at this curious juncture. Wellington and Canning were both great men, but upon their reputations, too, the crisis cast a shadow. Canning, indeed, stood honourably and faithfully by his belief in Catholic Emancipation, but he made it a reason

[1] Temperley, *Unpubl. Diary, etc., of Princess Lieven*, p. 107. The allegation is dated in 1826.

for insisting that he should be Prime Minister, or, at least—and this was a measure of his patriotism—for saddling the Country with a dummy at the head of the Government if he were not. And Wellington, because he could not see his way to take office under Canning, must needs endeavour to embarrass him the more by asking for an apology when no real offence had been given, and resigning the post of Commander-in-Chief because it was not sent. A finer nature than that of the one would have placed his abilities unreservedly at the King's disposal, without inquiring too closely to what precise reward they were entitled; a longer vision than that of the other might have admitted from the beginning that Canning's talents set him a head and shoulders above his fellows, and that Canning's defects were the defects, as we say, of his qualities and by no means useless in bridging the gulf between two ages.

The cleverer politician won in the end; and Canning, amidst much popular applause, formed an administration from which Wellington, Eldon, Peel, and some other less famous Tory statesmen, had dropped out. For a hundred days, as Metternich observed, he reigned as Premier. More bitterly assailed by Grey than by his former colleagues, he showed no sign of failing wit or energy, but there can be little doubt that he was wounded to the quick, and, above all, by Grey's assault upon his foreign policy. There were some who, as the midsummer pomps of that eventful year went by, saw death most plainly written in his face. Lady Holland, under the spell of some strong presentiment, warned him urgently not to go to Chiswick, which Devonshire had lent him and where Fox had died. But, like the hero of another short and tragic premiership of recent times, he held upon his way, making light of labour until nature could no more. The first days of August ushered in an awful tale of pain; and on the 8th he was gone. For the briefest moment he had stood upon the pinnacle of Fame's temple; then, before he could use the opportunity of his great position, he lay buried beneath the temple floor.

What shall we say of him and to whom in all the roll of our Foreign Secretaries shall he be compared? Castlereagh—a man of his own time and generation—had a longer reign, a larger purpose, a more disinterested spirit, a more diplomatic mind. Palmerston, his chief disciple, gave to his notions a bolder expression and a louder sound, could rouse the nation to as high a pitch of passion and seem every jot as terrible abroad. If, therefore, we are to follow Acton's judgment and place him foremost on our list, it must be because we rate his intellect the highest or esteem his philosophy the most. Canning's political philosophy—his 'system,' as his contemporaries would have called it—was a very well-defined compact body of opinion, and can be gathered up easily into a bundle of phrases almost too familiar to repeat. At the root of his ideas lay the thought of the nation as the unit of statesmanship. He saw so far clearly and scarcely troubled to look beyond. Thus we find him abandoning the more catholic conceptions of Castlereagh, contending not only against the Holy Alliance, but against a concert of Europe, forswearing congresses, refusing conferences, exclaiming against 'Areopagus and the like of that,' and bidding every nation look to itself and leave it to a God apparently deprived of all human co-operation, to afford a point of unity in a warring world. It was all of a piece with this enlightened selfishness that he made the notion of a balance of power prominent in his speeches, accepting as a matter of course a conflict of interests, groups, and principles as the basis of foreign policy. "Some years ago," he told the House of Commons in the last months of his life, " . . . I stated that the position of this country in the present state of the world was one of neutrality, not only between contending nations, but between conflicting principles; and that it was by neutrality alone that we could maintain that balance, the preservation of which I believe to be essential to the welfare of mankind." [1] Even more significant of the character of his nationalism was his candid admission that it was "much better and more convenient for us to have neighbours, whose institutions cannot be compared with ours in point of freedom." [2] This was cynical enough, yet Canning was not immoral. He believed in treaties and the maintenance of treaties, and he believed in peace and justice; but he had no clear sense of the unseen foundations of society, and no regard for that common will towards a common welfare that forms the root of international civilisation. There was a shortness of thought latent in his determination to break up the machinery of discussion that his predecessor had so care-

[1] Speech on the affairs of Portugal, 12th December 1826.
[2] Temperley, *Foreign Policy of Canning*, p. 458.

fully prepared, and even perhaps from one angle in the emphasis that he laid upon the distinction between the Old World and the New. His influence upon his countrymen was, it may be, all the greater for that. He appealed to their native instincts in the grandest language, dwelt magnificently upon their proudest traditions, took them into his confidence and called them to his aid. Though he was no democrat and opposed to parliamentary reform, he cared for public opinion—cared to instruct it, valued its support. He was in this way wise in his generation. The most brilliant expositor of 'the mean' in foreign policy—of England as a mediating influence in international affairs between the contending principles of monarchy and democracy—he seemed peculiarly qualified to act as the forerunner of the English middle-classes as they entered upon their fifty years of sovereign power. Perhaps it was for this that Mackintosh, with bold, prophetic vision, called England 'the land of Canning.' For all his Eton education and all his sparkling scholarship, Canning's sympathies were with a grade of society which has seemed to many to be the backbone of the Country. He had the practical efficiency, the strong assurance, the material outlook that were to make the middle-period of Victoria what it became in politics and trade. As certainly, even though he never formally went back upon the pledges of his predecessor and professed to the end that he had always stood by the Quintuple Alliance,[1] he lacked the great manner, the high international courtesy, the sense of European solidarity, and the spirit of peace and counsel that so nobly distinguished Castlereagh. Combative, competitive, and insular, he broadened a path for British policy, where Palmerston was presently to strut, crowing with crest erect. To some this will seem to afford the soundest tradition of British foreign policy; and they will exalt Canning above all his fellows. Others, who set greater store than he did by conciliation, co-operation, and an impartial mind in international affairs, will, whilst not forgetting his great gesture westwards, content themselves in general with milder praise.

[1] See Temperley, *Foreign Policy of Canning,* p. 453.

III

ABERDEEN

[GEORGE HAMILTON GORDON.—Born 1784. Succeeded, as
4th Earl of Aberdeen, 1801. *Foreign Secretary*, 1828–1830,
and 1841–1846. Prime Minister 1852–1855. Died 1860.]

ABERDEEN

AMONG those who sat at the feet of Pitt and practised in the
school of Castlereagh was a young man of much promise and great
possessions, who was destined to occupy both the high office
of the one and that of the other. Posterity has dealt hardly
with Aberdeen. Lacking in self-esteem, insensible to ambition,
indifferent to applause, incapable of crediting either Whigs or
Tories with a complete monopoly of wisdom, solicitous from first
to last to do his duty by God, by man, and by his country, he has
seemed to succeeding generations, with their growing affection for
the vivacious, the flamboyant, and the bizarre in character to be
but little worthy of attention. Few British Foreign Secretaries
deserve this treatment less in a time like ours. No one in his own
day, unless it be Clarendon, was his equal in the practice of a
certain sort of diplomacy which some of the wisest judges amongst
us have come to reckon high. He understood that the first
principle of international business is to dispel distrust, and that
the evangelical counsels offer in the long run a better textbook
of foreign policy than the works of Machiavelli. For to none is it
said more emphatically than to the diplomatist that in quietness
and confidence shall be his strength. The voice of wisdom, here
as elsewhere, is still and small. It neither bluffs nor boasts. If
it threatens, it does not falter; if it triumphs, it raises no hymns of
victory. It is first peaceable, patient, void of offence, easy to be
entreated; then, if need be, firm and faithful, yet so as equity be
not sacrificed to opportunity, nor aggression substituted for
defence. Against such diplomacy, if it could be persistently
pursued over a long period of time, there would be no standing.

More than any foreign minister of his time, or perhaps of any
time since, Aberdeen represents an attempt to establish Christian
methods in the conduct of foreign affairs; and his tenure of the
Foreign Office illustrates in a peculiar degree the advantage of

such methods just as the period of his Premiership emphasises the difficulty inherent in their application. This circumstance in itself gives to his career a singular interest and the colour of a tragedy. Behind the austere presence, the reserved manner, the costume suggestive, as someone said, of a nonconformist minister, there lay the romance of a mind seeking to bring the counsels of Christianity to bear upon the troubles of the time—seeking this at first with a large measure of success, and then at last worsted by the obscurity and complexity of a situation that was none of his making, and falling both in public esteem and into pathetic self-reproach. A good man, a wise man, an honourable man, struggling in the toils of human passion and adverse circum-stances—perhaps the most moving spectacle that public affairs can show!

The background of the portrait, the shifting scenery of Aber-deen's private life, is in keeping with the rest; and little is left wanting to complete the melancholy splendour of the whole. The morning of his days is bright with promise; before long the clouds have gathered; at midday the storm breaks in fury over him. Bruised and battered he pursues his way bravely through an inclement afternoon; yet still in the evening there is no radiance of declining light. Job is not more afflicted, more trustful, more resigned. But not to him as to Job does there come any day of restoration. Life continues in the main, so far as he is concerned, to be an exercise in virtue, a school of suffering, a pilgrimage to be patiently performed. He leaves no high achievement of which orators might speak or poets sing, but just to the student an example of duty nobly done, and to the statesman—and that statesman Gladstone—the memory of one who of all the public men of his time seemed first in tran-quillity of mind, in freedom from egotism, in the love of exact justice, in far-reaching tolerance of spirit, and, above all, in an "entire immunity" from the suspicion that "makes our minds in general like a haunted place." Of that last quality, springing as it did in him "not from defect of vision, but from thorough nobleness of nature" his colleague speaks with particular warmth.[1] It seemed, in public life at least, his most endearing gift, affording "an indescribable charm to all intercourse with him in critical and difficult circumstances." By virtue of it

[1] See Gladstone's estimate printed in Stanmore, *Earl of Aberdeen*, p. 308.

especially, rather than by virtue of his intellectual abilities, he enjoyed, so the same witness affirmed, a "remarkable power of winning confidences without seeking to win them." The mind must be diseased which thinks so rare a nature dull.

Aberdeen was born in the first year of Pitt's first administration and came of age in the last year of Pitt's last administration. Thus he grew to manhood in full view of a career that has stirred young men's ambition more, perhaps, than any other in British political history. Circumstances gave him the chance of actually sitting at the feet of Gamaliel. His father was accidentally killed whilst he was still a child; his grandfather, to whose estates in Aberdeenshire he was heir, had made of Haddo a house where no good woman could wish to see her son brought up; and, to make his destitution complete, his mother died soon after she became a widow. Thus, under the provision of Scottish law which gave a minor at the age of fourteen the right to name his guardians, he passed completely into the hands of Dundas, an old friend of his parents, and of Pitt, Dundas's friend and leader. In the house of one or other he passed his vacations, learning the science or art of politics from greater tutors than either Harrow or Cambridge could provide.

The Peace of Amiens opened the closed door of the Continent at the very moment when he was grown old enough to see the world to some purpose; and his intimacy with Pitt procured him the entry to the First Consul's presence. He visited Malmaison, several times saw Napoleon, and was half vanquished by the romance of his rise, the brilliance of his talk, the beauty of his face, the magic of his eye and smile.[1] His experience is not peculiar. Even still, with no better medium than portraits on page or canvas, we have many of us fallen at first sight under the fascination of a personality that has no equal in range of mind, force of will and versatility of fortune—have fallen under it only to recognise, as life goes on, how largely evil was this giant example of human power, whence its magic sprang, and of what spirit it was born. Aberdeen, if not insensible to the charms of Napoleon, fell no victim to his politics. "Évidemment le grand conquérant était resté à ses yeux un personnage malfaisant

---

[1] Stanmore, *Earl of Aberdeen*, p. 9: "I have often heard him say that Napoleon's smile was the most winning he ever saw and that his eye was wholly unlike that of any other man."

autant que sublime," reports Jarnac forty years later.[1] No public
or private principles ever ran more surely counter to one another
than those of the Corsican adventurer and the Aberdeenshire
magnate.

From France, in these two wander-years [2] of his life, the young
student of the various humanities of men and books passed on
to Greece and Turkey, exploring, excavating, cultivating with
an even hand the twin fields of politics and history. His exploits caught the notice of a poet, whose ways ran also to those
regions; and he appears as "the travelled Thane" in Byron's
Caledonian black-list. In time to celebrate his majority, he
returned to those Scottish estates of which he retained no more
than childhood's memories. He found them strangely bleak
and bare, the very antithesis to the realms of sun and civilisation,
now ill-exchanged for home. All the young man's instincts
recoiled from the sacrifice demanded of him, and only a sense
of duty kept him faithful to his inheritance. With an energy
that lasted his life he set himself to plant, to build, to drain, to
teach the arts of living to a people that had sat long in ignorance.
He lived to reap his reward in personal revenue as well as in
the growth of general prosperity around him; and a forest of
fourteen million trees remained, after he was gone, for remembrance amongst other memorials of an unwelcome obligation
faithfully performed.

In those vast plantations a poet might be tempted to descry
a symbol of the planter—a symbol of his tenacity, his unceasing,
patient effort to improve, to fertilise, to draw from the not too
friendly soil of human nature a richer and a kinder growth. Burke
has a passage where, in his magnificent way, he compares "people
of great families and hereditary trusts and fortunes" to "the
great oaks that shade a country." Aberdeen was an aristocrat
of this stamp. Over all the countryside round Haddo and beyond
it his personality towered and gave rest. Enlightened counsels
in his time and country were still recommended rather than embarrassed by the possession of great estates. His compatriots
heard him gladly; and he spoke not the less persuasively that he
was as one having authority. Only by a little did he fail to
reconcile the turbulent enthusiasts who between 1834 and 1844

---

[1] *Revue des Deux Mondes* (July 1861), p. 447.
[2] 1802–4.

split the Church of Scotland from the top to the bottom on an issue no graver than whether the congregation of each parish should or should not be entitled to exercise a veto upon the nominations of the lay patron. Disposed to gratify the natural wish of the sheep to have a say in the selection of the shepherd, and at the same time satisfied by the experience he had had in one of his own parishes that they were by no means competent to do so, he proposed in a Bill which almost secured the assent of both parties to substitute a presbyteral for a popular veto, or in other words to give to the clergy of the district the power of rejection which was claimed for the congregation of the parish. Into the reasons of his failure to stop the secession of that which subsequently constituted itself the Free Church of Scotland we need not stop to inquire. But this chapter of his life will not be entirely neglected by any who desire to bring before their eyes a complete picture of the man. It throws into relief his deeply pacific, religious nature; it was probably the foundation of his sombre reflection—so often echoed and so ill-disproved by the inexhaustible sectarianism of numbers of Christians— that "the language and conduct of what is usually called the religious world is not encouraging" and that "did it not excite pity . . . (it) could only produce disgust." [1] Profoundly convinced that love is the fulfilling of the law, he took the most alluring of short cuts to reach his end, too careless, perhaps, of the adage that the longest way round is often enough the shortest way home. He took his faith with him whether he went north or south, allowing the form of it to be determined by local custom. In Scotland he called himself a Presbyterian, and sat, quite literally, in the seat of the elders. But he made his communions in England under the ægis of a Church which, for the second time in its strange history, was even then falling again under Catholic influences.[2]

Such breadth of mind or haziness of thought, whichever we happen to think it, was as unpalatable to Aberdeen's Anglican as it is to his Presbyterian biographer, yet must be reckoned entirely characteristic of his outlook in this direction. The

[1] Lady F. Balfour, *Life of George, Fourth Earl of Aberdeen*, ii. 322.
[2] Stanmore, *The Earl of Aberdeen*, p. 129. "While he never in his life attended the administration of the Sacrament in a Scotch Church, he was in the habit of receiving the Holy Communion in an English Church every year on Good Friday."

practical point, as he saw things, was to afford to organised
religion the utmost assistance in his power; and he was content
to worship God in the manner of his immediate ancestors and
according to the expectation of his tenants and retainers, whatever
his private preferences might be. But it would, of course, be
an error to suppose that he had anything in common with the
grim fanatic who conceived the theology of Geneva or the murder-
ous [1] pulpiteer who made it a household word in the Scottish
Lowlands. All his faith was summed up in a prayer which any
child—or any man to whom age and experience have left the
birthright of the childlike mind—might say in any church:
"Lord, I believe, help thou my unbelief." [2] And all his practice
lay enshrined in the text that he gave his grown-up children for
a sermon on the Christmas Day of 1844: "Love one another." [3]

The character of a mediator which he displayed so eminently
in matters connected with churchmanship clung to him in
politics. His nature was so generously and wisely blended that
liberal ideas flourished easily in a patriarchal framework. It
was a saying of his that no Government could be too liberal for
him, provided it did not abandon its conservative character; [4]
and he spoke for the most part of his countrymen when he coined
the epigram. He was indeed a Scotsman born, if not a Scotsman
bred; a man of parts, blessed with a grave humour and an
ethical disposition, but with all this the owner of a mind enlarged
by travel, by study, by goodness of heart and participation in
great affairs.

Aberdeen's character carried him well through a series of
private trials such as comparatively few men have to undergo.
The early death of his Hamilton wife—clever as she was beautiful,
and devoted as she was clever—shattered a lovely idyll; and the
subsequent loss of his boy in infancy and of his girls before they
reached maturity, deprived him of children not undeserving to
be called, with the moving simplicity of the old Greek epitaph,
"his high hopes." All his days he continued to wear mourning
for one in respect of whom, laconic and reserved as he was in the

---

[1] Knox consorted with the murderers of Beaton. ["I think no one who
carefully reads what he (Knox) has written on this subject can doubt that
he justified the action of the conspirators," M'Crie's *Life of Knox*, i. 48.]

[2] Balfour, *Life*, ii. 322.

[3] Unpublished Memoir by the first Lord Stanmore.

[4] Balfour, *Life*, ii. 166.

expression of his feelings, he wrote that "most undoubtedly," as long as he lived, he should believe that in her he had "seen human nature under a form in which it never before existed." [1] Not till Aberdeen was dead was Patmore to speak for the mourning husband in these supreme tragedies of affection, and invest the dread hour of the woman's departure and the man's desertion with a radiant pathos never before achieved; but it is to that exquisite 'reproach,' [2] which seems to track for the last time through all "her great and gracious ways" the passage of 'the angel' who has fled 'the house,' that a student may well turn in the effort to envisage, if only for a moment, the emotional intensity of Aberdeen's existence. His case seemed desperate. As in his public aspect he may, as we have seen, be likened to such an oak as Burke took for an image of the worth and weight of British aristocracy, so in these private griefs he claims comparison with that stricken tree whose evil case was depicted by the same master-hand in illustration of the supreme melancholy of his own latter days: "The storm has gone over me, and I lie like one of those old oaks which the late hurricane has scattered. I am stripped of all my honours; I am torn up by the roots and lie prostrate on the earth . . . I am alone. I have none to meet my enemies in the gate. They who ought to have succeeded me have gone before me. They who should have been to me as posterity are in the place of ancestors."

Burke was, however, sixty-four when his son died; Aberdeen but twenty-eight at the date of his wife's death. Though such a first marriage as his really suffered no second, he was content, under the strong pressure of his father-in-law, to be married again to Lady Hamilton, his brother-in-law's widow. The arrangement brought him other children and new responsibilities. The guardianship of a step-child—the future Duke of Abercorn—lent him for many years another home to which at one time at any rate he gave the palm as "the place he liked best in the world." This was the Priory at Stanmore, a place near enough to London to afford him exceptional facilities for entertaining the great world of politics and fashion. For the rest this *mariage de convenance*, which continued until he was near fifty, proved to be what is generally described as a qualified

---

[1] Balfour, *Life*, i. 67.
[2] "Departure."

success. Then, after his second wife died, he became dependent for such happiness as he had upon the charities of a younger generation. A daughter-in-law—Lady Haddo—took the woman's place in the concluding period of his life, winning his affections at a bound and fulfilling by grace and charm of character his utmost remaining expectations. Thus the last twenty-five years of his blighted existence passed over to the end they were created, —and brought him at the last unto a quiet grave.

An urn that he caused to be placed at the end of a vista at Haddo bears the inscription, "Haud immemor." Whatever the precise significance of the words for him, they echo, happily enough, the dominant note in a private life conspicuous for pathos and fidelity. Not unmindful of his first and best affections, of the ancestral pieties of his home, of the obligations and traditions of great place, his figure stands out against the background of Haddo, low-lying, with the purple hills of high romance upon the one side of it and the grey North Sea upon the other—the figure, as a forgotten article in the *Revue des Deux Mondes* of July 1861 [1] may yet serve to remind us, of a *grand seigneur* of the purest type, noble by nature and by name, and yet more ennobled by suffering. We have no call here, indeed, to see him so. He moves for us upon a wider stage, and into the reserves and domesticities of that sad life of his we need no further pry. But, without some notion of what he was and suffered in his own home and country, we might miss the charm of his disposition, the meaning of his melancholy, the rounded perfection of his public virtue. He was, indeed, the same man in all the relations of his life. Only, just as a face will wear a different look according as the mind turns outwards towards humanity or gazes inwards upon its buried memories, so did he make another word than that inscribed at Haddo, his own at Westminster—a single word—Δικαιότατος. And this they wrote upon his monument.

Aberdeen's public life began with the contemplation of one of the worst and hardest of human injustices—the evil that allows one man, moved by pride or greed or glory, to tear other men from their homes and families and set them to fight against their fellows. The fact that he had followed in the wake of the armies of Napoleon as the Allies forced them back across the Rhine, and had seen at first hand the havoc, the horror, and the

---

[1] By the Comte de Jarnac.

desolation of war, left beyond all doubt a mark upon his mind as permanent as his own private sorrow. His position, a considerable one in the case of a man without previous diplomatic experience, gave him, indeed, every facility for studying both the cost and the splendour of military operations. Castlereagh had accredited him to the Court of Austria in the summer of 1813 as a special envoy with large powers, though without any precise rank, but his appointment was from the first recognised by the Austrian and eventually regularised by the English Government as that of an ambassador. His instructions were to do his utmost to bring Austria into the coalition against Napoleon; and he carried with him the promise of a subsidy. Events, however, moved quicker than his means of locomotion; and he found that Austria had thrown in her lot with the Coalition before he arrived. His immediate efforts were, therefore, directed towards persuading Metternich to adopt the full programme of restitution approved by Castlereagh; and in this he largely succeeded. An agreement was signed at Comotau which included in its scope, together with the more immediate war-aim of the liberation of Germany, the restoration of Spain, of Portugal, and of Sicily to their legitimate sovereigns. It was also understood that Austria would honour, subject to certain reserves, the British pledge to join Norway to Sweden and to set Holland free. Of the agreement itself Aberdeen wrote to Castlereagh that "it does all you desire and more than we could hope"; and he was in a position to add that Cathcart and Stewart—his colleagues, but not the more friendly or the less critical for this— both thought it better by a good deal than they had expected.[1]

All treaties in time of war lie at the mercy of military operations, and it is easy to make too much of Aberdeen's achievement. But it is also easy to belittle it unduly. He had got what he was sent out to get; and there does not appear to be any ground for insinuating that he fell either now or later a prey to Metternich's astuteness. "He saw only with the eyes of Metternich," observes Professor Webster.[2] Aberdeen's correspondence does not confirm this conclusion.[3] His narrative

---

[1] Corresp., Aberdeen to Castlereagh, 9th October 1813.

[2] *Camb. Hist. of British Foreign Policy*, i. 412.

[3] Neither does Jarnac's observation about him: " Aucune prédilection extrême pour le prince de Metternich dont il signalait les terreurs incessantes avec la plus fine raillerie " (*Revue des Deux Mondes*, July 1861, p. 450).

has all the virtue of direct observation; his estimate of the leading personages in Court and camp all the air of considered opinion. He thought the Emperor an abler man and Schwarzenberg a better general than was commonly supposed. In the case of the former he had the opportunity of correcting by constant intercourse a first impression of foolishness, conveyed, as he notices, by an awkward, diffident address[1]; and in the case of the latter he enjoyed every means of appreciating the difficulty of commanding a heterogeneous army with three autocratic monarchs following close upon its heels and one of them aspiring to lead it himself. On the other hand, with opportunities for forming an opinion greater than have been enjoyed by any Briton before or since, for they lived together upon the terms of the closest intimacy, he judged Metternich's intelligence to be overrated. The passage deserves quotation, and the more that it incidentally refutes the charge of subserviency directed against himself.

"Metternich," he told Castlereagh, "is not a very clever man, but he is tolerably well informed. He is very agreeable in society and in transacting business, without any stiffness or formality. He has considerable quickness and may be acute: but I do not think him a difficult man to deal with. You must not imagine that he has blinded me by his fine speeches, or turned my head by his praises in all quarters. As we are a great deal together, I think it very possible that my society may suit him, and, as I am perfectly fair and honest with him in whatever I say, it is possible he may like this proceeding, if for no other reason, at least for its novelty. *Au reste*, I am perfectly on my guard." And then comes the curious sentence which lays bare the almost inconceivable obscurity in which the figure of one of the great foreign ministers of the time was cloaked from the eyes of another. "So far as I recollect, you had quite an erroneous notion of his age, he is a young man, only forty, I believe not quite that." [2]

"Do not be afraid of me," he repeats a day or two later. "There is a sort of half-confidence and intimacy which ambassadors may enjoy which perhaps is likely to mislead. My intercourse with Metternich is of another description. Living with him at all times and in all situations, is it possible

---

[1] Balfour, *Life*, i. 117.
[2] Corresp., Aberdeen to Castlereagh, 10th November 1813.

I should not know him? If indeed he were the most subtle of mankind he might certainly impose on one little used to deceive, but this is not his character. He is, I repeat it to you, not a very clever man. He is vain, but he is a good Austrian. He may, perhaps, like the appearance of negotiation a little too much, but he is to be trusted."[1]

Aberdeen wrote from Frankfort, where he had assisted at the triumphal entry of the Austrian Emperor a month earlier, and where the Allied statesmen paused to take counsel whilst the Allied armies held upon their march. The diplomatic situation was calculated to test the metal of which the Grand Alliance had been made. There was the danger of not pushing the defeat of Napoleon far enough to be convincing; there was the danger of pushing it so far as to fill the tired people of France with new energy to resist; and there was the danger, which we have long forgotten, that the Russian troops, clamorous as they were for peace,[2] might cause the Allied combination to break up. In the hour of decision Metternich was all fight and firmness; it was "impossible," Aberdeen tells Castlereagh, "to be more warlike or decided."[3] This did not mean that he was unwilling to negotiate on terms conformable to the existing military situation, provided that they gave adequate security for the future. At Frankfort Napoleon was offered the so-called natural frontiers of France—the Rhine, the Alps, and the Pyrenees; and both British Foreign Secretary and British Envoy approved the offer. It was characteristic of Aberdeen's mind that he objected to the Russian plan of stating the Allied terms too high in order to bargain the better. "I told Nessel-rode," he wrote to Castlereagh, "that if the propositions were made with the hope of being accepted, common sense dictated that they should be rendered as palatable to Buonaparte as was consistent with the fixed views of the Allies. If the propositions were made without any such hope, I deprecated the whole proceeding as being most erroneous in principle and calculated to produce the greatest injury to the common cause. I observed that it would be much better to defer making any overture at all, if it was not thought that we were in a sufficiently commanding

---

[1] Balfour, *Life*, i. 154–5, 12th November 1813.
[2] Corresp., Aberdeen to Castlereagh, from Frankfort, 8th November 1813.
[3] *Ibid.*

situation to make that which we were determined to press." [1]
It might seem superfluous to lay emphasis upon the merits
of a diplomacy based upon a constant good-will to negotiate
and firm offers of peace, upon a clear-cut conception of the end
to be reached, a resolute determination to be content with
nothing less than this, nor to pursue anything further, if it
were not that we must soon become familiar with a diplomacy
widely removed from it.

For the rest, Aberdeen's influence in the counsels of the
Allies was a shining example of what straightforwardness can
do. He pleased everybody, except the colleagues who were
jealous of him, lived with Metternich, rode daily with Pozzo,
dined every night with the Emperor, and so bewitched Sir Robert
Wilson, the British military attaché, with his fair-mindedness
as to make that ardent Liberal declare that a man of so independent a spirit and reasonable an intellect could be no Tory at
all. Liberalism, however, enjoys a more limited monopoly of
political virtue than its ardent advocates sometimes suppose;
and Aberdeen in no way found the creed of Pitt incompatible
with the exercise of freedom or the pursuit of sense. His
diplomacy was indeed the complement of Castlereagh's policy,
and, though it is impossible to allot to each his respective merit
in the formation of the permanent alliance of the Great Powers
that was achieved at Chaumont, we can at least make sure that
his intimacy with Metternich had laid a good foundation for
Castlereagh to build upon.

There was another feature of Aberdeen's character which,
in any review of the incidents of his mission to the Court of
Austria, must strike the student even more forcibly than his
calmness of judgment; and this is his tenderness of heart. It
was a trait which, as we shall see, remained conspicuously his
to the end of his career. Amidst the glamour of great place,
great persons, great issues, great events, he never lost sight of
the meaning for common folk of a situation, intoxicatingly
exciting and dramatic, when viewed from the high altitude of
a Cabinet Council or the General Staff, but pregnant with
wretchedness for the rank and file of humanity. The ugliness
of the business in which he was engaged more than eclipsed for
him its burnished splendours. "The near approach of war

[1] Corresp., Aberdeen to Castlereagh, from Frankfort, 8th November 1813.

and its effects," he wrote from Teplitz to the sister-in-law who had taken his dead wife's place as his closest correspondent, "are horrible beyond what you can conceive. The whole road from Prague to this place was covered with waggons full of wounded, dead, and dying. The shock and disgust and pity produced by such scenes are beyond what I could have supposed possible at a distance. There are near two hundred thousand men round this town. There is much splendour and much animation in the sight, yet the scenes of distress and misery have sunk deeper in my mind." [1] The scenes were indeed appalling enough, and Tolstoi makes them no more vivid in *War and Peace* than does this pained and meditative spectator. Well before the hardest fighting of the campaign began he had stumbled as he walked in a shrubbery upon "a great heap of arms and legs." "The continual sight of the poor wounded wretches of all nations," he wrote, "haunts me night and day." [2]

At Leipzig, of course, things were even worse. " How shall I describe the entrance into this town? For three or four miles the ground is covered with bodies of men and horses, many not dead. Wretches wounded, unable to crawl, crying for water amidst heaps of putrefying bodies. Their screams are heard at an immense distance and still ring in my ears." [3] At Schlüchtern irony added a new element of pathos. "The most affecting sight, I think, that I ever beheld, I have seen to-day. Houses were burning, the owners of these cottages (were) in the deepest misery, and their children were playing around and were quite delighted with the fire which consumed the whole property of their parents and condemned them to cold and hunger." [4]

Cynics have suggested that War might be suppressed if only, at every outbreak of hostilities, all the diplomatists involved were systematically hung. It would be a milder but perhaps not less efficacious expedient if a diplomatic education included such glimpses as Aberdeen had of Mars as he mangles human flesh and murders human happiness.

If man was vile, there were at least, what modern warfare no longer spares, pleasing prospects to be seen on every side. To such charms Aberdeen was very happily susceptible. "You know," he writes to his sister-in-law, "there is nothing which

---

[1] Balfour, *Life*, i. 82.
[2] *Ibid.*, p. 99.
[3] *Ibid.*, p. 125.
[4] *Ibid.*, p. 129.

at all times has so benignant an influence over me as the enjoy-
ment of Nature.   It is so pure and unmixed, it is so perfectly
within our power at all times and in all places, and it is so intense
that I think those persons who do not possess it are much to be
pitied.   They have a sense the less." [1]

We must not linger over passages like this.   Enough has
been said to show with what manner of man we have to deal,
and how gentle and gracious a character was now afloat on the
rude sea of circumstance.   Urgent for peace yet patient of war,
he still continued, even after Castlereagh had himself joined
the migrant Council of Monarchs and Ministers, to be in charge
of the negotiations for a peace by agreement.   The Châtillon
offer to Napoleon of a France with a frontier such as it had had
in the first phase of the Revolution was entrusted to his hands,
and, when this also failed, he passed on to Paris with his Chief
in the wake of the winning armies.   A more ambitious man
would have gone to Vienna and taken his opportunity of joining
in the work of the Congress.   It was characteristic of him that
he preferred to regain at once the large simplicities, amenities,
and liberties of a British peerage and a feudal principality; a
Cincinnatus, as we might say, returning to a gilded plough and
unreclaimed acres.   For fourteen years, while Castlereagh's
slow star rose to its meridian-height, waned and fell, and
Canning's radiant meteor shot across the sky and was lost to
view, he remains in obscurity, busy with the care of a delicate
child, with an essay on Grecian architecture, and a Bill for the
modification of Scottish entails.   Yet he was not quite forgotten.
Now and again Castlereagh consulted him about foreign affairs;
and all the while his friendship with Wellington grew.   Then,
when the Duke formed his Administration in 1828, Aberdeen
became Dudley's auxiliary [2] at the Foreign Office, and, within
a month or two, on Dudley's resignation, his successor.   He
had from the first been Wellington's choice for the post.   The
two men were not entirely agreed in opinion, but completely
at one in sentiment; both of them great lovers of integrity, duty,
and peace.   At this point we may conveniently pick up once
more the main thread of British foreign policy.

---

[1] Stanmore, *The Earl of Aberdeen*, p. 5.
[2] He held office as Chancellor of the Duchy of Lancaster on this understanding.

The curtain was dropped, as the reader may recall, over the death-bed of Canning whose final orientation, under the influence of events and Madame de Lieven, was towards Russia and even towards combined action in the Near East with Russia, if action there had to be. Rather more than two months later, but still as a result of Canning's handling of the Eastern Question, Navarino was fought—a naval encounter which threw diplomacy into confusion. It came about, as such things will, contrary to intention and without prevision. The French and English Admirals, manœuvring in Greek waters with vague instructions, had on a sudden found their neutral police measures challenged and their ships temerariously engaged by the Turkish and Egyptian Fleets which they had pinned in the Bay of Navarino. Compelled to assert themselves, they did so with a·hearty good-will. By the evening of 20th October the ships of Sultan and Pasha, which numbered at sunrise some 120 sail, had as really ceased to exist as the navy of a more famous sovereign, on a more memorable occasion, in adjoining waters, of which it had been lately written:—

> " He counted them at break of day—
> And when the sun set, where were they ? "

The British Admirals had laid the Turkish Empire upon a sick-bed from which it never rose again to real health, but British statesmen were by no means ready to assist at its obsequies. Wellington, in particular, like many another Conservative since, feared the break-up of an institution whose existence had become part and parcel of the European system. Aberdeen, as one might expect from what has already been said of him, had long envisaged the question from another standpoint. A letter, addressed to Castlereagh in 1821, shows a strong sympathy for the cause of Greek independence, but rests it expressly, not upon the fascination of classical studies, but upon a kinship of Christian ideas. "The Christian population of Greece," he wrote, "is a bastard and mongrel breed derived from many sources . . . still they are Christians, quick-witted, and capable of any degree of improvement." [1] And he went on to argue that, as their present condition could not be prolonged indefinitely, we should be well-advised ourselves to further their struggle for independence

[1] Stanmore, *The Earl of Aberdeen*, p. 71.

and not leave it to Russia to gain the credit of their liberation. This opinion presently reappears in a more developed form in a despatch addressed, when he is Foreign Minister, to his brother, the British Ambassador at Constantinople; and the sentence in which it is enshrined is the key to his Near-Eastern policy. "The principle of the arrangement which we ought now to desire to see accomplished is that which should most effectually secure the tranquillity of the Levant during the remaining existence of the Turkish Government and which, at the period of its dissolution, should offer in the Greek state a substitute whose interests we should naturally be called on to support in preference to the pretensions of all others." [1]   The real difficulty, as he saw, was to keep Turkey going until the Christian people of the Balkan Peninsula had become equal to taking over its international functions; otherwise the dissolution of Turkey must mean the extension, actual or effectual, of Russia; and to that he was not prepared to be a party.   A waiting policy was what he wanted, but it was a policy which Navarino made it uncommonly hard to pursue.

For that "untoward event," as Wellington's Government, conscious of all the inconvenience that it had given them, pathetically styled it, had caused the Sultan to tear up a treaty which he had just concluded with Russia, and declare for a holy war, and the Russian Emperor to set his legions marching towards Constantinople.   Critics of Wellington and Aberdeen have argued that, if only Canning had been still alive, he would have kept Russia in hand by acting up to a point in conjunction with her. It may be so.   But the usual fate of moderates who yoke themselves to extremists is that they are swept off their legs and dragged further than they at all want to go.   Neither Wellington nor Aberdeen was prepared to take the risk involved.   They held to the Treaty of London, which Canning had concluded in favour of Greek autonomy; they were willing to turn the Egyptian garrison out of the Morea and had, in fact, the satisfaction of seeing it shipped off, with Mehemet Ali's connivance, in British vessels; but they were not ready to approve direct military operations against the Turks.   These, however, Russia undertook on her own account, and, after meeting with greater difficulties than she had perhaps anticipated, compelled the Porte

---

[1] Stanmore, *The Earl of Aberdeen*, p. 86.

in the Treaty of Adrianople to swallow, together with other distasteful matter, a settlement based upon Canning's plan of combining Greek autonomy with Turkish suzerainty. This was so much the more open to objection that a pre-eminence among the signatories of the Treaty of London [1] seemed now more than ever assured to Russia, already secure as she was of a dominant influence in Greek affairs owing to the presence of Capodistrias, formerly a Russian Minister, at the head of the Greek insurrection.

It was in these circumstances, and as a direct consequence of the Treaty of Adrianople, that Aberdeen reached the opinion that the Turkish Empire was certainly moribund, and that to keep it alive, once there was something to put in its place as a counterpoise to Russian influence in the Near East, would be a profound mistake. He set himself, therefore, to do what he might with the not very promising material afforded by the population of the southermost part of the Balkan Peninsula, and got into close touch with Metternich who had for some while maintained that, if the Greeks were liberated at all, they had better be liberated altogether. He was too finished a student of the history of ancient Hellas not to know that width of territory has no necessary relation to worth or power, and, in attempting to win back for Greece some effective fragment of her old prestige he threw his weight rather upon the side of fulness of freedom than extent of soil. "Much more will depend," he wrote to his brother, "upon the character of the Government than upon the precise limits of territory to be assigned." [2]   A king was the best symbol of sovereign rights, and he desired to find for the Greeks a king who would be a king indeed. But for the intrigues of Capodistrias he would have succeeded in placing a Coburg prince, the admirable Leopold—once the husband of Princess Charlotte, and some day to be king of the Belgians—upon the throne of Greece. Even as it was, he secured for the new State at its birth full freedom instead of mere autonomy, and an independent monarch in place of a president in the grip of Russia.   In one

---

[1] The Treaty of London, as explained above in the article on Canning, was signed on 6th July 1827, a month before Canning's death. It committed the three signatory powers—England, France, and Russia—to the policy of Greek autonomy under Turkish suzerainty. Persuasion was to be used with the Turks to bring them to sign, but by a secret article force also might be brought into play.

[2] Unpublished Letters.

material though not essential point, indeed, the settlement fell short of his intentions. In view of opposition in the Cabinet the Protocol of February 1830 gave Greece a frontier less advanced than the Arta-Volo line where he would himself have fixed it; and Palmerston later on had the satisfaction of moving it forward. So that, if one were required to apportion merit for the creation of modern Greece, one might perhaps say that Canning conceived it, Aberdeen brought it to birth, and Palmerston fostered it in the first phase of childhood. With so much care devoted to its production it is impossible not to regret that the baby did not grow up to be a fairer and a finer child.

The affairs of Greece and Turkey exacted the greater share of the Foreign Secretary's attention between 1828 and 1830, but out of the revolutionary centres of Lisbon, Paris, and Brussels there sprang other problems to be considered. In the early spring of 1828, Dom Miguel, the male candidate, as the reader will recall, in a disputed succession, had landed in Portugal; and it was almost instantly plain that he was king in all but name, and would be king in fact before many months were out. The Wellington Government prudently decided to withdraw the force which Canning had imprudently despatched, before it became further involved in the dispute between the rival pretenders; and to the principle underlying this policy, Aberdeen steadily adhered. The Portuguese in his view must settle their own domestic difficulties, which indeed they were very ready to do, and quickly did in Dom Miguel's favour.

The French Revolution of 1830 gave the Foreign Secretary a good deal more trouble. He had no direct reason to regret the fall of Charles X., whose policy in Algiers, as conducted by Polignac, had had about it an unpleasantly shifty air. But the July Revolution seemed to challenge the settlement of 1815, which made the maintenance of the French Monarchy and the suppression of revolutionary agitations a matter of international concern. Wellington was half-disposed to think that in fact the prescribed condition of interference was present; and it was Aberdeen who counselled neutrality, but a neutrality alert and armed. Nothing, as the Foreign Secretary saw things, was to be gained by giving offence once the change of régime had been effected; and if the Duc d'Orléans proved able to retain his newly-acquired throne, the claims of the monarchical principle would still be satisfied.

As the event showed the July Monarchy of Louis Philippe had pretty nearly as good a life in front of it as any form of government that the French hit upon in that century of revolution; and in due course Aberdeen was to find in the Anglophil constitutionalist, Guizot, a far more congenial collaborator than in the Anglophobe absolutist, Polignac. But at the first sight the situation looked black enough. No matter who reigned in Paris there were Frenchmen intent upon recovering the Rhine frontier for their country. Polignac had indeed, before he fell, laid a powder-mine destined to blow to fragments the forced union between Holland and Belgium; and the July Revolution in France seemed to many as a lighted match fortunately provided to fire the train. For the rest the Eastern Powers were not, perhaps, as entirely displeased as their principles required by the prospect of a convulsion in the West. Every democratic agitation offers some excuse for the iron hand of despotism; all disorder opens the way to a new and perhaps more advantageous shuffle in the perennial game of grab; and there is fruit to be had for the asking whenever the winds of dissolution shake the laden trees. Were France but occupied with an internal crisis, Russia must get the freer hand in Turkey, Austria in Italy, and Prussia in whatever direction she might happen to cast her watchful eyes. The maintenance of a European peace, which was not yet fifteen years old, hung to all appearance upon a *rapprochement* between the two great Powers of Western Europe and their capacity to present a common front.

Aberdeen had no sentimental love of France, nor any consuming faith in her disinterestedness or fidelity. That great country was to him just a fact and a factor in a complicated international situation; and he dealt with it as such. The July Monarchy offered a chance of co-operation, absent in a Government more White or Red. This possibility he desired to exploit for all it was worth. It seemed to him useless, in circumstances wholly unforeseen fifteen years before, to inquire whether the supplanting of the elder line of the Bourbons by the younger was a violation or not of the post-Napoleonic settlement; and he brought Wellington round to his view that the accession of Louis Philippe should be acknowledged without delay. Quickness of decision had given him, at no cost, the credit of a friendly gesture; and he led the great Chancelleries of Europe in the

recognition of one who, poaching partly in royal and partly in
imperial preserves, called himself adroitly "King of the French."

The new Sovereign was, perhaps, as good a friend to England,
not that this is saying much, as ever sat upon the throne of
France—a friend good enough anyhow to cause his own countrymen to nickname him "the Englishman." He understood the
value of Aberdeen's advances, and returned the compliment by
the despatch to England of one who has lately been described
as "le plus brillant messager de toute une école de diplomates
inspirée par le sentiment de la solidarité Européenne." [1] Talleyrand was at this time well past seventy; but only now at last
had the fortune of circumstance played into his hand and
offered him an occasion of bringing about that alliance between
France and England which he had always desired. The approximation of forms of Government had, he thought, given him his
chance. "Ce sont les progrès de la civilisation," he wrote, "qui
formeront désormais nos liens de parenté." [2] He was thus,
perhaps, never more truly himself than when at last he came
forward as the ambassador of a constitutional monarchy to a
country where constitutional monarchy may be said to have
its hearth and home. We cannot but smile, indeed, at the
irony which caused this bleached and hardened cynic to be
associated with such a limpid spring of honour and conscience
as Aberdeen in laying the first, tremulous foundation of that
good understanding with France which in our own day has
grown to seem so stout a fortress against despotic aggression.
Credit, however, to whom credit is due!

Talleyrand, so Wellington assured Madame de Dino, was the
only man capable of preserving the solidarity of France and
England under any English administration. [3] Can we not see
him still, fixing the eye with the sins of two centuries reflected
in his face, charming the ear with the oracles and epigrams
that came tripping off his lips, cracking his last consummate
jokes at the expense of the old Sailor-King, and all the while
sapping and mining the ancient prejudices and well-established
distrusts that made English society fight shy of the fair words
of France; a figure not to be lost sight of by those who seek

---

[1] Sindral, *Talleyrand*, p. 209.
[2] See *Ibid.*, pp. 139–41.
[3] *Mems. of the Duchesse de Dino*, 23rd May 1832.

to trace to its first beginnings in the 'thirties of the nineteenth century the history of the Franco-British *rapprochement*'? Between 1830 and 1834, in Aberdeen's time and in Palmerston's time, he reigns at the French Embassy, the classical embodiment of the old diplomacy accomplishing the ends of the Orleans Monarchy. But present services could not eclipse the recollection of past deceits, and it was Louis Philippe who wound up the tale of the old cynic's life with a witticism as fine, as piercing, as pitiless as any he had coined himself. "Sire," someone is said to have observed to the King of the dying man, "il souffre tous les tourments de l'Enfer." No sense of propriety stops a Frenchman's tongue. "Comment! Déjà!" came the quick reply. And the last word in Talleyrand's dispraise had been said by the Sovereign he had served the best.

The most famous Ambassador that France ever sent to England arrived only in the late September of 1830, and the Wellington Government fell from power in mid-November. In the last two months of his administration, however, Aberdeen, backed by this powerful auxiliary, contrived so to readjust the relations of the two countries as to render a settlement of the Belgian issue only a matter of time and patience. He associated Great Britain with the policy of non-intervention which Louis Philippe was maintaining both against the protagonists of the Holy Alliance and the military and civil interventionists of France; and he proceeded to drag the great Powers of Europe into a conference in London. The successes of the Belgian insurgents against their Dutch masters did the rest. It became clear that Belgium could no more be tied to Holland in the nineteenth century than Holland and the Provinces adjacent could be tied to the Spanish Netherlands in the sixteenth; and it only remained to fix the manner and extent of their liberation. Before he left office, Aberdeen had arranged an armistice which left each party in possession of the territories that it had held before the too zealous activity of the Congress of Vienna had sewn them together into a single kingdom. It rested with Palmerston to bring the freedom-violating yet freedom-praising Dutchmen to consent to unfasten from off their neighbours' necks the yoke they could not bind there.

Aberdeen, after his manner, relinquished office in 1830 with a sense of satisfaction that far outweighed any possible regrets.

His views upon the actual issue which produced the downfall of the Conservative Government will not be doubtful to anyone who has caught the temper of his mind. He was wholeheartedly in favour of Catholic emancipation, not merely as a measure of expediency but as a measure of justice. The course taken by Wellington and Peel was, therefore, entirely acceptable to him; and he went with them and indeed beyond them on the road. But he had no illusions as to the perils and penalties of fair-mindedness and moderation in a world like ours. "The Catholic question," he wrote to his brother,[1] "has utterly destroyed all party attachment, and, having separated the Duke and Peel from their natural followers, has thrown them on the mercy of the candid and impartial, who, I fear, will never give the necessary strength to any Government."

It is the weakness of a biographical treatment of foreign policy that the sequence of events is obscured, as it is the shortcoming of the chronological method that the personal and teleological elements in history tend to disappear from view. To follow Aberdeen's career at this point is to lose contact for a decade with the dominant controlling influences in foreign affairs. The Whigs were in power between 1830 and 1834, and again between 1835 and 1841; and for all that time Palmerston was in power also. Aberdeen, it is true, had he wished it, might have resumed his old place during Peel's brief administration in the winter of 1834-5; and Wellington desired that he should do so. But he was never susceptible to the charms of office at any time and very sensible of the fact that the Duke's European prestige gave him at the moment the better qualification to fill the post. Instead and under pressure he took, first the Admiralty and then the Colonies. But within a few months the Bedchamber Question had given the Conservative Administration what, with his constant appreciation of domesticity as against publicity, he probably viewed as a happy despatch. For six years more Palmerston reigned at the Foreign Office; with what results to Franco-British relations we shall presently have to consider in greater detail. Provisionally, however, Princess Lieven's opinion, delivered as it was from the vantage-ground of her Paris salon, may be allowed to stand. "Lord Palmerston," she writes in the February of 1841, "a un ennemi dans chaque

1 Balfour, *Life*, i. 279.

Français, tenez cela pour certain. . . . Si je dois vous dire le fond très intime de mon opinion, jamais avec lui il n'y aura un sincère retour de la part de la France à de bonnes relations avec l'Angleterre." [1]

This ill-feeling between the two countries it was that needed, above all things, to be changed in the interests of peace when Aberdeen returned to power as Foreign Secretary in Peel's last Government; and it was the great feather in Aberdeen's cap that, without being, as he warns Princess Lieven, "a passionate lover of France or a French alliance," [2] he recreated a good understanding which lasted during the six years of his administration, only to be lost again the moment that Palmerston got back to power. He accomplished his object by the simple expedients of good faith and good manners. "I can willingly honour and esteem a Frenchman," he told his famous correspondent; and by good fortune the two Frenchmen, to whose hands at that moment the destinies of France were entrusted, were both numbered amongst those whom he had come to hold in repute and estimation. Louis Philippe and Guizot were alike well-acquainted with England—the one from long residence during the Napoleonic wars, the other from a study of her institutions. Their presence at the head of affairs seemed to confirm, what it had partly caused, that approximation of the French to the English Constitution, so arresting to the imagination of the time. People supposed, innocently enough no doubt, that the French Revolution of 1830 was the equivalent of the English Revolution of 1688, and that the same sort of finality would attend the one as had attended the other. The political theorists of the day, brilliant as they were, made, as we can see, two elementary mistakes. They believed that political science could hold its own against political sentiment; and they supposed, which was perhaps only another aspect of the same delusion, that the form of government, once it has attained to theoretical perfection, is *ipso facto* protected against the ravages of time and the eccentricities of place. All things considered, the Constitutions of England and France in the 'forties of the last century would have deserved finality, if finality had any place in the

---

[1] Corresp., Aberdeen, from Princess Lieven, 7th February 1841. Jarnac confirms this view in the *Revue des Deux Mondes*, July 1861, p. 436.

[2] Corresp., 24th April 1840.

politics of mankind. They were eminently sensible, keeping privilege, which everyone likes for himself and no one relishes in his neighbour, within bounds, and giving equal play to the monarchical, aristocratic, and democratic elements in the community, so that none could be certainly affirmed to be greater or less than another. To the philosopher, the political developments of Western Europe might seem at last to have satisfied the subtle doctrine of the mean; to the man in the train—for it was in that new-found means of transport, and not yet in the street, that opinion was formed—it might reasonably appeal as a practical demonstration of the simpler precept, "In medio tutissimus ibis."

In that hour of golden mediocrity the middle classes, both intellectual and industrial, entered into their own. Their interests prevailed, their ideals triumphed; and the chief of those interests is trade and the best of those ideals peace. In France, if possible more even than in England, the Sovereign satisfied the temper of the time. Louis Philippe cared little for glory; the Court lacked something in splendour; and the Prime Minister,[1] so the gossips declared, was so definitely a *bourgeois* that Princess Lieven, although she opened her heart to him and he was to her in lieu of a husband, could never be persuaded to give him her hand. Lafitte, the banker, and Thiers, the professor, had done their work as well as was possible. Sagacity sat upon the throne; learning was honoured in the council-chamber; in the Senate good-sense had got its say. If reason were the end, this might have seemed at last the reign of reason. But in France, or at least in the capital of France, they follow reason, not as an end, but as a diversion. Would a city, adorned with so many trophies of war and stirred by so many memories of revolution, ever rest content with the dowdy platitudes of common sense? The 'bourgeois' King was Parisian enough and statesman enough to have that question ever present in his mind; and his anxiety is the key to much in his foreign policy that might otherwise appear obscure. He entertained a secret regard for absolutism abroad, because it suppressed revolution with a high hand and he was afraid of revolution at home. But with regard to militarism, of which also he was afraid, he thought it expedient to adopt another procedure. He pretended

[1] Guizot.

to be ready to go to war. Not once only did he place a Marshal of France at the head of his Cabinet; with peace all the while in his heart, he rattled the sword and made ready to battle; for the sake of bringing his own unadventurous monarchy into some sort of connection with a hero, and staining his own drab version of the Tricolour with a streak of imperial purple, he, a Bourbon still, whatever his advocates might pretend,[1] did even consent to beg the ashes of Napoleon from the British Government and inter them with much pomp in the heart of Paris. At his best a wise sovereign and a courageous man, there are moments when Louis Philippe may make us think of M. Jourdain, if it were not for an uncomfortable, perhaps unjust suspicion that we are dealing, after all, with one even greater than M. Jourdain—the far-famed Tartuffe.

It was Aberdeen's good fortune that his tenure of the Foreign Office fell within the period of the 'bourgeois' Monarchy; and it was his merit that he made the most of his good luck. Great gentleman though he was, or, rather, as he was, he sympathised instinctively with the best preoccupations of the middle class and made straight the ways for commerce and for peace. Palmerston, indeed, might equally with himself have welcomed those buxom sisters, but it was he who best understood the conditions of their coming. His whole administration of foreign affairs was calculated to instil confidence, and it was this that enabled him to take advantage of the sort of planetary conjunction that had occurred in the history of the French and British Governments. A similarity of organic structure furnished them, as he saw, with a similarity, though not an identity of vision, and this again with the basis, not of an alliance, but of an *entente cordiale*.

The Sovereigns of France and England played their part in the business of *rapprochement*. Once and again Queen Victoria visited the Château d'Eu, that pleasant country house, situated some two or three miles from the coast of Normandy, where still amongst deserted halls and forsaken gardens the ghost of the Orleans Monarchy may be sought and seen. And Louis Philippe also, in his turn, came to England and received the Garter and was applauded by the crowd and approved by public opinion.

---

[1] They did, in fact, most absurdly pretend that he was only a Valois. He was either a Bourbon or a changeling.

But it was, above all, in Guizot, a scholar, a Protestant, a Conservative with Liberal ideas, or, if we like it better, a Liberal with Conservative reserves, a man, anyway, having certain salient characteristics in common with himself, that Aberdeen found his best auxiliary. The Foreign Ministers of France and England became close personal friends ; and this fact governs the relations between the two Countries in the period between 1841 and 1846. Europe could have hoped for no better security that peace would be maintained.

And peace was in fact maintained, though by no means without difficulty. A trivial incident in the wilds of the Pacific —the substitution of French for British influence in the island of Tahiti and the detention for a few days by the French of a turbulent British missionary who had exercised consular functions and been guilty of indiscretion and intrigue— brought the two jealous Nations to the verge of war and the two cool-headed Ministers to the verge of resignation.[1] The incident is and deserves to be forgotten, but it furnished the occasion for what deserves to be remembered. Just when the excitement was at its height, the Emperor of Russia, Nicholas I., unexpectedly landed in England, compared Turkey, in a parable that was long remembered, to a sick man, and proposed that England, Russia, and Austria, to the exclusion of France, should divide his inheritance. Or so, at least, it was believed, for the exact tenor of what passed is lost in the obscurity of verbal communications. No sinister impression, however, was left upon two of the principal actors in the business. The Queen tells her uncle Leopold that "Nicholas asked for nothing whatever," and "merely expressed his great anxiety to be on the best terms" with us, but not to the exclusion of others.[2] And Aberdeen writes to Princess Lieven that "our friends at Paris have no reason to regret this visit, for I think we shall all be the better for it."[3]

For all that, both the hour and the man deserve attentive scrutiny. The Crimean War was just ten years ahead, and by these antecedents of it Nicholas must in part be judged. Who would not have sought to penetrate, if he might, the soul of the handsome autocrat, so distinguished and so melancholy,

---

[1] Balfour, *Life*, ii. 106.   [2] *Letters of Queen Victoria*, ii. 17.
[3] Corresp., 25th June 1844.

as he sat at an English breakfast-table in the long June days of
1844? Victoria, as she did the honours of Windsor, with no
more than twenty-five summers of experience behind her to
dull her curiosity, felt all the strangeness of his presence.
"Really," she writes to King Leopold, now safely seated on
the new throne of Belgium, "it seems like a dream when I
think that we breakfast and walk with this greatest of all earthly
potentates as if we walked . . . with Charles or anyone." [1]
Aberdeen, too, had good reason to study the man, for here was
the sovereign whose policy was to prove his own undoing.
If we cannot be certain that Nicholas was, as he so earnestly
protested, wishing England well, we know at least that the
Foreign Secretary judged him kindly. "The visit of the
Emperor," Aberdeen informed Princess Lieven, "was most
successful. All ranks were equally charmed with him. He
is, as you say, a remarkable man. He is not quite what I
expected, but the impression is more favourable. He speaks
well, and his speech carries conviction; but in spite of his
commanding appearance and manner and power, there is
something about him which always inspired me with a sensation
of melancholy. I believe it is the expression of his eye, which
is very peculiar." [2]

If Nicholas's thoughts about Turkey were obscure, his mind
in regard to the Orleans Monarchy was clear as daylight, at
least to the British Ministers who spoke with him in confidence. He disliked that institution with all the conviction of a
Legitimist; and he had no wish to see it survive its maker into
another generation. Neither Peel nor Wellington nor Aberdeen
could follow him here; and they told him so. He was nevertheless
to be gratified. The Fates were already planning the downfall
of Louis Philippe; and, as has happened both before and since
when a dynastic catastrophe was impending in France, they
wove their webs in Spain. Rightly or wrongly—for no immediate
connection of cause and effect can be established—the affair
of the Spanish Marriages has long been held responsible for
the French Revolution of 1848; and Aberdeen's part in it
constitutes, by force of contrast with Palmerston's, the most
obvious tribute to his diplomatic talent.

The tie between the two Countries separated by the Pyrenees,

[1] *Letters of Queen Victoria,* ii. 14.   [2] Corresp., 25th June 1844.

which was formed when the Bourbon grandson of Louis XIV. succeeded to the throne of the Spanish Habsburgs, had gained a new importance as Louis Philippe developed the policy of making the Mediterranean into a French lake.   A total indiffer-ence to Spanish domestic politics was in the circumstances hardly to be expected of France, and the less so that Spain had for some time shown herself singularly incapable of managing her affairs for herself.   At the death of Ferdinand VII., which occurred in 1833, the throne had fallen into dispute between the followers of Don Carlos, the nearest male heir, and of the child-Queen Isabella, the late King's daughter, and as soon, or even before the followers of Isabella got the better of it, new factions had arisen under pretty names which had but little relation to what we understand by them.   There were Moderados and there were Progressistas, but the passions of the one were not moderate nor the politics of the other progressive.   Christina, the Queen-Mother, after much wavering, declared for the former, only to find that she had put her money on the wrong horse. She fled to Paris, leaving Espartero, a soldier and the hero of the Progressistas, at the head of the Government.

So matters had stood when Aberdeen took over the adminis-tration of foreign affairs in 1841; and an armed attempt of the Moderados, with which the French Government were suspected of being in sympathy, failed to alter them.   Not long after this the diplomatic battle for the hand of Isabella may be said to have begun.   The attitude of Louis Philippe was as typically French as that of Aberdeen was typically British.   The one instinctively assumed the functions of the head of the family in arranging a *mariage de convenance*; the other instinctively shrank from interfering with a freedom of choice in the party primarily concerned.   The King of the French was bent upon confining Isabella's selection within the circle of her relatives, whilst Aberdeen was not less eager to leave to the Spanish sovereign and the Spanish people the choice of a consort for the throne. One thing, however, emerged clearly in the preliminary com-munications between the Foreign Secretary and the French emissary.   England would tolerate no marriage, so Aberdeen declared, between any of the French King's sons and the Queen of Spain; to that extent the British principle of safeguarding the balance of power must bar the path of Isabella's affections.

Each Government sought to shift the other from its stand-point. Events favoured the French. The confusion in Spain increased, and with it the claims of intervention. Espartero fell and the Progressistas who rested on British support were obliged to make way for the Moderados, who were the friends of France. It seemed even possible that with this new turn-ing of the tables Isabella might be rushed, in spite of British opposition, into a marriage with one of the sons of the King of the French. In these circumstances Aberdeen was compelled to move some inches from his first position. At Eu, whither he accompanied Queen Victoria in the September of 1843, he discussed the Spanish problem with Guizot, and, whilst reiterating the view that to leave the Spaniards free to make their own selection was a more excellent way, agreed to support the French Government to the extent of representing at Madrid that a husband for Isabella might with advantage be sought among the descendants of Philip V., or, in other words, amongst the Spanish or Neapolitan branches of the House of Bourbon. Thus, upon the understanding reached at Eu, the two candidates for Isabella's hand most acceptable to her mother [1] and most desirable in themselves were put out of court—the Duc de Montpensier, because the British Government would not permit a son of Louis Philippe to sit upon the throne of Spain, and Prince Leopold of Saxe-Coburg, because the French Government would have no consort for Isabella except a Bourbon prince.

Among the scions of the House of Bourbon established in Spain and Italy there were four eligible, or rather possible young princes to be found—all of them, of course, Isabella's near relations. Two might, perhaps, with any luck have made tolerable husbands, but the Queen-Mother ruled out one as a Carlist, the other as a Liberal. There remained the Count of Trapani, who was a dolt, and the Duke of Cadiz, who was a degenerate. Thus, through the machinations of her relatives and the compliance of Aberdeen, the greatest match in Europe was required before she had reached the age of a French or English débutante, to look for a husband amongst specimens of manhood such as no village-maiden would have lightly wedded. If royalty has its privileges, it has also most assuredly its pains.

The first conference at Eu upon Spanish affairs had the

---

[1] Guizot, *Mémoires pour servir*, etc., etc., viii. 217.

incidental effect of drawing from Aberdeen, when a few weeks later at Haddo he discussed the political situation with the French Chargé d'Affaires,[1] a phrase so nicely descriptive of the best that can be hoped from Franco-British relations as to have entered not only at once into the pacific vocabulary of Louis Philippe and his favourite Minister, but also into the womb of time, to spring forth in due season armed like Athene from the head of Jove. The Foreign Secretary called the new relationship between France and England "a cordial, good understanding." [2] And so it was whilst he was there to see to it. As long as he remained at the Foreign Office good sense and good feeling were victorious over intrigue and suspicion.

Everything was outwardly the same as it had been two years earlier, when the Sovereigns of France and England met once more in 1845. The time was again September; the place again the Château d'Eu; Queen Victoria came as before by sea; and in her train there followed once more Aberdeen. Only Isabella and her sister were two years older, and by just so much were their marriages a matter of more concern both to their mother and the French and British Governments. Louis Philippe and Christina had already come to a sort of understanding in favour of making Trapani the husband of the Spanish Queen; and then had gone on to explore the possibility of bringing forward the Duc de Montpensier, the youngest son of the King of the French, as a match for the younger. The Infanta was rich in her own right, and Louis Philippe was not averse to money. A message had been sent by Guizot to Aberdeen in July to the effect that it was not proposed that the younger pair should be married at present, or at all unless Isabella had children; and this assurance was confirmed verbally at Eu. There Aberdeen, as he told Peel at the time, was content to leave the matter; sufficient unto the day of Isabella's being twice a mother, seemed the good or evil of wedding the French King's son to the Spanish Queen's sister.

All the vigour of French diplomacy was now concentrated upon the conclusion of the Neapolitan—the Trapani—marriage. But, hard as Guizot worked to persuade the King of Naples to allow Trapani to be put forward and the Spanish people to accept him as the consort of their Queen, he could not prevail.

---

[1] See Jarnac. Lord Aberdeen, *Revue des Deux Mondes*, 15 juillet 1861.
[2] *Ibid.*, pp. 451-2.

The Queen-Mother veered once again and in the direction of
Prince Leopold of Coburg. Aberdeen, in spite of much pressure
from Paris energetically to countenance the designs of France
and resolutely to oppose any scheme at variance with them,
scarcely shifted at all from an attitude of benevolent neutrality,
even when Jarnac warned him that, if any project of marriage
unacceptable to France began to take shape, the French Government would consider itself free to put forward Montpensier as
a candidate for the hand of either sister. He was probably
wise enough. The diplomatic and domestic sides of the question
were hopelessly involved, and a new turn of the kaleidoscope
in Spanish politics might upset the nicest plans of chancelleries
and kings. One thing alone he could safely do; and that was
to play his hand with perfect correctness and keep himself above
suspicion of intrigue. Circumstances gave him the chance of
proving that he did so.

Henry Bulwer, subsequently Lord Dalling, at this time a
very rising diplomatist, had been placed by Aberdeen himself
at the Court of Madrid. As Bulwer understood his trade, his
business was to steal a march upon the diplomatic colleagues
with whom he was associated and gain a hold upon the sovereign
to whom he was accredited; and this idea of his functions was
stimulated by the fact that Bresson, the French Ambassador,
whom he cordially disliked as a bourgeois and a bounder,
entertained an almost identical conception of them. Accordingly the Representatives of two Countries, supposed to be
united in a cordial understanding, intrigued against one another
for a predominant influence in the counsels of Christina. The
Queen-Mother, a Bourbon and a Neapolitan, was in point of
fact no bad match for them both. She used Bulwer as the
medium of her negotiations with the Duke of Coburg, en-
trusting him with a letter offering Isabella's hand to Prince
Leopold, and making him aware of its contents. Christina,
whether or not this was her object, had him thus at her mercy.
A word to the French Government, and the British Ambassador
stood convicted of dishonouring the compact of Eu!

It was Aberdeen and not Christina who spoke it. The moment
he learnt what Bulwer was doing, he made a clean breast of
the intrigue to Sainte-Aulaire, who represented France in London,
adding that Bulwer had infringed both the letter and the spirit

of his instructions and would accordingly be reprimanded. The reprimand was administered; but, with characteristic gentleness, Aberdeen refused to let his reckless subordinate resign. It is difficult to suppose, however, that he could have left him at Madrid, for, so far as the French were concerned, Bulwer was hopelessly discredited. But, just after the incident occurred, the Government fell. In the new Administration Palmerston once more took the Foreign Office; and Bulwer, a man after Palmerston's own heart, was retained at his post and resumed his operations. In due course, as we shall see, he concluded the affair of the Spanish marriages in much the same style as he had begun it.

On the eve of resignation, and in circumstances so singular that they gave rise to the legend of "Diana of the Crossways," Aberdeen brought to a successful, or at least satisfactory, close a protracted negotiation with America which covered two distinct issues, but constituted in its entirety a milestone on the long road that lay between the recognition of American Independence by George III. and the reception of an American President in London by George V. Two boundary questions stood obstinately in the way of so much as the pretence of a good understanding between the two peoples when Aberdeen took office in 1841; and his biographer is perhaps justified in suggesting that in no part of his administration is his quality as a peace-minister more admirably shown than in his tenacious determination to settle them without a row.[1] The areas in dispute lay on the Canadian frontier, the one to the north-east the other to the north-west of the States. In neither case was the territory particularly valuable, but in Maine considerations of strategy, in Oregon considerations of principle gave importance to its possession.

The frontier between what is now the State of Maine and the Province of New Brunswick had been insufficiently established at the close of the War of American Independence, and attempts to settle it, first by a boundary-commission and then by arbitration, had alike failed. The land in dispute offered the best communications between Quebec and Nova Scotia, and on this account British military opinion, as represented by Wellington, set its face against any sort of compromise. Aberdeen, however,

---

[1] Balfour, *Life*, ii. 125.

though upon taking office in the very year of these events, he had
written to a Quaker friend that "Americans would find him very
obstinate where he felt it necessary to be firm," [1] envisaged the
issue from a more generous standpoint—a standpoint that had
permitted Castlereagh as early as 1818 to conclude a naval treaty
of disarmament in respect of the Great Lakes [2] and has enabled
the two great nations of Anglo-Saxon origin to face one another
for the best part of a hundred and fifty years along three thousand
miles of frontier without any surer defence than a will to peace.
It was a bold business to defy the greatest soldier of the age on a
question of security, but Aberdeen took his courage in both hands
and commissioned Lord Ashburton to cross the Atlantic and
settle the dispute as well as might be, subject only to the retention
of at least one-third of the area in dispute.   Before Ashburton
had reached his destination, however, the Foreign Secretary
had been so far shaken by Wellington's protests that, probably
for the first and last time of his life, he sent a despatch open to
the charge of confusion and inconsistency.   Ashburton was
irritated.   He would brook no revision of instructions whose
purport had been with him a prime condition of undertaking the
mission at all; and his firmness steadied Aberdeen's purpose.
Wellington was reasoned with and placated by a trifling concession; and Ashburton proceeded to set the matter at rest by
securing five thousand square miles for his country out of the
twelve in dispute.   This was more than had been conceded to
Great Britain under the arbitration-scheme which the States
had rejected some years before; and Aberdeen, though the
settlement did not pass without vigorous criticism, had no cause
to be dissatisfied.

It was the pressure of the American population on the border
that made a settlement of the Maine frontier, so particularly
urgent from the British standpoint.   The same consideration
operated after 1843 with still greater force in Oregon.   There,
in the far West, Canadian furriers, or rather the furry creatures
for whose skins they came, were gradually retreating before the
advancing tide of American civilisation.   No precise agreement
distinguished, in a region too remote to be considered in 1783, the
territory of the British Empire from that of the States; all that

---

[1] Balfour, *Life*, ii. 137.
[2] The Rush-Bagot Agreement.

had been settled under a convention of 1818—subsequently renewed—was that the subjects of either Power might occupy land at will. With time very certainly in her favour, America had little reason to press for any immediate change in this arrangement, and, had it not been that some counterweight on the side of freedom to the coming addition of Texas to the slave-owning States of the American Commonwealth was needed, the issue might perhaps have been held in abeyance until with the spreading tide of population all its legalities were submerged. As things were, the Presidential Election of 1844 raised Polk—a President, as it proved, of the baser sort—to sit in the seat of Washington. There followed reckless talk in high places of the unquestionable title of the States to the whole territory of Oregon, and irresponsible babble in the highways and hedges about "Fifty-four forty, or fight"—the figures being those of a latitude well-advanced into what is now the province of British Columbia. To Polk's thundering defiances as to the shrill outbursts of Yankee Doodle, Peel and Aberdeen opposed speeches of measured resolution; and in due course the President returned to his senses, which it is possible he had never really lost. He had reason enough to come to terms. His policy in Texas involved a war with Mexico; and, even if he had his hands free, the transport of an American army across the Rockies was in those days a more serious operation than the transport of a British army from Madras.

The proposed settlement, whilst retaining for Great Britain what is now British Columbia and Vancouver, gave to America the existing states of Oregon and Washington. It was a fair compromise, but there was room for delay on the American side; and delays, with the fall of the Government impending and Palmerston, who got on as badly with the Americans as with the French, looming in the distance as prospective Foreign Secretary, were evidently dangerous. Desiring earnestly to complete his work before he fell from power, and convinced that the adoption of free-trade by the Cabinet would disperse American alarms, Aberdeen, on the eve of Peel's change of economic faith, took what was, at least in those days, a very unusual step. He informed Delane, the enterprising young editor of the *Times*, that the Government was going to renounce protection. This alteration of economic policy by sweeping away tariffs swept away also the last hesitations of the American Government; and the Convention was approved. "This is an immense thing for the peace of the world," wrote Queen Victoria with her customary emphasis and bold disregard of grammar. ". . . It is a very great satisfaction to us that Lord Aberdeen should have settled this question, which he alone, she fully believes, could have done."

His days at the Foreign Office—the happiest of his public life— had indeed ended in peace and honour. The world was definitely the better for his labours. He had reached a lasting settlement with America; he had created a good understanding with France; and, though Europe within two years was to be shaken by a revolutionary upheaval, international relationships had as healthy an appearance as they can ever be expected to possess. His charity indeed knew no exclusions. To Palmerston especially, who had bitterly assailed him as an imbecile and a traitor, he returned good for evil. "He means to show Lord P.," the Prince Consort noted, "the contrast by declaring his readiness to assist him in every way he can by his advice . . . as if he was his colleague." [1]

It would have been well, therefore, for Aberdeen's reputation, if his public service could have ended with his resignation of the Foreign Office in 1846. A greater post was reserved to him, but one which he neither sought nor desired, nor, at the age of sixty-eight, could have hoped to fill with the energy that it rightly demands. Circumstances, however, were too strong for him. Peel's fatal accident threw the leadership of the Peelite group into his hands in 1850; and though, in 1851, his judicious, unpopular condemnation of the Ecclesiastical Titles Bill, at a moment when the nation, with "Johnny" Russell at its head, was mad to get it carried, gave him an excellent reason for refusing the Queen's invitation to form a government, the excuse no longer held good when the Conservatives fell in December 1852. Palmerston would not serve under Russell, but was willing to serve under Aberdeen; and Bedford himself, whose position, both as a Whig magnate of great power and some parts and as Russell's brother, gave weight to his opinion, urged the old statesman to take office on the ground that "no other arrangement would give us any chance of a strong and

[1] *Letters of Queen Victoria,* ii. 101.

lasting government." [1]   Accordingly, upon the understanding
that, as soon as the Administration was well-set in the saddle,
Russell should have his place, Aberdeen none too willingly
took office and became the head of that motley, many-talented
group of Whigs and Peelites which evoked Disraeli's long-
remembered observation that England does not love coalitions.
Man proposes but does not dispose.   For a few months all went
admirably, and Gladstone carried his famous Budget, owing
not a little of his success to the Prime Minister's tenacious
assistance.   Then out of the blue—out of those blue Eastern
skies where political storms silently gather and suddenly burst
—there rose the fiercest tempest that Europe had seen for close
upon forty years.

Of the diplomatic negotiations which led up to the Crimean
War something will have to be said when we come to speak of
Clarendon who, as Foreign Secretary, was immediately responsible for them.   Here we have only to take notice of the
Prime Minister's particular standpoint.   In some words that he
set down in reference to the War he has given us with great
exactness the key to his mind both before and after it began.
"It is unquestionably just," he said, "and it is also strongly
marked by a character of disinterestedness.   But, although just
and disinterested, the policy and the necessity of the war may
perhaps be less certain.   It is possible that our posterity may
form a different estimate on this head from that at which we have
arrived.   The policy or necessity of any war must always be,
more or less, the subject of doubt, and must vary according to a
change of circumstances. . . . It is true that every necessary
war must be a just war, but it does not absolutely follow that
every just war must also be a necessary war." [2]

It was a scholar's opinion, and it suffered the fortune, both bad
and good, to which a scholar's opinion upon questions of great
public moment and interest is necessarily subject.   It lacked the
fire and fury, the uncompromising certitude, the pronounced one-
sidedness that uneducated minds, and, very often educated minds
also, require, or suppose that they require, to support them
through the strain of hostilities.   But in the light of time it has
become the wisdom of history.   "I did not condemn the Crimean

[1] Stanmore, *The Earl of Aberdeen*, p. 213.
[2] *Ibid.*, p. 303.

War," observed Salisbury, "because the grounds for fighting were insufficient, but because it was not our interest to undertake the championship of a power so clearly moribund as Turkey." [1] Aberdeen's calm, unflinching judgment had taken, even in the hour of battle, the just measure of his cause. He knew that Britain was fighting against the best hope of civilisation in that part of the world where the war was waged. "Almost every Christian man, woman, and child throughout the Turkish Empire," he wrote to Russell, "must in their hearts pray for the success of the Czar. This is the great original vice of our position." [2] He perceived that at the outset Russia had had "a just ground of complaint," even though he thought that she had subsequently extended it "beyond the bounds of moderation." [3] The sounding phrases about securing the freedom of Europe, the advance of civilisation, and the overthrow of barbarism, which perfervid patriotism has always in store, left him cold. Such things were, in his eyes, "objects too vague to be easily understood," and, as he observes to Russell, with a touch of Castlereagh's cool common sense, "it is better that we should confine ourselves to such as are more comprehensible and which are capable of attainment," [4] He was not so blind as to be unable to see that the Turks had gradually manœuvred the British Government into a position in which it was more or less committed to their support; [5] nor so simple as to imagine that Stratford de Redcliffe, whom Russell, when for a few months he was Foreign Secretary at the beginning of the Administration, had sent back to Constantinople as British Ambassador, and would not, any more than Palmerston, have agreed to recall,[6] had not hurried his principals with imperious speed along the path to hostilities.[7] He had a right to blame others for the catastrophe, but he blamed himself most of all. He believed that there were two occasions when

---

[1] Gooch, *Life of Lord Courtney*, p. 376.
[2] Balfour, *Life*, ii. 215.
[3] Stanmore, *The Earl of Aberdeen*, p. 238.
[4] Balfour, *Life*, ii. 215.
[5] Corresp. to Mr Gladstone, 17th October 1853.
[6] Stanmore, *The Earl of Aberdeen*, p. 254.
[7] *Ibid.*, pp. 270, 271. Aberdeen's words are: " I thought that we should have been able to conquer Stratford, but I begin to fear that; . . . he will succeed in defeating us all. Although at our wits' end, Clarendon and I are still labouring in the cause of peace ; but, really, to contend at once with the pride of the Emperor, the fanaticism of the Turks, and the dishonesty of Stratford is almost a hopeless attempt."

want of support had prevented him from securing an honourable
and advantageous peace, but as he wrote to Russell with his
habitual humility, "the want of support, though it may palliate,
cannot altogether justify to my own conscience the course which
I pursued." [1]

In truth he never forgave himself; and the evidence of his
self-reproach is among the most touching of his memorials.
Some ecclesiastical buildings in the neighbourhood of Haddo had
fallen into disrepair; and his family had expected that, in his
munificent way, he would renovate them. He rebuilt the manse,
but there his charities unaccountably stopped short; the
restoration of the church, he said, he should leave to his son to
deal with. No one guessed the cause of his decision until death
had laid bare his papers; but these left it no longer doubtful.
Again and again he had scored across chance scraps of paper, the
text recording David's relinquishment of the work of building
the Jewish Temple into the hands of Solomon on the ground
of having shed blood.

So deep a mark, as the Prince Consort noted, had the iron of
Leipzig left upon the soul of this gentlest of British Foreign
Secretaries, or, for that matter, of British Prime Ministers.
Gentlest but by no means weakest! His courage was, if we only
look close enough, beyond praise. He carried the burden of his
years, the burden of his doubts, the burden of a coalition Cabinet,
distracted as well by disputes over a Reform Bill as by divisions
about the war, the burden of Russell and Palmerston, which was
perhaps the greatest burden of all. He carried these, and might,
but for two things, have carried the War itself to a conclusion.
The stars in their courses fought against him. Transports laden
with stores for the troops were wrecked and their cargoes lost;
and the winter of 1854–55 was unusually bitter. It was idle to
expect that the general public would apportion the blame for
the suffering that followed with impartial hand. But also—and
this was the second circumstance that caused Aberdeen's government to fail—Russell, who was his first lieutenant, partly perhaps
from pique, of which there were signs enough, at not becoming
head of the Government, but also in the conviction that he could
not put up an adequate defence for the Ministry's conduct of
the War, deserted him on the eve of Roebuck's famous motion

---

[1] Balfour, *Life*, ii. 212.

of censure. It is possible to behave honestly and yet not honourably; and this was Russell's case. His resignation at the critical juncture was condemned by the Queen, who frankly conveyed her disapproval; by his colleagues, who refused, after Aberdeen's fall, to serve under him in a new administration; by Aberdeen, who though incapable of showing heat or harbouring resentment, spoke of his conduct as 'scurvy'; and eventually, in the light of reflection, by himself.[1] He had in fact done that which no society great or small can afford to condone; he had left the ship just as she met the storm, just as all hands were called to action and every officer required in his place. There was indeed a time when he might have pressed to a conclusion his wavering wish to resign, but that time had gone by. In the hour of stress and danger he owed it to his accepted leader to afford him every assistance in his power. As a direct consequence of this unmannerly desertion, Aberdeen fell, and, after Derby had refused and Russell failed to form an administration, Palmerston took his place as Premier as he had before now taken it as Foreign Secretary. Aberdeen's private life had still some six years to run, but his political career was ended.

Diplomatic history owes him some amends. The shadow of the Crimean War has obscured both his merits as a diplomatist and his services as a Foreign Minister. He is, as his son observes, one of the suppressed characters of history.[2] His high purpose, his conciliatory temper, his quiet achievement, and the delicate balance of his mind, if he were to be more fairly judged, would place him high upon the roll of British Foreign Secretaries.

[1] See Gooch, *Later Corresp. of Lord John Russell*, ii. p. 383. Mr Rollo Russell's Appendix gives the case, such as it is, for Russell's conduct.
[2] Stanmore, *The Earl of Aberdeen*, p. 310.

IV

PALMERSTON
With some mention of RUSSELL

[HENRY JOHN TEMPLE.—Born 1784. Succeeded as 3rd Viscount Palmerston to an Irish peerage in 1802. *Foreign Secretary*, 1830–1834, 1835–1841, 1846–1851. Prime Minister, 1855–1858, 1859–1865. Died 1865.]

[LORD JOHN RUSSELL.—Born 1792. *Foreign Secretary*, 1852–1853, 1859–1865. Prime Minister, 1846–1852, 1865–1866. Created Earl Russell, 1861. Died 1878.] ·

PALMERSTON

PART I

THERE is often said to be a continuity in British foreign policy; and there might with quite as much truth be said to be a discontinuity in British Foreign Secretaries. Canning's personality differs profoundly from that of Castlereagh. Clarendon seems as cosmopolitan as Russell seems insular. Granville is all that Salisbury is not. And Sir Austen Chamberlain, if set beside the late Lord Curzon, bids fair to embody one age as contrasted with another. But of all the possible varieties in this kind there is none greater than that of Palmerston and Aberdeen; nor are there any administrations which illustrate better than theirs the complex play of character and circumstance to which allusion has been made.

Wellington, when he warned Malmesbury, on being appointed to the Foreign Office at the close of the half century, to stand well with France and to distrust the Emperor of Russia like a Greek of the Lower Empire,[1] laid his finger in rough soldierly fashion upon the two outstanding features of British policy in all the period that we are traversing—as well upon that astonishing gravitation of the two great Western Powers of Europe towards one another, which has proved stronger than all the instinctive suspicion and temperamental dislike of their nationals and every adverse incident, as upon that hostility of Great Britain to Russia, which no minister, however powerful—not Canning at his height, nor Palmerston at his best, nor Clarendon, nor Salisbury, though they all of them tried—could break down for more than a moment, if so much, and which may well seem to us, with the Bolshevists in power, no less than an inexorable decree of Fate.

Here, then, was continuity—a compelling continuity of policy.

[1] Malmesbury, *Mems. of an Ex-Minister*, i. 317, 318.

133

But, between the diplomacy of Aberdeen and that of Palmerston as they surrendered to it, how great a discontinuity! *Le style c'est l'homme!* At every turn the student is conscious of the gulf that divides these two men—a gulf embracing character, purpose, physical vitality, and intellectual culture. At every pause he will be sensible of a preference for the outspoken Anglo-Irishman, who had so much about him of what we revere in John Bull, or else for the quiet Scot, who in his political theory was so much of a scholar and in his political practice so nearly a saint. And in any final review of their respective careers he may reflect that in the one he has chanced upon a singularly pure example of the national system of Canning and in the other of the international method of Castlereagh.

Henry Temple, the subject of this study, came of a stock which in its time had borne that distinguished man, half-statesman and half-diplomatist, who was also the patron of Swift. His father, the second Lord Palmerston, seems to have been a good, easy man, a lover of society, a friend to pleasure, a dabbler in the fine arts, and a master of 'the graces'; and if only we could suppose that his mother was, as Bulwer alleged, the daughter of a Dublin tradesman, many things in his character could be neatly explained on hereditary lines—his social charm, for instance, and his breezy temper; his business-like habits; his bluff and blarney; as well as a certain ill-bred arrogance in his manners that makes us sometimes wonder whether he was really quite what is meant by a gentleman. Unfortunately his more recent biographers [1] will have it that Miss Mary Mee sprang from no famous preserve of pretty women, such as Dublin's gay city produces, but of a family drawn from the west of and associated with the Bank of England. Be it so, then, since we cannot have it otherwise, and let us admit at once that no more romantic strain than this had added its ethos to the blue blood of the Temples.

Harry Temple's education deserved all but the highest praise. If one could not be Eton and Oxford, one did well in those days to be Harrow and Cambridge; and to the learning to be got at these famous institutions the boy had the good fortune to add a period of residence in Italy, and the young man some terms at Edinburgh University, where owing to a local association with

---

[1] See on this, Lloyd Sanders's *Palmerston*, pp. 2 and 3, and Guedalla's *Palmerston*, p. 26.

certain famous names—Hume and Robertson, Adam Smith and Dugald Stewart—schools of History and Political Economy just then flourished exceedingly. For the rest, an extant letter, written at the age of thirteen, shows that young Temple was early posted in elementary ethics and was busy posting himself in the Spanish and Italian tongues. "I am perfectly of your opinion," he informs his schoolboy correspondent, "concerning drinking and swearing, which, though fashionable at present, I think extremely ungentlemanlike; as for getting drunk, I can find no pleasure in it. . . . I have begun . . . to read *Don Quixote* in the originall (*sic*). . . . I can assure you I have by no means left off my Italian but keep it up every holidays with Mr Gaetano, who has published a new Italian grammar. . . . I cannot agree with you about marriage, though I should be by no means precipitate about my choice." [1]

The man proved not unfaithful to his own early precept. Late in life he married one of the most charming women of that which Englishmen call the great, and Frenchmen the beautiful world—Emily Lamb, Lord Cowper's widow, and Lord Melbourne's sister.

Through his father's decease, Harry Temple became a peer before he went to Cambridge. He had inherited the most desirable sort of peerage that the Constitution affords to a young man of talent. As an Irish viscount he enjoyed all the social amenities of nobility, and yet, not being a peer of Parliament, he was free to enter the House of Commons without fear of being forced to leave it for the lethal splendours of another place. He made the most of his advantages, and, with an abundance of vitality to back his versatility, used them to the full. We see him now gay, now grave—one day, a man of pleasure and fashion, shooting, speculating, whist-playing, or convivial over a bowl of punch; another day, a politician in the making, standing for Cambridge University before he has so much as taken his degree, administering and reorganising his Irish property with a shrewd eye to business as well as to the welfare of his tenants, getting elected to Parliament as member for Newport and into communication with the leading Tories of the time; in a word, everywhere and always a model of intelligent energy, "going in for life," as his biographer puts it, "at every corner of it." [2]

---

[1] Bulwer, *Life of Palmerston*, i. 8. [2] *Ibid.*, i. 113.

Palmerston carries the first fences of his political career with an ease that leaves us breathless. He is a Junior Lord of the Admiralty before he has a seat in Parliament. His first speech, characteristically dedicated to a defence of the most disputable act in the annals of British foreign policy—the seizure of the Danish Fleet in 1807—and of the Minister who became his model, brought him a flood of compliments. "It was impossible," he tells his sister with an assurance that promises breezy morals in international questions, "to talk any very egregious nonsense upon so good a cause."[1] In the very next year[2] he receives from Perceval one of the most brilliant offers that ever fell to a young man of twenty-five—the Chancellorship of the Exchequer. With a rare sagacity he judges it to be beyond the measure of his political ability at the time and contents himself with the office of Secretary at War—a post which, though its functions went no further than the equipment of the armies which the Secretary for War was there to set in motion, seemed important enough to satisfy any modest ambition, whilst the country was fighting and the adversary was Napoleon. In a departmental squabble with the Commander-in-chief he sustains successfully the rights of the civil as against the military establishment. Perceval's assassination proves no check to his fortunes. He continues still in the same employment under Liverpool's long administration, and some six years later escapes by a lucky twist of his body at the critical moment the consequences of an attempt upon his life.

The appointment of Canning, his master in statecraft, to be head of the Government brings him for a second time to the threshold of the Exchequer, whose doors the Prime Minister first flings open to him and then closes again, either, as he supposed himself,[3] on account of the King's opposition, or, as Princess Lieven affirms,[4] because he was too much compromised by speculation on the Stock Exchange. In compensation he is offered India—for the second time[5]—but once again his cool judgment rejects a prize that might have placed him beside Clive and Hastings. The fulness of his time had not yet come, and some uncanny instinct kept him patient. Still at the War

[1] Bulwer, *Life*, i. 80.
[2] 1809.
[3] See Bulwer, *Life*, i. 183.
[4] Temperley, *The Unpublished Diary of Princess Lieven*, p. 164.
[5] Liverpool had also offered it to him. Bulwer, *Life*, p. 186.

Office, though now at length included in the Cabinet [1] and clearly
marked for high promotion, he watched the star of Canning shoot
to its final splendour, blaze, and vanish. Still at that relatively
obscure post he served the transient and embarrassed Goderich,
and, still as Secretary at War, he joined that divided Ministry of
Wellington's upon which all the ends of the doomed dogmas
of a bygone age seemed to have concentrated. An advocate,
like Canning, of Catholic Emancipation, he passed with Huskisson
out of the Government, pledged himself a year later to the cause
of Parliamentary Reform, and was offered, as Princess Lieven
fondly but incorrectly supposed at her instigation, the post of
Foreign Secretary in Grey's memorable Reform Administration.

During those critical years between 1828 and 1830 he had
passed from the camp of the Tories to that of the Whigs, and
from the preoccupation of domestic to that of foreign affairs.
The circumstances of his conversion do not, however, confirm
the popular idea that he was a Tory at home and a Whig abroad.
Rather they prove that he believed in a constitution such as
England enjoyed between 1832 and 1867—a constitution which
so fair a judge as Lecky pronounced the best in her history—
and that he wished to assist foreign nations to reach a similar
point of development. Russell, so his biographer warns us, is
wrongly nicknamed "Finality John." "Finality Pam," however,
would be appropriate to Palmerston. He believed in a certain
measure of popular government and no more, and having once
shot the rapids of an extended suffrage, he did his utmost to
avoid having to shoot them once again.

Thus only at the age of forty-six had Palmerston found his
Party and his place. Without being a Whig of the straitest sect,
he was well fitted to stroke the boat of a Liberal aristocracy as
it floated serenely between the Reform Bill of 1832 and the
Reform Bill of 1867. He brought with him more energy and
decision than Whigs commonly possess, and yet he had no cranks
nor fads nor unseasonable doctrines, but was well content to
leave things as they were and to be guided by interest and expediency. He was indeed so evidently the man for the time,
that in the thirty-five years of life that remained to him after
he joined Grey's Government, some eight only were spent out
of office. In spite of a blunder that would have ruined a lesser

[1] Bulwer, *Life*, i. 191.

politician, he gained continuously in popularity and power, until he overshadowed all his contemporaries and at an age when many men are content to retire seemed but just to have touched the summit of his prestige. Physical energy, a breezy way of treating things, an instinctive understanding of the mentality of common men, a cleverness sufficient but not too great for the House of Commons, one of the most skilful hostesses in Europe for his wife and one of the finest houses in Piccadilly for his abode—all these things helped prodigiously to give him a place amongst his contemporaries such as no man, perhaps, after him except Gladstone has occupied. He was one of the greatest of Prime Ministers. Whether he was also a great Foreign Minister, we have now to inquire.

It was upon Canning's decease—so Princess Lieven informs us [1]—that Palmerston began to apply himself to the study of foreign affairs; and his particular qualifications for the post of Foreign Secretary, as they probably appeared to the mind of Grey in 1830, were these three years of reflection coupled with an admirable knowledge of French. The subtle arts and polished graces that we associate with the very thought of a diplomatist were always wanting to him. His manners were detested alike by the subordinates whom he drove with untiring energy and the foreign representatives whom he badgered with bluff resolution, and sometimes even with bluff that had behind it no resolution. Talleyrand—"Old Talley" as the Foreign Secretary characteristically called him—aged and famous, fared in this respect no better than his fellows, and bitterly resented it. And Bulwer, Palmerston's best disciple and apologist, who had exceptional opportunities for seeing behind the scenes, can do no more than explain upon the score of youth—a score singular enough in the case of a man of forty-six who had enjoyed twenty years of office—a defect which, for the rest, all the weight of age and long experience did not avail to cure. The footnote in which Bulwer makes his chief's excuses is indeed so significant as to be worth recalling from the page where it lies buried, for it conveys in the phrases of a friend as much as any counsel for the prosecution could desire to prove.

"Lord Palmerston, I think," says the astute and accomplished man of the world who became Lord Dalling, "did not quite

[1] Temperley, *Unpubl. Diary of Princess Lieven*, p. 165.

understand M. de Talleyrand's meaning. He was then a young negotiator; but an experienced one, whilst he bears constantly in mind the important points of his case, avoids being too emphatic about them. One should glide to one's point, and not rush—stamping one's foot—up to it." [1]

So they thought, at least, who followed the methods of the old diplomacy! But Palmerston placed his trust elsewhere—in the Press which he was at pains to manipulate; in Parliament, which he learnt better than any man then living to manage; in the Country, whose temper he knew how to catch and the weight of whose name and resources he brought to bear upon every negotiation with a patriotic effrontery that has never been excelled.

The issue that provoked those strained relations with Talleyrand, to which reference has just been made, was an incident in the troublesome business of separating Belgium from the Kingdom of the Netherlands. Aberdeen—to pick up the tale of policy where we left it—had prepared the way to that end by summoning a conference in London in the last days of the Wellington Ministry. Unfortunately the liberation of "the cock-pit of Europe" from the tyranny of the House of Orange was bound to be a matter of more than local interest. It involved, in the first place, the extraction of a corner-stone out of the edifice erected by the Congress of Vienna; and consequently the creation of a dangerous precedent. Also, as a challenge to authority and a concession to rebellion, it was certain to excite the attention of the despotic Monarchies of Eastern Europe, and not the less that the King of the Netherlands was the brother-in-law of the King of Prussia. But it was, above all, the French who felt the most vital interest in any political reconstruction of the Belgian provinces. Here lay their Naboth's vineyard—those fertile lands but lately theirs, which, according to the newest patriotic doctrine, Providence must be supposed to have designed to form their 'natural,' their rightful boundary. And here, too, lay the abomination of their late desolation—that chain of barrier towns, fortified against their ambition under the provisions of the Vienna settlement of 1815, memorials of their defeat and pledges for their good behaviour. For the French Government to allow the Belgian imbroglio to be settled

---

[1] Bulwer, *Life*, ii. 52, footnote.

without snatching some tangible advantage would have been, in those early days of the Orleans Monarchy, to incur a perilous diplomatic disgrace. And Great Britain, to whom the mainten-ance of the throne of Louis Philippe represented an escape both from Royalist intransigence and Republican revolution, had reason enough, whilst protecting her own vital interest in Antwerp and preserving Europe from the desire of military glory which is indigenous in Paris, not to cause the Orleans Monarchy to be discredited. No one knew this better than Palmerston, to whom Sebastiani, the French Foreign Minister during the most part of his first foreign administration, had already observed that no cordial alliance could exist between England and France so long as England set her face against extensions of French territory towards the Rhine.

It was in face of these considerations that Palmerston had to endeavour to compose the internal dissensions of the Nether-lands; and his conduct of the long negotiation, with its attendant, continuous risk of a general war has seemed to more than one well-qualified critic to be the *chef-d'œuvre* of his diplomacy. Space does not allow an affair which lasted pretty nearly a decade to be treated in detail; nor, perhaps, would his merit show the clearer if it were. All the puzzle of the problem is apparent in its leading terms; all the difficulty of the negotiation in its principal incidents.

The liberation of Belgium from the Dutch embrace was a foregone conclusion when the Conference of London began to sit; and it was quickly agreed to. But to bring the contending and arbitrating Powers to a common conclusion about the bases of separation was another matter altogether. There were three main issues to be settled—one personal, another geographical, and a third financial—and the first two were eminently con-tentious. The new State had to be provided with a king; and a king who satisfied the wishes of all the parties concerned was hard to come by. There was, of course, an endless preserve of princes amongst the royal houses of Germany, and Louis Philippe was always ready with a son or a nephew; but it was not in either direction that the eyes of Palmerston at first were turned. He hoped, it must be confessed a little innocently, that by the choice of the Prince of Orange the independence of the people of Belgium could be secured without putting a

slight upon the Sovereign who was soon to be no more than
King of Holland. But the Belgians had no stomach for so
naïve a solution. So deeply had the oppressions of the Dutch
scarred their soul that they were prepared for any arrangement,
even to re-incorporation into France, which would set them
free from their northern neighbours. In this mood they took
the step of electing the Duc de Nemours, the second son of the
King of the French, as their Monarch. The election, had it taken
effect, would have given France almost as good a hold on Belgium
as the restoration of the Tricolour itself; and Palmerston would
not hear of it even at the price of war. To Charles of Naples
there was only so much less objection on the part of England
as a nephew by marriage is less objectionable than a son by
blood. The Duc de Leuchtenberg, not otherwise an ineligible
candidate, had the misfortune to be the son of Eugène Beau-
harnais, and, being thus embedded in the tradition of the
Bonapartes, was inacceptable to the Bourbons. In the end,
therefore, the High Conferring Powers came little by little to
him whom his father-in-law, George IV., had irreverently styled
'Le Marquis Peu-à-peu'—Leopold of Saxe-Coburg, the widower
of Princess Charlotte of England and the uncle of Queen Victoria.
The Belgians accepted him in default of Nemours, and, thus
fortified by a symbol of independence, immediately developed
a new phase of successful obstinacy.

The Conference in its optimism had thought to cut the knot
of the geographical and financial problems involved in the
separation of Holland and Belgium by a compromise. In the
beginning of 1831 the High Powers assembled in London had
agreed that the frontier between the two projected kingdoms
should follow the line of division existing between the Dutch
and Austrian Netherlands before the French Revolution, and
that Luxemburg and Limburg should constitute a grand-duchy
with the King of Holland for its sovereign. As for the Netherlands' public-debt, the Conference had proposed to halve it.
To these ideas the Dutch Government was willing to give a
grudging assent. But the Belgians had already learnt the value
of resistance. Blest with the possession of the territories they
claimed, and not unwilling to fight for them, they presently
induced the Conference, in spite of some reckless boasting that
its terms were irrevocable, to submit these to revision. All

Palmerston's brass melted before the fear that the German Confederation might advance an army into Luxemburg to drive the Belgians out, and the French push up troops to keep the Belgians in.   Well had they nicknamed him "Protocol Palmerston" at the Foreign Office, for of protocols in relation to the severance of Belgium from Holland he produced no less than seventy-eight.   And now upon a well-devised protocol hung the peace of Europe.   With characteristic, easy-going opportunism Palmerston drafted the articles of separation anew; and this time there was the appearance of a bias towards Belgium.

It was the turn of the Dutch to be angry; and their indignation with their neighbours got the better of their famous phlegm. They armed; they invaded; and they conquered.   Had not a French army been pushed across the frontier to save the routed Belgians, Brussels would have fallen.   But the forces of the King of Holland were no match for those of the King of the French.   The Dutch retreated as quickly as they had advanced; and the soldiers of France were left in possession.   They had not been sent from motives of pure disinterestedness, and they were not prepared to leave unless France were paid her price. That price was the reduction of the barrier-fortresses, or rather of some of them, to the rank of unfortified towns.   Palmerston had already agreed to so much, if for no better reason, then because the new State of Belgium would be in no position to take over the expenses of their up-keep.   But to leave the French in Belgium after the Dutch had left would have brought a German army across the Meuse.   He insisted that they must retire at once and leave it to the Powers to select the fortresses destined for demolition.   The situation had grown to the last degree tense; and diplomacy was nearly at its wits' end to relieve it.   "One thing is certain," the Foreign Secretary wrote to the British Ambassador in Paris, "the French must go out of Belgium, or we have a general war, and war in a given number of days." [1] Lord Granville was equal to the occasion.   Backed by his colleagues at the two Imperial Embassies and by the Ambassador of the King of Prussia, he induced the French Government, as if on its own initiative, to withdraw its troops from Belgium. In due course, but at the will and choice of the Powers, five

[1] Bulwer, *Life*, ii. 109.

fortresses—Menin, Ath, Mons, Philippeville, and Marienburg
—were dismantled.

Palmerston had thus secured two subsidiary points to which
he attached much importance, though the main body of the
business in hand had yet to be dealt with. Dutch obstinacy
and Belgian tenacity required still to be pared until, like the
pieces of a jig-saw puzzle, they fitted into a common frontier;
and this had to be accomplished without setting all Europe
by the ears. Palmerston, pushing his way through a thicket
of hopes and fears, threatened on the one hand with a con-
centration of the Eastern Powers behind Holland, and on the
other with the possibility of Belgium throwing herself bodily
into the sinuous embrace of France, besides being worried at
home by the Conservative Opposition with its Dutch sympathies
and Belgian antipathies, proceeded to draft another protocol
with the same admirable sang-froid, the same breezy disregard
of abstract principles of justice, that characterised his treatment
of the problem throughout. The proper bases of separation
were determined in his eyes—for he was a thorough man of the
world—by no more obscure consideration than the military
and diplomatic assets of the two parties at the moment. As the
falling stocks of Holland were reflected in the second project
of settlement,[1] so the falling stocks of Belgium were reflected
in the third;[2] though the fear of a Franco-Belgian understanding
behind the back of the London Conference gained for the
Belgians better terms than they could otherwise have got.[3]
In this—its final utterance—the Conference gave them a slice
of Luxemburg, a section of Limburg, Antwerp with its citadel,
a right of navigating the Scheldt with a partial administrative
control over the estuary, and a share of the debt unacceptably
larger than it had been before.

The scheme was a compromise and as much open to attack
as are all compromises, grounded as they must be, not on
principle but expediency. The Belgians were furious at getting
so little, the Dutch at having to give so much. Good sense,
embodied in the House of Coburg, triumphed at Brussels;
unyielding purpose, the tradition of the House of Nassau, got

[1] The so-called Eighteen Articles, June 1831.
[2] The so-called Twenty-four Articles, October 1831.
[3] *Camb. Hist. British Foreign Policy,* ii. 147.

its way at the Hague.   The King of Holland refused to give in.
He firmly declined to surrender Antwerp; and the Belgian Government was therefore in a good position to decline to surrender the
Dutch pieces of Luxemburg and Limburg.   A dozen expedients to
bring the contending parties to agreement failed of their purpose.
All Europe was thrown into agitation by the quarrel; and the
statesmen of the Greater Powers showed no little impatience at
that same unbending temper of mind in the inhabitants of the
Smaller, which on occasion they take for high mettle when it
appears in their own fellow-countrymen.   "What is to be done
with these damned Dutch and Belgians?" wrote Grey to Holland,
in the autumn of 1832; and Palmerston would doubtless have
enforced the sentiment and perhaps strengthened the expletive.

What indeed was to be done with them, or rather with the
King of Holland, who was the fount and origin of all the trouble?
Palmerston certainly had not found out, when, after Wellington's
short-lived attempt to collect an anti-Reform Administration in
the May of 1832, he returned to the Foreign Office.   In September,
with popular opinion in England opposed to hostilities with
Holland, and royal opinion in Russia, Prussia, and Austria opposed
to any pressure except economic, his mind still ran on protocols
and compromises.   But a stronger will than his was now making
itself felt in the counsels of France.   The Duc de Broglie, the son-
in-law of Madame de Staël, a man noted for culture, integrity,
and purpose, but not for good manners, had lately consented to
accept the Ministry of Foreign Affairs on the clear understanding
that something drastic should be done to determine the doubts
and delays of the Dutch.   His representations, apart from the
merit of terminating a really intolerable situation, had this to
recommend them—that his resignation might have compelled
Louis Philippe to look for a Foreign Minister in the party of the
Left, and that the party of the Left fostered the old revolutionary
idea of a union between France and Belgium.

It was in these circumstances that Palmerston at length consented to the military coercion of the Dutch, on the assurance that
the French armies would not remain after the fall of Antwerp.
An ultimatum was presented to King William and, upon his continued obduracy, the mouth of Scheldt was closed by the French
and British fleets.   Then, after a short interval had elapsed
without producing compliance, a French army, sixty thousand

strong, advanced upon Antwerp, and before the year (1832) was out the city had surrendered.

The Belgians had now got all and more than all that they were entitled to have under the provisions of the Settlement, but even still King William would not give way. To raise the blockade of the Scheldt he assented, indeed, to a convention, binding him to refrain from attacking Belgium and therefore perpetuating the existing situation until a treaty was arranged. For five years he sulked on these unsatisfactory conditions. Then in 1838, under pressure from his subjects, he decided to content himself with what the Conference had given him; and the Belgians were compelled to hand over districts of Luxemburg and Limburg which they had come in the interval to regard in the light of permanent possessions.

Palmerston was still in power when the Dutch at last surrendered, and it was his hand which guided the long negotiation firmly through its final stages. The separation and re-settlement of the Netherlands has, as has been said, been held to be the masterpiece of his diplomacy. It was, doubtless, a diplomatic achievement to have revised so important an item in the Treaty of Vienna without a general war. But students of British foreign policy may do well to temper their praise of Palmerston's "firm and skilful" [1] handling of the affair with some critical reserves. They might with justice point out that the opportunism which distinguished the work of the Conference caused its credit to be scarred with one, if not more than one humiliating rebuff; that, if a general war was averted, there was nevertheless bloodshed and bombardment; that it was Talleyrand who, by suffering with patience Palmerston's bad manners and incurring with courage the rebukes of his own Government, kept France and England more or less in line in the earlier stages of the negotiation, and who deserved the credit of fixing upon Leopold as the best-qualified candidate for the Belgian throne; that it was Broglie, who, in the later phase of the affair, insisted upon terminating delays which had seemed interminable by a bold, effective stroke; and finally that, when all was said and done, the settlement itself left something to be desired, even if nothing that can, in the circumstances, be legitimately condemned. Upon that last count a word needs to be said.

[1] Hall, *England and the Orleans Monarchy*, p. 143.

In breaking down, under the pressure of circumstances too strong to be denied, the provisions of Castlereagh's Vienna settlement as regards the Southern Netherlands, Palmerston failed, as the event showed and as he himself suspected, to substitute a plan affording any adequate protection against its powerful neighbours to this, from the British point of view, most interesting locality.   If Belgium was too poor to maintain even the existing barrier-fortresses against France, much less could she be expected to make good her defences on her newly exposed frontiers to the north and east.   The Treaties of 1832 and 1839 gave her indeed a guarantee of neutrality, but so carelessly was this drafted that no one could tell for certain what it imported any more than what it was worth.   To this day historians and lawyers debate whether the pledge given by the Great Powers was "joint" only or "joint and several"—whether, that is to say, the compact to defend Belgian neutrality was binding only if all the Powers were willing to act together, or binding also upon each guarantor alone.   That Great Britain chose, both in 1867 and 1914, to treat it as if it were the latter is inconclusive, in face of the fact that the technical phrase required, and carefully inserted in a similar treaty relating to the Ottoman Empire, is wanting here.[1] But it is scarcely worth while to inquire how it may stand with the legalities when the moralities of the guarantee have been in so bad a case.   To France in 1867, as to Germany in 1914, the Treaty of 1839 seemed no more than a piece of paper; and, if William II. saw no great harm in passing his armies through neutral territory, it has to be remembered that Napoleon III. had felt no difficulty at all about swallowing that territory whole.

Palmerston would, perhaps, have manifested but little surprise had he lived to see either the attempted or the actual violation of so solemn an undertaking, since he declined to remonstrate at Brussels in 1855 against the erection, by the Belgians, of certain frontier fortifications, observing to van de Weyer that all history showed the advantage of fortifying frontiers with something better than sheets of parchment.[2]   In that piece of well-judged cynicism from its own author's mouth there is latent the obvious criticism of a scheme that substituted a guarantee too weak to work for Castlereagh's conception of a buffer-state strong enough

[1] See on this point *Camb. Hist. British Foreign Policy*, iii. 15.
[2] *Ibid.*, ii. 157.

to hold its own against its neighbours. A longer view, a wider survey of the whole situation, might conceivably have preferred, after bringing Antwerp and the mouths of the Scheldt under some sort of international control, to allow the Belgians to work out their own salvation in a closer connection with France. The small kingdoms of Germany were within Palmerston's life-time to be drawn into the Prussian orbit, adding thereby more and more to the power of the Prussian king. It would have been in no way inconsistent, therefore, with the doctrine of balancing one international combination against another, in which Palmerston himself believed, nor contrary in the long run to the interest of Europe as a whole, had France been allowed to assert her so-called 'natural rights' and embrace Belgium definitely within her system, if not actually within her borders. Doubtless in 1839 to adopt so visionary and temerarious a course as has been here suggested would have needed an eagle-eye and a lion-heart. Nothing short of the one would have availed to span the years that hid the August of 1870 from view, still less to reach beyond them to the August of 1914; and only the courage of a masterful conviction could have compelled the British Public, already disposed to represent Palmerston as the dupe of Talleyrand, to approve a step that must anyhow have set France some distance upon the road towards her old ambition. As a matter of fact the Foreign Secretary took the line of least resistance throughout the whole negotiation. It would be unfair to blame him, but also easy to give him too much praise.

To the crisis in the West there had been a pendant in the East of Europe. The December of 1832, which saw the fall of Antwerp, saw also the defeat of the Sultan's last army at Konieh by the troops of Mehemet Ali. Nothing, except foreign intervention, stood between the Pasha of Egypt and the conquest of Asia Minor up to the very shores of the Bosphorus. Three Powers, besides the two combatants, were especially interested in the event—Russia, whose long fingers, even if, as would appear, they had for the time being ceased to clutch at Constantinople, still played shiftily about the Bosphorus; France, whose gleaming eyes, mesmerised here, just as in the West, by the growing charm of the Napoleonic legend, were fixed upon the Pyramids, and visualised in Egypt the easternmost prop of a Mediterranean empire; and Great Britain, impatient always of external change and excogitating already that innocent faith in the capacity of the Turk to be reformed, for which the greatest giant in her diplomatic annals—Stratford de Redcliffe—must be held chiefly responsible, but to which Palmerston also lent his countenance. The Foreign Secretary committed himself, indeed, more than once and with much confident emphasis, to an idea that was to be so perpetually disproved for the next three-quarters of a century that there is probably no one left so foolish as to believe in it. "All that we hear every day of the week," he wrote to Bulwer, in the very hour of decision, "about the decay of the Turkish Empire and its being a dead body or sapless trunk, and so forth, is pure and unadulterated nonsense." [1] And to the same correspondent at another time. ". . . I much question that there is any process of decay going on in the Turkish Empire. . . . I should be disposed to think that, for some years past, the foundations, at least, of improvement have been laid." [2]

With such optimism at his disposal it is not surprising that Palmerston regarded the appeal of the Turks for British assistance as deserving of consideration, though to his colleagues it seemed otherwise. Russia, meanwhile, was pressing upon the Porte the very attentions which Britain had refused, for it was no part of her policy to let the Egyptian army reach Constantinople. Low as he had sunk, the Sultan could not for the moment bring himself to accept an offer of naval and military assistance from the arch-enemies of his race and faith. In his palace on the side of those mysterious Straits, where age after age War and Diplomacy have held high revel, he had every reason to view the gifts of these Greeks-by-creed with as much suspicion as the gifts of the Greeks-by-birth were viewed by the hapless Laocoon. Rather than take the hand of Russia, he made a last attempt to come to terms with his adversary. But Ibrahim, in command of the Egyptian army in Asia Minor, was inexorable, and would not be delayed whilst Constantinople negotiated with Alexandria. In despair the Sultan turned again to Russia, and agreed to accept the aid that he had lately declined. Ships and troops were ready at Sebastopol and appeared forthwith on the Bosphorus. Turkey had apparently committed herself to the Russian embrace.

The British Chargé d'Affaires was disturbed; the French

[1] Bulwer, *Life*, ii. 299, 1st September 1839.
[2] *Ibid*,, 287, September 1838.

Ambassador distracted; and the Porte was pushed hither and thither and torn by divergent counsels. Whilst the Russian forces were collecting, new concessions were offered to Ibrahim, and, before they had fully assembled, a Convention,[1] for the surrender of all that Mehemet Ali demanded had been arranged. Pashaliks and provinces—Egypt, the sacred cities of Arabia, Palestine, Syria, Adana—were poured into his lap, and he was confirmed by his overlord in the possession of them all. To all intents and purposes he had rent the Turkish Empire asunder.

There was, it is true, a moment of final hesitation, when the Sultan saw the legions of Russia gathered around his capital; but those very legions proved to be his undoing. We suppose the Turk to be acute; he can be much more stupid than other people. The fact that armies require to be fed only occurred to the Turkish authorities after the Russians had arrived. As soon as they had discovered it, there was nothing, even to the half of their empire, that they were not prepared to surrender to get their new friends away again. For the armies of Russia eat up the food of Constantinople; and the food of Constantinople was already short, since Ibrahim's advance had impaired their ordinary sources of supply. The Russians therefore retreated, but their generalissimo remained to present the reckoning. The Treaty of Unkiar Skelessi (8th June 1833), and, above all, its secret article was the cash that paid the bill. It is possible that in the 'thirties of the last century people exaggerated the value of this compact. It is perhaps true that in actual warfare it would have counted far less than appeared.[2] But, at any rate, in the history of Palmerston's oriental diplomacy it forms a landmark of the first magnitude. Its conclusion in 1833 represents for him a diplomatic defeat as grave as any that he suffered, and its supersession eight years later a diplomatic triumph as great as any that he secured.

The patent terms of the Treaty bound the parties, in the event of one or other becoming engaged in hostilities, by a contract of mutual defence. A latent provision enabled the Porte to compound its obligations under this arrangement by closing the Dardanelles to the Russian advantage against the warships of other nations. The broad effect of the undertaking, therefore,

---

[1] The Convention of Kutaya, 1833 (April-May).
[2] See Hall, *England and the Orleans Monarchy*, p. 254.

as the negotiators interpreted it, would have been to enable Russia to pass her navy at will backwards and forwards through the Straits. So long as such a document, violating as it did the old rule by which Turkey closed the Straits to all foreign warships without exception, remained operative, the primacy of Russia in the counsels of the Porte was indisputable. Palmerston was resolved to recover the ground that had been lost, but he had to do so at the price of the friendship of the French.

For five years, indeed, the opportunity for a diplomatic counter-stroke was wanting. Neither Sultan nor Pasha regarded the Convention, which held them prisoner within their existing frontiers, as a final settlement, for to each it seemed that his position was susceptible of improvement, and the one was dominated by the furies of revenge, the other by those of ambition. But the pressure of the Powers for peace [1] and the time required for preparation delayed the crisis until 1839. Then, in the April of that year, the Sultan, seeking a military advantage at the sacrifice of a diplomatic point, ventured the preliminary blow. He was impressively and decisively defeated at Nisib. Many people, and among them the French, whose wish tended to confirm their thought, were from that time fully convinced that the Egyptians were better soldiers than the Turks, and made their calculations accordingly. Only a few eyes were keen enough to notice that Moltke—the great Moltke, then a young man, engaged in training the Sultan's troops and actually present on the field of battle—had been overborne by the Mullahs and his tactics thwarted. Palmerston, however, was so advised,[2] and the advice worked in well with his previous dispositions.

For the moment, however, crown and sceptre seemed to be slipping from the stricken head and listless hands of the Turkish Sultan. His army was scattered; his fleet had deserted to the enemy, with the French conniving at the treachery; and he himself in that hour of catastrophe went to his long home. Well might the mourners go about the streets of Constantinople! And well might Palmerston, facing the Eastern question squarely in his room at Whitehall, have felt that he stood in the valley

---

[1] This is true of Palmerston at any rate, if not also of Ponsonby. M. Bourgeois's statement that Palmerston encouraged the Sultan to declare war (*Camb. Mod. Hist.*, x. 512) is very well refuted by Hall, *England and the Orleans Monarchy*, p. 240.

[2] See on this, Hall, *England and the Orleans Monarchy*, p. 251.

of decision. For, against the judgment of Clarendon and other of his colleagues, he was now to fix the Oriental policy of Great Britain for three-quarters of a century. The French might follow or not as they pleased; he had resolved—discarding with scorn familiar metaphors,[1] symbolical of decay, as totally inapplicable—to set Turkey on its legs again, in the fond faith that the legs were very good legs and the sick man a capital subject for the doctor's hands.

At the first consultation Palmerston seemed to have all the Diplomatic Faculty at his back. So as to prevent the new Sultan, still a boy in his 'teens, from surrendering to the victorious Pasha, the Great Powers intimated to the Porte in a memorable Collective Note,[2] that they intended to assist in the impending settlement and that an agreement amongst them was secured. The first proposition was certainly true, and the second as certainly false. England and Russia were backing the Sultan for all they were worth; Austria and Prussia—the least interested Powers—were for something like an even compromise; and France, whose foreign affairs were for the time being in the incompetent, easy-going hands of old Marshal Soult, was heart and soul behind the Pasha. The only concord that had been really secured by the Collective Note was concord between Great Britain and Russia. As by a miracle the exclusive Russian protectorate over Turkey, which had been established by the Treaty of Unkiar Skelessi, vanished into air. The protection of the Porte had in fact been transferred to the Concert of Europe, but it should have been obvious to the French Government that those Powers which were prepared to get Turkey the better bargain in the coming negotiations would become the more influential among its advisers. Both Soult, however, and Thiers after him, made the fatal mistake of supposing that they could gain a good footing in the camp of the Turks and at the same time demand the largest concessions in the interest of the Egyptians.

Great Britain was not the only Power which could register a solid advantage by the substitution of the European Concert for the Russian protectorate in Turkish affairs. The Emperor Nicholas, who seemed to give way, had yielded only to achieve a greater end. Collaboration with England enabled him to gratify

[1] Bulwer, *Life*, ii. 298.　　　　　　[2] 27th July 1839.

his dislike of Louis Philippe. At last he had succeeded in driving a wedge between the Cabinets of London and Paris. He was quick to follow up his advantage. Baron Brunnow, one of the best diplomatists in the Russian service, appeared in London, and proposed to allow the Treaty of Unkiar Skelessi to lapse in return for an Anglo-Russian understanding in the Near East. The terms of that understanding were suggested. Mehemet Ali was to be granted a hereditary pashalik in Egypt, and to be obliged, by force of arms if necessary, to restore Arabia, Syria, and Crete. These were precisely the terms that Palmerston himself approved; and he conveyed his willingness to adhere to them, provided that, in the event of a Russian fleet passing the Bosphorus to defend Constantinople against the troops of the Pasha, a British fleet should enjoy the right to pass the Dardanelles. To this, a few weeks later, Nicholas consented. He had, by dexterous concession at a decisive moment, broken down the surface structure of the old wall of partition between England and Russia and laid the foundation of a new wall of partition between England and France.

Soult, in his innocence, had not believed that such things could be. He had relied confidently, first, on the Treaty of Unkiar Skelessi, then upon the notion of a British fleet passing the Dardanelles, to hold England and Russia apart; and he fell from power in the spring of 1840, leaving to his successors a diplomatic situation hopelessly complicated by the fact that he had signed the Collective Note without arriving at a clear understanding with England before he did so about the terms of the future settlement. The downfall of the Marshal and his hotch-potch Cabinet produced a very different type of administration in France. Palmerston, from the March until the December of 1840, found himself fencing with three of the ablest Frenchmen alive; one of them on the throne, another at the Ministry of Foreign Affairs, a third French Ambassador in London.

Of Louis Philippe there is no occasion a second time to seek to draw a portrait. As Palmerston saw him, he was at once 'a man in whom no solid trust could be reposed' [1] and 'prime mover of the foreign relations of France'—a conception of him and the part he played, which, whether correct or not, evidently vitiated

[1] Bulwer, *Life*, ii. 310.

any cordial understanding between the great Western Powers. Once and again the Foreign Secretary declares the King of the French to be the rival of the Grand Monarque in love of aggrandisement—'as ambitious as Louis XIV.';[1] and Granville's warning from the Paris Embassy that want of candour may just as well have its root in time-service and men-pleasing, where a throne is insecure, as in any malignant desire to deceive, fell upon deaf ears. Palmerston judged, so he said, not by motives but by acts.[2] In point of fact he was not well qualified to be a judge at all when a charge of double-dealing was in issue. His candid biographer imputes to him the inspiration, if not the actual composition, of articles in the *Morning Chronicle*, attacking the King of the French in a manner utterly inconsistent with friendship,[3] and one might add, totally incompatible with the character of a Foreign Secretary required to conduct diplomatic relations with a friendly Power. Upon this allegation, as upon David Urquhart's wild suspicion that Palmerston was the tool of Russian diplomacy, and perhaps even the recipient of Russian gold, there is no object in dwelling. The way in which he dealt with and doctored the unfortunate Alexander Burnes's despatches from Afghanistan [4]—burking inquiry, with the aid of a Parliamentary majority, in a case strongly supported by a man as honest and intelligent as John Bright—suffices to show that at best he fell nothing behind Louis Philippe in sharp practice, and at worst was a man whom Louis Philippe might very properly mistrust. Nor was Palmerston in a much better position to accuse Thiers of swaggering and bullying [5] than Louis Philippe of dealing underhand, for those were habits in which he himself excelled all Foreign Secretaries who have been before him and all who have come after him. The accusation was the more unfair that Thiers, as Bulwer who knew him well was at pains to point out to his chief, though, of course, quite ineffectually, was as eager as any French statesman had ever been to maintain good relations with England,[6] and gave

---

[1] Bulwer, *Life*, iii. 19, 23.   [2] *Ibid.*, ii. 311, footnote.

[3] Lloyd Sanders, *Palmerston*, p. 75.

[4] The case against him is set out in Miss Gertrude Robinson's *Life of David Urquhart*, pp. 142–46. John Bright used the words, "mutilated, false, and forged" in regard to the opinions with which Burnes was credited in the official Blue Book published under Palmerston's authority as Foreign Secretary.

[5] Bulwer, *Life*, ii. 319; *cf.* pp. 316 and 327.

[6] *Ibid.*, 313.

in fact some actual evidence of goodwill by offering to arbitrate in a dispute between Great Britain and Naples.

With the third member of the French diplomatic triumvirate —with Guizot, now established as French Ambassador at the Court of St James and resident at Hertford House—Palmerston got on as well as a rollicking opportunist can be expected to get on with a solemn and studious doctrinaire. In one respect at least he gauged his three antagonists well. They were all of them both by nature and conviction men of peace, and each of them, perhaps, even more a man of peace than even the others suspected. "M. Thiers," Louis Philippe had assured Bulwer, "est furieux contre moi parceque je n'ai pas voulu faire la guerre. Il me dit que j'ai parlé de faire la guerre; mais parler de faire la guerre et faire la guerre . . . sont deux choses bien différentes." [1] But Thiers had also communicated to Bulwer a piece of information. "Le Roi," he had said, " est bien plus belliqueux que moi." [2] By the comparison of such little confidences are the secrets of hearts revealed.

Palmerston, as has been said, had had two principal disfigurements to remove in his attempt to rejuvenate the wrinkled face of Turkey. One of them—the Treaty of Unkiar Skelessi— was as good as gone before Thiers succeeded Soult. The too powerful Pasha remained to be dealt with. Guizot, at the first interview he had with the Foreign Secretary, scored an academic victory by showing, in face of Palmerston's contention to the contrary, that the Turks were over the border and into Mehemet Ali's dominion when the first collision occurred, and must therefore be reckoned the aggressors. It was the only victory he got, and one to which his interlocutor was probably quite indifferent. The practical point for Palmerston was to take Syria from the Pasha and give it to the Sultan. He became quickly aware that he would not be able to accomplish this with the approval of France, and he saw that he could not take the risk of showing the French his hand for fear that they might pass on their information to Mehemet Ali. He was obliged, therefore, to prepare the diplomatic stroke that he had in view without taking the French into counsel. Fortunately for his operations the triumvirate enjoyed a false security. Thiers and Louis Philippe supposed that he would not be able to overcome the

[1] Bulwer, *Life*, ii. 352.   [2] *Ibid.*

opposition to his policy of the Francophil section of the Cabinet; and Guizot, who was better informed, cherished the fond belief that he would never despatch a Note without first submitting it for French approval. They were alike mistaken. Whilst Thiers imagined that he himself was mediating between Sultan and Pasha, greatly to the Pasha's advantage, Palmerston had squared both his colleagues and the rest of Europe. Not, it is true, without difficulty! To carry his policy in the Cabinet against the opposition of Clarendon and Holland, he had been reduced to the expedient of tendering his resignation; to satisfy Austria and Prussia he had consented, in the event of an immediate acceptance by Mehemet Ali of the terms agreed upon, to add southern Syria as well as the hereditary governorship of Egypt to the Pasha's acquisitions. These corners turned, and all the necessary naval dispositions made, there remained nothing but to explode the mine. One fine morning Palmerston confronted and confounded Guizot by reading to him a memorandum embodying an agreement between the Four Powers. For some days afterwards he had the fun of seeing the Ambassador look "as cross as the devil," and finding him scarcely able "to keep up the outward appearances of civility."[1] England and Russia, Austria and Prussia stood together behind the Sultan; France alone behind the Pasha.

It is, perhaps, superfluous to add that the eyries which flank the Seine were tremendously fluttered, and that for two or three months there was loud flapping of wings to be heard all over Paris. But it presently appeared that there were nothing but agitated doves in the eagles' nests; and in due course the turmoil subsided. Thiers gave place to Guizot at the Ministry of Foreign Affairs, and Louis Philippe pursued his way without a war. Meanwhile the British Fleet was working wonders. A landing at Acre caused Ibrahim to take to his heels; a demonstration at Alexandria brought Mehemet Ali to his knees. The Pasha became thankful to accept what time had left of the offer of the Allies; and the difficulty was rather to compel the Sultan, who had solemnly deposed his vassal, to concede even so much. Thus the *débâcle* of French diplomacy was complete, and it only remained for the French themselves to make the best of a bad job. Too late to save their reputation, and only just not

[1] Bulwer, *Life*, ii. 318.

too late to save their face, they became a party to Conventions embodying the Anglo-Russian agreement in regard to the Pasha and the Straits. But there was no getting away from the fact that they had been outmatched by Palmerston, even though he had been pitted against the three ablest statesmen in France. His harshest critics were compelled to murmur his praise. He had made indisputably a diplomatic master-stroke, and British prestige had not stood so high as he had raised it for some while past.

Adverse criticism, if there was any room for it, lay along a line for which no immediate hearing could be expected. The brilliant *coup* had been bought, as Clarendon and other surer guides perceived, by taking the ship of state out of its safe anchorage in a good understanding with France into a sea dotted with reefs and breakers and of which neither the pilot nor any one else possessed any certain chart. Aberdeen, indeed, gradually restored for the period of his administration the lost goodwill between France and England; but no one could bring back the psychological moment that had gone by in the history of the Near Eastern Question. For sixty years and more Great Britain strove, according to Palmerston's prescription, to regenerate, reorganise, or at least reform the Turkish Empire, until at last a Foreign Secretary had the courage to confess in a metaphor, reminiscent of Palmerston's habitual phraseology, that we had chosen the wrong horse to back. Had we in 1840, when opportunity crossed our path, been wise enough to take the decisions which were forced upon us by circumstances at a later date; had we left Russia beside the sick bed in Constantinople to nurse, or not, the dying man as pleased her best; had we registered the final loss to the Sultan of provinces that, but for our intervention, were already gone—Syria, Egypt, and the parts of Arabia about the holy cities and along the sea; and had we established there in conjunction with the French, or without them, a protectorate sufficient to safeguard our Eastern interests, some events would have been conveniently hastened, some wars mercifully averted, and some stones of stumbling opportunely shifted from the road which the nations of Europe were about to tread. So at least it may seem to close students of policy. But to Palmerston it seemed otherwise.

Diplomacy of whatever kind does wisely not to look for its reward at the polls. The Foreign Secretary had his brief hour of triumph, but it was past and gone before the Government had resolved to appeal to the country. By the midsummer of 1841 the desire to be quit of the Melbourne Ministry was widespread. Not the least count in their indictment was the incompetency of their finance; not the least factor in their difficulties the expenditure upon foreign affairs.[1] By the autumn Aberdeen was once more installed at the Foreign Office, and the change of temperature was quickly registered on the diplomatic chart by some advance both in France and America in the negotiation of treaties for the better suppression of the slave trade.

It is, perhaps, as well that we have no occasion here to follow the course of foreign affairs during the five years of Aberdeen's administration, for the true sequence of policy is to be found in personality and not by chronology. Palmerston, that is to say, when he returned to power in 1846, took up his own tale and not the tradition of his predecessor. So apparent, indeed, was it that this would be the case, that it was not without difficulty that Russell reinstated him in his old position. Grey's view[2] that he was unfit to be Foreign Secretary in face of the opinion entertained of him both at home and abroad, and especially in France, was in fact the circumstance upon which Russell's attempt to form a Free Trade Government, in December 1845, broke down, for Palmerston and Grey were equally necessary to him, and Palmerston would be satisfied with nothing less than the Foreign Office.

The fact that so strong an objection was raised to his administration of foreign affairs was probably not without its effect upon Palmerston's mind and movements. In the Easter recess of 1846, we find him in Paris making himself pleasant in every direction. Lady Palmerston went with him, and between them they had what only the French language is adequate to describe —a *succès fou*. "Ce terrible Lord Palmerston" became in two little weeks "ce cher Lord Palmerston." So agreeable is it to flirt with the devil and discover that he is not so black as one had painted him! For we have always to remember that it was

---

[1] "Lord Palmerston's foreign policy, by creating alarm and increasing expenditure, indirectly occasioned a fresh deficiency." Spencer Walpole, *Life of Lord John Russell*, i. 365.

[2] See for this Spencer Walpole, *Ibid.*, i. 415.

to the family of Beelzebub, that Palmerston in Continental circles
was considered to belong!

> " Hat der Teufel einen Sohn,
>   So ist er sicher Palmerston "

ran the famous distich, which, presumably because it expressed
with great exactitude the feelings of many contemporary critics,
has resisted with singular success the ravages of time.

Mephistopheles returned to England when Easter was past,
resumed in the course of the summer his old place at the Foreign
Office (for Grey's objection was not pressed a second time), and
was once more black as pitch in the sight of Louis Philippe and
Guizot before the year was out. The sable pigment for this
final portrait of him as he appeared in the eyes and days of the
Orleans Monarchy was brought from Spain.

In that distracted country, where Carlists and Christinos,
Moderados and Progressistas explored all the avenues of violence
and intrigue, Palmerston, in his previous administration, had
already found occasion to steal a march upon his friends, the
French. Afraid of another intervention by France such as
had occurred under Louis XVIII., he had abandoned with
breezy indifference that theory of non-intervention in the
domestic concerns of independent states which Great Britain
had once opposed to the doctrines of the Holy Alliance, had
taken sides vigorously with the Liberal (or so-called Liberal)
elements in the Peninsula, had despatched a fleet to Spanish
waters, and, by suspending the Foreign Enlistment Act, had
countenanced the addition of a fresh supply of dare-devil ruffians [1]
under the title of the British Foreign Legion to the indigenous
resources of Spain. These things were done in the name of that
which Palmerston reckoned among the greatest of his diplomatic
successes—the Quadruple Alliance of 1834. He boasted that
he had carried it through the Cabinet by a "*coup de main*," and
included France amongst its signatories by "a great stroke of
diplomacy." In theory, of course, the Quadruple Alliance was
intended to provide the Peninsula with the blessings of peace
and liberty. In practice it produced, or contributed to produce,

---

[1] This is not an idle expression. The men fought well, but Clarendon
(Maxwell, *Life of Clarendon*, i. 147), then British Minister at Madrid, wrote
to his brother: " As to the Legion—if you did but know how they have disgraced and degraded the name of England."

the dispossession of a pair of uncles with tolerable titles and moderate abilities in favour of a pair of nieces, of whom one was almost a stranger to her country and the other proved no better than she should be. Of peace or enlightened government —despotic, democratic, or mixed—there was no sign in Spain either then or for a long while afterwards. Nor had the French much more reason to be grateful to Palmerston for his master-stroke than the Spaniards. Their diplomatic prestige had been injured, and for no object except that Palmerston might crow. They had been included in the Alliance only as an after-thought, and their part had been plainly that of a second, and not a brilliant second at that. The slight did not go unnoticed; it is hardly to be supposed that it went unremembered.

All this had happened in the 'thirties. By 1846 the world had moved a long stride on. Isabella of Spain was now a marriageable young woman, and her sister after her. Aberdeen had consented, as early as 1843, to recommend that the selection of the Queen's consort should be made from the descendants of Philip V.,[1] and Guizot in 1845 had responded with the famous pledge that no marriage should be concluded between the Infanta and a French prince unless her sister, the Queen, had first been married and was the mother of children. The essence of the bargain was plain enough. Confronted by the purpose of the Queen-Mother to strengthen a precarious position by marrying Isabella within the pale either of the French or British reigning Houses—for preference to a son of France, but, if not, to a cousin of the Prince-Consort of England—the two Govern-ments had agreed to accept one another's exclusions. The French, in a word, renounced the candidature of Montpensier, Aumâle, or any of Louis Philippe's children, and the English undertook not to promote the candidature of any prince born of other than Bourbon blood. Each country, whatever might be said about leaving the Spaniards free to choose their sovereign's consort, had really barred a class of eligible candidates.[2]

Thus, then, matters stood when Palmerston returned to power

[1] *F.O. France*, 664. Aberdeen to Cowley, 15th December 1843 (printed in Hall, *England and the Orleans Monarchy*, p. 349).

[2] See Guizot, *Mems. pour servir, etc.*, viii. 110, 205–6. Compare Bulwer, *Life of Palmerston*, iii. 223. " . . . the general spirit of my instructions—though it did not command me to oppose a marriage without the Bourbon pale—prevented me from assuming the character of promoting one." This describes the position in 1846 before Aberdeen resigned.

in July 1846 with Bulwer for his second at Madrid. We must
forgive the French if in face of this combination they felt
a little suspicious. The Foreign Secretary had overreached
them twice in spite of the Franco-British understanding; the
British Ambassador had just been caught in the act of transmitting an offer of Isabella's hand to a quarter where Great
Britain had engaged not to recommend it. One can imagine,
without imputing to them any unnatural degree of distrust,
that Louis Philippe and Guizot may have made up their minds
that, if there was going to be any sharp practice, they would,
this time at any rate, be beforehand with Palmerston.

And Palmerston took no trouble to allay their fears—was,
in fact, beyond all question wildly indiscreet, and worse. In
the very month in which he took office he wrote a despatch to
Bulwer, calculated to set the French Government thinking hard
and the Spanish Government thinking furiously. It mentioned
three candidates as Isabella's suitors, and it placed Leopold
of Coburg first of the three. It then proceeded to discuss the
domestic politics of Spain and to denounce the Moderados, who
were in power, for their arbitrary methods, their denial of liberty,
their violence, their—for these words did not seem to Palmerston
to be too strong—"grinding tyranny." Not for such a rule
as theirs, he continued, had Great Britain intervened to expel
Don Carlos. The despatch was, in short, as reckless a production as ever Foreign Secretary penned, and it would in all
probability have never been permitted to start for Spain if
the Prime Minister, at the moment when it reached his hands,
had not been starting for church.[1] Lord John, intent that
Sunday morning upon his religion, gave to Lord Palmerston's
politics no more than a casual glance. Virtue is its own reward;
he had let a document slip through his fingers that was to
undo all Aberdeen's labours for five years past.

In Whitehall Palmerston appears to have felt well satisfied
with his performance. He was, in fact, so well satisfied that, not
content with sending the despatch to Bulwer with instructions to
convey its contents in his own language to the Spanish Government, he must needs also cause a copy of it to be delivered at
the French Embassy. Bulwer declared that he could never
make out why this was done. It was not unnatural that a

[1] S. Walpole, *Life of Lord John Russell*, ii. 2.

diplomatist should wonder. Those of us who are not diplomatists are in less difficulty to find an answer, for we are better acquainted with the pleasantness of sometimes letting people know exactly what we think of them. The French were delighted both to know and to make known what Palmerston thought of the Spaniards. The astonishing despatch passed from London to Paris and on from Paris to Madrid. It was truly a document that killed two birds with one stone. It killed the good understanding of Great Britain with France; it killed the influence of Great Britain with the *Moderado* Government of Spain; and it consummated its work by uniting the Bourbon Monarchies by the strongest of all political ties—the hatred of a common foe. "Les Anglais et la Révolution nous menacent," exclaimed the Queen-Mother to the French Ambassador when she had had time to digest the Foreign Secretary's communication.[1]

One final act was required of Palmerston to crown the high structure of his indiscretions; and he committed it. Fatally influenced, as was also Clarendon, by the Spanish Progressistas then in exile in London, he produced a new candidate for the hand of Isabella, and instructed Bulwer privately to put forward Don Enrique, the Duke of Seville, as her consort. This prince sprang, indeed, from the charmed circle of the Spanish and Neapolitan Bourbons, but found no favour with Louis Philippe and was an abomination to the Queen-Mother. So mad did it seem to propose him that Bulwer delayed to act upon his instructions until he had made plain to the Foreign Secretary their manifest disadvantage. He received for his pains a smart rap across the knuckles. The best title of an agent to the confidence of his chief—so Palmerston reminded him—is that of obedience.[2] Bulwer obeyed, and had the satisfaction of seeing his diagnosis of the situation immediately vindicated. The Queen-Mother threw herself into the arms of Louis Philippe. On 28th August she made up her mind to marry Isabella to the Duke of Cadiz, and, immediately after, the Infanta Louisa was affianced to the Duc de Montpensier. On October 10th these marriages were celebrated.

Palmerston had lost the game, and there was nothing left to be done but to borrow a familiar jeremiad from the French and to

---

[1] Guizot, *Méms. pour servir, etc.*, viii. 303.
[2] Bulwer, *Life*, iii. 230.

exclaim with the utmost possible vociferation that one had been betrayed. This he did, and with great effect, even in France itself. Among the principal causes of the downfall of the Orleans Monarchy historians are wont to give a foremost place to the discredit incurred by the episode of the Spanish marriages. To this day there are those who think that Louis Philippe, even though in fact he would really have preferred to marry the Queen to Trapani,[1] was counting on the impotence of the Duke of Cadiz to bring the succession to the heirs of the Duc de Montpensier. To this day he is supposed to have planned an act of treachery under cover of a promise of cordial co-operation, even though his private correspondence with Guizot makes it plain that, as late as the date of Palmerston's despatch, and after it, he would have none of Bresson's intrigue for the simultaneous marriage of the Queen and the Infanta, and was, in fact, extremely concerned to keep good faith with England.[2] From such accusations a study of Palmerston's private correspondence with Bulwer ought to exonerate him. For in those letters, whose purport at any rate was probably being all the while conveyed, as Stanmore suggests,[2] by Bulwer to the Queen-Mother Christina, and by Queen Christina to Louis Philippe, Palmerston plainly throws over the undertaking that Great Britain would not promote the candidature of Leopold of Coburg. He does so eventually in the plainest manner: " In a few words, then," he writes, "the upshot of the matter is: we hold ourselves free to recommend to the Spanish Government any one of the candidates whom we may think the best, whether he be Coburg or any other." [3] Here is the understanding gone. What of the cordiality? " The great object to be accomplished in the interest of England is to prevent a French prince from marrying the Queen or the Infanta." [4] And finally, " I have not yet broached in conversation with Jarnac the question of Montpensier's marriage with the Infanta. I have purposely abstained from doing so, because the impediments to that marriage had better, in the first instance at least, be created in Spain." [5]

If Louis Philippe and Guizot knew these things, or even if they merely divined them, their swift, sudden change of front about

[1] See Hall, *England and the Orleans Monarchy*, p. 402.
[2] Stanmore, *The Earl of Aberdeen*, p. 168.
[3] Bulwer, *Life*, iii. 273-4.   [4] *Ibid*., p. 266.   [5] *Ibid*., p. 272.

the middle of August, and the stroke that followed it, is both explained and defended. The condition underlying the promise at Eu was gone. There was no reason why the promise itself should be observed. Palmerston was following a course definitely unfriendly, definitely designed to thwart and disappoint a kindred Power that had made no secret of its own desires. He had cause enough to complain, not of himself, but because he had been found out. If Aberdeen seemed to side with him at the moment [1] it was, as Aberdeen's correspondence with Russell [2] discloses and as Stanmore warns us, [3] because the case for Guizot was not yet available nor had the secrets of Bulwer's letter-bag been yet revealed. Had Aberdeen been himself at the Foreign Office "the whole thing," as Queen Victoria tells her uncle, a little recklessly in view of her contention that the King of the French was all to blame, [4] "would not have happened." Louis Philippe was very well aware of it. "I don't consider Montpensier's marriage an affair between nations . . ." he told a friend who had read him Stockmar's memorandum on the subject, ". . . it is much more a private affair between myself and . . . Lord Palmerston." [5]

Even the jauntiest souls amongst us are apt to lose their sense of humour when they are challenged and worsted with their proper tactics. Palmerston did not escape that droll misfortune. In a final fling at his enemy, he invoked the Treaty of Utrecht with its out-of-date precautions to avoid the union of the crowns of France and Spain upon a single head. Wellington is said to have characterised this forensic argument as "damned stuff," and it was but little better. Time made a mock of it; in a couple of years it had come to seem as idle dreaming. For Louis Philippe fell from his throne, and the House of Bourbon with him, to return no more. And Isabella took her own measures, even if they were not those of an honest woman, to

---

[1] See Bulwer, *Life*, iii. 305. " I happen to know that Peel, Aberdeen, and Graham are indignant at the conduct of the French. Peel sent a message to this effect confidentially to John Russell." Palmerston to Bulwer.

[2] *Later Correspondence of Lord John Russell*, i. 128. ". . . believing him (Guizot) to be as honest as myself, or as any public man in England, I thought it no more than justice to wait for the requisite explanation. I am now fully disposed to believe that Guizot acted under a real apprehension of the intention of the British Government to promote the marriage of Prince Leopold of Coburg." Aberdeen to Russell, 17th November 1846.

[3] Stanmore, *The Earl of Aberdeen*, p. 170.

[4] *Letters of Queen Victoria*, ii. 122.

[5] *Ibid.*, p. 123.

secure the succession to her children. As for Montpensier, he and the Infanta passed into an obscurity from which neither they nor their descendants have ever emerged. There had indeed been made the most possible ado about next to nothing.

PART II

Palmerston, had he not enjoyed the stress of competition, the straining for a goal, the plaudits of the crowd, and the victor's wreath—had he not enjoyed them in point of fact a little too much for one whose ministry ought to be in the first place, and the second place and even the third place a ministry of peace—would have had every right in the last period of his career at the Foreign Office to recall his brother-in-law's memorable definition of life. "One damned thing" came tumbling "after another" with inconsiderate rapidity, and no sooner had the agitation of Courts subsided than the agitation of Kingdoms began. The central crisis of the century was reached very much as the half-century was completed, and the champions of hope, credulity, and change, decked out in contemporaneous frills and fashions, stood ranged once more against that strange alliance of cynics and epicureans who, whilst good men doubt and wise men discuss, are a sure prop in every age of the existing order. The feebleness of the great Governments, as Beust advises us in his Memoirs,[1] already in 1847 had become evident to the fomenters of revolution; and it is from that year rather than its successor that he would have us date the beginnings of troubles.

Palmerston kept well abreast of what was going on. He had a good, though no infallible eye for a situation, and there was no sounder quality in his composition than his power of recognising and accepting the large evolutionary movement of society onwards and yet distinguishing its content from all the sublime and heroic attributes with which political and doctrinaire enthusiasts are apt to invest it. Not for nothing had he served both as Whig and Tory; nor was it without significance that he had passed from one camp of politicians to another without any show of difficulty—with, in point of fact, something of the sporting indifference of a schoolboy or a professional to whom the game's the thing and who can play up with equal vigour on either

---

[1] *Memoirs* (English translation), i. 44.

side. He had, indeed, his ideas, but they were those that consort well with many philosophies and capture the admiration
of the majority of men. He liked generosity, jollity, energy,
and efficiency; and he disliked cruelty and tyranny and maladministration and the desolation and devastation of war. And
in this way he satisfied to a degree unusual in politicians
the sentiments of the ordinary Englishman who does not care
much about those who think closely or take their political
creeds for sacred dogmas, but fancies a fellow that takes a
party in his stride, yet strides beyond party into the country
of common-sense.

It was Palmerston's especial strength that he countenanced
the Liberal movement of his time without any animus against
princes or priests or standing institutions. He was as ready to
think well of Pope or King, if they would but go along the road
that the world was trying to travel, as of Lamartine with his
Republican ideals and Girondist enthusiasms. Change for the
sake of change was no part of his philosophy; and he had no
public nor private quarrel with the structure of society. But he
realised that there were certain things in certain countries that
cried aloud for alteration, and he knew that the world would not
wait for ever to see them altered. Autocracy, above all incompetent, irresponsible autocracy, was one of these things; persecution another; alien-domination a third. As the Liberals were at
the time the best friends that representative government, free
opinion, and nationality possessed, he was prepared to throw all
the moral force of British influence abroad upon the Liberal side.
To his eminently British mind it appeared that in foreign policy
there were two ends chiefly to be held in view—the general
advancement of right and justice and the particular advancement
of British interests.[1] Happily for his peace of mind these objects
never seemed to him to disagree.

It was of a piece with all this that Palmerston must be reckoned
the reverse of a revolutionary. For himself, no doubt, he liked
'a scrap' well enough, but only with the gloves on and in accordance with the rules of the game. War and civil war and all the
by-products of blood and iron he regarded, not indeed with any
holy horror, but as Englishmen mostly do, in the light of costly
surgical operations that a good doctor and a well-judged treatment

[1] See his remarks printed in Ashley, *Life*, i. 61-3.

should avert.   His best efforts in 1847, and indeed still in 1848, were devoted to pulling Europe through a climacteric with the minimum of suffering and disorder.

In other words and other metaphors he set himself, in the changed condition of the international atmosphere, to persuade the powers that were to put their houses in order, to agree with their adversaries quickly whiles they were yet in the way with them, to be wise in time.   Wherever opportunity offered, his influence was felt encouraging the adventurous, fortifying the weak-kneed, and recalling the lapsed or the reluctant to their labours: upon Portugal and later upon Greece his hand lay heavy: even amidst the strange turmoil of Swiss politics, where State and Canton were fighting out their differences over the bodies of inoffensive Jesuits, his voice could still be heard.

It was, however, above all upon Italy that Palmerston's eye became fixed.   There, as with no little prescience, if prematurely, he had anticipated, the new wine of France, if Guizot fell or Louis Philippe failed, stood in danger of bursting many ancient bottles. The moment Liberalism triumphed in France, Liberals, he realised, would rise in revolt in Italy; and upon that the Austrians would intervene to suppress, the French to sustain the movement for reform.   In the clash of arms the latter, with the Italians at their back, were likely to win.   France would swell again with love of glory; Austria, the pivot as he held, upon which the balance of power in Europe was poised, be shaken from its place; and war spread from one locality to all the Continent.[1]   He wrote such things to Russell in the summer of 1846, and Russell —already cast for an Agamemnon to his Achilles and some day to play Castor to his Pollux—in general agreed with him. Together they decided to send out Minto—a Cabinet Minister who, as Russell's father-in-law, carried the greater weight—and entrust him with a strange, roving commission which a rising young Hebrew politician of the day described, in true Disraelite style, as a commission to teach politics in the country where Machiavelli was born.   In practice what Minto was required to do was to assure any of the princes and potentates who were disposed to reform their own ways or their countries' constitutions that the British Government would view such performances with great satisfaction.   He was not, however, authorised to offer them

[1] See his letter in Bulwer, *Life*, iii. 195–6.

anything more than moral, as distinct from material support in the event of Austria's taking exception to their proceedings.

Minto's main idea of carrying out his instructions was to cry "Viva l'Independenza Italiana!" without any further explanatory phrases, whenever he was asked for a speech. The Italians, as yet unversed in the British system of affording to foreign patriots no more than rhetorical aid, not unnaturally supposed that he was the herald of an active interference so soon as the times were ripe for it. Palmerston and Russell, however, had no such idea. All they intended was to give Pio Nono, who had burst upon the astonished world in the character of a Liberal Pope, a pat upon the back accompanied by a warning not to let his reforms embroil him with Austria,[1] and for the rest to sermonise for their good all the petty princes of Italy. For both the Prime Minister and the Foreign Secretary in their several ways had a taste for international preaching; both took England to be the appointed pulpit of the world; and both believed in the efficacy of a few plain-spoken words.

There were, however, fascists in Italy then as there are now, and before Minto had completed the delivery of his exhortations the long-impending storm was upon him. Almost as the New Year—that great year of Revolution, 1848—opened, it burst in Sicily, raging there with ungovernable fury, as befits a place where the population can turn to massacre at the sound of a vesper bell. In a few weeks the Neapolitans were swept back across the Straits; and for a year or more the Sicilians enjoyed a state of independence without discovering any particular aptitude for freedom.

The lightning of revolt ran up Italy, striking the great cities as it passed, rending the topmost towers of autocracy, substituting constitutions for the old order, dragging impracticable concessions from trembling and reluctant hands. It coursed through Naples, Rome, Florence, Turin, and before anyone had guessed what was coming, it had reached Paris and brought the Orleans Monarchy crashing to the ground. On the spot where in February Louis Philippe and Guizot were standing secure, sheltered by good sense, the *juste milieu* and the *bourgeoisie*,

---

[1] " Lord Minto . . . had given the Pope clearly to understand that should the Reform movement degenerate into a provocation of Austria, England would not put out a finger to help." *Camb. Mod. Hist.*, xi. 78.

there stood in March the figure of Lamartine, noisily declaiming yet in secret diplomatising. He knew what was expected
of him, had a mint of fine phrases, revolving round natural
rights and natural frontiers, for the consumption of the mob,
and shook his fist energetically at all that was illiberal in Europe,
and more especially at the Treaty of Vienna. But also he knew
what was politic, and quietly intimated to Wellington that all
his cosmopolitan sentiments must be translated into terms of
peace and an English alliance.[1]

The Paris Revolution gave a new impetus to the avenging
current. It turned eastwards, firing the powder magazines of
Liberal opinion across the Rhine and shaking all the thrones of
Germany. The only possibility of staying its advance seemed
to lie in Vienna, where old Metternich still kept vigil. For
three and thirty years, from that vantage-point with its sacred,
memories of the Congress and the Treaty that had brought the
old order back to life, he had kept watch over European institutions and ideas, both foretelling and forestalling disaster in a
manner to excite admiration, if not approval. Would he prove
able to ride the whirlwind now that it was no longer a question
of burking the wind? To Palmerston, always brooding over the
problem of Italy and fearing to see there "a war of principles,"
it was a matter of great concern to know what Metternich would
do.[2] But the Revolution gave the old Chancellor no time to
move, caught him at last half-napping, smothered him in its
embrace and tossed him like a bag of old bones on the dust-
heap of Time. In a moment he was gone.

Then, indeed, all was wild confusion. East and west, south
and north, the lightnings shot and shivered. In Berlin and Buda,
in Milan and Venice, it was everywhere the same. The old order
passed away, and on every side men declared that they would
make all things new. Their notion of novelty was a constitution.

Palmerston contemplated the chaos of the times not without
sympathy nor without apprehension. He had a feeling, attribut-
able perhaps to Stratford Canning, who was furnishing him with
ubiquitous information,[3] that Europe would pull through, and

---

[1] The correspondence is to be found in Walpole's *Life of Lord John Russell*, ii.
32–7.
[2] See Palmerston's letter to Ponsonby of 11th February 1848, printed in
Ashley's *Life of Palmerston*, i. 63.
[3] *Camb. Hist. of British Foreign Policy*, ii. 310.

he liked to see liberty, or its likeness, advanced. Yet it was not altogether without a sentiment of satisfaction that he recollected that the forces of order had still a surviving representative in his old enemy at Petersburg. "Assure Count Nesselrode," he writes genially, "that our feelings and sentiments towards Russia are exactly similar to those which he expresses to you towards England. We are at present the only two Powers in Europe (excepting always Belgium) that remain standing upright, and we ought to look with confidence to each other." [1]

In this sea of difficulty, Italy was, at least from an English window, the most interesting object, and upon Italy Palmerston kept his eyes. He had not judged the situation there very correctly before the crisis, for the measure that he took of it was Minto. Neither did he judge it very correctly afterwards, for his measure was now Metternich or rather the fall of Metternich. In other words, he underrated the forces of revolution in 1847 and the power of reaction in 1848. The one had carried Italy far beyond a federal solution—that friendly league of states, of which his protégé, Pio Nono, was to have been the sponsor—but the other was still strong enough to regain Venetia and Lombardy and prevent the realisation of national unity. With so imperfect a grasp of the problem as he had, his treatment of it was of necessity faulty. Fearful of such another international encounter as he could himself remember between the Ancien Régime and the Revolution, as exemplified respectively by Austria and France; prematurely certain that the Austrian hold on Italy was irretrievably lost; [2] perfectly satisfied that French military intervention was a very present danger; and rightly convinced that Austria would in the long run be the stronger for the surrender of her Italian provinces, he made it his main endeavour to get the Austrians out of Italy before the French marched in. But this was to misconceive the relative strength of the forces in play. The Italians did well enough at their first rising, whilst Austria was embarrassed by the revolution in Vienna, by a change of dynasty and by the national movement in Hungary; but they were no match for her when she recovered herself, still less when Russia came to her aid. One of the

[1] Ashley, *Life*, i. 91.
[2] See his letter of 15th June 1848 to the King of the Belgians : " If Austria waits till she be forcibly expelled—which she soon will be—she will get no conditions at all."

Western Powers, it became plain, would have sooner or later to fight the battle of Italian unity. The English were ready to fight it with words, but the French with arms. In Palmerston's eyes, the first kind of ammunition was much to be preferred to the second. He was, therefore, not sparing of good advice at Vienna. "The cheapest, best, and wisest thing which Austria can do is to give up her Italian possessions quietly and at once," he wrote to the British Ambassador in April 1848. There were, however, he thought, no men at the head of affairs wise enough to take this course. The Emperor, he observed, was "an *implumis bipes* . . . a perfect nullity; next thing to an idiot . . . a mere man of straw, a Guy Fawkes . . ." [1] and his heirs-apparent were but little better. The Ambassador, who himself came in for some share of Palmerston's intolerant contempt,[2] was, therefore, to recommend Ferdinand's resignation and the discovery of some substitute in the family. As the correspondence continued, the Foreign Secretary found the professor's chair more and more to his liking, and passed from a dissertation on the *implumis bipes, genus imperiale*, to some authoritative observations on the counsels of the Deity. "Providence," he informed the suffering but not long-suffering Ponsonby, "meant mankind to be divided into separate nations, and for this purpose countries have been founded by natural barriers, and races of men have been distinguished by separate languages, habits, manners, dispositions and characters. There is no case on the globe in which this intention is more marked than that of the Italians and the Germans, kept apart by the Alps and as unlike in everything as two races can be." [3]

Fortunate professor! Anthropologists had not as yet discovered the *Homines Nordici, Alpini*, and *Mediterranei*, whose geographical disposition, providential or casual, would appear to split both Germany and Italy, racially-speaking, in twain—or, at any rate, if they had, Palmerston had not got wind of it. Doubly fortunate professor! To have been able to satisfy himself that as regards the claims of nationality the cases of Ireland and Lombardy were "wholly different," [4] and to feel, not only

---

[1] Ashley, *Life*, i. 102–4.

[2] See Walpole, *Life of Russell*, ii. 53 (footnote). " Lord Ponsonby went so far as to tell Lord John that he had received from Palmerston letters which are not to be submitted to by any man."

[3] Ashley, i. 109. The letter is dated 31st August 1848.   [4] *Ibid.*

righteous indignation, but an immaculate conscience as he looked
now on this picture and now on that. Most fortunate professor!
And yet most ill-timed lecture! Already when he wrote, the
tide had turned. Custozza had been won by Radetzky; from the
Italian ranks there was a fatal defection; in the Italian prospects
a manifest decline. The military intervention of France alone
could have saved the situation; and he had made this impossible
by diplomatic interference. Both the Italians and Austrians
had reason to welcome his mediation; the former because it
seemed to promise them some advantage in terms, the latter
because it afforded them every advantage of time. *Rusticus
expectat, dum defluit amnis*—it was very much that! Whilst
Palmerston was negotiating, the Austrians were recuperating,
well-satisfied to have had so many weeks gratuitously given them
to set their house in order, but innocent of any real intention of
returning what they had already regained. Thus the issue was
not determined, as Palmerston had designed, around a conference
table in Brussels, but upon the field of battle at Novara, where
the Italians lost the last throw in a game which they were too
weak to play alone.

Austria, for all Palmerston's conviction of her helplessness,
had emerged from the struggle with her Italian provinces intact;
and his action had had no better effect than to defer the war of
Italian independence for a decade, and incidentally to discover
to our old Allies, the Austrians, the value of our friendship and
to our new protégés, the Italians, the limitations of our power.
A conflict had been stayed but not stopped; the intervention
of France postponed but not averted. When at length the
memories of Custozza and Novara were buried at Magenta and
Solferino, and Italy rose again from out her ashes, it was French
guns, and not British counsels that wrought deliverance; and
the end attained was no federal league of traditional states,
preserved with all their local character unimpaired, yet freed
from alien influence and flushed with the hope of a new renaissance
—no such solution, in fact, as Palmerston had favoured and all
the Greeks of politics and culture might wisely have approved
—but the union of the Italian people in a kingdom that would
some day seek to think imperially after the manner of old
Rome and reckon strength to be a sounder aim than beauty.

Palmerston groped with imperfect logic in a Europe given

over to change. His own system was rooted in the conception of a balance of power, and in the last resort he judged each new development by its possible effect upon that to him supreme consideration. Thus, whilst he favoured independence in Italy, he would have none of it in Hungary, for Austria without Hungary attached would have lost too much weight in European counsels. The Habsburg Empire, with all its follies and all its crimes,[1] remained for him the ark of the European covenant;[2] and this, though with impulsive generosity, he took the risk of war with Austria and Russia, in order to support the Sultan in refusing to surrender the Hungarian Nationalists who had fled to Turkey. Any shifting of the weights in the balance, in fact, alarmed him. Thus in the problem of Schleswig-Holstein, which began to lift its head about this time and in connection with which his mediation was invited, he was quite as much interested in keeping Denmark strong enough to play doorkeeper at the gate of the Baltic as in the rights and claims of Dane and German.

All this while Palmerston was increasing not in wisdom, but stature; so that by the middle of the century he had become too big for any boots that the British Constitution provides. There can be little doubt that he irritated the larger proportion of the people with whom he had to do, from the Queen upon her throne down to the clerks of his Department, who were in a mood to illuminate the Foreign Office when he lost his seat in Parliament in 1835.[3] The evidence of the unpopularity of his administration far exceeds that which can be adduced in the case of any Foreign Secretary, with the possible exception of one too recent to be named. Subordinates, colleagues, foreign ambassadors at home, English ambassadors abroad, men like Greville and Bear Ellice who were in the know of things—from all these directions there comes a testimony too lucid and too frequent to be convincingly disbelieved. Everybody, we say, quarrels with somebody, but nobody quarrels with everybody.

[1] " The Austrians are the greatest brutes that ever called themselves by the undeserved name of civilised men." To Ponsonby, 9th September 1849. Ashley, i. 139.

[2] See, for example, his speech in the House of Commons on 21st July 1849. " The political independence and liberties of Europe are bound up in my opinion with the maintenance and integrity of Austria as a great European power, etc., etc."

[3] Greville, *Mems.*, iii. 139, 203, 216.

almerston in his official relations came perilously near to
e the exception to the rule. If it was his business to get on
ell with any one at all, it was certainly his business to get on
ell with the great Powers of Europe. Yet the witness of one,
ho knew the Continent better than any Englishman of the
me and whose words were as a rule both modest and measured,
ands recorded against him like a judge's summing-up at the
ose of his diplomatic career. "Lord Palmerston," wrote
e Prince Consort in 1850 to the Prime Minister, "is bringing
e whole of the hatred which is borne to him—I don't mean
ere to investigate whether justly or unjustly—by all the
overnments of Europe upon England, and . . . the country
ns serious danger of having to pay for the consequences." [1]

The tale of Palmerston's indiscretions is long, but some
ention of them must always form a vital part of his story;
singular, dramatic, and constitutionally important is the
tuation which they gradually create. His imprudences begin
ith his extraordinary attempt in 1833 to send Stratford Canning
British Ambassador to Russia. Etiquette prescribes that
e sovereign to whom an envoy is accredited should be first
all sounded as to whether the nomination is acceptable.
anning's long connection with Constantinople and long opposi-
on to Russian designs in Turkey made any departure from
recedent in his case peculiarly unfortunate. But Palmerston
ad his own way of doing things and appointed Canning, as he
ad formerly appointed Durham, without troubling to notify
is intention. The discourtesy was no careless solecism.
urham, on his return from Russia, had cautioned him that if
ere was one man who was unacceptable there, it was Canning ; [2]
nd Lieven had endorsed the warning. But he met their
epresentations with unblushing cynicism. "Canning," he
ld the Russian Ambassador, "is of my party, and I must
rovide for him." [3] And he proceeded to argue, though indeed
o one disputed it, that the King of England, or, to be more
ccurate, his Foreign Secretary, could nominate whom he
ould. Nicholas made what in the circumstances was the only
ossible rejoinder. He withdrew his own ambassador—Prince

---

[1] *Letters of Queen Victoria*, ii. 288.
[2] Stuart Reid, *Life and Letters of Lord Durham*, i. 315.
[3] *Ibid.*, p. 316.

Lieven—from the Court of St James's, thus incidentally bringing to a close the English phase of Princess Lieven's career; and he made it clear that he would never receive Canning as British ambassador at St Petersburg. In face of so crushing a snub, Palmerston's common sense and sense of humour alike forsook him. Not only did he decline to appoint anyone in Canning's place, but he insisted on sending him, invested with the title of "Ambassador to the Emperor of all the Russias," on a special mission to Spain. In the castles of that country the envoy may perhaps have perceived the similitude of his distant embassy. At all events he never approached appreciably nearer to it. Always for him it remained a castle in Spain. And, after a year or two, Palmerston, recollecting perhaps that the Diplomatic Service is maintained by the tax-payer in the hope of greasing and not of rusting the wheels of international intercourse, reappointed Durham to the vacant post and closed an incident almost too trivial to be worth recalling, if it were not that it illustrates thus early an essential trait in his character, and explains why, for all the *réclame* that had attended his diplomacy in 1840, he seemed to Grey wholly unfit to resume the conduct of foreign affairs in 1845.

It was not, however, until the end of his third term at the Foreign Office that the ripe harvest of Palmerston's imprudences was gathered. The Year of Revolution seems to have doubled his want of tact and deepened his need of manners. Between 1848 and 1851 his misdemeanours grew in weight and volume from month to month; and he developed an autocratic procedure which would not have disgraced the monarchs whose unconstitutional habit of mind he took so much trouble to correct. His colleagues resented it, but to the Queen it appeared insufferable. He treated her, indeed, with an insouciance insulting in the case of a sovereign, unchivalrous in that of a woman. Her counsels went ignored or undervalued; her letters were opened at the Foreign Office before they were sent on to her; [1] drafts that she had altered were despatched unchanged, and despatches were sent off that she had never seen; important information was withheld from her; and decisive action was sometimes taken without her consent or that of the Cabinet. A duel between the Crown and the Foreign Secretary gradually

---

[1] *Letters of Queen Victoria*, ii. 227.

developed—a duel as curious as any in our constitutional history. Victoria could scarcely have fought it unaided, but she had behind her, as it happened, at the time, two of the closest and best-informed students of foreign politics and international custom in Europe—her husband, just reaching the maturity of his very considerable talents, and, behind him, his tutor, the excellent, the judicious, the admirable Stockmar.

Two Germans and a Queen, German on her mother's side, and of a German house! It is difficult to escape at first sight the suggestion that there was in their attitude some reminiscence of courts that are not as our Court and kingships that postulate a larger influence on the part of the sovereign than is customary in our Constitution. And Palmerston's defenders will always find their best defence along some such line as this, taking, if they are clever, a text from Clarendon, who can be quoted as saying that the Queen and the Prince Consort were claiming "a right to control, if not to direct, the foreign policy of England."[1] There is this much truth in the suggestion—that the precise relations of the Crown towards the administration of foreign affairs were still imperfectly defined, and that a greater influence over, or at least interest in, the Foreign Department had always been tacitly accorded to the Sovereign, if only because, whenever he wills, he must always be the first diplomatist in his kingdom. But, so far as policy was concerned, it was rather upon a better knowledge of the British diplomatic tradition than upon any exaggerated conception of her prerogative that Victoria based her interference. "The country," she wrote to the Prime Minister in the June of 1848, "is at this moment suffering . . . particularly with regard to Spain, . . . under the evil consequence of that system of diplomacy which makes the taking up of party politics in foreign countries its principal object. This system is condemned alike by the Queen, Lord John, the Cabinet, and, the Queen fully believes, public opinion in and out of Parliament."[2]

The occasion of this outburst was the concluding episode in Bulwer's career at Madrid, and we may as well glance at the fading fortunes of so old an acquaintance as he passes off our stage. "I quite agree . . . that our policy must now be to

[1] Maxwell, *Life and Letters of the Fourth Earl of Clarendon*, i. 341.
[2] *Letters of Queen Victoria*, ii. 213.

try to form an English party in Spain," Palmerston had written
to him [1] after the episode of the Spanish marriages was ended;
and faithfully had he striven to carry out his master's wishes.
"Sir Henry Bulwer," observed Victoria when all was over, "has
for the last three years almost been sporting with political
intrigues. He invariably boasted of at least being in the
confidence of every conspiracy, 'though he was taking care not
to be personally mixed up in them,' and after their various
failures generally harboured the chief actors in his house under
the plea of humanity. At every crisis he gave us to understand
that he had to choose between a 'revolution and a palace intrigue,'
and not long ago only he wrote to Lord Palmerston, that, if
the Monarchy with the Montpensier succession was inconvenient
to us, he could get up a Republic." [2]

All this vast activity on the part of Palmerston's *fidus
Achates* produced very little result upon the strongly entrenched
Conservatism of Spain; and eventually Palmerston could no
longer refrain from his incurable, recurring desire to try the
effect of a lecture. Bulwer was consequently instructed to
recommend the Spanish Government to "adopt a legal and
constitutional course of government in Spain"; to warn them
"how great was the danger of attempting to govern a country
in a manner at variance with the feelings and opinions of the
nation," and, in a word, to advise the Queen to call some Liberals
to her councils. [3] He did as he was told, but, fearing some
embarrassing affront at the hands of a prime minister, noted
for his brutality, if he attempted to paraphrase his instructions,
he communicated the despatch itself as on the whole the least
offensive and dangerous method of discharging his commission.
Those who habitually run races with the devil can afford to
think lightly of encounters with "the devil's son." Marshal
Narvaez—that same who informed his confessor as he lay dying
that he had no enemies to forgive because he had killed the lot
of them—went in no fear of Lord Palmerston's pulpit utterances.
The despatch was, accordingly, returned to Bulwer as a piece
of ill-bred impertinence, and the British Government obliged
to stomach an indignity which, as Aberdeen observed, [4] was
without precedent in British diplomatic annals. As for Bulwer,

---

[1] Bulwer, *Life*, iii. 307.   [2] *Letters of Queen Victoria*, ii. 207.
[3] Bulwer, *Life*, iii. 245, 246.   [4] Martin, *Life of the Prince Consort*, ii. 66.

some real or supposed complicity in a Liberal insurrection that occurred soon afterwards caused him to be presented with his passports, and he returned to the Foreign Office breathing fire and sword. Palmerston was prepared to gratify him by blockading Cadiz and demanding an apology; but to these measures the Cabinet took exception.[1]

Russell, when the Queen's strictures upon his Foreign Secretary reached him, was in more minds than one. He approved Palmerston's general policy and Liberal leanings; he shared his taste for homily and reproof; he feared to break up an Administration none too securely based; but he could not disguise from himself the departure from British tradition involved in foreign intrigue, nor was he prepared to justify his colleague's uncovenanted asperities. In these circumstances he temporised, not without chivalry so far as the Queen was concerned, nor without generosity so far as Palmerston was concerned, but of course in a quarrel between two such strongly marked and determined personalities without affording to either any particular satisfaction.

Palmerston's policy, in truth, very well exemplified the nemesis of the system of Canning. Starting with the principle of every nation for itself, he was perpetually confronted with the fact that no nation is, or can be, purely self-regarding, that, unless or until society is, if it ever is, set upon the rock of a rational Christianity, there will always remain a side to be taken in international as in domestic affairs. It has been no assumption of this book that such partialities are reprehensible, for they form part of that inevitable, constant pressure of ideas upon institutions which no one can really confine within the limits of any individual state. Every insalubrious or convulsive locality, whether stagnant pool or stream of lava, becomes of necessity in a world of change, even if not of progress, a legitimate object of solicitude, of remonstrance, and ultimately of intervention to neighbouring countries. But this much may at least be asked— that external interference, if it must be at all, should at least be rare, effective, and the considered expression of the armed conscience of a Continent. The charge against Palmerston is that his interventions were frequent, personal, ill-considered, sometimes misleadingly impotent, and often sadly ineffectual.

[1] Bulwer, *Life*, iii. 250, 251.

Queen and Cabinet were to experience the consequences of the Foreign Secretary's methods twice more before the Year of Revolution was out. Sicily early in 1848 had risen in revolt against the rule of Naples; and the insurgents stood, of course, in need of all the arms of which they could get hold. Palmerston was quite ready to assist them to the best of his ability. Without a word to the Cabinet he allowed some guns, already supplied to the War Office and actually stored in Woolwich Arsenal, to be removed by the manufacturers, who undertook in due course to make the deficiency good. The matter became known; questions were asked; and in the end he was compelled by his colleagues to offer his apologies to the Neapolitan Government.

The other matter vexed the Queen no less and touched her more nearly. She had keenly resented Palmerston's undisguised sympathy with the attempt of the King of Sardinia to wrench Lombardy from Austria—sympathy inconsistent as it seemed to her with the Treaty of Vienna, with our obvious obligations towards a Power on friendly terms with us and in fact our old ally, and with his own attitude towards the German claim in Schleswig-Holstein—and she told him with feminine vigour in so many words that she was "ashamed" of his policy.[1] It was therefore a slight, all the more galling that she felt it to be justified, when, upon Francis Joseph's accession to the Austro-Hungarian throne, the announcement to her of that event was not communicated in the customary manner by the mouth of an archduke. To Palmerston, on the other hand, the absence of a member of the imperial house seemed rather a subject for congratulation than regret; and to the fuming, furious Ponsonby he conveyed with manifest delight his satisfaction at his escape from the bother and trouble of entertaining a royal visitor.[2]

1848 passed into 1849 and Queen and Minister continued to exchange passes in the long constitutional duel. So strained had their relations become that early in the year there was some talk between the Queen and Russell [3] of getting Palmerston out of the Foreign Office by moving him to Ireland, where Clarendon, most self-effacing of men, was willing to vacate in his favour the Lord Lieutenancy. Palmerston, however, compounded with his chief

1 *Letters of Queen Victoria*, ii. 215.   2 Ashley, *Life*, i. 113.
3 *Letters of Queen Victoria*, ii. 251.

by apologising to the Neapolitans for the Woolwich incident; and the duel with Victoria went upon its way.

In the course of the summer, however, the Queen got upon surer ground. About her right to approve despatches before they were sent there could be no manner of doubt, and Palmerston's habit of ignoring her existence, when it suited him, played, therefore, straight into her hands. It is doubtless true that he had some excuse for what he did. The Year of Revolution had multiplied the labour of the Foreign Office out of all belief, so that where, twenty years earlier when Palmerston first came to the office, there were but ten thousand despatches to be dealt with, he had now to deal with twenty-eight. And, besides this, the Queen was not always expeditious in attending to business, whilst the foreign-messengers who carried the bags were like posts that go out perhaps twice only in the week and must be caught at all hazards if important communications are not to be seriously delayed. But, though all this was true, a wise man would have found his way through the difficulties—and in point of fact a wise man had already done so. The problem of reconciling the Queen's constitutional rights with the exigencies of business had been discussed during Peel's Administration by Victoria and Aberdeen; and Aberdeen had undertaken that drafts of all despatches that were not mere matters of course should be submitted to the Sovereign before sending, subject only to the reservation of a right of prompt action in urgent circumstances.[1] This accommodation appears to have worked perfectly so long as Aberdeen remained at the Foreign Office, and would have given Palmerston all he required if he had been content to show any ordinary discretion. But he observed it neither in the letter nor the spirit, and in the summer of 1849 the Queen resolved to submit to his infractions of her prerogative no longer. To meet her views Russell was obliged to insist that all drafts of foreign despatches should pass through his hands into hers; a procedure which, so far as it went, deprived the Foreign Secretary of his traditional right of direct communication with the Sovereign. Palmerston submitted readily, having in fact surrendered nothing that he very much cared about, and continued to act to all intents and purposes as he had acted before. By the spring of 1850 the Queen was once more rampant.

[1] See S. Walpole, *Life of Lord John Russell*, ii. 54, footnote.

The trouble had arisen this time in Greece; but neither Pagan nor Christian had the leading *rôle*. The Jews are a great race, and Gibraltar a proud possession, yet it remains one of the melancholy ironies of British diplomatic history that Don Pacifico, whose name is for ever yoked to the thought of the pride and range of British citizenship, should have been no more than a Jew of Gibraltar, and not a very honest Jew at that. A chance and no more appears to have persuaded Palmerston to take up his cause. A squadron had been sent out to Constantinople to strengthen the Sultan in the refusal, already alluded to, to surrender Kossuth and his companions to the Austrians; and it struck the Foreign Secretary that as the ships returned home they might very well call at Athens and enforce some unsatisfied claims of long standing. Of these claims Don Pacifico's was the most exciting, if not the most important. Three years before, his house had been plundered by a Greek mob in the effort to celebrate Easter; and he had suffered personal inconvenience and material loss in consequence. What that loss amounted to in cash was by no means clear. Don Pacifico undoubtedly put it rather high. One item in his estimate affords the measure of his ability as a valuer—or of his character as a man. He computed that £21,000 would not be too much to compensate him for some vanished papers representing claims upon the Portuguese Government, in whose employ, notwithstanding his British birthplace, he had formerly served as consul-general at Athens. An international commission subsequently valued these same claims at £150. In other circumstances, we might suspect that Palmerston would have been the first to contend that so great a rogue would be no worse for a 'drubbing' and had got off full lightly with the loss of his goods. But there was on the present occasion a rival attraction, such as a pedagogue may be suspected of experiencing when he birches an incorrigible schoolboy. The Greeks stood in as much need of castigation as Don Pacifico himself; and if, as it seemed to Gladstone and others, the home of the Humanities was no place for humiliating executions, Palmerston might perhaps have retorted that the rod had been long esteemed the best road to the Classics. Let that be as it may. In spite of Russell's protest that Don Pacifico's wrongs, even when coupled with the injury done to George Finlay, the historian, by the absorption, some ten or fifteen years before, of some land of his in the Royal Garden, and with one or two other small matters, were "hardly worth the interposition of the British Lion," [1] the Fleet anchored before Athens; the Piraeus was blockaded; a Greek war-ship was seized as a "material guarantee"; other property, both public and private, was made hostage; and, in short, the Greek Government was given plainly to understand that the 'terrible' Lord Palmerston did not stand any nonsense from little nations, and that they must compound at once with Don Pacifico and Mr Finlay in satisfaction of their claims, and for the rest apologise for having been so long negligent and naughty.

All this, however, was not accomplished without a great to-do both abroad and at home. Neither of the other protecting and, as it happened, creditor Powers liked the sudden, single-handed action on the part of Great Britain; and the French promptly offered mediation. Palmerston would, however, have rejected it, but for the Cabinet's insistence. Compelled to be conciliatory, he permitted himself to be careless; and twice in quick succession his carelessness fully and promptly to instruct the British Repre-sentative at Athens rendered the French mediation useless.[2] Everyone was furious—the Queen, the Cabinet, and not least, the French, who withdrew their ambassador and even thought of war.[3]

The new crisis brought the constitutional issue another stage forward; and Palmerston's failure to communicate to Russell a letter of the Queen's regarding the choice of a minister for Spain added explosive vigour to Victoria's growing determination to be quit of him. "Lord Palmerston's conduct," she wrote to Russell, ". . . is really too bad, and most disrespectful to the Queen; she can hardly communicate with him any more; indeed it would be better she should not." [4]

The Prime Minister—reluctantly enough, for he both admired and feared his colleague—felt that the Queen's case against Palmerston had become too strong, concluded that he must make a change, and, after consultation with Lansdowne, resolved to take the Foreign Office himself and to relegate Palmerston, if

[1] Walpole, *Life of Russell*, ii. 56.
[2] The best account of this incident is in S. Walpole, *Life of Lord John Russell*, ii. 119.
[3] Malmesbury, *Mems. of an Ex-Minister*, i. 361.
[4] *Letters of Queen Victoria*, ii. 285.

that old political hand would only consent, to the charge of the Colonies. Thus for a moment it seemed as if the end of the long duel had come. But just when he looked as if he had been brought at last to his knees, Palmerston recovered himself by one of the smartest thrusts of parliamentary fence on record—a lunge, learnt in the school of Canning and worthy of that master of penetrating phrase. A development for which neither the Queen nor Russell were to blame gave him his occasion.

Whilst the Prime Minister was turning over in his mind how best to oust the Foreign Secretary from his place, the Ministry were defeated, on this very question of the treatment of Greece, in the House of Lords; and at once it became necessary for them, if they were to continue in office, to retrieve their reputation in the Commons. For this purpose, therefore, Roebuck, whose name survives as the mover of resolutions on memorable occasions, proposed on the midsummer day of 1850 a vote of confidence in the foreign policy of the Government. In the debate that followed many great speeches were made, but the greatest, whether we judge it by effort or by effect, was Palmerston's. The discussion reached, indeed, far further and deeper than the claims of Don Pacifico, and, as Morley observes,[1] "it stands to this day as a grand classic exposition in Parliament of the contending views as to the temper and the principles on which nations in our modern era should conduct their dealings with one another." Peel spoke then for the last time with stately and splendid eloquence; Gladstone made then his maiden entry into the discussion of foreign affairs;[2] Bright, reckoned by some a greater orator than either, poured forth his evangelical counsels in Saxon English; and with him pleaded the twin soul of Cobden; also Disraeli spoke after his manner. All these—and they were among the greatest of contemporary parliamentarians—urged according to their weight and measure, with high hope or caustic sneer, the claims of human solidarity, of doing as one would have others do by us, of a Christian civilisation, of a small people and a classic soil, of a just proportion between punishment and misdemeanour. But Palmerston was a match for each and all of them. Rising on that short summer night, after the last glimmer of day had fled the northern sky, and speaking till the sun was once more faintly warming eastern

---

[1] Morley, *Life of Gladstone*, i. 369.   [2] *Ibid*, i. 369.

windows, the Minister, to that dramatic accompaniment of darkness followed by dawn, traversed all the range of his policy.   He
spoke not only of British relations with Greece, but with Spain
and Portugal, with France, with Switzerland, with Hungary,
vindicating by a dexterous shortness of thought his confused
manœuvres in a Europe distracted by revolution and deluged
with blood.   He spoke—not to the international jurist who might
find difficulty enough in the application of his doctrine as to
the enforcement of private claims in foreign countries; not to
the historian who might doubt the value of the British Constitution as a prescription for all peoples and a panacea for all ills;
not to the statesman who might question the wisdom of countenancing armed revolt against established governments even
when prompted by the purest ideals or stimulated by the pressure
of a rising tide; not to the Christian with his instinctive tendency
patiently to suffer wrong and hopefully to look to the slow march
of faith and love as the best foundation for a new world of
righteousness—he spoke to none of these, but to his countrymen,
with their confused thoughts, loose generosity, upright purpose,
and noble pride in a land where liberty and order had alike found
rest, where rich and poor could live, not comfortably, yet in
peace together, where honesty and self-help were reckoned to
be the fulfilling of the law, both human and divine.   He spoke
to Englishmen in a language that they understood and he concluded in a peroration that they remembered.   Once again,
though it be for the hundredth time, those famous words must
be recalled, for the secret of a man's influence has never been so
completely enshrined in a single sentence, nor the character of
this man's genius elsewhere more perfectly explained.

"I therefore," he said as the night wore on towards morning,
"fearlessly challenge the verdict which this House, as representing
a political, a commercial, a constitutional country, is to give on
the question now brought before it—whether the principles on
which the foreign policy of Her Majesty's Government has been
conducted, and the sense of duty which has led us to think ourselves bound to afford protection to our fellow-subjects abroad,
are proper and fitting guides for those who are charged with
the government of England; and whether, as the Roman in days
of old held himself free from indignity when he could say, '*Civis
Romanus sum*,' so also a British subject, in whatever land he

may be, shall feel confident that the watchful eye and the strong arm of England will protect him against injustice and wrong."

The debate continued two days longer, but the battle was already won, and the division proved all and more than all that the Government had hoped for. Palmerston was left victorious over his enemies within and without the House, having secured by something perilously like clap-trap the sympathies of his countrymen. He had indeed shown himself in every way worthy of Morley's delicately malicious description of him as a "masterful and expert personage . . . the ruling member of the weak Whig Government" . . . and one, moreover, who "made sensible men tremble." [1]

Russell was a sensible man. As he had been alarmed at the sight of Palmerston in opposition to the Queen, so now he was even more alarmed at the vision of Palmerston in alliance with the people. In vain Victoria wrote to him that she felt she owed it to the country "not to allow a man . . . who had conducted himself in anything but a straightforward and proper manner to herself, to remain at the Foreign Office." [2] His majority was threatened; his resolution failed him; and an interview with "the masterful and expert personage" settled the matter. Palmerston diagnosed the position with brutal precision. There had been, he told his leader, a great conspiracy against himself. He had been put on his trial, accused, and acquitted. The country was delighted at the verdict, and he had now a strong party behind him. He added, with a concluding touch of sarcasm, that his deliverance from the snare of the fowler was not a little due to the handsome support he had received from Lord John and his colleagues in the Cabinet. [3]

If the situation was provoking for Russell it was a hundredfold more provoking for Victoria. Her annoyance lies exposed in the preamble to the famous memorandum of August 1850—a preamble carefully suppressed when the memorandum was first made known. "The Queen thinks it right," ran the exordium with its characteristic, significant underlining, "in order *to prevent any mistake* for the *future*, shortly to explain *what it is she expects* from her *Foreign Secretary*." So much she said; but it was the

---

[1] Morley, *Life of Gladstone*, i. 368.
[2] *Letters of Queen Victoria*, ii. 306.
[3] See for the conversation *Letters of Queen Victoria*, ii. 313.

judicious Stockmar who phrased the substance of her expectations. They were to all appearance simple enough—nothing in
fact more serious than a distinct statement of the Foreign
Secretary's intentions in any given case; subsequent action in
strict accordance with the measures sanctioned; regular information as to the Foreign Secretary's intercourse with foreign
representatives; and sufficient time to master the drafts of foreign
despatches. No one could reasonably take exception to this;
and Palmerston did not take exception to it. But it is also true
that, whilst the Memorandum seemed as if designed merely to
deliver the Sovereign from the position of a cipher, it suggested
vaguely, obliquely, by implication only, that she possessed some
sort of a voice in the direction of foreign affairs. Not certainly a
controlling voice; hardly so much as an advisory voice; perhaps
just no more than a delaying voice, to make sure that the measure
to be sanctioned had been thoroughly considered and possessed
the full assent of the Cabinet; but still a voice distinct from
that of the Minister and having a right to be heard. For otherwise the sanction upon which so much stress was laid must have
been an idle form, and the work of mastering the despatches a
fruitless labour. The Memorandum when subsequently laid
before the House of Commons may thus properly be said to have
preserved to the Sovereign, in an epoch of waning prerogative
and increasing Parliamentary control, something of that peculiar
authority in the sphere of foreign affairs which the Crown had
until lately exercised, and which is even now, perhaps, not
absolutely gone.

Palmerston undertook without a murmur, to attend to the
Queen's wishes, and resumed without delay the course of his
indiscretions. In the autumn of 1850 some London roughs
assaulted General Haynau, whose unlucky name, with its
obvious suggestion of hyæna, added no doubt to the fervour
of the belief in his exceptional cruelty. He was very probably
a pretty good Tartar, though, as Victoria took occasion to
remind her Foreign Secretary, one should be careful how one
accuses or condemns on hearsay evidence public men of other
countries who have to act in circumstances of great difficulty
and high responsibility.[1] But, whatever he was or whatever he
had done, an old Austrian soldier, over seventy years of age,

---

[1] *Letters of Queen Victoria*, ii. 322.

had as good a right as Don Pacifico or anyone else to be protected from ruffians, at any rate until he had been properly tried and convicted of crime. Palmerston thought otherwise. "The draymen," he wrote to the Home Secretary, "were wrong in the particular course they adopted. Instead of striking Haynau, which, however, by Koller's account they did not do much, they ought to have tossed him in a blanket, rolled him in the kennel, and then sent him home in a cab, paying his fare to the hotel." [1] These singular notions may have exemplified the Foreign Secretary's conception of that combination of law with liberty which he had so lately held up as one of the loftiest merits of his country, but they have inconvenient consequences when they are associated with diplomacy. A formal apology to the Austrian Government for what had occurred was accompanied by a rider, conveying tacit approval of the action of the mob; and as usual the document was sent off before the Queen had given it her assent. There followed, according to a by this time more or less established precedent, a strong representation on the part of the Sovereign, a mild rebuke on the part of the Prime Minister, an angry protest on the part of the Foreign Secretary, and finally a graceless and worthless surrender where to many it would have seemed that there should have been a manly, straightforward resignation.

A political crisis in the spring of 1851 brought no relief. The seals of office—tossed to and fro between the Conservatives, the Whigs, and the Peelites—reverted in the end to Russell's hands; and those hands were powerless to hold them without Palmerston's support. A promise, half extracted by the Queen, that Palmerston should be removed from the Foreign Department in the Easter [2] recess was revoked ten days later [3] on the unanswerable ground that it would break up the Whig Government and leave Victoria with the responsibility. So Palmerston reigned again, and indiscretion, his inseparable consort, reigned once more beside him.

In the autumn of 1851 Kossuth landed in England, and the Foreign Secretary made ready to bid him welcome. The Queen drew Russell's attention to the grave impropriety of the suggested reception; and there ensued a controversy between the two

---

[1] Ashley, *Life*, i. 240.   [2] *Letters of Queen Victoria*, ii. 377.
[3] *Ibid.*, p. 381.

Ministers concerned more acrid than any that had preceded it.
Palmerston endeavoured, as he endeavoured again at a later
date, to establish a distinction between his private and his public
conduct, taking the line that his house was his castle and that
he could entertain there whom he would.   Backed by the Crown
and backed by the Cabinet, Russell eventually, though with
great difficulty, carried the day.   But Palmerston's stock of
imprudence was as rich in recuperative power as the widow's
cruse of oil.   He had hardly abandoned the interview before he
was receiving a deputation of Islington Radicals conveying an
address which stigmatised the sovereigns of Austria and Russia
as odious and detestable assassins.   The Queen was again
annoyed; the Prime Minister again reproachful; and the delicate
mechanism of Cabinet government once more agitated.   But,
for all that appeared, Palmerston's hold on the Foreign Office
was at the end as strong as ever, confirmed rather than shaken
by such a multiplicity of storms.   Yet the hour of the Queen's
deliverance was at last at hand.

Louis Napoleon, who for the next twenty years was to be
the preoccupation of European diplomacy, was just then climbing
the last flights of his extraordinary ascent into the midst of the
political heavens.   Palmerston had presumably met him in
the days of his exile—at Lady Blessington's perhaps, where
dashing young men had been wont to congregate, or at some
other rendezvous of a society still small enough to assure the
intercourse of men of mark.   Be that, however, as it may, the
Foreign Secretary undoubtedly preferred the Prince-President
(to give him the singular and suggestive title by which he was
just at this time known) to those able and distinguished princes
of the House of Orleans—sons of Louis Philippe and one of
them related by marriage to Queen Victoria—who from the
melancholy retreat of Claremont [1] were balancing the chances
of a constitutional restoration.   His enduring hatred of a family,
which he was presently to place first amongst his enemies and
to credit, absurdly enough, with having poisoned the Queen's
mind against him and brought about his downfall,[2] was certainly
not without effect upon his attitude towards the bloodshot

---

[1] I had better perhaps say that I use the expression more or less figura-
tively, lest some critic should take the trouble to point out that Aumâle was
actually in Naples at the moment I am writing of.

[2] Ashley, *Life*, i. 317.

coup d'état of December, which, at the expense of a suppression of parliamentary government and the imprisonment of the more powerful friends of free institutions, laid the imperial crown of France at the Prince-President's feet, leaving him at liberty, whenever he chose, to raise it to his head. Palmerston was even convinced, by evidence too slight and ill-substantiated to be treated with respect, that the Prince de Joinville and the Duc d'Aumâle were actually on the point of heading a revolution, and that—to use his own language—"if the President had not struck when he did, he would himself have been knocked over." [1]

Perhaps, and also perhaps not! In Paris the Orleanist plot was regarded as moonshine, and the Bonapartists did not even bother to exploit it as propaganda.[2] But Palmerston was, as ever, quite sure of his opinion, and could not restrain himself from expressing it even to the person, of all others, in whose presence he had most occasion to be reserved. The French Ambassador at the Court of St James was by general admission, though not according to the laws of God or man, the son of the First Napoleon; and to him, when he called on December 3rd at the Foreign Office with an account of the events of December 2nd in Paris, the Foreign Secretary made known his approval of the latest proceedings of one destined within a year to be called Napoleon the Third. Walewski was naturally delighted, naturally assumed that Palmerston's attitude was official, and naturally communicated the knowledge of it to his master at home. Two days later, however, after Queen and Cabinet had taken counsel, the Foreign Secretary informed the British Ambassador in Paris that by Her Majesty's desire nothing must be done by her representative which might wear the look "of an interference of any kind in the internal affairs of France." Normanby was, in other words, to carry on his duties as if nothing had occurred, passing no judgments and waiting upon events. Sure of his instructions and much too sure of his chief, he hurried off rather unnecessarily to see the French Foreign Minister, only to have his non-committal attitude immediately undermined by the information that Palmerston had already expressed to Walewski his complete approval of what had been done.

The fat, which had been sizzling and sputtering on the grill for

---

[1] Ashley, *Life*, i. 289.　　　　[2] *Letters of Queen Victoria*, ii. 409, 410.

three or more years past, was now at last in the fire.   Normanby,
protesting like a well-trained servant that he knew his place,
wrote a vigorous protest against the ministerial methods that
had placed him in so awkward a hole.   Lady Normanby simultaneously conveyed to Colonel Phipps, who was about the Court,
her opinion that Palmerston was pretty nearly mad,[1] for, as
it seemed to her, the publication of his letters to her husband,
with their jocular references to the outrages in Paris and apparent
indifference to the peril incurred by British residents, must have
ruined his reputation in the eyes of a party that revered him
as the champion of Don Pacifico and the author of the immortal
peroration upon Roman safety and British citizenship.   Victoria,
for her part, professed herself at first politely, if perhaps
insincerely, incredulous that Palmerston could have advanced
opinions so directly contrary to her wishes.   And finally,
Russell, perceiving, as is generally suspected, that this sudden
vindication of despotism and violence had delivered his eternally
troublesome colleague into the Queen's hands, took his occasion
and demanded from the Foreign Secretary the seals of office.

It was no doubt unfortunate for the Prime Minister that, as
Palmerston was in a position to point out, when the matter came
up for debate in the House of Commons some few weeks later,
both he and some other of his colleagues had also, at chance
encounters with Walewski during the critical days of December,
signified some sort of approval [2] of the Prince-President's
proceedings, even though their imprudence had neither the
stamp of a formal interview nor the confirmation of a com-
muniqué placing it upon record.   For Palmerston, as it appeared,
had not been able to refrain from informing Normanby, actually
in an official despatch,[3] of the private satisfaction that he had
felt at the success of the *coup d'état*; and this when he had for
some days known the Queen's and the Cabinet's pleasure to the
contrary.   This repetition of his indiscretion constituted the
very core of his offence [4]—the sin against precedent and propriety that could not be forgiven.   But it was not for this, nor

---

[1] *Letters of Queen Victoria*, ii. 410. " It is the letter of a man half-mad."
[2] It is difficult to say what really passed between Russell and Walewski.
Their statements conflict (*cf.* Walpole, *Life of Lord John Russell*, ii. 142, with
Ashley, *Life of Palmerston*, i. 326).
[3] Ashley, *Life*, i. 229 (the despatch is dated 16th December 1851).
[4] See Walpole, *Life of Lord John Russell*, ii. 142.

any other aspect of his final blunder, that the House of Commons judged him to be in the wrong and heard him, as his friends sadly noted, less willingly than usual. What impressed them and undid him was the Queen's hitherto secret memorandum of August 1850, defining her requirements in respect of her Foreign Secretary. Russell, it is true, suppressed its damaging preamble, but even without this the document spoke volumes. The fallen Minister, taken by surprise and convicted at best of stark discourtesy towards a woman and his Sovereign, put up no effective defence. The sense of the House was plainly against him; and the passage of the Address without a division left him discredited, the Queen triumphant, and the constitutional issue settled in the Sovereign's favour. No Minister had, perhaps, so gravely compromised himself since Dundas stood convicted of misfeasance by the Speaker's casting vote and Pitt pulled his hat over his eyes to hide his strong emotion. For the moment people even wondered whether the 'game' old man was not, as the phrase is, 'finished.' "There *was* a Palmerston," observed Dizzy sententiously, as he exchanged some words with Bulwer on the staircase of the Russian Embassy. And the Russian Ambassador had more reason than he knew to wish that Disraeli had been right.

So far, however, as the Foreign Office was concerned, the end had really come. Palmerston had still a great part to play and a great influence to exercise in the conduct of foreign affairs; but in the Department, with which he had been associated for fifteen years and over, they knew his face no more. He had made, as indeed any man must have done with so long a record of service, a vast impression there, and we may pause with advantage in a tale that must henceforward seek to move more swiftly to its close, in order to sweep into a few concluding observations that salient impression of his personality and measure of his achievements which remains to one after following him into the arcana of his office and through the contradictions of his policy.

Palmerston was, in the first place and evidently, as great a driving force as any his Department had yet experienced at its head. He worked incessantly, energetically, autocratically; expanding a regular eight-hours' day into a ten-hours' day on occasion; displaying in that private correspondence, which he

made, more than those who went before him and sometimes
much to the inconvenience of those that came after him, a
main channel of official information, the exquisite qualities of
his penmanship; utilising to good advantage his rare knowledge
of French and his competent acquaintance with German;
punishing with caustic minutes the slips of his subordinates,
so that there were men alive but a few years ago who could
tell strange tales of the provocations he offered and received; [1]
and, in a word, compelling admiration of a kind, if not always
of the pleasantest kind.   There is a cry of pathos to be caught
in the name that was given him of Protocol Palmerston—the
exceeding bitter cry of the junior clerk dreaming of high
diplomacy and required to copy out projects, each duller than
the last, and all, except the last, condemned to limbo.   And
there is a world of knowledge to be gained about the way in
which he could treat even the more distinguished, agreeable,
and promising members of his staff in a little confession of
Granville's, evidently noted down by the Prince Consort among
his memoranda as curious and interesting.   "Lord Granville,"
we read, "has been Under-Secretary for Foreign Affairs under
Lord Palmerston for three years, from 1837–40, but, as he
expressed himself, rather the sandwich between his principal
and the clerks.   Lord Palmerston had in these three years
hardly once spoken to him upon any of the subjects he had to
treat." [2]

This is the same fault that meets us everywhere in Palmerston's
operations—a protean tactlessness, tactlessness without parallel,
sometimes even without point.   His apologists, unable to screen
a failing which confronts and confounds one by its frequency
and magnitude at every turn, have urged that it stands alone.
"To be impolite and insulting," observes one critic quoted by
Dr Temperley,[3] "is a mistake, but it was Palmerston's only
mistake."   One might almost as well say of a soldier that

---

[1] The late Lord Sanderson told me a few years ago that Palmerston
made such stinging comments on the fact that some personal letters, addressed
to him at the Foreign Office, had been sent up with the envelopes opened, that
Mellish, a Foreign Office clerk (the same who had the Schleswig-Holstein
question at his fingers' ends) came up and challenged him to a duel.   I possess
Lord Sanderson's memorandum of this curious picture of the old Foreign
Office.

[2] *Letters of Queen Victoria*, ii. 423–4.

[3] *Edinburgh Review*, October 1925, p. 400.

cowardice was his only shortcoming, or of a clergyman that immorality was his only vice. Tact in diplomacy is of the essence of the matter. No foreign minister can reasonably hope to make his country loved by all alike; but a Foreign Secretary who carries on his business so that an Englishman, returning from the Continent, can report that "the only chance one had to avoid being insulted was to say *Civis Romanus non sum*," [1] or a foreign sovereign complain "This (change of Ministry) is a blow to me, for so long as Lord Palmerston remained at the Foreign Office it was certain that you (English) could not procure a single ally in Europe," [2] is pretty clearly a Foreign Secretary not very well adapted to his work.

This is not to say that Palmerston did not have his successes. No strong personality could well have wielded the power of Britain for fifteen years without enjoying his hours of prestige and triumph. The creation of Belgium, even if it did not prove to be the strong rampart of civilisation against both Goth and Gaul that Europe required, countered with sufficient skill the urgent perils of the time. And, though doubtless the finest diplomacy does its work without threat of arms or blare of trumpet, Palmerston showed himself more than once, but notably in 1840, a past-master in those second-rate diplomatic achievements which consist in outwitting, to the admiration of the crowd of onlookers, a by no means artless neighbour in what may be euphemistically styled the international game.

On any long view, however, of the two main issues of his time—the issue in the East and the issue in the West—the historian may wisely hesitate to pass any complimentary judgment. In the Near Eastern Question it is idle to deny that he put his country's money upon what, after endless testing, proved unmistakably to be a rotten horse. Of that, however, more than enough has already been said. But there was also a great issue in the West—the issue of Liberalism in its double significance of independent nationality and constitutional government; and here, too, it is not clear that Palmerston's long tenure of the Foreign Office carried Europe much nearer to its goal. There occurred indeed no general war such as the world had known in the first years of the century and was to know again in the early years of the next;

---

[1] *Letters of Queen Victoria*, ii. 423.
[2] Quoted by Morley, *Gladstone*, i. 367.

but it is a little insular to suppose that, in the city of confusion to which the Continent may well be likened in 1848, all the states-men were strong incendiaries and Palmerston a solitary but sufficient fire-brigade. Be that as it may, his sympathy with Liberalism bore no fruit in Italy, where the federal solution unfortunately failed, and turned in Spain and Portugal, if not also, as some might argue, though perhaps with less show of justice, in Switzerland and Greece, to a nagging interference. Still sympathy it was for a cause, whatever may be the final verdict of Humanity upon it, unmistakably generous, inspiring, and powerful to promote heroic sacrifice and high devotion. Unfortunately, in the very last lap of his career at the Foreign Office, he belied all the tenor of his former ways and cast grave doubt upon the sincerity of his first professions. The suppression of Mazzini and the Roman Republic by French troops in 1849, if the dishonourable diplomacy that facilitated it be left out of consideration, may be condoned by those who take Rome for a universal city and the presence of foreign soldiers within its precincts no intolerable disaster; and, equally, the *coup d'état* of December 2nd in France, stained though it was with slaughter and involving as it did the destruction by the Prince-President of a constitution that he had sworn to defend, may yet seem to such as would have stood by Cæsar at the passage of the Rubicon to be worthy of praise. But one who had administered as many lectures as Palmerston in support of Liberal institutions and national independence must in common decency be held to have been estopped from volunteering his approval—his private and personal approval, as he was at great pains to explain—of actions as plainly illiberal as any the century brought forth and incident-ally of an actor whose foreign policy had, with some added marks of treachery, put down a free Republic to replace an exiled Pope. Incapable of working harmoniously with the French Government when it stood for constitutional monarchy, he took it to his heart precisely when it had assumed a form and function repugnant to his principles. Self-stultification could no further go.

Palmerston fell; Granville took his office; and Russell became undisputed master of his Cabinet for just nine weeks. Then on a motion relating to national safety, which the advent of a new Napoleon was thought to threaten, the Whigs were turned out.

Palmerston was the author of the motion, and its passage was his famous 'tit for tat.'

A weak Conservative Administration took over the government of the country, but it was out again before the end of the year and Aberdeen, with something like a Ministry of All the Talents, other than those of Derby and Disraeli, behind him, at the head of affairs. In this strange coalition of Whigs and Peelites, Palmerston figured as Home Secretary. He was sensible of the incongruity involved in serving under Aberdeen, his constant opponent of twenty-five years' standing: a fiery race-horse might as well have been set to go in tandem behind a sober roadster. But, as he tells his correspondents candidly enough, interest mingled with patriotism in persuading him to make the attempt. The times seemed to demand as strong a Government as could be found; and to refuse to serve might have left him stranded, a political animal that was neither fish, flesh, nor fowl—neither Whig nor Tory nor numbered among the fine and faithful spirits that still clung to the name of Peel.

So for a few years we find him busy with various matters, some grim, some grimy, such as the Home Office connotes—intra-mural interment, for example, or smoke-consumption, or that ever-recurring desire of the more sombre-minded Victorian clergy, both Scottish and English, to seize every possible opportunity to secure days of national fasting and humiliation. It was in regard to the last of these issues that he found, to the excitement of his contemporaries, an opening for one of those lectures in which he took delight. The curious dissertation, in which he expounds to the Presbytery of Edinburgh the mind of the Deity in regard to an outbreak of cholera, and discovers to them with nice exactitude the point where sanitation may be said to end and prayer and fasting may properly begin,[1] is worthy to be placed beside his address to Lord Ponsonby upon the international designs of Providence. His observations got him into trouble with a certain school of theologians; yet he was, in spite of appearances, neither sceptic nor scoffer, and among the tributes that have been paid to his character, the most impressive is that of "the good Lord Shaftesbury." [2]

It is not, however, with such matters that we are here concerned, but with his swift recovery of his lapsed contact with foreign

---

[1] Ashley, *Life of Palmerston*, ii. 13.   [2] *Ibid.*, p. 315.

affairs. He had wisely made up his mind, as soon as Aberdeen
invited him to join the Government, that he would not go back
to the Foreign Office; and he had been well satisfied to see first
Russell and then Clarendon sitting in his former seat. But the
imbroglio in the Near East made every Minister with diplomatic
standing a kind of minister of foreign affairs. There were, as it
happened, no less than four men in the Cabinet who had in their
time controlled the Foreign Office—Aberdeen, Palmerston himself,
Russell, and Clarendon—all of them possessed of ability and
character. This circumstance contributed rather to the weakness
than the strength of the Administration. How was it possible
that Palmerston who was cheerfully writing to Sidney Herbert
about "the progressively Liberal system of Turkey" [1] should
work well in harness with a Prime Minister who did not think
that Turks were worth defending against his fellow-Christians,
or a Foreign Secretary who had long ago perceived that the
fate of Egypt and not the fate of Turkey was the thing that
mattered? [2] Or Russell either, who, during his brief two
months' tenure of the Foreign Office at the beginning of 1853,
had refused without any apparent consideration the Russian
proposal for a settlement of the Eastern Question along the
lines that in spite of a thousand hesitations and backslidings
in high places, the course of history has in the main pursued;[3]
who, to make refusal doubly sure, had proceeded to drag from
his retirement Stratford de Redcliffe, the best friend of Turkey
and the worst foe of Russia, and send him out once more as
ambassador to the Sultan; and who, for the rest, had had as
Clarendon observed to Victoria,[4] but 'one idea from the first
day of entering Aberdeen's Government, and that the idea of
tripping Aberdeen up '!

Not here, however, but in relation to Clarendon, is it apposite
to follow the actual course of the negotiations that led up to the
Crimean War. For the moment it is enough to make clear
Palmerston's own part in the proceedings. Believing that
Russia had no more iron in her purpose than could be dispelled

---

[1] Ashley, *Life of Palmerston*, ii. 37.
[2] Clarendon's Memorandum is to be found in Maxwell's *Life* of him, i. 186–93.
[3] The proposal was to emancipate the European Provinces of Turkey and
organise them as independent principalities under Russian protection. Great
Britain was to be free, if she pleased to take Egypt and Crete.
[4] *Letters of Queen Victoria*, iii. 117.

by a brave show of brass,[1] he became the protagonist in council
of a hot and strong diplomacy, which so far prevailed as to cause
the Allied Fleets to enter the Black Sea just in time to destroy
the last hope of peace by negotiation; and, believing that war is
easiest waged with jovial jest and robust bellicosity, he delivered
his soul, after hostilities had begun, in language that brought
down upon his head the thunders of John Bright's noncon-
formity.   His quips and crotchets were in truth better adapted
to the post-prandial oration in honour of a gallant sailor going
to the war, for which in fact they had been intended, than to
the grave deliberations of the senate-house where, to the seeing
eye, once battle has been joined, the spectral shroud, as in the
lore of Highland seers, clings high about the neck of Youth—high
and ready to rise higher.   The two old parliamentary hands exchanged passes across the floor of the House and, not for the last
time, the members witnessed the clash of a mind, all taut and stiff
with militant patriotism, with another, stretched to the point
of strain by cosmopolitan humanities.   In one of Palmerston's
five or six opening words, all the essence of his argument was
contained.   "The honourable and reverend gentleman," he
began as the eloquent old Quaker resumed his seat; and one is
left to moralise that, if much is lost of the accomplishments that
we acquire at Eton and Harrow, there are yet certain happy gibes
and crushing sarcasms, learned in the course of a young gentleman's education, that remain with us, or at least with the
sprightliest of us, always even to the end.[2]

Whilst Palmerston threw himself with singleness of heart into
the prosecution of the war, Russell found time not only to
prosecute the war, but to undo the Prime Minister.   The latter
enterprise came to fruition before the former.   On the resignation of their Leader in the House of Commons on the very eve
before their conduct of the war was challenged in debate, the
Aberdeen Government fell.   A prolonged political crisis ensued.
Not indeed that there was wanting a man to take office as Prime
Minister, for Russell was more than ready to do so!   But just
that almost everybody shrank from serving under one who had
so lately played the part of Zimri and slain his master—a master,

---

[1] See his Cabinet Memorandum of 12th July 1853 (printed in Ashley, ii. 32).
[2] Macaulay's judgment on this performance is worth preserving in any
study of Palmerston : " Palmerston's want of temper, judgment, and good
breeding almost incredible." (Trevelyan, *Life of John Bright*, p. 234.)

as it happened, as remarkable for his loyalty to his subordinates as for his modesty about himself. Their reluctance came as a great surprise to Lord John, whose thoughts upon such matters were not as other men's thoughts—or, perhaps, as we who were witnesses of the formation of Mr Lloyd George's Government in 1916 might prefer to say, were ahead of the age in which he lived. For it was observed at the time that his conduct had a good following of supporters in the second-class railway carriages though not in the first; [1] and "sixty years after" he might have met with better success. As things were the dying code of public ethics, or, if we like it better, etiquette, found no stronger supporter than Clarendon who, supposing that political morality would suffer if Lord John were to succeed, virtually compelled the Queen, by his repeated refusal to serve under a potential usurper, to send for Palmerston.

The country wished for nothing better. People had got it into their heads that Palmerston possessed the qualities that prevail in war; and Russell, who, in the reconstruction of the Cabinet that he had tried to force upon Aberdeen, had allotted to Palmerston the War Office, had encouraged the idea. The French, needless to add, were enchanted at the prospect of turning the terrible energy of their old antagonist against the common foe; [2] and, though Derby in the course of some private advice to the Queen had depicted the incoming Prime Minister as "very blind," "very deaf," "seventy-one years old," and "totally unfit for the task," [3] he was still as hearty a belligerent as the country contained, and even, it may be, with the aid of the rouge which he put on his cheeks,[4] in appearance as hale a one. It was to his credit that he had behaved throughout the recent Cabinet crisis with admirable propriety; supporting Aberdeen's government as long as it was there to support; declining to join a Conservative administration, when Derby tried to bribe him back with the offer of the Conservative leadership in the House of Commons, which Disraeli was willing to relinquish; promising, none the less, to give the Conservatives the best help he could in the prosecution of the War if they came

---

[1] *Letters of Queen Victoria*, iii. 109. Lansdowne's observation to the Prince Consort.
[2] *Ibid.*, iii. 102.
[3] *Ibid.*
[4] Buckle, *Life of Beaconsfield*, iii. 113.

into power; and placing himself very much at the Queen's disposal when she intimated to him her desire that he should assist
Russell in the formation of a government, although not, in truth,
without the *arrière-pensée* that he would in this way be able to
counter any charge of personal ambition.[1]

Thus it was, through no manœuvring of his own, but in the
fulness of a week's ineffectual search to determine how the
Queen's Government might be carried on, that Palmerston rose
to the height of his power and in due course to the height of his
opportunity. The strangeness of his fortune struck his own
imagination. "A month ago," he wrote to his brother, "if any
man had asked me to say what was one of the most improbable
events, I should have said my being Prime Minister. Aberdeen
was there, Derby was head of one great party, John Russell of
the other, and yet in about ten days' time they all gave way
like straws before the wind, and so here am I, writing to you
from Downing Street, as First Lord of the Treasury."[2]

History, when it does not belie, repeats itself; and a plausible
analogy has been found between the fall of the Coalition Government in 1855 and the fall of the Coalition Government in 1916.
As Palmerston was to Aberdeen, runs the theorem, so was Mr
Lloyd George to Lord Oxford; and it is tempting to institute a
comparison between the characters of the men to whom, in rather
similar circumstances, the country turned for help. Doubtless
they had some points in common, though perhaps more of
difference. But in any likeness that can be established one
consideration ought in fairness to be remembered to Palmerston's
advantage. It was no act of his, nor act to which he gave
approval, that hurled Aberdeen from the saddle; and this
although no personal nor party tie bound him to his Leader.

So, then, in the February of 1855, with threescore years and
ten behind him, Palmerston came into his own—into the leadership of a nation that loved above measure, at any rate in those
days when Philistinism was the fashion and Art and Science
were looked upon as the dowdy mistresses of a German Prince,
a game old cock full of fight and assurance, good spirits and
common sense—a "he-man," as the Americans say, but tempered
and, one must charitably suppose, mellowed by age. He had
hit off, vocalised, and embodied the spirit of his time and country;

[1] See Ashley, *Life of Palmerston*, ii. 76.   [2] *Ibid.*

he had grown to be the idol of mid-Victorian, middle-class England; he had become the hope and stay of Britain in her hour of crisis; he was amongst his patriotic compatriots what every proper man would wish to be; he seemed, just for a decade, as if he had caught and interpreted at last to general satisfaction the enigmatic character of John Bull. "It has made us all proud of him," Peel had declared, almost with his dying breath, of Palmerston's Don Pacifico speech in 1850; and the pride in him had grown and flourished until now, in 1855, he had reached the summit of his power and fame. There, as it will seem to some, we might well leave him, since the arts of parliamentary management and popular appeal in which the strength of this Samson really lay, lie beyond the province of this book. Yet this would be to leave his portrait as Foreign Secretary but three parts painted. For, though in the life of most Prime Ministers foreign affairs have only an incidental and subordinate place, with Palmerston they were always a preoccupation. There were two reasons for this—his lively desire to promote reform abroad and his vigorous resolve to postpone reform at home.

He came into power as the champion of war and efficiency; and in both issues he proved faithful to his trust. The fighting went on; but the troops fought under improved conditions, as indeed, without any change in the personnel of the Cabinet, was almost bound to be the case, once the war was fully launched and the wants of the army were clearly known. What all the fighting was about, however, was no longer so obvious as it had been even in Aberdeen's time. "General Février turned traitor" [1] just as Palmerston came into office; and the amiable figure of the "Tsar Liberator" filled the place which the masterful personality of Nicholas I. had until then occupied. For the rest, the dispute about the custody of the Holy Places had lapsed into limbo, and the provinces of Moldavia and Wallachia been long evacuated under Austrian pressure by the Russian forces. As happens sometimes when a war has been some while in being, the primary aims of the combatants had been lost sight of and other aims had come into view. Even here Russia was evidently ready to go a good way to meet the Allies. A Conference at Vienna

---

[1] The reference is, of course, to Tenniel's famous cartoon of Nicholas's death-bed, which was suggested by the Emperor's remark that he had two excellent generals—Generals Janvier and Février.

between the Powers interested, which, almost as soon as Palmerston's Government had been formed, Russell set off to attend as British representative, made it plain that the Russian Government would raise no objection to the substitution of a European for a Russian guarantee of the autonomous Balkan provinces, and made it probable that they would equally consent to a European in place of a Russian protectorate over the Orthodox subjects of the Sultan.   But neither the Emperor of the French nor the Prime Minister of England were in any hurry to agree with their adversary.

Napoleon, with his armies closing in upon Sebastopol, forgot his famous declaration of 1852 that "*l'Empire c'est la paix*," and recollected more and more his uncle's military reputation.   And Palmerston, always Russo-phobe to the core, and elated at seeing that his enemy was getting the worst of it, cheated his countrymen with the cant phrase of a good fighter, and urged that he was indeed seeking peace and ensuing it, but that the peace he sought and ensued must be no other than a good one; all of which, being interpreted, signified nothing more nor less than an intention to leave the enemy saddled with some humiliating condition that he would try to throw off at the earliest convenient opportunity.   The drift of the Prime Minister's thoughts had, even before the Queen sent for him, been apparent to some of the astutest of his colleagues.   Both Lansdowne and Gladstone supposed him to have a secret understanding with the Emperor of the French; and he did, in fact, to Victoria's alarm, give ground for the suspicion by initiating a sort of secret correspondence with Napoleon.[1]   But, whatever we make of this, it is clear that the two principals effectually suppressed the over-zealous activities of their agents at Vienna in the cause of peace.   Both Russell and Drouyn de Lhuys, the French plenipotentiary, were alike repudiated and alike driven to resign.

The actual point upon which negotiations broke down was the question whether or not Russia should be permitted to retain a fleet or any part of a fleet on the Black Sea.   By fighting for the best part of a year longer the Allies secured a negative decision.   For fourteen years, therefore, the Black Sea was neutralised;   then, when in 1870 France and Prussia were endeavouring to cut each other's throats, Russia took the oppor-

[1] *Letters of Queen Victoria*, iii. 120, 133, 134.

tunity of throwing off the incubus of a stipulation not much
more reasonable than if Great Britain were denied the right to
have warships in the Ægean Sea or coaling-stations in the Indian
Ocean. Thus the actual "good" peace of 1856 was reduced to
the level of the abortive "compromise" peace of 1855; and all
its distinctive virtue for the next generation resolved itself into
a choice between shouldering single-handed a second Crimean
War or stomaching with idle protests an unpalatable humiliation.
The Englishmen of 1870, dominated by Gladstone, selected the
milder, the more reasonable alternative. For Palmerston was
dead; and his fine fighting spirit was buried with him.

To what extent Palmerston swept Clarendon from his native
moorings in the negotiations arising out of the Crimean War is
open to discussion; but there can at least be little doubt that the
Prime Minister's judgment dictated the decision in regard to the
project of the Suez Canal. Amongst all examples of his self-
confidence and obstinacy, this particular affair inevitably stands
out, so completely did he commit himself, so unanswerably did
the event disprove his theories. Lesseps, who saw him about
the scheme which was to make his own name famous, tells us
that, as the interview progressed, he asked himself from time to
time whether the man he was speaking to was a statesman or
a maniac, so violent was the prejudice, so absurd were the objections with which he found himself confronted.[1] And well he
might! For Palmerston's own considered memorandum of five
years later addressed to Russell declares that "it may safely be
said . . . that, as a commercial undertaking, it (the proposed
canal) is a bubble scheme, which has been taken up on political
grounds and in antagonism to English interests and English
policy."[2] On the political side he is equally certain that the
project stands condemned: "It requires only a glance at the map
of the world to see how great would be the naval and military
advantage to France in a war with England to have such a short
cut to the Indian seas, while we should be obliged to send ships and
troops round the Cape." All this preposterous nonsense—the consequence, as the memorandum shows, of his first fatal error in
taking Turkey, and not Egypt, for the British key to the Near
Eastern situation—might well be allowed to drop into oblivion

[1] *Recollections of Forty Years*, i. 291.
[2] Ashley, *Life of Palmerston*, ii. App., p. 327.

if it were not that the judgment is no casual one, the responsibility of a Prime Minister no light one, and the construction of the Suez Canal and subsequent acquisition by England, under Disraeli's wiser auspices, of the Khedive's holding in its shares,[1] no incident in British imperial history but an event of vast and outstanding importance.

There occurred, at the close of Palmerston's first premiership, another foreign affair which bears the unmistakable impress of his hand and exemplifies the vice or, as some may think the virtue, of that "strong, coercive policy" in the Far East, peculiarly associated, as a high authority points out,[2] with his presence in a Government and designed to force an entry into a provokingly self-satisfied and self-sufficient China for the Western world in general and Great Britain in particular, for British trade as a whole and the opium traffic in especial. Wherever the tale of Don Pacifico is told, no better story than that of the 'lorcha' Arrow need be sought to cap it. The hero, this time, whom Britain extended her long arm to succour, was no Portuguese Jew, endowed by fortune with a British birthplace, but a notorious Chinese pirate, in flight from justice, and in hiding on a vessel, owned by Chinamen and improperly flying a British flag. That was, however, all one to Palmerston. He had a bone to pick with China—a bone as old as his own time at the Foreign Office, and of which the pith and marrow was the desire of the Chinese to keep the foreign devil out of their country; a bone, when one comes to think about it, that had a curious look of likeness to certain notions that he himself seemed sometimes to entertain about nationality and independence. Possibly the resemblance was superficial. At all events the Prime Minister felt no difficulty in approving the conduct of Sir John Bowring, Mr Harry Parkes, and Admiral Seymour when they dealt in a smart, summary fashion with the conduct of the Chinese official concerned. Twelve of the Chinese crew of the lorcha Arrow had been taken by Mr Commissioner Yeh and tried, and of the twelve three had been found guilty, and the others released. But when the Commissioner found that such potentates as the Governor of Hong-Kong, the British

---

[1] This represented 177,000 (out of a total of 400,000) shares, and cost only £4,000,000.
[2] Satow (*Camb. Mod. Hist.*, xi. c. 28).

Consul at Canton, and the British Admiral on the China station were dissatisfied with his ideas of justice, he decided to release his prisoners one and all, guilty and innocent alike. Even so he fell short of the British requirements. Nothing less than a public apology for the arrest of suspected Chinese criminals and a public restoration of the whole lot of them to their ship seemed to Sir John Bowring and Mr Harry Parkes and Admiral Seymour compatible with the honour of the British flag. So Canton was blockaded and Mr Commissioner Yeh's official residence was shelled.

It was all one to Palmerston whatever might have happened; and he defended the British case not the less vigorously that he knew the facts vaguely. A robust faith in racial loyalties and vicarious punishments pervaded his mind. He had left far behind him Wellington's curt reminder, addressed to Napier, that the King's Government desired to establish intercourse with China not by force but by measures of conciliation. He who, some fifteen years before, had seized Hong-Kong and caused British subjects to be withdrawn from Chinese criminal jurisdiction, was, indeed, about to seek occasion to force foreign legations upon Pekin. He held that East is East and West West, that we must always stand by our compatriots, that it was high time that these Orientals should get what he characterised as another "exemplary licking." In the House of Commons his argument failed to convince. There sprang up against him a holy, or unholy alliance, as we may prefer to call it, between Conservatives, Radicals, and Peelites, and the Government was defeated. But in the Country he was more fortunate. His pluck, his conception of a flag of England that covered all deficiencies of conduct and knew no limitations of race, carried the day. The Electorate gave him the majority that he desired, and the Manchester School such a beating as it had never yet received. "Old Pam," as they lovingly called him in the constituencies, was thus returned to power just in time to fight "the Mutiny"; and "Cupid," as his colleagues more cryptically named him in their private communications,[1] immediately signalised his new lease of authority by passing a Divorce Bill. With neither the one matter nor the other are we here concerned,

---

[1] See Maxwell, *Life of Clarendon*, ii. 95. The name apparently originated in his good looks when he was a schoolboy. (See the D.N.B. article on him.)

though the former, with its sequel [1]—the transfer of the government of India from the Company to the Crown—was his most
notable contribution to imperial and the latter to domestic
politics.

History has preserved among its archives an incident which
falls to be recorded at this point and contains, besides a familiar
moral, an instance of the spectacular brilliancy of Palmerston's
political position at the commencement of 1858. It was after
one of the debates upon the Indian Bill, when his majority,
contrary to expectation in the case of so contentious a measure,
had been amply and splendidly sustained, that Bethell, better
remembered as Lord Chancellor Westbury, observed to him as
they walked home together, that he needed an attendant to
remind him, in something of the same way as was done in the case
of the victor in a Roman triumph, that his power and place were
subject to the usual laws of political mortality. The warning
was well-timed. A week later his Government fell.

For once Palmerston had failed his countrymen—had failed
them precisely in that quality which almost every critic has
reckoned to be his outstanding defect—in patriotic truculence.
Orsini's plot, hatched upon British soil, to murder Napoleon III.
proved to be his enemies' occasion. It had produced some not
unreasonable representations from the French Government to
the effect that English toleration went too far for the proper
security of a neighbouring and allied sovereign; and Palmerston
met them by the introduction of a bill converting conspiracy
to murder from a misdemeanour into a crime. At the critical
moment, however, when the measure was under consideration in
the House of Commons, some fire-eating Frenchmen, supposed by
English opinion, under the influence of inherent if erroneous
probability, to be of the grade of "colonels," made their voices
heard and threatened with final destruction the too hospitable
country which had given Orsini and his confederates shelter.
Palmerston took no notice of the fire-eaters and proceeded calmly
with his Bill, without so much as taking the precaution to see that
Clarendon, in his reply to the French official despatch, conveyed,
under diplomatic forms, the conviction, dear to the English
people at that time, that one Englishman is as good as three
Frenchmen and better too. Old Derby, sitting up in the gallery

[1] Not completed in his term of office.

of the House of Commons, is said to have seen his chance and to have sent word to bid Disraeli cast consistency to the winds and play for office. Be that as it may, Palmerston was defeated, when this was least expected and least deserved. For the only time in his life he was really unpopular. Suddenly, as a curious memorandum of Prince Albert's remains to show, the House of Commons took a violent dislike to the very man whom it had been returned to support, held him actually, we are told, "in abhorrence" —would hardly listen to him, must vote against him, might even hoot him down.[1] He took it all lightly, gaily, after his manner; but Lady Palmerston was seen to be very unhappy and greatly pained.

A year, or a little more than a year, sufficed to disperse these humours. Like a capricious woman the Country returned to the man with whom it was never long out of love. After a poor sixteen months of administration in more than twenty years the Conservatives were put out, and in July 1859 Palmerston was back again, firmly entrenched in power for the remainder of his days. The decision to send for him had afforded an illustration of one of the few remaining, unchallenged political prerogatives of the Crown—the prerogative of choosing, when two men's claims to the Premiership are equal, which shall have the lead. Victoria had, however, tried to save herself from deciding between Russell and Palmerston by sending for Granville; and Granville, with admirable loyalty, had attempted a task which, had he been successful, would have left him as much master of his Cabinet as is the owner of a field who puts a pair of rampageous prize-bulls out to grass in it. His advances, recommended by a letter from the Queen, were met by Palmerston with characteristic generosity, but by Russell with not less characteristic disdain. Lord John's refusal to meet Granville's advances obliged the Queen to make her choice. She sent for Palmerston, perhaps because she really liked him the better of the two, perhaps because of all living statesmen the Country liked him best. It followed, as a matter of course, that Russell claimed the Foreign Office, which he took to be the post of highest dignity after the Premiership. His action threw out Clarendon, to the regret both of the Queen and the Prime Minister.

It was not the first time that Lord John had been entrusted

[1] *Letters of Queen Victoria,* iii. 381.

with the conduct of foreign affairs merely because no one knew how else to keep him contented. Also he had been sent to the Vienna Conference in 1855 by Palmerston and Clarendon mainly to prevent his making trouble in the House of Commons; [1] and twice in that year "Satan," if the Germans were right about Palmerston's descent, had taken occasion to reprove sin. Russell's habit of acting upon sudden impulse, his dry, stiff manners, his want of practice in dealing personally with artful negotiators, his unfortunate way of suddenly surrendering on matters in regard to which he had previously made an apparently immovable stand, and "his aptitude to be swayed by others," [2] all came in for Palmerston's criticism of him as diplomatist. But of the last of these failings the Prime Minister had little reason to complain, for it redounded to his own advantage. He now resumed, with his former chief as his henchman and with the immense prestige of an admittedly personal victory at the polls, that battle with the Crown which he had lost in 1851. To borrow and a little extend a happy criticism of Lady Theresa Lewis's, he took, in the drama of "Offhand Despatches and Random Shots" which was forthwith staged, the part of Robin Hood and Johnny Russell that of Little John. [3]

In the guise of those romantic characters we may, if we will, figure the Twin-Brethren during the six years in which they tried to run away with the Constitution and stampede the Country into foreign commitments that it had not properly measured and foreign adventures the bearing of which it had imperfectly understood. Or we may think of them just in Victoria's matter-of-fact phraseology, lately made public, as "those two dreadful old men." [4] Against them were ranged the Queen and the Cabinet —the Queen, at first with the Prince Consort at her side, then, distracted, almost to the loss of dignity in her official correspondence, by the overwhelming misery of her loss, yet still inspired by her husband's precepts and bent upon following in the path that he had marked out; the Cabinet, led in its cogitations upon foreign affairs by Granville subsequently reinforced by Clarendon, and deriving further strength from the presence of Charles Wood and Sidney Herbert, and, except when his enthusiasm for

---

[1] Maxwell, *Life of Clarendon*, ii. 63.
[2] *Ibid.*, pp. 63, 81.
[3] *Ibid.*, p. 197.
[4] *Letters of Queen Victoria* (second series), i. 168.

the liberation of Italy deflected his judgment, of Gladstone, the friend of peace and of economy.

The trouble began almost immediately and raged round the two great foreign issues of the period—the union of Italy and the question of Schleswig-Holstein. We shall do best to glance at the former first. Whilst Great Britain was passing through the political crisis which brought Palmerston back to power, Napoleon III. had been liberating Lombardy at Magenta and Solferino. At the Peace of Villafranca the new Bonaparte initiated, though not in name, the union of Italy, and thus, as critics ought perhaps more often to remind us, incidentally commenced the grand attack upon the work of Castlereagh. Negotiated at Vienna, whose name it bears, the Treaty of 1815 had derived the corner stone of the European system that it set up from the country of its origin. The Austrian Empire exemplified two notions long assumed to be just—the notion that royal houses such as the House of Habsburg had the right to rule and to retain their territorial possessions, and the notion that the violation of international treaties, and above all of recent international treaties, which had the signature of the Great Powers of Europe upon them, was a breach of faith. These ideas had not lost their validity in the eyes of Queen Victoria.

Russell and Palmerston moved in a different order of ideas. They supposed that sovereigns are bound to govern well; they supposed that a nation has the right to throw off a government, and more particularly an alien government, that it dislikes; and they were inclined to suppose that the provisions of treaties of which they themselves no longer approved need no longer be kept. There was consequently a great gulf fixed between their principles and those of Queen Victoria. In her correspondence [1] there is even to be found the record of a very sharp and curious exchange of opinion with Lord John, in the course of which he defends the conduct of King Victor Emmanuel with the help of the conduct of King William III.

It was a far cry from the future hero of Italian Unity to the "Whig Deliverer," but, even had they been within closer call, the Queen might fairly have been excused for failing to perceive in the uncouth creature with his strange talk and stranger habits, who had visited England some four years earlier, the up-to-

---

[1] *Letters of Queen Victoria* (second series), iii. 505, 506.

date embodiment of her title to reign.   Russell, however, was in
a position to approach the Italian problem by other than royal
roads.   His political creed taught him to look at countries
and not at kings, and together with Palmerston he beheld,
even if with nothing better than an old man's vision, that
same sacred fire which had lit up in Canning's time the heights of
Olympus and the mountains looking upon Marathon and the
Ægean Sea beyond, but was now coursing madly along the
Apennines, turning their peaks to flame and rousing to richer,
more abundant life the spirit of the Italian people.   We catch
that glow nowadays only with difficulty—we, who have seen the
nemesis of Liberalism, of Nationality, of all that was once the
very passion of faith and freedom; we, who see the faithful
Tyrolese now standing where once the Venetians stood; we, in
whose time, not Italy alone, but the other Mediterranean Penin-
sulas also, have passed adverse verdicts upon parliamentary
institutions.

The charm of an Italy set free and made into one hardly lives
for us outside of Mr Trevelyan's magic pages, where it is perfectly
rendered by one of the most eloquent voices of our generation.   But
"Johnny"—for so they all called him when his back was turned;
the Queen in her correspondence with her good uncle, Leopold,
as well as his colleagues in their correspondence with one another
—"Johnny" in his own dry way caught the enthusiasm of the
cause and envisaged it, "Pam" acting as his tutor, with the
understanding of a schoolboy—in point of fact, if the truth must
absolutely all be told, of Macaulay's schoolboy.   Granville and
Clarendon, as they watched him closely, noted his youthful
weaknesses.   "He is always dying to connect his name with
something," [1] the former wrote of him to a correspondent.   And
the latter in a very confidential epistle to the Duchess of Manchester, which he implored her to burn, but which, woman-like,
she left to be exposed to Posterity, advised her that "John
Russell has neither policy nor principles of his own and is in the
hands of Palmerston, who is an artful old dodger, and whose
monomania against Austria has reached the point of phrenzy." [2]

Russell's policy was, indeed, as Cowley saw, a thing of dabs
and dashes.   "One never knows where one is with him.   One

---

[1] Fitzmaurice, *Life of Lord Granville*, i. 355.
[2] Maxwell, *Life of Clarendon*, ii. 206.

day it is one thing and one another." [1]   So it was bound to be if
one starts to promote an Italian federation and ends by blessing
Italian unity.   Principles, too, of public conduct as well as of
public policy, were wanting.   Despatches that bore a closer
resemblance to what Palmerston and Russell wanted than to
anything that the Cabinet had settled or the Queen approved
began to be drafted and even presently to be despatched.   It may
have been, as Granville thought,[2] " Johnny's " loose way of doing
business, or it may have been, as the Queen thought,[3] that same
calculated resolve to direct policy without regard for Crown or
colleagues that had characterised Palmerston's own management
of foreign affairs.   But at all events Victoria found herself once
more battling for the right to appeal from the Foreign Secretary
to the Cabinet as a whole.   The Cabinet, fearful of what the
"Twins" might do if left to themselves, entered into alliance with
her against them.   A secret correspondence, of which a few
sentences will show the character, grew up between Granville and
the Prince Consort to sustain the cause of the allies.   "Sir," the
former writes to the latter at the end of August 1859, just about
two months after the Government came into power, "the Cabinet
was very satisfactory.   Lord John looked ill and evidently
ashamed of much of his case . . .   The Cabinet thoroughly understood what had passed between the Queen and her two ministers,
although we could not get Lord John to show us all we required." [4]
In a letter to Argyll, Granville added another amusingly significant
detail: "Pam asked for fuller powers to act during the recess,
which was met by a general assurance of readiness to come up by
night trains," [5]

The "two dreadful old men" were rightly suspect, from the
point of view of those who thought, like the Queen, that Austria
was in the right, or, like the majority of the Cabinet, that the fate
of Italy was no affair of England's.   Great Britain had nothing to
gain by the transfer of Northern and Central Italy to Sardinia,
and something conceivably to fear from the creation of a strong
Mediterranean Power.   But Russell could never be stopped from
giving advice and was now possessed by the idea that, for want

---

[1] Cowley to Clarendon (printed in Maxwell's *Life of Clarendon*, ii. 219).
[2] Fitzmaurice, *Life of Granville*, i. 351.
[3] *Letters of Queen Victoria*, iii. 490.
[4] *Ibid.*, p. 468.
[5] Fitzmaurice, *Life of Granville*, i. 358.

of it, we might be compelled in the end to intervene in Italy "against the ruthless tyranny of Austria or the unchained ambition of France." [1]

His advice—his "friendly and judicious advice," as he hopefully styled it in writing to the Queen—was first directed towards the substitution of the vote of a national assembly in Tuscany, Modena, and the Romagna for the terms of the Peace of Villafranca which restored these Duchies to their former rulers and kept the States of the Church still in the hands of the Pope. He was so far successful that, first in parliament and then by plebiscite, Central Italy voted itself into the arms of Sardinia. This was all very well and nothing to be objected to. But it had escaped Russell's notice that the increase of Sardinia and Piedmont could not reasonably be effected without also some increase of France, whose armies had after all initiated the work of liberation. Napoleon claimed as a set-off to the growing size of Sardinia the Duchy of Savoy and the region around Nice. Cavour made no difficulty; and Russell was left idly protesting. His meddlesome diplomacy had brought him this rebuff. He chose to emphasise it by demanding that certain districts of Savoy—Chablais and Faucigny—neutralised by the Treaty of 1815, should be transferred to Switzerland, and then stomaching Napoleon's refusal to do anything of the kind. "We have been done brown in the affair," Clarendon had written to Reeve, when he heard of the cession of Savoy, and had proceeded to prophesy that, in the endeavour to extricate himself from the mess, the colour of the Foreign Secretary was likely to change from brown to verdant green. [2] And so it had come to pass.

The fortune of Central Italy was no sooner made than the fate of Southern Italy came forward for decision. Garibaldi and the Thousand did not land in Sicily till the May of 1860, but the Sicilians themselves rose in April, the sympathies of Sardinia were immediately engaged, and the intentions of Cavour became hardly doubtful. It was in these circumstances that Victoria cautioned her Foreign Secretary to make it clear in his despatches that any attempt on the part of the Sardinian Government to overthrow the Government of the Two Sicilies was not merely, as Russell admitted, politically inexpedient, but also morally

---

[1] *Letters of Queen Victoria*, iii. 462.
[2] Maxwell, *Life of Clarendon*, ii. 208.

reprehensible. Great Britain had as a country no quarrel
with the Bourbon Kings of Naples, whatever might be the
case with their subjects, and was in fact responsible for
placing them where they were under the terms of the Treaty
of Vienna. This opinion was not agreeable to Lord John, and,
as he was no less accomplished a professor of ethics than of
politics, he proceeded to explain to Victoria that, whilst it would
be "criminal" for the King of Sardinia to assist Sicilian
insurgents "for the sake of making new acquisitions," he was
altogether within his rights in disinterestedly aiding in the
overthrow of a tyrant.[1] Unluckily for the argument, Victor
Emmanuel was aiming at nothing less than the domination of
Italy and had as good as said so in open Parliament a month
before, when he declared that the Italy of the Italians was born.
Before the year was out, the British Foreign Secretary had been
swept completely from his academic moorings and was loudly
approving what he had some months before described as crime.
The motive of this rapid change of front was rather dislike of
France than love of Italy. Napoleon III.'s intervention in the
affairs of Sardinia had caused both Russell and Palmerston to
wonder whether he might not be modelling his policy upon lines
reminiscent of that of his uncle. The annexation of Savoy and
Nice, and the suggestion of a French expedition to Syria to relieve
the Catholic Maronites from their traditional foes, the Druses,
deepened this suspicion. Yet the idea that the Emperor was
an enemy was probably groundless. A letter of his to Persigny,
which bears every appearance of good faith even though its
contents were intended to be retailed to Palmerston, affirms
in the most explicit way his unchanged desire for a cordial
understanding with Great Britain: " Depuis la paix de Villafranca je n'ai eu qu'une seule pensée—qu'un but—c'était
d'inaugurer une nouvelle ère de paix et de vivre en bonne intelligence avec tous mes voisins, et surtout avec l'Angleterre." A
frank talk with his old friend, Palmerston, would, he thought,
make that plain.[2] But Palmerston no longer trusted the
Emperor of the French—the ruler of a people, whose memory
was, he declared, all the longer that they took so little share

---

[1] The correspondence is to be found in the *Letters of Queen Victoria*, iii.
505–6.
[2] Printed in Maxwell's *Life of Clarendon*, ii. 217.

in current politics and whose actual ill-will towards England was a matter of common knowledge.[1] And, writing as he was in French to Persigny, he took occasion to snatch a plume from the Imperial Eagle's tail! " Il n'y a certainement pas de nation qui puisse se vanter d'être plus brave que la nation française mais je crois que nos hommes ont quelques dix minutes de ténacité de plus que les vôtres ; et lorsque le courage est égal des deux côtés, c'est la ténacité qui décide du sort du combat." [2]

The rift in the Anglo-French understanding proved to be the making of Cavour's schemes—the making of Italy. Neither Great Britain nor France had much wished to see Italy united; both would have been well content to see the liberation end in a weak federation. But, with the throne of Naples rocking under Garibaldi's hammer-blows and the possibility that, if the Bourbons fell, Napoleon might slip into their place a Murat or a Bonaparte, or alternatively, that if Victor Emmanuel got possession of the Sicilies, France might exact more Italian territory in compensation, Russell, after some ineffective wriggling, came down, still talking loudly of the Whig Deliverer and the glorious Revolution of 1688, on the side of Italian unity. The fall of Naples to Garibaldi and the subsequent march of the Sardinian army into the States of the Church had in some mysterious way removed from his moral philosophy the reservation which he had so carefully made in his letter to the Queen. As he saw things now it was no longer "criminal" to aid insurrection, even with the view of making new acquisitions. So, whilst all the great Powers of Europe thundered in the name of international right against the invasion of Umbria by the troops of Victor Emmanuel, and some actually withdrew their representatives from Turin, Russell penned a new despatch contesting the justice of their strictures and bidding them raise aloft their eyes and behold the "prospect of a people building up the edifice of their liberties." Brunnow might declare that this was not diplomacy but roguery, Vitzthum assert that diplomatic history contained no similar performance, and the Cabinet protest because they had never been shown the despatch before it was sent,[3] but the British Public had got what it liked—a

---

[1] Ashley, *Life of Palmerston*, ii. 195.
[2] *Ibid.*, ii. 194.
[3] *Camb. Hist. of British Foreign Policy*, ii. 449.

piece of generous sentiment that cost them nothing. "Well said, Johnny Russell!" wrote the weekly spokesman of London opinion:—

> "Well said, Johnny Russell! That latest despatch
>   You have sent to Turin is exactly the Thing;
> And again, my dear John, you come up to the scratch
>   With a pluck that does credit to you and the Ring."

It had escaped Mr Punch's notice—or was perhaps beyond Mr Punch's immediate means of information—that "Johnny's" pluck had been more assisted by fear of the French and the swift, astute, not to say Machiavellian moves of Cavour than by any native decision or determination of his own.

The despatch, nevertheless, is Russell's supreme contribution to the diplomatic history of the period. It met the precise requirements of Cavour at the moment, and bestowed upon his disregard of treaties a blessing the more effective that it came from a quarter accustomed to maintain their sacred obligations. Also, it had the effect of convincing the statesmen of the Continent, then, and as Dr Reid supposes, for some years after, that Great Britain was in reality "consistent only in self-interest,"[1] or, if we like to strip the mask off this soft rebuke, that Great Britain was as arch a hypocrite about the binding nature of treaties as they were themselves.

Let the remote consequences of Russell's proceedings be as they may have been, the effect at the moment was all that a schoolboy, wanting a splash, could possibly have desired. The Foreign Secretary had achieved the ambition with which Clarendon credited him. He had 'connected his name with something'—and that something "the making of Italy." Not the Thames alone was on fire with his fame, but the Seine, the Spree, the Danube, the Tiber, even the cold Neva up in the distant North! He was so delighted with the power of his words that he would fain have gone further. He wished to announce that, not Naples and Umbria only, but Venetia and Rome also, ought to be added to the Kingdom of Italy, and that if anybody liked to take practical measures to bring this about, the British Government would "hold themselves free to act in such a manner as the rights of nations, the independence

---

[1] Dr Rachel Reid, in *Camb. Hist. of British Foreign Policy*, ii. 449.

of Italy, and the interests of Europe may seem to them to require."
These fine words, however, seemed to Victoria, like other fine
words, to butter no parsnips. In her common-sense way she
pointed out that, as England is free to do as it pleases, the
Foreign Secretary's language constituted either an empty menace
or a threat of war. The former was undignified; the latter, so
far as she was concerned, unintended.[1] She therefore requested
that the despatch might be referred to the Cabinet; and the
Cabinet, in our modern phraseology, 'turned it down.' They
had not the smallest intention of backing up Young Italy in
any attempt to wrest Venice from Austria, or Rome from the
protectorate established there by Catholic France. A decade
must go by, Napoleon fall and Bismarck rise, before these things
could be. Not by such aid as Russell had to offer, not with
high-sounding words and opportune despatches, but with blood
and iron, by the help of the long arm of Prussia and across the
breach at Porta Pia, were Venetia and the Eternal City to be
joined to the Italian Kingdom. Russell was to live to see that
final consummation, but he had no hand in it, nor his country
either.

How much in all this question of Italian unity Palmerston
pushed Russell forward we shall never precisely know, or at
least not until the tenaciously-guarded Broadlands Papers have
given up their remaining secrets; but we need not doubt that
it was the hand of the Prince Consort that held Russell back.
Albert's judgment in matters of foreign policy was now as much
worth attending to as that of any Englishman of the time; and,
before his life untimely ended, he was able to render England
a final service. The American Civil War was in full swing by
the last months of 1861; and the conduct of a neutral Power,
when both Secessionist and Federalist had in their different
ways an unanswerable case, had become a matter of increasing
difficulty. Palmerston's sympathies are not in doubt, for the
suppression of slavery was the one great passion of his politics;
but a declaration in favour of the North, even if all his colleagues
had agreed with him, would not have been in point, for as the
Northern Government well knew, the issue was no straight
fight between servitude and freedom, but between the rights
of the individual State and the rights of the whole Federation.

[1] *Letters of Queen Victoria*, iii. 523.

In the circumstances Great Britain gave to the North official, but did not deny to the South unofficial, recognition. It was a half-way house which promised no permanent shelter. The rape by a North American vessel from off the British liner *Trent* of the two Southern Commissioners—Messrs Mason and Slidell of famous memory—raised a definite issue and gave the Northern States a chance, which they did not fail to take advantage of, to express their feelings about their old-world cousins. British anger rose in response; and it needed all the dry common sense of Anglo-Saxon statesmanship to calm the storm, and a few courtly phrases besides, to act like oil upon the troubled waters. Russell's draft demanding the surrender of the envoys, set out the British case forcibly enough; but it was the disclaimer, which the Prince Consort inserted as he lay dying, of the idea that their seizure had been authorised or approved by the American Government, that made the despatch politely persuasive. Before the year was out Lincoln and Seward had decided to give way; but, before they had reached their decision, Albert was dead. What he had accomplished for the thankless cause of Anglo-American friendship had, however, no long endurance. Russell quickly squandered in the case of the *Alabama* [1] what had been gained in that of the *Trent;* and for ten years his omission to stop that illicitly-equipped vessel from leaving a British dockyard embittered the relations between Great Britain and America.

In Albert a much greater figure had passed off the diplomatic stage than a facetious Posterity, bored with the bare idea of right and wrong, can recognise. Palmerston had small cause to love this Sir Galahad with his high conception of the place of the Crown in the Constitution and, above all, in the sphere of foreign affairs. Yet it was Palmerston who, taking as his measure the mystery-man of the 'fifties, had estimated the Prince Consort to be "far greater and more extraordinary than Napoleon III," [2] and in the crisis of the Prince's illness had gone out of his way to try to wrench the invalid out of the hands of those "not even

---

[1] The *Alabama* was secretly fitted out at Liverpool in 1862 in the interest of the Confederate States. Representations from the American Minister failed to induce Russell to act in time to prevent her from sailing. She carried on hostilities against the North American Government with success. Her depredations, when eventually assessed by arbitration, cost the British Government three millions and a quarter.

[2] Martin, *Life of the Prince Consort,* ii. 429.

average old women," [1] as Clarendon irreverently styled the royal physicians. He had but little success; and it may well be that the Prince was fatally stricken from the very first. But it is curious to reflect that Palmerston, had he succeeded in saving Albert's life, would almost certainly have given the Crown such an influence in the conduct of foreign affairs as might have set back, by fifty years, the hands upon the dial of time. The width and wisdom of Albert's views upon foreign affairs, coupled with a continuous growing experience, must have made him such a master in European diplomacy as few Foreign Secretaries could have found it easy to oppose with an equal weight of knowledge. Even as it was, the Queen, working singly but with religious fervour along the lines of the Albertine tradition, became a power in foreign policy, dangerous to challenge, impossible to ignore, and of much importance in the counsels of Europe.

It was characteristic of Palmerston to have done everything he could to save the Prince's life. It was perhaps not less characteristic of him that, when he went down to Osborne shortly afterwards to visit the inconsolable, widowed Queen, he was dressed in a costume that might have graced a racecourse—brown overcoat and light grey trousers, blue studs and verdant gloves. [2] His critic was no doubt justified in surmising that these garish garments—or, to take the word back to the ampler sense of its original, garnishments—did not escape the royal eye.

The untimely death of the Prince Consort opened the way for the most famous, the most amusing of Palmerston's epigrams. It must have been within a year or two of Albert's death that developments in Schleswig-Holstein compelled the Prime Minister to turn his mind again to a problem that had engaged his attention first as Foreign Secretary; and the prospect provoked the remark that there were only three people in England who had ever understood the question thoroughly—the Prince Consort who was dead; Mellish (a clerk in the Foreign Office) who had disappeared; and himself—who had forgotten it. The affair has, indeed, as many mazes as a German sentence, and by the time one has worked through to the end of it one has as likely as not lost the thread of the beginning. The

---

[1] Maxwell, *Life of Clarendon*, ii. 253.
[2] *Ibid.*, p. 257.

outstanding feature of the business is, however, clear enough. The new principle of nationality, which Palmerston had been so intent upon in Italy, had in Schleswig-Holstein, ever since 1848, been cutting clean across the old attachment of the two Duchies to the Kingdom of Denmark. Only the link of a common sovereign held them together; and that link threatened to snap with the death of the reigning monarch. The Danish Government, fearful of losing territory, and with territory power and prestige, took time by the forelock and endeavoured to unite the Duchies to their country, before these slipped altogether from their grasp, by the new expedient of a common constitution. The Schleswig-Holsteiners resented the attempt, rose in revolt, and amid the chaos of the Year of Revolution established a provisional government and a contested independence. This was the beginning of troubles. Palmerston was at that time in power and rushed to the rescue, not of a nationality struggling to be free, but of a sovereign anxious to do as he would with his subjects. His mediation was so far successful that the resistance of the Duchies eventually broke down. In due course, though no longer under Palmerston's administration, a Conference of the Powers chiefly interested, which included the Great Powers of Europe, decided the fate of the Duchies pretty much in the Danish sense.

The Treaty of London of 1852 which embodied the collective wisdom of the European statesmen of the time has met with scant praise from posterity. This is the less surprising that the people most nearly concerned in the settlement were of the least account in the deliberations. Neither the German Confederation of which Holstein was a member, nor the Schleswig-Holsteiners themselves, nor the Duke of Augustenburg, the next heir to the ducal throne according to the accepted principles of inheritance, assisted or assented. The Duke, it is true, was content to waive his birthright in return for cash, but his renunciation could hardly affect the claim of his grown-up sons. The Conference, however, pleading international necessity, put all other claimants aside in favour of Christian of Glucksburg, the father of one whom Great Britain was one day to know as Queen Alexandra. In this arrangement Prussia and Austria concurred, but on the definite understanding that Schleswig should not be united to Denmark, nor Holstein to Schleswig, and that the Germans of Schleswig should receive equal treatment with the Danes.   A proclamation on these lines and amplifying their significance, was issued by the Danish king; but there, to all intents and purposes, the matter ended.   The Government of the Duchies was carried on from Denmark as if they were dependencies; and in Schleswig the German-speaking population were denied the use of their mother-tongue in church and school.   So things continued for a decade.   Protests from Austria and Prussia, threats of 'federal execution' from the German Diet, judicious lectures from Lord John, and finally a despatch embodying a project of settlement—all proved unavailing;   and in 1863 matters came at last to a head.

That year is, in some respects, of crucial importance in the study of the Palmerston-Russell diplomacy, for events and circumstances combined to test the measure of their ability. Bismarck had just entered the lists where Napoleon had held the championship so long;   and these two great diplomatists, with the fortunes of the two chief Powers of the Continent in their keeping, were thus in the field together.   Also there were difficulties in the east and in the west, and there was a diplomatic interaction between the two.   Over and above all this the foundations of Metternich's and Castlereagh's great settlement at Vienna were plainly out of joint, and the structure everywhere in need of repair.   A better occasion for skilful diplomacy could hardly have been found.   Palmerston took to himself the management of the issue in the East, dictating the policy and drafting the despatches.[1]

Poland, emboldened by the liberation of Italy, had begun rattling its rusty chains;   and the liberal measures initiated by the Grand Duke Constantine went no way to quiet it.   Of the rights and wrongs of that unhappy country, an Englishman has need to speak with caution.   The Poles were the Irish of Eastern Europe.   Religion and temperament, internal dissension and political ineptitude had long made them a trouble to their neighbours;   and the Russians had adopted the method of alternately beating and coaxing them, which is not without its milder analogies in the proceedings of the English in Ireland even so late as the recent Premiership of a Welsh Liberal.   But whether or not Palmerston might have been better advised to clear the

[1] Russell, *Speeches and Despatches*, ii. 235.

mote—if, indeed, it was no bigger than a mote—out of his own eye before he set to work to remove the beam from the eye of the Russian Emperor, it was at any rate unpardonable to take the larger operation in hand without a pure motive, a clear policy, and a firm resolve to see matters through. Palmerston had none of these. His motive was the fear that the Emperor of the French, acting under the pressure both of nationalist and Catholic opinion, might gain a prestige that Britain did not share; his policy was moral platitude; his resolve went no further than pen and paper could carry it. A despatch, for which Russell was at any rate technically responsible, raised the plea, dismissed already and not unreasonably by the Russian Government in 1831, that Britain derived a right of interference in Poland from the Vienna Congress and invited Russia to do what Gortchakoff was in the position to retort had just been in a manner done under the benevolent régime of the Grand Duke—to endow Poland, that is, with national and representative institutions. "The despatch," observes a modern critic,[1] "did unbounded harm, both by encouraging the Poles to hope for foreign aid in a hopeless struggle and by enabling Bismarck to keep France, who might have aided the Poles, in play, whilst he was improving Prussian relations with Russia."

Embarrassed by Palmerston's diplomacy, Napoleon eventually fell back upon the idea, which was never at this period far from his mind, of a European Congress; and Russia might possibly have fallen in with it if she had been assured that the negotiations would enable her to barter the concession of Polish autonomy against rescission of the Black Sea Clauses of the Treaty of Paris. But Palmerston dallied, and as tales of Russian atrocities in Poland poured in, Russell got excited. It was in vain that the British Ambassador in Petersburg emphasised the urgency of clear decision. "The revolt," he wrote, "is spreading in the hope of foreign intervention. If the English Government do not mean to fight, let them say so, and stop the loss of life and the suffering attendant on a rising which, unaided, cannot succeed."[2]

The two old men neither meant to fight nor yet to say so. To do the former without French aid—and none was now

---

[1] Dr Reid, *Camb. Hist. of British Foreign Policy*, ii. 460.
[2] *F.O. Russia*, **631**, No. 335 (quoted in *Camb. Hist. of British Foreign Policy* ii. 462).

available—would have been silly; to do the latter would have been to shorten those academic exercises in putting other nations straight that they loved so well. But, where action was really intended, matters were moving. The criminals who had spoiled Poland of her liberties had got together; and France and England suddenly found themselves confronted with an understanding between the Three Powers of the Polish Partition. Napoleon made a final effort to save his face by suggesting a Congress that should review the whole settlement of 1815; but Russell would have none of it. Baffled and discomfited, the Western Governments were left to their reflections and recriminations and the Poles to take their beating.

The crisis in Poland exercised a marked effect upon the crisis in Schleswig-Holstein by dividing France from England and drawing Russia towards Prussia. Napoleon, with no more effective ally than Britain at his side, felt no disposition to thrust himself between the contentious Danes and the pugnacious Prussians; and Alexander, with a debt for aid in Poland to be paid off in Berlin, had no wish to cross the path of Bismarck. But in its earlier stages the Polish crisis had also exerted an effect upon the Danish Government by encouraging the belief that Europe was too busy or too distracted to attend to them. In March 1863 there was published the project of a new constitution for the Duchies in which, contrary to the undertaking given in 1852, Schleswig was formally united to Denmark, and Holstein brought into a kind of financial servitude. The German Confederation thundered again; and this time there were thunderbolts behind the thunder. The Danes, however, went fearlessly and foolishly on. The project of a constitution was replaced by an edict actually establishing it. Then at last, tired out, the German Confederation, with its odd assortment of Powers both small and great, resolved to move. A federal execution, or in plainer language the occupation of Holstein by the forces of the Confederation was decreed.

At this juncture the last sovereign of the House of Oldenburg —the King-Duke who had united Denmark and the Duchies— died. Christian of Glucksburg succeeded as of right to the Kingdom. But in the Duchies Legitimism and the German people alike declared for the Hereditary Prince of Augustenburg, the son of him who had renounced his claims.

The Treaty of London had, as the reader may remember, vested the double succession in Christian of Glucksburg—"the Protocol Prince," for so someone with a taste for alliteration was good enough to style him—or, as he had now become, Christian IX. of Denmark. With this arrangement, to which both the Prussian and Austrian Governments were party, rather than with the sentiment of the German people, Bismarck found it advisable for the moment to identify himself, for he had no use in his schemes for the Hereditary Prince of Augustenburg nor any wish needlessly to provoke the interference of France or England. It was, therefore, rather as the champion of those flouted conditions precedent to the Treaty of London, which had provided for the autonomy of both Duchies and the equality of the German and Danish inhabitants of Schleswig, than as the agent of the German Confederation, that Prussia, pushing some Saxon and Hanoverian troops before her and dragging an Austrian army in her wake, entered into occupation of Holstein at the close of 1863, and then, after dexterously separating herself from the honourable purpose of the Confederation to restore the Duke of Augustenburg, and cunningly persuading Austria into a kind of partnership in an indefinite but already ill-looking enterprise, proceeded in the beginning of the next year to occupy Schleswig also, not without fighting.

Neither Russell nor Palmerston had watched the development of the issue between the Danes and the Germans with an indifferent eye. Of Russell's notes and negotiations, both before and after the seizure of the Duchies by the great German Powers, it is indeed almost impossible to speak, so many were they, so complicated in detail, so empty of consequences. One despatch, however, inspired by Robert Morier, at that time a rising young diplomatist with a rare knowledge of German affairs, and soon, if not already, to be marked out for the distinction of Bismarck's hatred,[1] stands out conspicuous. It was drafted in 1862 before Frederick VII. died or Bismarck had got to work; and it was designed to enable Great Britain to extricate herself with credit from obligations that might become inconvenient. Its proposals were simple and sensible— autonomy in Holstein; autonomy in Schleswig with a consequent power to adjust the linguistic difficulty in that latter

[1] *Letters of Queen Victoria* (second series), i. 461.

Duchy by local arrangement; the apportionment of taxation amongst the three, or more accurately four integral parts of the united monarchy; and the adoption of local budgets. The plan had indeed but one defect; it was inacceptable to both parties to the dispute. The Prussians, it is true, countenanced it, but only on Morier's assurance that the Danes would refuse it, as in fact they did. Its defect was, however, from a British standpoint, its virtue. Russell had but to have left the matter there, and Britain must have been exonerated from further responsibility—would at the worst have lost no diplomatic battle, and at the best have brought the Danes to reason. He was not, however, constituted after this manner,[1] and in numerous communications continued to humour the Danes, whilst Bismarck in turn humoured him.

In the course of the next summer—the summer of 1863—Palmerston spoke with decision on the Danish side, unfurling the Union Jack, waving it grandly and wrapping up Denmark in its folds. His words were long remembered. If any attempt were made, he said, to interfere with Danish rights or Danish independence, "those who made the attempt would find in the result that it was not Denmark alone with which they would have to contend.[2] In his private correspondence with Russell just five months later and at the time when the occupation of the Duchies began, he was still more explicit in his language: "Holstein is part of the German Confederation; and if the Germans determine to commit therein an act of gross injustice and of diplomatic perfidy, we should content ourselves with a strong and indignant protest. But Schleswig is no part of Germany, and its invasion by German troops would be an act of war against Denmark, which would in my clear opinion entitle Denmark to our active military and naval support."[3]

So he thought, and so unluckily he had already to all intents and purposes implied. But his letter to Russell contained a caution which his speech in the House of Commons had lacked: "You and I," he said, "could not announce such a determination

---

[1] Morier asserts that Russell saw the point of the despatch and apparently thinks the Cabinet was the obstacle upon which he foundered (Morier, *Memoirs*, i. 385). I must confess I see nothing in his subsequent action to confirm this view.

[2] Speech in the House of Commons, 23rd July 1863.

[3] Walpole, *Life of Lord John Russell*, ii. 388.

without the concurrence of the Cabinet and the consent of the Queen." He had too often forgotten it; for in all this business they had had neither the concurrence of the one nor the consent of the other. A contest with Crown and Cabinet had proceeded all the while alongside of the contest with Bismarck. The Queen had never liked the Treaty of 1852: in the first place because the Prince Consort had disapproved of it—wisely enough, as it seems, since the English historian best qualified to judge has warned us that it was "in some of its consequences beyond all doubt one of the most unfortunate of the achievements of European diplomacy";[1] and in the second place because it drove a wedge between her own country and the country of which her eldest daughter would one day be queen. Victoria was consequently as determined as she could be not to go to war over Schleswig-Holstein; and to this end she scrutinised severely every despatch that Russell sent, and brought Palmerston sharply to book for one unauthorised, bellicose conversation.[2] Her services did not pass unrecognised by the rank and file of the Ministry. "The insistence of the Queen," wrote Granville,[3] "that all doubtful propositions should be well considered by the Cabinet has not only saved the Country, but the Government itself from many false steps." Ministers did not, perhaps, go all the way with the Sovereign, but they were at least resolved not to commit Great Britain further without an assurance of the co-operation of France.

"Timidity and weakness," Palmerston called it in a letter to Russell;[4] yet it was rather wisdom. To fight the great German Powers without France would have been folly; and Palmerston's policy in Poland had made co-operation impossible. There was no denying, Napoleon told Clarendon, that the French and British Governments had received one good box on the ear[5] over the Polish business, and a second was more than he could stand. Terms, indeed, existed, as Rouher intimated somewhat later, upon which the Emperor of the French would fight— terms that included the conquest of Venetia for Italy and a move forward towards the Rhine for France, but they were

---

[1] Sir A. W. Ward, in the *Camb. Hist. of British Foreign Policy*, ii. 538.
[2] See Walpole, *Life of Lord John Russell*, ii. 392-3.
[3] *Letters of Queen Victoria* (second series), i. 208.
[4] See Walpole, *Life of Lord John Russell*, ii. 392, footnote.
[5] *Gros soufflet.*

not such terms as Russell would accept. And of his own final expedient for settling the future of the Duchies without war—a new conference in London on the basis of the old London treaty—the Foreign Secretary made nothing. Neither Dane nor German had a will to peace. Bismarck, however, managed his case the more cleverly. Obstinate as ever, the Danes still fondly fancied that Britain was ever at their back. They fought; and Russell failed them. They were beaten; and Russell got them no redress. Schleswig and Holstein with Lauenburg passed into the keeping of Austria and Prussia. Not, however, so far as Austria was concerned, to remain there long! Bismarck was only waiting till he had done with his enemies to deal with his friend. The Danes had been first eliminated from the Duchies; then Augustenburg's claim had been disposed of; and finally the turn of Austria was come. Holstein was taken from her; she fought and was defeated at Sadowa; and her place in Germany knew her no more.

Palmerston, to whom the coming might of Prussia was as a book still sealed, did not live to see the end of these things; but we know that he would have viewed it without regret or apprehension. In a letter which has been described as his 'legacy to the nation,'[1] he affirmed with all the emphasis of repetition that "Germany ought to be strong in order to resist Russian aggression," and that "a strong Prussia is essential to German strength." So little do the opinions of John Bull in one age accord with his opinions in another!

Two rebuffs, then, formed the inglorious conclusion of Palmerston's diplomatic story, and if we look for an *envoi* we may find it in a document newly published. "When we had been praising Lord Granville," notes Victoria amongst her private memoranda, "Lord Halifax alluded to how badly foreign affairs had been conducted by Lord Russell and Lord Palmerston, saying it was not to be told what good I had done in that time by checking their reckless course, and that he would repeat that at any time to the world at large."[2] Halifax knew what he was talking about, for he had sat long in the Cabinet with the men of whom he spoke. But with the world at large other considerations outweighed the misconduct of foreign policy. Englishmen

---

[1] Lloyd Sanders, *Palmerston*, p. 237.
[2] *Letters of Queen Victoria* (second series), ii. 125.

saw in Palmerston a fine old fellow, eighty years of age yet still brimful of pluck and fight; and a general election in the summer of '65 left him strong in power.

It was his final triumph—a laurel wreath crowning his brows just before the virile, hard-worked body passed over into the cypress shade. In the autumn, before Parliament had met again, he was gone, suddenly, an unfinished letter and a half-open despatch box upon his writing-table showing both the haste of his departure and a vigour of industry continued to the end. Jaunty old man—let us think of him kindly as we pass 94 Piccadilly, where he entertained so genially, with Lady Palmerston, all charm and grace, confirming her husband in power by receiving at the head of the stairs. But, if we would see him only in relation to foreign policy and can bring ourselves to strip him of the glamour of great age, long service, incomparable energy, and a singular gift of leadership, we may find the epitaph that Victoria wrote upon him not so much amiss:—

" He had many valuable qualities though many bad ones, and we had, God knows ! terrible trouble with him about foreign affairs." [1]

Of Palmerston's coadjutor in so many enterprises—of his "oldest and best friend," [2] as Lady Palmerston called Lord John—a parting word remains to be said. The death of the Prime Minister enabled the Foreign Secretary to resign the Foreign Office, for which he was never made, and resume the Premiership, where his abilities secured their proper reward. Russell had, however, already outlived his political generation, and 'the last Whig Ministry' was no great success. After his defeat in 1866 he retired to the house which the Queen had given him in Richmond Park, contenting himself for the last decade of his life with excursions into politics and incursions into history. Upon him, too, Victoria's verdict may pass muster:—

" A man of much talent . . . kind and good, with a great knowledge of the Constitution, who behaved very well on many trying occasions ; but . . . was impulsive, very selfish . . . vain, and often reckless and imprudent." [3]

---

[1] *Letters of Queen Victoria* (second series), i. 279.
[2] Walpole, *Life of Russell*, ii. 434 (footnote).
[3] *Letters of Queen Victoria* (second series), ii. 625.

V

THE THREE WHIG EARLS

[George William Frederick Villiers.—Born 1800. Succeeded as 4th Earl of Clarendon, 1838. *Foreign Secretary,* 1853–1858, 1865–1866, and 1868–1870. Died 1870.]

[Granville George Leveson-Gower.—Born 1815. Under-Secretary of State for Foreign Affairs, 1840–1841. Succeeded as 2nd Earl Granville, 1846. *Foreign Secretary,* 1851–1852, 1870–1874, 1880–1885. Died 1891.]

[Archibald Philip Primrose.—Born 1847. Succeeded as 5th Earl of Rosebery, 1868. *Foreign Secretary,* 1886 and 1892–1894. Prime Minister, 1894–1895.]

THE THREE WHIG EARLS

A Whig, says the dictionary, is a Liberal opposed to further progress in democracy. Evidently then, as democracy is fulfilled, Whiggery must cease to be, and Whigs withdraw into private life. And thus in fact it has been. That feudal eminence rising oddly in a champaign of equalitarian ideas, where the greater Whigs were wont to dispense and the lesser Whigs to receive benevolent counsels in praise of freedom, has been gradually undermined by the destruction of privilege, so that of the party which shot so gracefully the rapids of 1688, 1714, and 1832, instituting constitutional monarchy in the person of William III., a premier responsible to Parliament in the person of Walpole, and popular government through the wise action of Grey, there remains now nothing to be seen but here and there some human anachronism cast in the mould of a more spacious or gracious age than our own. With the resignation of Russell the last Whig Administration passed away—how completely only became apparent when, some three years later, after Gladstone's retirement, the transient and embarrassed struggles of the last Whig Prime Minister were disclosed to view.

At the Foreign Office, however, Whiggery was longer welcome. In that "last choice preserve of administration, practised as a sport," [1] in that last home of aristocratic privilege whose communications were still so largely mixed up with courts and kings, the officials were well pleased, amid the doubts and fears attending any 'progressive' Government in a time of change, to have some unexceptionable representative of the old order at its head. And Gladstone never failed them. Whatever his mistakes in foreign policy his three Foreign Secretaries stand out as the exquisite, polished products of that exclusive political academy where rank and birth and a liberal education are the

[1] Professor J. S. Phillimore.

presiding, equivalent graces. Clarendon and Granville, indeed, he inherited, but Rosebery was of his own finding, most brilliant yet most industrious, a bright particular star. We shall speak of the three first together and then one by one.

Whigs then they were, and as Whigs the student of diplomacy may do well to see them; for they filled no place in either of the great schools of British foreign policy. They are neither in the line of Castlereagh nor yet of Canning. They framed no system, embodied no principle, and have left no lasting mark upon the road we travel. They did but bridge the gaps of a period of change, carrying forward the foreign business of the nation in the best manner of gentlemen of their persuasion, with fine courtesy, shrewd observation, and more or less dexterous opportunism. Yet, for all that the nation owes them the praise of remembrance. They were for compass in a party that otherwise had sailed on foreign waters by naked theory; cosmopolitan when National-ism was but too ready to drive blindly into revolution, imperialist when Little-Englandism threatened to fill the canvas. In the middle part of the reign of Victoria, after Castlereagh's system of congresses was dead and before Salisbury's method of a European concert had yet been evolved, Clarendon and Granville kept alive, informally and unobtrusively, that sense of international relation-ship which is the first word and the last in diplomatic wisdom; and later, when Britain was still but half inclined to welcome her heritage of empire, it fell to Granville to take a momentous decision, pregnant with remote consequences, both foreign and colonial, in regard to Egypt, and to Lord Rosebery to uphold by precept and example the standard of imperial destiny.

The foreign touch of Palmerston had been rough and that of Russell cold. The touch of Clarendon, of Granville, and of Rose-bery was a courtier's touch; and they were the better Whigs for that. It formed some part of the propriety of their appointment to the conduct of foreign affairs that the greatest Whig of the period was seated on the throne. We ought never to forget that Victoria was in her day and in her way as good a diplomatist as her son. She had once, though the fact has been long forgotten, the same power as he of evoking enthusiasm in the European capital, whose plaudits we commonly associate with jovial souls like François Premier or Henri Quatre, or great conquerors like Napoleon. "I hear from various quarters," writes Clarendon of her visit to Paris in 1855, "that no foreigner—royal or other—has ever had the same success with this fastidious people. . . . The unaccountable dignity with the short stature, the *bienveillance* of manner and the gracious *sourire* seem to have walked into their hearts." [1] Victoria's services to the Franco-British understanding were indeed incalculable. As she had a way with the people so she had also a way with the shifting dynasties that ruled them. She was well liked both by the Bourbons and the Bonapartes; her affectionate nature, honesty of purpose, and goodness of heart winning their affections; her Whiggery making it easy for her to accept in turn Louis Philippe who had the semblance of a usurper, and Napoleon III. who had the aspect of a *parvenu*. A genius for friendship with crowned heads sparkles among her political qualities; and her own and her husband's relationships and the marriage of her children strengthened her hands. In this manner her private correspondence came to possess such an international importance as a world more or less republicanised can hardly hope to see again; and her Foreign Ministers used and valued her help in maintaining the peace of Europe. France, which covered her with scandalous abuse in her extreme old age, owes to her direct intervention in 1875 its deliverance from German menaces, and perhaps from those menaces put into effect; and it would be unjust to dissociate the comparative immunity from war of Great Britain during her long reign from her presence on the throne. Of those who, during her time, controlled in turn the finest armies of the Continent, the Third Napoleon would have shrunk from attacking her; and as much might be said of the first German Emperor, and the second, and even, perhaps, the third. She had become, by the end of her reign, a kind of mother in Europe, whose advice could not be lightly disregarded, whose very personality afforded her country a sort of protection from its enemies. Her abilities will be differently estimated, her character variously judged; but about the greatness of her place in the Europe of her time there can be no serious disagreement. She was, on the whole, the most regal figure that had sat upon the throne since the famous days of Elizabeth; and of such a sovereign the Whig Earls were well fitted to be the foreign ministers.

Clarendon—to treat of these three now each in his turn—was

[1] Maxwell, *Life of Clarendon*, ii. 90.

born on the eve of his century,[1] with the blood of Cromwell as well
as of Hyde coursing through his veins, the great name of Villiers
to his back, an impecunious valetudinarian for a father, a woman
of the world for a mother, and the expectation without the assurance of inheriting an earldom from an uncle.   Nature endowed
him with a courtier's manners, a linguist's talents, and a statesman's address.   Fortune added what hardly any other British
Foreign Secretary can be said to have possessed, a diplomatist's
training—Fortune, that is, with Palmerston for her agent.   It
was Palmerston who picked the young man out of the com-
missionership of customs, into which poverty had persuaded
him, and sent him off as British Minister to Madrid.   Thus
began the singular connection between the two men—a connection, on Clarendon's side, never wanting in gratitude; on
Palmerston's part, kindly and paternal at the start, coloured
later, when Clarendon had grown in wisdom and stature, by
jealousy and suspicion, but again, in the conclusion, intimate
and frequent.[2]

The young diplomat found at Madrid every possible opportunity
of practising his trade.   " I am convinced," he writes to his sister,
who was perhaps his most intimate confidant and his best adviser,
"that I have improved more in my profession during two years
here than I should in twenty as ambassador in Paris." [3]   He
was, in fact, required to play between 1832 and 1837 the part
which Bulwer played so badly later, and to meddle without
giving offence in the internal politics of Spain.   Of the quarrels
of Carlists and Cristinos, of Moderados and Progressistas, however, enough has already elsewhere been said.   Clarendon did
his work as well as a man might and returned with a great
reputation for ability.   He had incidentally also acquired a
reputation—too great a reputation—for gallantry; and his
candid biographer is not proof against the temptation of telling
us, what is indeed curious enough in view of the subsequent close
relations of the two men principally concerned, that Napoleon III.
himself taxed Madame de Montijo with a liaison that would have
made Eugénie Clarendon's daughter—a charge repudiated indeed
so far as the Empress's parentage was concerned, yet in such a

---

[1] January 1800.
[2] Maxwell states that in one year (1857) Palmerston wrote to Clarendon
310 letters, some very long (*Life of Clarendon*, ii. 299).
[3] *Life of Clarendon*, i. 99.

manner as to confirm the rest of the story.[1]   It is to be feared in
fact that, golden as were the opinions Villiers at all times won by
being, as his family doctor was pleased to phrase it, "more
actively kind than a hundred parsons put together," [2] he was in
some respects ill-calculated to be the exemplar of that superiority
of Protestant to Catholic morality, which Borrow, carrying his
Bible with him into Spain just at this time, attempted to enforce.
Although, after some preliminary hesitation, he favoured that
singular enthusiast with so substantial an order for New Testa-
ments that Borrow forthwith credited him with having received
a particular illumination,[3] Lady Verulam was not a little agitated
at the prospect of accepting the gay diplomatist as a son-in-law,[4]
and not the less perhaps that he made his advances to her
daughter, almost without concealment, from the standpoint of a
mariage de convenance.   But the event falsified high romance
and vindicated cold calculation.   Clarendon had told his brother
that without being in love, he was satisfied that Lady Katharine
was the person of all others best suited to him, and he in his turn
suited to her; [5] and he proved to be correct in both points.

The twelvemonth that lay between the Christmas of 1838 and
the Christmas of 1839 forms a landmark in Clarendon's life.   In
the course of it he received the news of his uncle's death and of
his own accession to the family title; he left Spain; he married
Lady Katharine Barham; [6] and he entered the Cabinet as Lord
Privy Seal.   The last event was a sufficiently high compliment,
and not the less so that he had never sat in a Cabinet before and
had just declined in succession to become Governor of Canada,
Master of the Mint, and Postmaster-General.   Melbourne was
evidently determined not to let such abilities as his go idle.

Foreign affairs, naturally enough, exercised the mind of the
ex-diplomatist, as with Palmerston at the Foreign Office they
might very well do.   The Government was in the throes of the
dispute, elsewhere described, between Sultan and Pasha,[7] with
Palmerston backing the former for all he was worth.   Clarendon
took occasion to submit to the Foreign Secretary a very remarkable paper urging that British interests lay rather in the direction

---

[1] The story will be found in Maxwell, *Life of Clarendon*, ii. 91.
[2] *Ibid.*, ii. 112.   [3] *Bible in Spain*, chap. xx.
[4] *Life of Clarendon*, i. 153.   [5] *Ibid.*, p. 155.
[6] She was a widow, *née* Grimston.
[7] The Sultan of Turkey and the Pasha of Egypt (Mehemet Ali).

of Egypt than of Turkey; that Mehemet Ali's administration had more life in it than Abd-ul-Mejid's; that Turkey would defend Constantinople the better and not the worse for the loss of Syria and Arabia, turbulent provinces likely to exhaust and not consolidate her strength; and, finally, that the support of Mehemet Ali was best calculated to maintain the good understanding between Britain and France.

This difference of policy led to a sharp difference of opinion in the Cabinet, and both Palmerston and Clarendon offered to resign. But Melbourne held his Cabinet together with familiar cynicism. "Either policy would do," he wrote to Clarendon, "if firmly and summarily adopted; otherwise neither." [1] As a matter of fact the occasion was crucial in the history of the Eastern Question; and Clarendon, had his regard for principle been the equal of his insight, might probably have pressed his resignation. "He is weak," one wrote of him who knew him well, "because he acts on expediency only." [2] And at this date expediency came to him clothed in all the strength of party feeling. He was, in fact, at no pains to conceal that his strongest reason for not going out of office himself was the fear that by so doing he might let a Tory Government in.[3] Thus Palmerston carried the day, not without personal as well as public consequences. The incident certainly served to deepen the growing distrust with which the older man was beginning to view his protégé. For all that, Clarendon contrived to execute with success the commission, entrusted to him as the member of the Cabinet most friendly to France by Thiers, of inviting the British Government to approve the removal of the ashes of Napoleon from St Helena to the Invalides. All his native tact appears in his letter to the French Foreign Minister acceding to the request, as no doubt it also appeared in his private communications with Palmerston upon a subject which lay properly within the province of the Foreign Secretary and not of the Privy Seal. He had acquired, by nature or by grace, that sublime knowledge of the management of human beings in general which is embodied in one of his particular observations upon Palmerston. "Like everybody else," he said of that jaunty, arrogant, yet not quite intractable creature, "he requires to be dealt with in his own fashion."

There is no point in following Clarendon's career through the

[1] *Life of Clarendon*, i. 195.   [2] *Ibid.*, ii. 112.   [3] *Ibid.*, ii. 368.

decade that elapsed between the fall of Melbourne's Administration in 1841 and the formation of Aberdeen's in 1852. He was partly in opposition, then for a brief moment in 1846 President of the Board of Trade, and finally from 1847 to 1851 Viceroy of Ireland, where his reign was signalised by the passing of an Encumbered Estates Act and by one of those too infrequent visits of the Queen to her turbulent but royalist subjects across the Irish Channel. For a moment, indeed, when in 1852 Palmerston was driven from the Foreign Department by the Queen and Russell, his claims to the succession were freely discussed by the Cabinet and openly admitted by the Prime Minister. But his love of office was never more than platonic; and on this occasion a scruple restrained him. He was aware that Palmerston regarded him as an ambitious rival, and he was under an old obligation to Palmerston that he could not forget. He made it clear, therefore, to Russell that he cherished no wish to fill the vacant place; and Russell, realising that upon Clarendon, had he accepted, would have fallen the brunt of Palmerston's powerful displeasure, was grateful for so handsome a withdrawal.

It was in these circumstances that Granville first came to the front. A diplomatist by nature and by birth the son of a diplomatist, Leveson—as he still was at that time—had made his ministerial *début* in 1840 as Palmerston's Under-Secretary at the Foreign Office and had subsequently consolidated his reputation for tact by organising with conspicuous success the Great Exhibition of 1851. All the rest that requires to be said of him by way of introduction can be compressed into a word, for nicknames are sometimes so happily chosen as to save the writing of a character. Granville was known as "Puss"; and neither cat nor man perhaps ever purred his way through business better. Two short months, which was all he had in his first term at the Foreign Office, gave him indeed but little chance to prove his merit. Yet, even so, Russell found it in his heart, when the Government fell, to write to him that the country was losing one of the best foreign secretaries it had ever had, and the Queen gave him an assurance of her satisfaction at seeing the methods and manners of Palmerston so admirably reversed. At her request Granville drew up a memorandum, unavoidably composed of full-bodied platitudes, on the subject of British foreign policy, the effect of which was to convey that every issue must be settled upon its own merits, and, for the rest, that Britain did best to cultivate intimate relations with countries having institutions accordant with her own.

Admirably as Granville had discharged his duties, it was Clarendon whom Aberdeen marked down as next choice for the Foreign Secretaryship whenever Russell should find it no longer possible to combine its duties with those of Leader in the Commons. Nor was the Prime Minister's judgment at fault, for Clarendon was unquestionably the abler man of the two. Granville, by way of compensation, was accommodated with the Presidency of the Council, which is the pleasantest arm-chair in the Cabinet, and subsequently with the Duchy of Lancaster, which has been irreverently styled its cushion. He accepted and indeed encouraged these diminutions of power, if not of dignity, in his usual handsome way.

Clarendon's first tenure of the Foreign Office covered the whole period of the Crimean War—its inception, its course, and its conclusion. It was by far the most important matter that he ever had to deal with, and by his handling of it his measure as a diplomatist must in the main be taken. To a man of Clarendon's temperament and opinions, the issue was bound to appear in a very different light than it did to Aberdeen or to Palmerston. To the former, as the reader will recollect, the cause of Christian civilisation, which the Russians, however imperfectly, represented, was always a larger consideration than the particular rights and wrongs of the conflict. To the latter, on the other hand, Turkey had always seemed a country susceptible of effective regeneration. And these two opinions were in practice, if not absolutely in logic, contrary the one to the other. Russell, the next leading personality in the Cabinet, followed Palmerston afar off, but had been—which was of much more consequence—responsible, during his few weeks conduct of foreign affairs, for sending Stratford de Redcliffe back to Constantinople. That famous cousin of George Canning's had in his bones the diplomatic ability of his more famous relative and a double dose of his diplomatic arrogance. "He is a pasha,"[1] wrote Graham, "too long accustomed to rule alone." Clarendon grew to be only too well aware of it before the Crimean business

[1] Or as Graham spells it ' bashaw,' *Life of Clarendon*, ii. 12.

ended. He had to his own undoing agreed with Russell that Stratford was the best man for the place, but his correspondence contains more than one bitter lamentation over the mischief that Stratford was doing to the negotiations through unbridled hatred of Russia. Cowley, he thought—calling to mind one who deserves, though he does not possess, a greater name than Stratford—or the like of Cowley, would have settled the whole trouble without delay.[1]

The effort to bring into line these contending wills and counsels without a rupture caused Clarendon's own essentially untheoretical point of view to be the more obscured. As little affected perhaps by that faith in Christian civilisation, which was to Aberdeen an anchor of hope and to Gladstone a flag of battle in international politics, as by Palmerston's faith in Turkish regeneration or Stratford's fear of Russia, his vision scarcely travelled—or at least travelled without gathering effective purpose—outside the province of diplomacy into those larger considerations of policy that lie beyond the urgent business of the day. It was Granville's belief that the war ought not to have occurred, and would not have occurred if either Palmerston or Aberdeen had had their way.[2] The interest of the opinion lies in the fact that it came from one whose habit of mind was not dissimilar from Clarendon's own. If it has substance, it is not merely a criticism of his colleague but of the whole Whig position in foreign affairs with its want of clear principles and ultimate aims and decisive values. And a phrase of Clarendon's which has become classic by reason of his use of it just as the negotiations merged in the catastrophe, but which occurs much earlier in his private correspondence with his wife—"drifting towards war"[3]—conveys a sense of helplessness in face of circumstances which may be read or not, as we please, in the light of a confession. If he failed for lack of purpose every allowance at least ought to be made for a man almost intolerably harassed. His correspondence shows him bored by Aberdeen's long, anxious conversations, provoked by that 'cockiness' in Palmerston which led him to suspect a secret understanding with Stratford, distressed by Russell's inopportune and contentious preoccupation with a

---

[1] *Life of Clarendon*, ii. 25. [2] Fitzmaurice, *Life of Granville*, i. 97.
[3] *Life of Clarendon*, ii. 30, 40.

Reform Bill, when nothing was more necessary than that the Cabinet should hold together, and, last and worst, increasingly distrustful of Stratford's conduct of affairs at Constantinople, increasingly convinced, whether with justice or not, of Stratford's determination to force on war.[1]   No man perhaps ever tried to control so complex an international crisis with a Cabinet, torn by the differences between three ex-foreign secretaries, behind him, and at the very seat and centre of diplomatic operations, a subordinate, too powerful to be compelled to obey, too dangerous to be recalled.[2]   In such circumstances the line of least resistance has much to make it tempting, and Clarendon followed it from the first.   Russell had just rejected the Russian Emperor's famous proposal of 1853 for the partition of Turkey; and Clarendon was content to leave things so.   The suggestion, nevertheless, so far as it had shape, proceeded precisely on the lines of his own earlier argument with Palmerston—some day to be triumphantly vindicated by events—that the essential interest of England lay in Egypt.   For the rest, France, in Nicholas's project, would have been invited to take Syria, which she has taken to-day; the Turks would have been replaced, as they ought to be replaced in Asia whence they came; Constantinople would have been converted into a free city; Serbia and Bulgaria would have become autonomous kingdoms under Russian protection, whilst Austrian assent to the project would presumably have been bought with the cession to her of Bosnia and Herzegovina.   In practice the project would have averted some Balkan wars and avoided several European crises; would, at the worst, have substituted tolerable for intolerable maladministration over a large part of the old Turkish Empire, and, at the best, have given to the luckless subject-races under Turkish rule the blessings of civilised government.   In principle it would have countenanced nothing more shocking than rebellion against an alien ruler which contemporary notions of the rights of nationalities had

---

[1] *Life of Clarendon*, ii. 29.   Clarendon to Cowley, 10th November 1853: " He (Stratford de Redcliffe) is *bent on war* and on playing the first part in settling the great Eastern Question, as Lady S. de R. admitted to me two days ago he now considered it to be—that the time was come and *the man was there* for curbing the insolence of Russia and resettling the balance of power in Europe."

[2] *Cf.* Clarendon to Cowley, 9th March 1855 (*Life of Clarendon*, ii. 68): " What a pest that man (Stratford de Redcliffe) is !   If I recalled him, however, he would make peace impossible."

already begun to approve, nor have established anything more questionable than the control of the less-advanced by the more-advanced people of mankind which the modern system of mandates now boldly affirms. It was, in short, an adequate plan for reclaiming for Europe the breeding-ground of half her quarrels from the ruthless race that kept it rank—how adequate the reader may decide by reflecting that the scheme represents substantially such a settlement as the three great combatant Powers in the Crimean War, who were also the three great Allied Powers in the Great War, would probably have agreed upon, had they emerged victorious with equal honours from the recent struggle for hegemony in Europe! One important difference, it is true, there would have been, yet that difference all to the British advantage. Had Bolshevism not overthrown the Romanoffs, Russia would have claimed Constantinople in 1919. In 1853 she would have been content to see it a free city.

The Russian offer was rejected by Russell with frigid politeness; and Clarendon, though the Emperor's advances had not ceased when on 21st February 1853 he took over the seals of the Foreign Office, made no effort to reverse his predecessor's decision. The light-hearted fashion in which this great refusal was made is susceptible of excuse in the case of both one and the other, for a deeper responsibility than theirs rests with Sir George Seymour, the British Ambassador at Petersburg, who had received and transmitted the Emperor's proposal. In Seymour's judgment Nicholas remained at heart in favour of maintaining the Turkish Empire as it was; and he destroyed all the significance of his official despatches by a private communication to this effect.[1] A reference to the Emperor's offer, subsequently so famous, in Lady Clarendon's journal [2] leaves the impression that Clarendon, too, was readily content to see Nicholas's fateful suggestion through Seymour's fatal eyes. The sibyl of the occasion, like the sibyl of the Roman fable, had twice tendered her full complement of wisdom only to find her gifts unvalued and have her treasure spurned. She appeared, indeed, again, but with a lighter load. To Clarendon, after that fag-end of an opportunity at the outset of his administration, there came no chance of effecting any final settlement of the Eastern question; some temporary accommodation and a war avoided was the best that he could hope for.

[1] Walpole, *Life of Russell*, ii. 180.   [2] *Life of Clarendon*, ii. 39.

Tout comprendre c'est tout pardonner, says the familiar adage. Nicholas's proceedings are at least very easy to understand, and perhaps to excuse. Alarmed at the sudden revival by the French Emperor of a long-forgotten interest, prejudicial to that of the Orthodox Greeks, in the Holy Places of Palestine, and disappointed of his hope that Britain would enter into an agreement with him for the partition of the Turkish Empire, he resolved to draw matters to a head and Turkey in Europe towards its coffin.

Clarendon, suddenly thrust, and for the first time, into the Foreign Office in the spring of 1853, was perhaps excusably slow in realising that what seemed to be a "churchwarden's quarrel" about the keys of the Holy Sepulchre was rather the gathering of eagles in expectation of a carcase. The 'hang' of things was hard to get—harder still to adjust. Russell, by hastiness, had queered the pitch as regards Russia; Rose—the British Chargé d'Affaires in Turkey—by more hastiness, queered it as regards France as well. When Menshikoff, charged with Nicholas's demands, descended upon Constantinople in a splendour almost more military than diplomatic, Rose caught the infection of the Turkish fears, and, without any orders from home, summoned the fleet from Malta. The French, of course, took alarm—Britain, they thought, might be stealing a march upon them—and the French fleet forthwith appeared at Salamis. Europe, as Dufferin used to say, is a bundle of nerves. All the great Powers of Europe became nervous, and Stratford's appearance on the scene added to their discomfort. He came to Constantinople, that historic figure, armed with the dignity of his office, the prestige of his personality, the long reach of his experience; armed with the authority that he rightly had, and the contempt of authority that he boldly dared; hating the Russians, despising the French, dominating the Turks; a man, the like of whom is not found in the annals of our diplomacy—he came to Constantinople, he saw, and swiftly he conquered. It was in the April of 1853 that he arrived, and, before May was out, he had sent Menshikoff packing, all his mission spoiled and all his plans discovered.

The affair was a nice example of neat diplomacy. The Russian Ambassador had bound up the business of the Holy Places with a larger demand for the recognition of a Russian protectorate over the Orthodox subjects of the Sultan. Stratford disentangled the two claims—advised the Porte to concede the former, persuaded the French Ambassador to concur in the surrender, and thus exposed to the world, in all its nakedness, the second point of Menshikoff's embassy. But, though the aim of Russia was made naked, there appears to have been no obvious reason why she should be ashamed. Her claim to protect the Orthodox Christians of Turkey differed in degree but not in kind from that of France to protect Turkish Catholics; and, what was more, Russell, in the course of his short term at the Foreign Office, had not only admitted its validity but had actually gone out of his way to declare that it fulfilled an obligation "prescribed by duty and sanctioned by treaty." [1] In these circumstances the rout of Menshikoff and the refusal by the Turks to sign the Russo-Turkish Convention that he proferred them, bore all the stamp of Stratford's personal and implacable hatred of Russia. Nicholas, of course, with his strong autocratic disposition—as strong and as autocratic as Stratford's own — was furious. After one last warning to the Turks that they must swallow the Convention with its recognition of the Russian protectorate or take the consequences, he caused his troops to occupy the Danubian Principalities. It would have been better for him if the Turks had fought; but Stratford was too clever for that. He left the Russian armies hanging inert between peace and war, whilst the opinion of Europe rallied and consolidated against the invasion of Turkish territory.

The great rulers of Europe, with the possible exception of Napoleon III., whose enigmatic purpose is to this day a matter of ardent dispute, were pacifically disposed. Above all was this true in Vienna, where Buol became the mediator of a settlement. The famous Vienna Note, inspired by France and secretly communicated to Russia, was his handiwork. Its language in regard to the vexed question of the Protectorate was vague, yet scarcely vaguer than the issue. Intervention of some kind on the part of Russia between the Sultan and his Orthodox subjects was evidently intended and was, in fact, recognised by a reference to the old treaty of Kutchuk-Kainardji. Was it possible so to police all the avenues of that intervention

[1] Quoted in *Camb. Hist. of British Foreign Policy*, ii. 340.

that Russia could not, if she would, abuse them? No treaty, drafted never so wisely, could have given effect to that. The safety of Turkey from hectoring interventions on the part of her northern neighbour rested in no form of words, but in the assurance, should she ever deserve it, of European support. So, at least, Clarendon, whose acceptance of the vague language of the Vienna Note has been sharply criticised,[1] presumably saw the situation. Stratford, however, whose business it was to press that Note upon the Turks, certainly saw it otherwise; and the Turks perceived, or, as many critics have supposed, were purposely allowed to perceive, the private sentiments that lurked behind his official representations. Sensible of his tacit approval, they amended the Note, which Russia had already approved in the form submitted by the Powers.

The amendments, as anyone may see who takes the trouble to study them,[2] were not of a character to put difficulties in the way of a strong Power resolved upon the coercion of a weak one. They were, in fact, as they have been called, 'puerile,' or, as Aberdeen more politely observed, "not of great importance." But, if their legal importance was small, their diplomatic importance was great, and Clarendon detected the master-hand of Stratford behind them.[3] To press the amendments of the feeble Turks upon the powerful Russians would be an intolerable offence to Russian prestige; to press the unamended Note of the mediating Powers upon the still more feeble Turkish Government would have provoked a palace revolution at Constantinople and substituted a Sultan bent on war for the existing, tractable occupant of the Prophet's throne.[4] The entanglement, as Clarendon wrote to his brother-in-law, was the most curious and embarrassing that ever six great nations were in.[5] The Russians had, however, so much the best of the position that Aberdeen, Palmerston, and Clarendon were agreed, much to Russell's annoyance, in approving pressure on the part of the Powers to make the Turks submit.

An indiscretion on the part of Russia—one of those accidents

---

[1] *Camb. Hist. of British Foreign Policy*, ii. 351.
[2] They are given in the *Camb. Hist. of British Foreign Policy*, ii. 370.
[3] *Life of Clarendon*, ii. 18. " I have all along felt," he wrote to Russell, " that Stratford would allow of no plan of settlement that did not originate with himself."
[4] *Ibid.*, ii. 20.   [5] *Ibid.*, p. 20.

that seem the finger of Fate itself—destroyed sympathy with her position and faith in her integrity. The Russian Minister for Foreign Affairs communicated his reasons for rejecting the Turkish amendments to the Russian Minister at Berlin; and these reasons made their appearance in a Prussian newspaper. They displayed a conception of the meaning of the Note at variance with that of the Powers. But for this the Turkish Government must have swallowed the Note in its original form with nothing better than an assurance from Nicholas and a guarantee from the Powers that nothing prejudicial to Turkish sovereignty was intended. As it was, the Note was discredited; the Conference, though not dissolved, was split; and both France and England were compelled from that time onward to lean in the direction of Turkey. The Turks perceived their new advantage, launched an ultimatum against Russia, and finally made war. Simultaneously the fleets of the Western Powers, anchored till lately in Besika Bay, moved up towards the Dardanelles.

Britain stood now at the parting of the ways; and Clarendon in the very valley of decision. More harassed, as his wife noted,[1] than she had ever seen him, he is most worth observing at this supreme crisis of his administration by those who seek to take the measure of his strength. Distracted by the rival counsels of his colleagues in the background, sensible of the strong hand of Stratford in the forefront of operations, he betrays himself by a kind of fatalism rather than a fund of resourcefulness. What else, indeed, are we to make of such admissions as these: " I verily believe that if two or three sensible people, meaning honestly and having real power to treat, were to meet together for an hour, the whole thing might be settled." " I see little chance of averting war, which, even in the most sacred cause, is a horrible calamity; but, for such a cause as two sets of barbarians quarrelling over a form of words, it is not only shocking but incredible." [2] Very able, very humane, very much trusted by both parties in the Coalition Government, very well alive to the triviality of the dispute and the magnitude of the impending consequences, Clarendon proved somehow unable to take control of the situation, with the inevitable result that it took hold of him. Whigs, perhaps, have never quite

[1] *Life of Clarendon*, ii. 26. [2] *Ibid.*, pp. 25, 26.

mastered the meaning of purpose with a big P. Negotiations were indeed kept going some few weeks longer, for Russia was in no hurry to assume the offensive against the Turks until the winter was past. But the presence of French and British ships in the Euxine rendered them useless; and a naval engagement in the Black Sea between the Russian and Turkish fleets revealed the partialities of the Western Powers. The "massacre of Sinope," where the vessels of Islam were sent to the bottom, was technically no more "a massacre" than the battle of Trafalgar; and its absurd nickname discovers as nothing else could do the excited mentality of the British Public.

At sea, in fact, as on land the Turks by strong aggression were drawing their patrons after them. Clarendon was not unconscious of it.[1] Still, however, whilst the busy mediators at Vienna fashioned yet another Note, the Western Fleets moved on and up, past Constantinople, through the Bosphorus, into the Euxine. Their new advance had been the especial care in France of the Emperor, in England of Palmerston. They carried explicit orders; they were to drive all Russian ships of war back into port, so that the Turks should suffer no new Sinope by sea or land. These orders came to Nicholas's knowledge the day before he received the new Note from Vienna. He rejected it angrily. So does it sometimes happen that the last hopes of such as strive for peace are baulked and beaten by the fears of such as seek to be betimes with war!

Not hastily, not under the pressure of some swift turn of events, but by slow and halting steps down a long valley of decision, Clarendon had brought his country into the only continental war with which it had to do between the fall of Napoleon and the European convulsion of 1914. There are still some who will judge that he acted rightly; that Russian ambition required to be curbed; that the Balkan States were not yet ripe for freedom. Such speculative considerations are in a way unanswerable; and Clarendon and his colleagues deserve the benefit of them. Yet they must weigh light in the balance against the fact that statesmanship, reluctant and resisting, has little by little been forced to take the road that Aberdeen weakly desired and Palmerston and Stratford boldly

---

[1] *Life of Clarendon,* ii. 33 (Russell to Clarendon, 8th December 1853: " You talk of Turkey making a war of aggression on Russia").

spurned. So much of the object purchased; what of the price that was paid? Of that let one of Clarendon's most vivacious and delightful correspondents speak first; and then the grave historian of the period. In the September of 1854 Clarendon received from Miss Emily Eden a letter conveying in a few sentences the three everlasting emotions of the onlooker in the day of battle—expectancy, admiration, wretchedness. "I am not fit," she wrote, "for anything but to sit and wait for the paper and then to cry over it . . . partly from excitement, for it is a stirring thing to read of our men marching through that river and up that hill as they did; and partly from thinking of the miserable wives and mothers and sisters then reading that same paper and the happiness of their whole lives sinking away from them. Une seule ligne pour l'annoncer— un instant pour le lire, et tout est fini pour elles—fini sans retour." [1] Six hundred thousand men, Spencer Walpole calculates,[2] perished in that shadowy contest about a Russian protectorate, nor is this yet for him the conclusion of the tale. He perceives in the Crimea the cradle of all that mass of fighting which, after a peace that had lasted forty years, rolls up for two decades in five successive storms, darkening the face of Europe with blood and iron. We may charitably hope that his thesis is exaggerated. So vast a weight of wars has policy seldom exacted to curb ambition! Be that as it may, the forty years during which Europe had rest were past and gone. The golden hours had slipped by, and their bowl was broken; the silver cord of international understanding that had seemed so strong after the First Napoleon fell was loosed; at the bidding of another Bonaparte, the pitcher of poor Humanity was to be broken once more at the cistern of life.

War came in the February of 1854 in response to the enthusiasm of war. Britons stood shoulder to shoulder in the simple faith that "the Tsar" was a tyrant and freedom in peril; any that looked back at the rights and wrongs of the quarrel seemed to their countrymen even as strangers and pacifists. Who does not know the rest? In due course the soldiers of the Queen gathered and went forth to die for Turk and Sultan. Late in time, Miss Nightingale—not then, nor till many years later, deemed to be a fitting subject for the pen of the satirist—took out

---

[1] *Life of Clarendon,* ii. 46.   [2] *Camb. Mod. Hist.,* xi. 324.

her devoted band of nurses and won by work and duty the highest prize of her generation. New names, long since forgotten, were added to the roll of honour; new battles, among which Balaclava towers, took their place in story. British valour was praised; British efficiency questioned; British authorities, both civil and military, cast into a like condemnation. The *Times*, which was edited by Delane, denounced the Government and the High Command; and Clarendon in his turn denounced the *Times*.[1] Everything in truth proceeded on lines all too familiar; and everyone was just as great in spirit, resolution, suffering, and speech as if the cause were greater. And all the while the mourners went about the streets!

Amid this turmoil of grief and fear, whilst reputations rose and fell, and the Premiership passed from Aberdeen's hands to Palmerston's, Clarendon kept his post, there being no man more generally acceptable to discharge its duties. Under his guidance Diplomacy, converted like other organs of the Body Politic to casual uses, was active at first in cementing and extending, or at least seeking to extend, alliances; then, later, in probing and exploring the possibilities of peace. The Foreign Secretary permitted himself all hopes and spared himself no pains in the search for allies. Austria, which depended for its existence upon diplomacy and not on war, proved, however, too old a bird to be caught by any chaff of his. Whilst others fought, she quietly manœuvred the Russians out of the Danubian Principalities, thus removing, almost before the war had properly begun, the main cause of the fighting. Secure, by virtue of the pledge that she had taken, against any attempt to exclude her from the settlement, she gave the Allies just so much countenance as was calculated to hasten peace, but nothing more. Of Prussia, Clarendon made still less than Austria; upon Spain and Denmark he tried his blandishments in vain. Only in Sweden and Sardinia, where solid interest prompted, and only then towards the close of the struggle, did he charm to any purpose. His main preoccupation, however, was, of course, Napoleon, for the Emperor of the French, though Palmerston was not disposed to recognise it, alone had troops

---

[1] *Life of Clarendon*, ii. 100, 101. " Three pitched battles would not repair the mischief done by Mr Russell and the articles upon his letters. . . . Of this I feel sure that every condition of treason is fulfilled by some of the recent articles in the *Times*."

sufficient to carry the war to a conclusion. Could Napoleon be trusted?—that was the question that haunted the minds of British Ministers. Granville had a talk with Thiers about it in the spring of 1855, of which he communicated the substance to Clarendon. "I do not say," Thiers had remarked, "that he (Napoleon) is a sincere man, but he is a perfectly sincere one with you." [1] We need not precisely disbelieve it. Yet a member of parliament takes account of the opinion of his supporters; and a popularly chosen despot is as much the creation of a constituency. France was, indeed, Napoleon; but also Napoleon was France—France as embodied in her army and in the toiling masses by whom that army was maintained. To French opinion, therefore, must British diplomacy bow. The course of events was to make that plain; and not all the cleverness of Clarendon could make it otherwise.

Johnny Russell was the first to feel the jerk of the Gallic lead around his neck. After his base desertion of Aberdeen and ignominious failure to form a Cabinet himself, he had been sent out, at Clarendon's instance, to Vienna in order to resume in that jovial, good-tempered city the negotiation of a settlement. Nicholas, as it happened, died about this time. His successor, though he could not afford a surrender, was not unwilling to consider an accommodation; and the compromise which Buol proposed commended itself as well to the judgment of the French Representative at the Vienna Conference as to that of Russell. The Western Powers had attempted, for the better security of the Turks, to secure either the neutralisation of the Black Sea or the limitation of Russian vessels upon it, but to neither plan would Russia agree. Buol's compromise was based upon the notion of counterpoise. If Russia increased her Black Sea fleet, Turkey was to be allowed to maintain an equal number of vessels, and France and Britain half so many. It seemed to Russell and to Drouyn de Lhuys that this plan should be adopted.

The compromise was in truth no bad compromise and invoked a principle that has since been constantly employed in naval discussions; but neither Palmerston nor Clarendon, who was perhaps as much under Palmerston's influence at this as at any time in his life, took kindly to it. The governing consideration was, however, to be found not in the East but in the West.

[1] *Life of Clarendon*, ii. 79.

Peace, until Sebastopol was taken, would have shaken Napoleon's throne. Drouyn was therefore tossed by his master into the deep sea, which is oblivion, and Russell thrown by his colleagues to the wolves, which were Parliament.

Six months later, with Sebastopol taken, the wheel came round full circle. The French became intent upon negotiations. "Granville, who sees everybody," Clarendon writes to his wife, "says that all the people coming home from different parts of France are unanimous in saying that, if we mean to go on with the war, we must do it single-handed, for France will have no more of it." [1] From that moment peace became inevitable, much as Palmerston would have liked to carry hostilities to another campaign. And the peace-negotiations, it was plain, would have to be carried on, so far as England was concerned, under the constant menace of French desertion.

This ugly diplomatic situation gave Clarendon the opportunity upon which in great measure his reputation rests. He had to pull the fat out of the fire; and it seemed to his more intelligent contemporaries that he accomplished it. The first step was to go himself to Paris, thus thrusting aside Sir Edmund Lyons, a sailor with some diplomatic experience and lately in charge of the Black Sea Fleet, whom Palmerston wished to appoint as British representative at the Conference. The second step was to take as his colleague the admirable Cowley; the third to play off for all it was worth that old friendship with Napoleon, which dated back to the Emperor's years of exile, against Walewski's presidency of the Congress and pro-Russian sympathies; the fourth to recognise the limitations of his strength. "We shall not get all we want," he wrote to Granville, "but I think it will be a peace of which we need not be ashamed, though a very different one from what we should have got if we could have had another campaign." [2]

The Peace of 1856 was, in reality, none the worse for being a negotiated and not a dictated peace—none the worse that it was the work of the Foreign Secretary and not of the Prime Minister. It laboured indeed under the fatal defect that the Turks in their political capacity were altogether past praying for, but, apart from this, it is no bad example of a generous and disinterested settlement. The victorious Western Powers took nothing for

---

[1] *Life of Clarendon*, ii. 104.   [2] *Ibid.*, p. 118.

themselves—neither indemnity nor territorial concession; the discomfited enemy suffered no vindictive humiliations, and, with the possible exception of the famous clause neutralising the Black Sea, no particular inconveniences. To the Turks, for whose benefit in fact the war had been fought, went all the outstanding advantages. They were received into the comity of nations; their coasts were protected from the menace of a Russian Fleet; their suzerainty over Moldavia and Wallachia, though subject to provisions for local autonomy, was confirmed; the independence and integrity of their Empire was guaranteed by the signatory Powers jointly and also by England, France, and Austria severally; their Orthodox nationals, in return for an illusory promise of equal rights, exchanged the effective protection of Russia for the ineffective protection of Europe; and, for the rest, their former frontier in Asia was restored to them and a strip of Bessarabia added to the Danubian Principalities. No state, in fact, was ever given a fairer chance of putting its house in order; and none has ever more fatally disappointed the vain imaginations of its friends. Yet, if the War was good, the Peace also was good; for that which the War had aimed at, the Peace secured. Turkey had been replaced upon such legs as it possessed.

Clarendon seized the opportunity of the Congress to settle some troublesome questions of maritime law. Both to the nature and effect of his proceedings, however, great exception was taken. It was urged that he had acted contrary to the spirit of the Constitution in deciding issues so important without intimation or reference to Parliament, and that by assenting to the doctrine that the goods of a neutral, under the flag of an enemy, and the goods of an enemy under the flag of a neutral are, unless contraband-of-war, alike safe from seizure, he had surrendered vital British interests. To the first charge there is no better answer than that of pure legality; and that answer is far from good. To the second it can be effectively replied that, since what was and what was not contraband-of-war continued to be undefined, the settlement left Great Britain well in command of the main position. Another provision of the Declaration of Paris ran counter to the famous Orders in Council which had parried the Continental System of Napoleon. A blockade had from this time forward to be made effective in order to be binding.

These things caused great opposition in England—so great indeed that, when the Treaty was officially proclaimed at Temple Bar, its provisions were received with hissing. The Declaration was hardly less unpopular in America. The abolition of privateering as well as the maintenance of contraband caused so much feeling that the States stood out from the agreement; and certain of the matters involved remain to exercise the temper of the Anglo-Saxon Peoples to this day. Yet, contentious though its merit was, Clarendon's work in maintaining at the Paris Congress both British prestige and the Anglo-French understanding obtained great praise from well-qualified judges; and recognition was not lacking in high quarters. Napoleon offered him the Grand Cross of the Legion of Honour, and Victoria a step in the peerage. Precedent required him to reject the one; prudence the other. Whilst he advised Cowley to become an earl for the sake of his daughters, he himself refused to be made a marquis for the sake of his sons. A courtesy title, he urged, was an advantage to women, whether married or unmarried, but to younger sons, with their way to make, no less than a misfortune.[1] It told in society, but in breadwinning hindered.

The War in the Crimea left like most wars a legacy of bothers, which were only by degrees cleared up. Granville, working as he did in constant harmony with Clarendon, was helpful here; and the account of his special mission to Petersburg for Alexander the II.'s coronation—of the sights that he saw, the splendours that he displayed, and the money that he spent in a prodigious competition with the French to impress their recent enemy—reads already, in our drab, democratic days, like some fantastic story conceived and cradled in Bagdad or Bokhara. We cannot stop to follow him on this adventure, nor yet Clarendon, as he pushes his way through the last diplomatic tangles of Palmerston's first Administration—the business of the withdrawal of the British Minister from Naples, where King Bomba, in spite of Gladstone's anathemas, still held upon his wicked way; the business of the faked plebiscite in Moldavia, which province the French, with prophetic wisdom, desired to unite with, but the British to keep separate from Wallachia, and the Turks to hold ever in subjection and distress; or again the business so full of trouble, both foreign and domestic, arising out of Orsini's plot.

[1] *Life of Clarendon*, ii. 122, 141.

Somewhat strained by the two first of these affairs, the Franco-British understanding all but foundered upon the last. It was lucky that one old friend of Napoleon's was at the Foreign Office when the trouble began, and not less lucky that another took his place when the crisis had reached its climax and produced a change of government. Malmesbury's periods as Foreign Secretary were indeed too hopelessly restricted by the long mid-Victorian enfeeblement of his party to make it possible to estimate his ability with any assurance. What he had time to do, however, he did well, and, before many months were out, the Franco-British understanding was restored. Restored—yet no more to work with its former ease! The Italian Risorgimento was in the air in 1858—an idea moving uncertainly across the face of the future. In 1859 it came to earth, bent its proud spirit to necessity, took shape and service under Napoleon's eye, and passed like a sword through Europe, sundering and scattering as it went. The results of its impact upon Britain were large and definite. It strained afresh the good relations between France and England, separated the British Court from the British People, severed the tenuous life of the Derby Government, split the new Palmerston Cabinet into contending camps. The Prime Minister and the Foreign Secretary, not to speak of the more famous man who had become Chancellor of the Exchequer,[1] were Italian to the core; and their strong, dominant personalities battled with the Queen and their colleagues for the mastery.

It does not need perhaps to be added that the Foreign Secretary was no longer Clarendon. Though both Victoria and Palmerston had wished him to return to his former post, Russell, with characteristic want of grace and in so many words, had claimed the Foreign Office as a right. The country had reason to regret it, but not Clarendon. He escaped the unpleasantness of a difference with Palmerston, with whom he disagreed about Italian unity. And also he escaped the ordinary toil of public business which he disliked, and the extraordinary toil of acting as a buffer between a masterful man at the head of the Government and a determined woman at the head of the State. He escaped a great deal, but he did not escape altogether. Everybody in the Government, from Palmerston downwards, wanted to have him back; indeed, when Russell grabbed the Foreign

[1] Gladstone.

Office, Granville had offered to stand aside so that he might have the Presidency of the Council and the leadership in the Lords. And at last in 1864 pressure proved successful and he agreed to take the Duchy of Lancaster with a seat in the Cabinet. His entry into the Government brought an accession of weight and wisdom to those who were struggling to curb the too youthful energies of the "two old ring-leaders"—to use his own significant description of Palmerston and Russell—in the matter of the Danish Duchies. Then in the next year Palmerston died, Russell took his place as Premier, and the Foreign Office was once more free for Clarendon's acceptance. He took it, to the immense satisfaction of his colleagues, who felt—what they had not felt for some while past—that nothing of importance would thenceforward be transacted without their knowledge.[1] But, with Hamlet dead, the play quickly petered out leaving the actors stranded. Russell's last Administration was nothing but the final scene in Palmerston's long drama. Clarendon, had he chosen, might indeed have held to his office under the incoming Conservative Government. But, firm in his Whiggery, unmoved in that "allegiance to party" which he declared to be "the only strong political feeling"[2] that he had, he remained proof against the urgent blandishments alike of Derby and Victoria, and Stanley was given the place that he would not take.

There is no end to the ironies of politics. Two years later the Queen was as eager to keep Clarendon out of the Foreign Office as before to get him into it. What exactly had occurred in the interval to change her feeling was matter for speculation even among those who knew her best. All we know for certain is that she spoke to her private secretary of Clarendon's impertinence, of his habit of sarcasm, of his friendship with the Queen of Holland and of her influence upon him, of his uncongenial opinions about German unity and about Russia; and for the rest, that, when her allegations had been brought to Gladstone's notice through the medium of Halifax, the incoming Prime Minister animadverted strongly upon the injustice of condemning a man upon hearsay reports which the accused had been given no opportunity to refute.[3] Clarendon's biographer,[4] indeed,

---

[1] See Granville's letter to him in the *Life of Clarendon*, ii. 312.
[2] *Life of Clarendon*, ii. 319.
[3] *Ibid.*, pp. 353, 354. |[4] *Ibid.*, p. 282.

supposes that the root of the trouble is to be found in some disparaging remarks about Germany which he had addressed to the Queen and the Crown Princess of Prussia [1] in 1863, and which are known to have made them angry. It may be so, but between 1863 and 1868 lies the Queen's statement of 1866 that she "cannot express *too strongly* her *hope* and *earnest* wish that Lord Clarendon may find himself able to accede to the proposal" that he should act as Foreign Secretary under Lord Derby.[2]

The incident is curious but trifling. Somehow or other Victoria's objections were overcome by Gladstone; and Clarendon resumed his now familiar office in December 1868. The Queen need not have been so much troubled at the thought of his return. Only eighteen months of life and service were left to her old, once beloved but now unacceptable servant—eighteen months, which, but for some transient yet momentarily serious trouble with America over the old *Alabama* dispute, passed with such an absence of diplomatic friction in Europe as to elicit at their close from Hammond, then Permanent Under-Secretary for Foreign Affairs, the famous observation that he had never in all his experience known so great a lull. Famous, because even as he spoke the biggest storm of the period was gathering—the storm that was to cause Europe, as was neatly said, to exchange a mistress for a master! There was one, deeply interested and deeply involved, who believed, or affected to believe, that, had Clarendon not died in the June of 1870, the Franco-Prussian War with all its memorable consequences would not have occurred. "Never in my life," observed Bismarck to Clarendon's daughter in 1871, "was I more glad to hear of anything than I was to hear of your father's death." Then, as she showed resentment at so apparently tactless a remark, he added, "Ach! dear lady, you must not take it like that. What I mean is that, if your father had lived, he would have prevented the war." [3] Unlikely as it seems that this neutral hand could have stayed the swift passage of events in the crucial forty-eight hours of July 1870, there was this much truth at least in Bismarck's view —that Clarendon had, by common consent, obtained and exercised an exceptional influence over the mind of Napoleon III. But, sincere or insincere, correct or incorrect, the compliment was

---

[1] The Empress Frederick.   [2] *Life of Clarendon*, ii. 318.
[3] *Ibid.*, p. 366.

well-deserved, for the British Foreign Secretary had striven hard enough in those last months of his life to bring about the disarmament both of France and Prussia. Thus it was that this fine gentleman justified to the full the title that the French bestowed upon him of "*le commis-voyageur de la paix*." Sarcastic and worldly-wise as he could be on occasion, yet, like the prophet of old, he had his Pisgah, surveyed a land flowing with milk and honey, and died with his eyes fixed upon the distant vision.

A few weeks after Clarendon was gone, the world of his day fell to pieces; the powerful Emperor—for in his time he had seemed very powerful—was cast down; the Entente was broken, England exclaiming at the folly of France, and France in her agony at her desertion by England; and Germany began to be lifted up. Clarendon's death comes, therefore, in the story of British policy like the fall of the curtain after a star player has played his best and his last. We part from him the more sadly that even in narrative his personality is fragrant with a peculiar charm. No figure so much suggesting a portrait by Vandyke [1] moves across our narrow stage; there is no other Foreign Secretary at once so graceful, so brilliant, so generous and so gay. To think of any such, rotting in cold obstruction, offends against that peculiar sense of beauty and the demands of beauty which is its own witness to the truth of survival; nor did Clarendon, few as were his commitments in the matter of religion, fear for himself so dark a fate. "I am no sceptic now," he wrote to a friend in the last autumn of his life, "but believe in the resurrection of man and his admission into Paradise." [2]

If, as Gladstone affirmed, of all the sixty men or so who had been his colleagues Clarendon was the easiest and most attractive, [3] his successor assuredly had a good claim to the next place in a calendar of Cabinet Ministers arranged in order of charm and courtesy. We have caught glimpses of Granville from time to time as he wins his way to great place by goodness of manner and generosity of heart rather than by any brilliant feat of intellect, fills with consummate tact, and vacates again with consummate disinterestedness, posts of first-rate political consequence, and practises in various circumstances and upon various occasions his peculiar gift of reconciling, in his own facile

---

[1] The comparison was made by Henry Reeve.
[2] *Life of Clarendon*, ii. 362.   [3] Morley, *Gladstone*, ii. 447.

and tolerant manner, the different contentions or divergent views of his colleagues or collaborators—a gift of peculiar value in the administration of a department of which it has been said by one well equipped to pass judgment both upon it and him that the Foreign Office "ought never to be, and certainly never was in his hands, as personal or even as predominantly departmental, as the administration of other great departments often is, and may safely be." [1] We have now to glance at his policy during two Liberal Administrations coincident with two pregnant periods of European and African history—1870 to 1874 and 1880 to 1885.

Granville came to the Foreign Office in July 1870 and immediately he was—as we should say in our expressive phraseology, destined doubtless some day to become classical—"up against" the Franco-Prussian imbroglio. He did the most sensible thing any man could do; he tried to get rid of the cause of offence. The cause of offence in this case was the wish of the Spaniards to place a prince of the House of Hohenzollern-Sigmaringen upon the throne from which the worthless and disreputable Isabella had at length been driven. The proposal was no more the concern of Europe than the elevation of a Stadholder of the United Provinces or an Elector of Hanover to be King of England; and so Gladstone was inclined to think. But the Bonapartes conceived that they had taken over with the Crown of France all the time-honoured interest of the Bourbons in the fortunes of Spain; and they were determined that no scion of the House of Prussia should sit upon the throne of Philip V.   As a matter of fact, neither the Hohenzollerns of Berlin nor those of Sigmaringen were urgent for the plan. Representations, which included a private letter from the King of Prussia to the father of the candidate, as well as pressure from Granville upon Madrid, resulted, therefore, in the abandonment of Prince Leopold's candidature, once its contentious character became apparent. And there Napoleon should have left the matter. He had got the substance of his demand; it was idle, and worse than idle to pursue distant shadows. He desired, however, to pose once more as the most powerful prince in Europe. He required, therefore, that the King of Prussia should formally associate himself with Prince Leopold's refusal and expressly undertake not to authorise

[1] The Duke of Argyll (quoted from Fitzmaurice's *Life of Granville*, ii. 506).

it again. These demands were presented to the King by
Benedetti, and firmly and finally declined. Their rejection,
however, was not left without a friendly rider intimating un-
reserved approval of the Prince's decision. Out of the telegram
from Ems recounting this incident, Bismarck, as all the world
knows, contrived, without altering a word, to produce by ex-
cision alone the impression that Prussia had been insulted. As
Napoleon had sinned for the sake of a diplomatic victory, so did
Bismarck now sin for the sake of a military one. Feeling rose
in a moment to fever-heat, first in Berlin and then in Paris.
Within two days of Prince Leopold's withdrawal, Napoleon had
decided to fight for as vain a shadow as man ever went to war
about.

Granville was helpless in face of this insanity. He suggested
a possible accommodation and attempted a final mediation, but
he might have spared himself the trouble. Both the French and
German Governments were bent upon battle for reasons not connected with the matter in dispute. The former hoped to rejuvenate an old empire, the other to bring a young one to birth.

In these circumstances British neutrality was a matter of
course; and Granville's path lay plain before him. Impartiality
was another matter. British opinion, indeed, was first with the
Germans and then with the French, so that on the balance neither
side had much to complain of. But the impartiality of trade,
which satisfies the needs of the first client that comes, consorts
ill with the impartiality of the statesman who seeks to show no
favour towards either combatant; and Granville had his troubles
about the supply of coal and arms to France. As always happens,
the parties to the fight trusted Britain none the more for her
scrupulous neutrality; and Britain in her turn had soon
occasion to trust them less than ever. Early in the proceedings
Bismarck disclosed the fact that Napoleon had discussed with
him a deal over Belgium in 1866, although both parties were
pledged by the Treaty of 1839. Granville took the opportunity
of obtaining from each combatant a new guarantee of Belgian
neutrality, but what such pledges would be worth, if interest
should ever prompt their violation, all the world was now in a
position to guess.

As the French reaped the reward of their foolishness and
Bismarck the harvest of his cunning, the cries of France for

help grew more insistent. The greatest of her statesmen became the mouthpiece of this clamour. Thiers, not sorry perhaps to become conspicuous in Paris by virtue of absence in London, arrived at the Foreign Office, interviewed Granville, grew warm with the effort of declaiming in eloquent, impassioned phrases the merit of his country's cause, and then sank back in a chair, with closed eyes, apparently overcome by the rigour of death. Granville, at all events, augured the worst, and was about to summon help when it occurred to him to make a second examination of the presumptive corpse. His precaution was fortunate. The old gentleman had merely dropped asleep, hypnotised, as Disraeli would have said, by the exuberance of his own verbosity.

Though upon this issue of military intervention Granville's course lay clear, on the question of pacific intervention there was room for serious debate. Here he had to wrestle, not with Thiers, but Gladstone, to whom it seemed that Great Britain should express disapproval of any acquisition of territory against the will of its inhabitants. He won, but came out of the Cabinet Council torn and bleeding—"quite exhausted," he records, "after the longest fight I ever had with Gladstone." [1] Doubtless he was right. The victor was too victorious, the vanquished too fully beaten to give a Neutral room to intervene. Yet it required no small measure of the pertinacity that lay concealed behind his engaging address to throw the giant-will of the Prime Minister in a tussle involving the fate of a nationality, and to recall, as he had to do not long afterwards, the vagrant, all-exploring tongue of his chief into the discreet and narrow paths of sound diplomacy. His letter to Gladstone on this latter point should probably be reckoned the *locus classicus* on the constitutional relationship between the Prime Minister and the Foreign Office. "I imagine," he wrote, "that the Prime Minister has an undoubted right to communicate directly either with our representatives abroad or with Foreign Ministers in London. But I think it is in his interest as much as in that of the Foreign Secretary's that he should only appear as the *deus ex machina*." [2] Gladstone does not appear to have shown resentment at being put back in his constitutional place; but, unfortunately, he retained his faith in the healing properties of language, and, to Granville's subsequent embarrassment, denounced Austria and

[1] *Life of Granville*, ii. 62. [2] *Ibid.*, p. 64.

its Monarch during the General Election of 1880 with all the eloquence and all the folly of enthusiasm. Apart, however, from the occasional outbursts which recur throughout his whole career against the wickedness of illiberal governments, he interfered as little perhaps as any Prime Minister of his time with the course of policy—less, certainly, than Palmerston or Russell or Beaconsfield.

To return to the eventful year 1870, when, as Lord Fitzmaurice puts it, "the defeat of France opened up the fountains of the diplomatic deep." [1]   In October Russia calmly announced by circular the cancellation, so far as she was concerned, of the Black Sea clauses of the Treaty of Paris—those clauses which had been the last-picked, ripest plums of the War in the Crimea and now turned out to be no better than Dead-Sea fruit. Britain was in the more uncomfortable position that she had bound herself to fight 'jointly' with France and Austria, or 'severally,' by herself, to maintain the independence and integrity of Turkey, and that both the Turks themselves and Elliot, who represented England at the Turkish Court, took the gravest view of the effect of the Russian action upon Turkish freedom. As things were at the moment France could not fight, Austria would not fight, and Britain had no wish to fight. In these awkward circumstances Granville crystallised his policy in an epigram which has its place and time amongst the aphorisms of diplomacy. "Promising peace," he said, "is as unwise as to threaten war." With that he sent off Odo Russell, the best diplomatist on the British active list, to see what could be made out of Bismarck, now just climbing, at Versailles, the last steps of the diplomatic throne, once occupied by Metternich and more lately by Napoleon III. The move was the bolder that Bismarck had put Russia up to the trick she had just played; [2] but Odo Russell was even bolder than the move. As he sat in conversation with the all-powerful Minister he decided to drop Granville's cautious equivocation and declare boldly that Britain would fight, with or without allies, unless the Russian Circular was withdrawn. His decision told. Provided Russia, to whom a debt was owing, triumphed in the substance, Bismarck was ready to let Britain triumph as to the form. In order, therefore, to comply with the stipulations of the Treaty

[1] *Life of Granville*, ii. 70.
[2] Bismarck, *Reflections and Reminiscences* (Eng. trans.), ii. 114.

of Paris and to make the dismissal of the Black Sea clauses to limbo an international instead of a unilateral act, he approved the project of a conference. The meeting-place of that conference Granville, by further pressure, contrived to fix in London. So much, then, he gained in mitigation of the rebuff Great Britain had received; and this much more. The Powers assembled recognised as a principle of the Law of Nations that no Power can free itself from treaty obligations except by amicable agreement with the other contracting Powers, whilst to Turkey was given the right to admit vessels of war into the Straits in time of peace should the Porte judge this to be needful in order to maintain the Treaty of Paris. These provisions constituted some sort of a sop to the parties flouted; but the broad fact remained that Russia had summarily brushed away the most contested clauses of the settlement of 1856 and taken no harm in doing so.

Granville had no luck in the hour of his administration. All the dregs of Palmerston's and of Russell's diplomacy were his to drain. He had no sooner cleared off the legacy of the one in the Eastern Hemisphere than he had to deal with that of the other in the Western.

The depredations of the *Alabama*, a cruiser which Russell, eight years earlier, had let slip from a British port to prey upon Federal commerce, still poisoned the relations between Britain and America; and beneath the immediate issue of compensation lay the larger question of adjusting the English and American doctrines of neutrality, particularly in regard to the diligence required of a neutral state in restraining its nationals from unneutral action. The prolonged, uneasy feeling between the two countries had, even during Clarendon's final administration, appeared pregnant with peril; and Granville was resolved, at whatever cost, to end it. A brilliant suggestion from one of the cleverest of his clerks [1] gave him his cue. He suggested publicly the appointment of an Anglo-American Joint High Commission on Canadian Fisheries, and he suggested privately to the American Government that they should make their assent conditional upon the inclusion of the *Alabama* affair within the reference of the Commission's business. On these terms, then, the Commission was set up—a Board, so far at any rate as the English Commissioners were concerned, very dexterously

[1] Lord Tenterden.

selected so as to give representation both to the Government and the Opposition, and thus commit both Parties in the State beforehand. In conjunction with their American colleagues the British Commissioners formulated rules which showed that there was no organic divergence between the English and American doctrines of neutrality, and incidentally showed up "the vacillation and defective knowledge of history"—to borrow the words of a recent high authority [1]—of which Russell had been guilty in 1862. On the understanding that these rules, embodied in the Treaty of Washington, would govern the finding in the case of the *Alabama*, the compensation claimed for that trouble-some affair was now submitted to arbitration at Geneva. Russell, though he recognised his error in not detaining the *Alabama*, was extremely annoyed that it should be considered in the light of subsequent events and not of contemporary law; and doubtless he received something that fell short of equity. But an error remains an error for all that; and he was the last man who ought to have complained, because, after ten years of delay, Granville paid for it in the only currency that commanded value. The price was, no doubt, as the times went, not inexpensive; and Houghton's epigrammatic observation that each of the four days of Russell's indecision in 1862 had cost the country a million pounds embodied the brutal truth.[2]

Had Granville been weaker and the Americans got their way, the *Alabama* incident would have cost the country even more. There were certain indirect claims, based upon the remote results of the depredations complained of, which seemed more than once to have been abandoned and then were revived again. Granville would have none of them, but the American Government lacked the courage to give in. It was therefore agreed between the principals, by means of what has been characterised as "secret diplomacy of almost childlike simplicity," [3] that the arbitrators were to rule out these pretensions and so enable America to save its face. Thus was the long quarrel settled and harmony dwelt again for a space between the jealous children of the Anglo-Saxons. Virtue is its own reward. The settlement brought no credit to its initiator. "There can be

---

[1] Professor J. E. G. de Montmorency (*Camb. Hist. of British Foreign Policy*, iii. 64).

[2] Quoted in the *Life of Granville*, ii. 81.

[3] *Camb. Hist. of British Foreign Policy*, iii. 70.

little doubt," says Lord Fitzmaurice, "that . . . the average British elector made the Geneva award one of the principal counts in the indictment which caused him to record his vote against the Government"[1] in 1874.

For six momentous years the Foreign Office passed into the keeping of the Conservatives—six years whose detailed history is best studied in connection with Salisbury, but whose broad result was to galvanise once again the old sinner of Eastern Europe, rotting on his bed of sickness, into some semblance of life, and to invest the German Chancellor with the dignity of consulting physician in a case which had long baffled the efforts of the physicians-in-ordinary. Or, if we prefer to adopt the German rather than the Russian metaphor, we might say that the enduring result of the Berlin Congress was that for all future dealings in Turkish stock Bismarck was broker, and that, whenever business was done, Germany was entitled to, or at least resolved upon a commission.

This was a new factor in the situation, and one that made itself quickly felt upon Granville's return to the Foreign Office in 1880. So powerful was it that all the history of his last administration may conveniently be grouped about his dealings with the land of the Pharaohs and with one who was worthy to be called the German sphinx. If Granville failed, as to his countrymen it seemed that he did fail, in the five years when he had the freest hand and the fullest opportunity, it must be in fairness remembered that he had to deal with Egypt in the very depth of its financial and administrative darkness and with Bismarck in the very height of his political and international power.

The burden of Egypt had begun to fall upon England some while before Granville resumed office. It was the immediate result of the incompetent extravagance of the Khedive Ismail, of whom it may be said with confidence that he was a prince of spenders, if not in other ways princely, and the indirect result of the position of Egypt on the road to India and of the acquisition by Disraeli of the Suez Canal shares. With the French, that eminent man had once observed, in especial reference to their Egyptian policy, dominated as it was by the powerful interest of the French bondholders, "finance . . . is politics." In the

[1] *Life of Granville,* ii. 107, 108.

case of the English in Egypt, subject and complement needed to
be reversed. Politics were for them finance. One might add,
not inappropriately, that in the view of the Egyptians the two
things were in no way related.   In the co-existence and collision
of these ill-assorted opinions lay the essence of the Egyptian
problem.

The Western Powers had at least this in common that they
found the actual state of things unendurable.   Whether primarily
as financiers or as politicians, they were alike interested in the
government of the regions of the Lower Nile and the Suez Canal,
and, after a futile attempt to reform the administration on
national lines, they procured the deposition of the extravagant
Ismail and the elevation to the throne of the feeble Tewfik.
The change signified, in terms too plain to be mistaken, the
presence of a dual Anglo-French control and the passing of
the Egyptians under its yoke.   It was so understood and as
such resented by the National Party which in Egypt, as in Italy
and Ireland, was of opinion that a people is best left to govern
itself.

Upon the stage of this troubled country, where the existence
of extra-national Consular Courts and Mixed Tribunals complicated the administration of justice, and into which a horde
of foreign officials were constantly pouring, there now appeared
the figures of Gladstone and Granville.   They came unwillingly;
they desired to do the least possible; they restricted the case
for intervention, in Granville's own words, to "the existence
of anarchy or some attack on the Canal."   But it was all to
no purpose.   The coming of England into Egypt was as surely
written in the book of fate as the exodus of Israel.   Just at
the fateful juncture, a personality exceptionally masterful,
impetuous, and determined crossed, though only for a moment,
the path that Granville was treading in his cautious, courteous
way.   It is hardly to be disputed that Gambetta, during that
brief ministry of his which lasted from November 1881 until
January 1882, dragged Granville further than he had intended
to go upon his appointed road.   A Franco-British Note, which
was communicated on 8th January 1882, and takes its name
from that date, promised the Khedive the support of the two
Powers and invited him to act with confidence on the strength
of this assurance.   This move gave the more furiously to think

that France had just seized Tunis. To Granville, indeed, the Note seemed to mean nothing; yet to Gambetta much; to Bismarck something; to Arabi, with the Egyptian Nationalists at his back and the Khedive in his power, perhaps everything. Developments, at all events, followed quickly, and, had Gambetta not fallen at the beginning of February, might have followed even more quickly than they did. Just as Gambetta fell, Count Herbert Bismarck—the son and, as was erroneously supposed, the eventual successor of the German Chancellor—arrived in London. He was received by the Granvilles with cordiality and entertained with the hospitality for which 18 Carlton House Terrace was at this time famous. His presence in London was the more noticeable from the circumstance that he occupied at first no official position. He was in fact his father's finger stretched out to stir the Franco-British pie and see that, when it came to pulling out the Egyptian plum, England and not France should have it. Neither a French protectorate nor an Anglo-French condominium consorted with Bismarck's plans. He reasoned perhaps somewhat thus. He wanted, first and foremost, peace—peace to consolidate the new German Empire that he had created. There were two obvious ways of getting it—by making alliances with states which also wanted peace, and by giving other countries plenty of occupation for their energies away from Germany. In the first connection he desired most of all, if he could get it, an alliance with England; and there is some reason to suppose that he chose Austria rather than Russia for the dangerous honour of becoming Germany's ally in 1879, principally because Austria was the traditional friend, Russia the traditional foe of Great Britain. In the second connection he had pushed France into her Tunisian adventure. Caring nothing for colonies himself, he viewed with grim contentment the dissipation of French strength involved in the annexation of Tunis. To invite Great Britain to take up the burden of Egypt was, perhaps, not less cunningly designed to produce a lasting condition of British dependence upon German support. Granville, however, could not afford to remain indifferent to Bismarck's proferred hand. Almost as soon as he came into office he had discovered the range of that far-reaching member in the course of his attempts to get the Turks to surrender what they owed to Greece of territory under the terms of the Treaty of Berlin. Until Goschen had made a special pilgrimage to Germany to flatter the all-powerful states-man by some recognition of his primacy, nothing seemed to get done; yet afterwards everything.

From the British Embassy at Berlin, where Odo Russell, now decorated with a peerage and become Lord Ampthill, was *persona grata*, there came strong pressure to put faith in the good-will and wise counsels of the German Chancellor. "For ten years have I preached confidence in Bismarck," wrote the Ambassador in 1881, "as a means of success in foreign policy, but in vain." [1] Granville was not unwilling to lend an ear to these exhortations. He had before this sought Bismarck's advice and been satisfied with it. He, perhaps, as well as Russell had still to learn that all the oracles of Varzin were no other than the lucubrations of the high-priest of a tribal god.

Everything, after Herbert Bismarck came to England, went according to plan—the Bismarck plan. The understanding between France and Britain, which Gambetta had tried to knit so tight, slackened under Freycinet. Ostensibly indeed the Powers co-operated, and together they moved naval squadrons to Alexandria. But all the while Freycinet was playing Gran-ville false. In Cairo the French agent was intriguing with Arabi and the Nationalists,[2] whilst at home Freycinet was planning the substitution of a new Khedive, devoted to French interests, for the feeble Tewfik. By midsummer Arabi was completely master of the situation in Egypt, except for the Allied squadrons; and in July he had so far advanced his preparations to secure command of the harbour at Alexandria that intervention became imperative. The French were, then, inevitably unmasked. Declining to co-operate, their squadron sailed away when the British opened fire. In the belief that Egypt was a trap which Bismarck had set for them and that they were evading his guile, the French Government left England alone to face a situation that looked already like ending in another addition to her heterogeneous Empire.

It might have been better, perhaps, if Granville had not shrunk from an admission, at least to himself, of this possibility, and had thus avoided any public denial of it and saved his country from

[1] *Life of Granville*, ii. 228.
[2] *Camb. Hist. of British Foreign Policy*, iii. 169.

a charge of hypocrisy. It might even have been better, as things turned out, if he and Gladstone had accepted instead of rejecting the Sultan's offer in 1882 to hand over to Great Britain "the exclusive control and administration of the whole of Egypt" subject only to Turkish suzerain rights. But, apart from all the inherent uncertainties of the problem, apart from the fact that a Liberal Government—and he as its Foreign Secretary—stood deeply committed to the principle of nationality, there was a particular consideration, so his biographer tells us,[1] that held him prisoner. He had been deeply impressed, just twenty years before, by the tragedy of Queretaro, and, throughout the developments that led up to the death of Gordon, the disastrous attempt of the ill-starred Maximilian to make himself Emperor of Mexico haunted his thoughts and made him fearful of committing himself to any reckless or uncertain enterprise. Unfortunately there is as much peril in tardy as in precipitate action.

The history of Egypt between the bombardment of Alexandria in 1882 and the death of Gordon in 1885 is a tale so often told that even to recall the main sequence of events seems to call for apology. The British contribution to it forms, however, an inevitable and bulky feature in any portrait of Granville as a Foreign Secretary, for upon his department the main responsibility for this imperial and administrative rather than strictly diplomatic venture was laid and by its partial failure he has himself been almost wholly, yet not quite fairly judged.

Briefly, then, matters fell out thus. The bombardment of Alexandria by sea was followed by a faultlessly organised attack on land, which eventuated in the rout of Arabi by Sir Garnet Wolseley at Tel-el-Kebir. Early in the next year (1883) Granville took occasion to issue a circular despatch abolishing—or at least intimating the coming abolition of—the Dual Control of France and England over finance and inaugurating a new era of financial administration and judicial reform under British guidance. Before Granville's despatch appeared, Dufferin was already on the spot, and, not many weeks later, had produced a report upon Egypt which is of the same family as Durham's more famous report upon Canada—not less generous, nor sympathetic. He came and went, but in his place appeared Baring—Cromer that was to be and is as such remembered.

---

[1] *Life of Granville*, i. 440.

So far all had gone well with Granville's Egyptian policy.   He had done the bold thing; he had got hold of the proper men; he had laid, for whatever time it might last, the foundation of British rule.   The Egyptians had been beaten; the French bowed out; the Turks put in their place; the Germans squared. But this excellent record of success was now to be completely spoiled in an unexpected quarter and by one no better than a savage and no wiser than a fanatic.

The insurrection of the tribes of the Sudan under the leadership of the Mahdi had begun in 1881, but it was not until 1883 that the Egyptian Government decided to take definite action against them.   This decision was combated, but not vetoed by the English authorities; and here occurred the first serious British mistake.   Hicks Pasha, in command of an Egyptian army, advanced against the Mahdi with the confidence that civilised man is accustomed to enjoy when he is pitted against barbarians. His confidence was in excess of his circumstances.   In the event he was defeated so thoroughly that it is obvious to compare the fate of his army with that of the Egyptians who in the proud days of the Pharaohs started to pursue the departing Israelites across the Red Sea.

This catastrophic disaster decided the British Government to do what they ought to have done before.   In the beginning of 1884 Granville intimated in no uncertain manner that thenceforward in all important questions the Khedive must adopt the advice tendered him by the British Agent.   But now a second fatality occurred, and one calculated to appeal with great force to the love of hero-worship always latent, sometimes patent, in all agreeably constituted human beings.   There were certain Egyptian garrisons and officials left behind in the Sudan and requiring to be relieved.   Someone had to be sent out to effect their release.   Granville had for some while had Gordon in his mind as a man who might well be made use of.   "He has an immense name in Egypt," the Foreign Secretary wrote to the Prime Minister, "he is popular at home.   He has a small bee in his bonnet." [1]   Baring in Cairo was, perhaps, not so sure that the bee in question was as small as Granville supposed.   But Granville was insistent.   Three times he asked that Gordon might be employed; and the third time Baring yielded.   On

[1] *Life of Granville*, ii. 381.

18th January 1884 the Foreign Secretary, as his biographer records,[1] himself took Gordon's ticket for the journey out. It was a piece of politeness which fixed a degree of responsibility.

"Good God! that I should have entrusted the fate of the country and of the administration to such hands," Pitt, according to Stanhope's famous story, exclaimed to Temple when they had parted with one whose memory was soon to be linked with the capture of Quebec and the conquest of Canada. Gordon was such another as Wolfe—a bold speculation in British imperial capacity. Both men abounded in spirit, in confidence, in leadership, and in courage—the very qualities that men so often lightly tell us make a certainty of success—and each secured a soldier's death and left a hero's name. Yet the latter end of the one was framed in gloom as that of the other had been framed in glory. Granville had wrongly hoped and Chatham idly feared. Circumstances calculated to clear our minds of cant!

Cromer, when he came to write twenty years afterwards what is probably the fairest account of the whole business, neither exculpated himself nor Granville for the events that followed the rash decision (taken, as it seems, so lightly at a meeting where only four Cabinet Ministers were present, and not even the Prime Minister among them) to send out Gordon to report, or maybe do something more than report upon the affairs of the Sudan. As the British Government had a great sin of omission already to their charge—the omission to veto Hicks's ill-starred expedition—so was the despatch of Gordon, as Cromer reckoned, their great sin of commission. And this for two reasons; first, because to send an Englishman at all was a mistake, when the presence of an Englishman might so easily implicate England and compel the despatch of an English army to the Sudan; and second, because Gordon, for all his talent for dealing with men, lacked stability of opinion. Herbert Stewart, as he soon saw, would have done better. There was, he thought, only one excuse for sending Gordon at all—and that not a particularly good one—the urgent desire of the British Public that he should be sent. Granville, though it may be true that his predilection for Gordon preceded the popular demand for Gordon's despatch, was not uninfluenced by this consideration. His act was to this degree the act of the nation; for the nation

[1] *Life of Granville*, ii. 383.

had made the same mistake about Gordon or the qualities of Gordon as he had himself.

Baring had a keener eye. He knew the man and was soon to know his communications. They streamed in from Khartoum— a mass of contradictory matter, revealing a nature as receptive as it was unstable. Gordon had received instructions from home —instructions all too vague and of which he proceeded to make all too light. As a consequence he passed almost insensibly from a policy of immediate evacuation to one of temporary occupation. Granville seems hardly to have appreciated the difference. " I believe," says Cromer, "that the original intention of the British Government was that Gordon should limit himself to reporting. . . . Lord Granville did not see that in authorising General Gordon to accept the appointment of Governor-General of the Sudan he changed the spirit of the instructions which he had issued on January 18th." [1] Some indiscretion and much vacilla- tion on Gordon's part followed this sharp shifting of purpose. It was difficult, as Baring felt, to find out what he wanted, except only that he wanted Zobeir Pasha whom, as an old slave-hunter, any Liberal Government was precluded from allowing him to have. Optimism carried him high—high as Dædalus's wings. He spoke of "smashing the Mahdi"; an army of twenty thousand men, he thought, would suffice for it. Then, like Icarus, he fell. Whilst he was telegraphing inconstant opinions from Khartoum, and the Cabinet was debating alternative but equally distasteful courses in London, and in Cairo Baring was trying to elucidate the policy of the one and to fortify the purpose of the other, the Mahdi attacked. Before a relief expedition could reach the beleaguered city, Gordon was dead.

A death in the desert such as he suffered threw judgment out of joint. His faults and foibles were buried with him; his character was magnified; his fate caused all the blame of the disaster to fall upon the living and be shifted from the dead. The whole Government suffered in reputation, but Granville's reputation suffered most of all. His best admirers can hardly complain of it. He was to blame not once nor twice but thrice. He blundered by allowing Hicks to march, by selecting Gordon, and finally by neither holding Gordon to his first instructions on pain of recall, nor yet, in the alternative, supporting him with

[1] Cromer, *Modern Egypt*, i. 452.

swift, effective aid in the bolder project that had seized his fancy. He recognised and partially admitted his mistake, but amidst the storm of criticism that assailed him and his colleagues, he kept a not uneven mind. "I have felt," he wrote, "great and deep regret, but no remorse at being one principally responsible for sending out Gordon." But it was rather the logical implica- tions of the relief expedition than its tardy despatch that dis- concerted him. "The sending out that army at all," he wrote, "perhaps somewhat weakens our case. I cannot admit that either generals or statesmen, who have accepted the offer of a man to lead a forlorn hope, are in the least bound to risk the lives of thousands for the uncertain chance of saving the forlorn hope." [1] Of which doctrine this commentator does not feel called upon to say more than that it raises in an acute form the old dispute between the utilitarian philosophy and its rivals.

Here, then, so far as Granville is concerned, we may take leave of Egypt and the Sudan. The serpent of Old Nile had caught him and his colleagues in its folds and held them tight and help- less as Laocoon was held. In its agony the Liberal Government undertook that Gordon should be avenged in the fall of the year. It was a reckless promise, and they went back upon it before they fell themselves. Not for a dozen years was Egypt good for another adventure in the desert, or England game to see it through!

It was as the British Government became more and more entangled in the affairs of Egypt and the fate of the Sudan that Bismarck began to show his hand. It may be, as he had repeatedly assured Ampthill, that he really took no interest in the creation of colonies, though this indifference postulates a blind- ness of vision damaging to his credit as a statesman; it may be only that by 1884 the pressure of the colonial movement both at home and abroad had become too strong for him and that he took action unwillingly and against his better judgment; but, at all events, from this time forward, he used the problem of Egypt as a lever to compel Great Britain to countenance certain German aspirations in Africa and elsewhere. The connection was open and declared. The price of German support in Cairo was the cancellation of the carefully considered and lately concluded Anglo-Portuguese agreement regarding the Congo, the admission

[1] *Life of Granville*, ii. 400, 401.

of German sovereignty over Angra Pequena, and a reconsideration of the German claims in Fiji. Granville decided to pay it. There was another matter mentioned, now for the first time—the cession of Heligoland by Great Britain in connection with a project for cutting a canal from the German Ocean into the Baltic. It was intimated that this favour would much facilitate British operations in Egypt. Granville gave the idea his serious consideration. The War Office, he found, had no objection to it; the Admiralty, on the other hand, was hostile; of its unpopularity with the general public he had no doubt, as they would see in the surrender submission to Bismarck and resent it accordingly. "Gladstone, Derby, and I," he wrote with truth, "would not be the best people to make it. But it sometimes occurs to me whether it would not be a price worth paying, if it could secure a perfectly satisfactory end to the Egyptian financial mess." [1]　Another and bolder Foreign Secretary was to reach a similar conclusion.

Meanwhile Bismarck—to borrow a phrase of Granville's making—'mumbled and grumbled,' [2] and the will of the Junker proved more powerful than the will of the Whig. The question of the Congo was referred to Berlin, where an international conference assembled under Bismarck's presidency. But the Foreign Secretary took the precaution of sending a strong body of experts to represent Great Britain, and reaped the reward of his carefulness. The Berlin Act which placed the Congo under an international commission and established there freedom of trade and freedom of navigation was an indisputable achievement, and not the less that in the case of undeveloped or unexplored countries it recognised the notion of spheres of influence and the principle that effective occupation gave a title to annexation.

The Congo Act of 1885 had been but lately signed when Granville, still wrestling in Africa with the situation produced by Gordon's death, found himself confronted in Asia by a crisis no less pregnant and acute. It is only since the diplomatic shuffle of the first years of the twentieth century that people have abandoned the belief in a great, inevitable clash between the Empires of Russia and India. In the nineteenth century the

---

[1] *Life of Granville*, ii. 362.
[2] Granville used it of Hartington (*Life of Granville*, ii. 471).

idea had its pigeonhole in every dogmatic mind, and would from time to time spring out, with the terrifying energy of a cuckoo in a cuckoo-clock, upon the childlike mortals who learn their politics from thrills and catchwords. Some danger of such occurrence on the North-West Frontier no doubt there was; how much and of what nature we need not stay to speculate. It is enough to say that in the spring of 1885 there occurred at Penjdeh a collision between the Russians and the Afghans, which seemed as if it might be the prelude of the expected storm. Granville was soon made aware that the clerk of this weather was no other than the demi-god at Berlin. Bismarck, if he had not exactly called up the clouds, had it certainly in his power to call them off. Sacrifice was consequently offered him as before.

A diplomatic slip on Granville's part happened to give the German Chancellor the better chance to take full advantage of British embarrassments. In the heat of debate the Foreign Secretary had made the ill-judged allegation that Bismarck had advised Beaconsfield 'to take Egypt.' Beaconsfield was dead; so, too, was Odo Russell, the probable source of Granville's information; and Salisbury disclaimed all knowledge of the story. Bismarck was thus in an excellent position to repudiate the charge that had been brought against him. He did so with all the effect possible, for to his denial he attached a general attack upon the dilatory methods and vexatious enquiries of British Foreign Office officials. Granville, already a target for criticism on account of the affair of Gordon, was further discredited by these strictures upon his Department. If nothing else was clear, it was at least plain that he had referred and deferred a little too much to the great man at Berlin. And yet, owing to the incident at Penjdeh and the possibility of a war with Russia, he had now to defer again, even though both he and the German Ambassador in London were equally aware that Bismarck had been guilty of false statement, or, at the best, of grave inaccuracy.[1] Large concessions, to the prejudice of Australia, were therefore granted to Germany in New Guinea.

The Bismarckian vapours once dispersed, the sky grew lighter as the year (1885) progressed. After an hour of intense anxiety, the Penjdeh incident was amicably referred to arbitra-

[1] For the full story, see the *Life of Granville*, ii. 426–8.

tion. In this common-sense conclusion, which eventually secured Penjdeh to Russia and the Zulfikar Pass to Afghanistan, Bismarck doubtless played once more his favourite part of honest broker. The *entente* between the Three Emperors had been revived in the preceding year, and German influence in Russia was again vigorous. Granville had already recognised its potency by inaugurating that policy of so-called "graceful concessions," which were to be a feature of Anglo-German relations for some while to come. He did more than this. In response to a gesture of Bismarck's he sent a brilliant student of politics and history on a special mission to Berlin, and in this manner ushered Lord Rosebery—his spiritual though not his chronological successor— into the world of diplomacy.

For Granville himself returned no more to the Foreign Office after the fall of the Liberal Government in 1885. Justly or unjustly, the affair in the Sudan had discredited him as a Foreign Secretary with the Electorate. About this he neither entertained illusions nor affected concealment, but was, as always in his public life, a model of high generosity. "Your first object," he wrote to Gladstone, when it came in 1886 to the formation of another Liberal Ministry, "should be to make your Government as acceptable as possible, which does not appear to be compatible with my taking the Foreign Office." [1] The graceful withdrawal was gracefully accepted. Gladstone mixed the pill with sedatives and Rosebery gilded it with compliments. The Leadership in the Lords was left to the aging Minister, and the Colonial Secretaryship added. But, all said and done, nothing could conceal the fact that he had exchanged a greater office for a lesser. Just the ill-luck of the advent of a mad prophet in the heart of the African desert during the last year or two of his administration had spoiled his record of service and exposed the weaker points of his character. So do circumstances mock our talents, and thus are we dragged to execution by the rude cart-wheels of chance!

Gladstone's Government of 1886 had no life in it; and Granville did not live to see another. He faded gradually in those critical years which saw the fading of the Liberals in the Lords and the latter end of the old Whig Party. Then in 1891, a year before Gladstone came for the last time into power, and in the seventy-

---

[1] *Life of Granville,* ii. 481.

sixth year of his own age, he came to that crisis which, patient like Love of inexhaustible simile, had seemed to the great poet of the time to be as the crossing of a bar. He set sail, it may be, by star rather than by compass. His published memorials give little or no indication of his theological views. He had had indeed strong Catholic influences all about him—a devout and charming wife,[1] a brilliant convert sister,[2] a Catholic stepson as widely versed as any man of his time in ecclesiastical and historical studies;[3] and during the last illness of the first of these he had witnessed the strange power of the last sacraments of the Church.[4] Such proximity is perhaps calculated to settle all the deeper problems in the simplest way, or else to leave them infinitely more complex and fluid than before. But, so far as foreign policy is concerned, we need the less to inquire in Granville's case that wherever Gladstone was, there also was Gladstonian theology. The oracles of God, as the Liberal Leader interpreted them, had declared for the merits of self-government. Granville subscribed without difficulty to this faith. In Ireland it made him an advocate of Home Rule; in South Africa a party to the surrender after Majuba; in Egypt an accomplice in delay. It was a theology, we may therefore perhaps infer, not exempt from practical difficulties.

Granville was succeeded, as has been said, by that distinguished student of politics and history, who took his first lesson in diplomacy in a bout with Bismarck. Industrious to know all that was to be known about great men in general and certain great men in particular—about Pitt, for instance, and Pitt's forgotten love-story; about Napoleon, more especially in his final phase; perhaps, too, in a more secret and secluded compartment of his mind, about Newman also—Lord Rosebery was indeed a student without, as we might say, the scholar's stoop. But also so much more than a student! An actor, too fond, it may be, of declaiming fine phrases and provoking dramatic situations to pursue high purposes down the dull lanes of circumstance or to convert patriotic airs into the hard stuff of life!

[1] Marie Pelline de Dalberg (Lady Acton *en premières noces*).
[2] Lady Georgiana Fullerton.
[3] The first Lord Acton.
[4] The reference is to two letters of Lord Granville's, published in Fitzmaurice's *Life of Granville*, i. 362, 363.

A race-horse trained to unusual swiftness and so outstripping all competitors at the outset of the race, but over a long course manifestly inadequate and stamped with lassitude! A statesman strong in promise but in performance disappointing or, as we say more shortly and simply—since the classic phrase really extinguishes every paraphrase—*capax imperii nisi imperasset*.

So we well may see him, not unjustly, in face of his record as Prime Minister, as Liberal Leader, and finally as free-lance! Yet at the Foreign Office he left another name. He seemed a hard worker, a wise counsellor, an engaging if sometimes imperious chief. He has to be judged, indeed, as a Foreign Secretary upon almost as short terms of office as are conceivable—a six-month in 1886, a year and a half between 1892 and 1894—and in relation to issues of which none seemed graver than a French ultimatum delivered at Bangkok and demanding a cession of territory on the Mekong. Yet, by virtue of the manner in which he handled this affair and the firm way in which he suppressed, on the strength of Granville's governing despatch of 1884, the attempt of the Khedive to break loose from British control in 1893, he has drawn from a critic the opinion that "in negotiation none better understood that genuine success consists in furthering the larger interests by the sacrifice of the smaller." [1]

Those larger interests Rosebery crystallised in the thought of Empire, and the advocacy of that "unswerving purpose to develop and to maintain," without which he warns us that "planting a flag here and there or demarcating regions with a red line on a map are vain diversions." [2] His words had charm and power, but his work lacked, perhaps unavoidably, the stamp of originality. He followed the path upon which Granville had reluctantly entered, and where Salisbury more boldly walked, for he understood the value of continuity. [3] We might say of his foreign policy that it has a bent towards Germany rather than towards France, not surprising in the case of one who declared that our relations with the latter were " really more troublesome than with any other power." [4] Here as elsewhere his native Whiggishness came out—that instinct to take the line of least resistance which makes Whigs what they are, and is sometimes

---

[1] W. H. Dawson, in *Camb. Hist. of British Foreign Policy*, iii. 198.
[2] *Miscellanies*, ii. 260.
[3] Grey, *Twenty-five Years*, i. 4.
[4] Quoted from the *Camb. Hist. of British Foreign Policy*, iii. 244.

their merit and sometimes their defect.   No one, perhaps, was better aware than he that friction with Germany meant friction with the master of the strongest army that Europe contained; no one, perhaps, more earnestly desired to have peace in his time; no one, as armaments increased and the two countries drifted into antagonism, viewed the international situation with more apprehension or characterised it with greater prescience.   It was the calm, he saw, before the storm; and he found it, as he says, "terrifying." [1]

The year in which those prophetic words were uttered was almost the last in which he made any play in politics.   He had always been meteoric.   As he was swift and resplendent in his rise, so he was still sudden and scintillating in his decline.   It is one of the extraordinary things about him that he made so much display and left behind so much reputation with so little actually to his credit in the way of accomplishment.   He was the latest child of the Whigs—interesting, rather pathetic, born out of time.   Only the Foreign Office could have afforded political opportunity at so late a date to a talent and temper such as his.   It framed his figure; and he embellished its roll of celebrities.   British diplomatic history will always salute him, yet as one about to die.   He was the last pure-blooded survivor of his race—of the old Whig breed that served us in a period of transition so well.   He carried his honours with excellent grace.   He seemed as if born to figure in such regal congresses as the world once knew, and to return the tennis balls of diplomacy in the grand manner of former times. Occasion failed him for this.   Yet not Clarendon nor Granville bore the old luggage of the Whigs into the lumber-room with a finer air, or left among the archives of latter-day diplomacy a more delicate perfume.

[1] " This calm before the storm is terrifying " (July 9th, 1909).

VI

SALISBURY
With some mention of LORD LANSDOWNE

[ROBERT ARTHUR TALBOT GASCOYNE-CECIL.—Born 1830. Succeeded as 3rd Marquis of Salisbury, 1868. *Foreign Secretary*, 1878–1880, 1885–1886, 1887–1892, 1895–1900. Prime Minister, 1885–1886, 1886–1892, 1895–1902. Died 1903.]

[HENRY CHARLES KEITH PETTY-FITZMAURICE—Born 1845. Succeeded as 5th Marquis of Lansdowne, 1866. *Foreign Secretary*, 1900–1905.]

SALISBURY

"We talked a little of Lord Salisbury," remarks Queen Victoria in 1874 with reference to a conversation she had had with Gladstone, "and of his great talents and uprightness but peculiarities." [1] A few years earlier Clarendon had written to an intimate correspondent in a position to give him information in something of the same sense. "Salisbury," he observed, "is an enigma to me, and I wish you could tell me what he really is." [2] So people wondered who saw him at close quarters in the days when he was building up his reputation. And less eminent persons than Victoria and Clarendon had not ceased to speculate on the matter when, some fifteen years after his death, his biography began to appear. He was plainly an unconventional man; and the biography, also, was plainly an unconventional work. It seemed, by virtue of a peculiar sympathy between the author and the subject—a sympathy so perfect as instinctively to eliminate uncritical admiration or extravagant praise—to realise Richmond's conception of finished portraiture and to be "the truth lovingly-told." It bore, besides, on every page the marks of unusual strength—strength of thought, strength of style, strength of feeling, strength of standpoint. It broke some ordinary rules. It proceeded towards its end without any particular regard for design or structure. In a work which could hardly run beyond five volumes, and perhaps not so far, the events of two years were allowed to engross almost the whole space of a single book. There was another singularity. Things that are usually considered in the last chapter of a Life were considered here fully in the beginning of it—the character and the religion of the subject. We were shown the interior man

---

[1] *Letters of Queen Victoria* (second series), ii. 322.
[2] Maxwell, *Life of Clarendon*, ii. 359.

almost before we began to take account of his exterior greatness; and we were thus persuaded to perceive how massive
he was in himself before the adventitious chances of rare fortune
and favourable circumstance began to affect our imagination.

This presentation of a character almost at the outset as if
it were a finished product might, in many instances, prove a
confusing anachronism. It ought not to be reckoned so in
Salisbury's case. He grew very early to maturity of mind
though not of talent. One chief reason for this is plain enough.
A boyhood of pathetic loneliness—a boyhood early deprived
of a mother's care and cursed beyond the ordinary by the
original sin sometimes to be detected in schools, schoolboys,
and even schoolmasters—made him intellectually and morally
a hermit. The story of his school-days is a very proper correc-
tive to the conventional picture of a troop of golden lads upon
a golden ladder, which did duty in those days, and later still,
for a more exact and detailed description of a young gentleman's
education. The boy in this instance was admittedly [1] of high
talent and character. Yet he spoke in later life of his time
at a reputable private school as "an existence among devils,"
and declared to his father, in regard, not to one but to many
days of his life at Eton as a lower-boy, that 'he was bullied
without ceasing from morning to night.' [2] A school, we are
sometimes assured by its thorough-going apologists, is a micro-
cosm where we are conveniently initiated into the mysteries
of the larger world that we shall presently come to inhabit.
It may be so; yet there are some of us who would gladly have
been spared the knowledge how coarse human beings can be
and how rough a place the world is, at least until the golden
hours of life are gone and, secure in the knowledge that at least
our houses, unlike our rooms at school, are, when we choose
to make them so, really our castles, we can better afford to
contemplate our fellow-creatures with philosophic detachment.
How deeply the iron entered into Robert Cecil's soul is apparent
from as curious a piece of evidence as one can well conceive.
Examined as to the source of his extraordinary acquaintance
with the alleys and bye-ways surrounding his London house,

[1] That is according to his tutor's reports. Lady Gwendolen Cecil, *Life of
Robert, Marquis of Salisbury*, i. 10. This book is that referred to simply as
Life in the footnotes to this article.
[2] *Ibid.*, p. 13.

he explained that his knowledge had been acquired in the early effort to avoid chance meetings in the holidays with the companions whom he saw only too much of at school.[1]

As the religious-minded men of the Middle Ages were apt to retire from the world in a sort of despair at its wickedness, so the boy, already deeply marked by the interest in religion which never left him, retired into himself in disgust at an experience which had outraged his deep-set faith in personal freedom. His father judged it necessary to take him away from school. Two years at home at Hatfield—two years of virtual seclusion from the companionship of boys of his own age—completed the solitary in him. When he emerged again he knew perhaps as much about men and cared as little about pleasure as Timon of Athens. Timon, however, by the time he had discovered what his fellow-creatures could be like at their worst, was in a position to make his everlasting mansion upon the beached verge of the salt flood. Cecil, on the other hand, had life before him; and energy and talent at his back. No mere cynicism could have satisfied him. He was fortunate, therefore, in meeting with a criticism of life which diagnosed human nature not very much more favourably than he had done, and yet stressed the existence, beside the uglier manifestations of humanity, of a new world governed by grace and love. Newman, when Cecil began residence at Christ Church, had been two years a Catholic, but Newman's early writings, "for which Cecil," as his biographer tells us, "always entertained a supreme admiration," [2] remained a model of what Anglican theology could bring forth. The *Parochial and Plain Sermons* are cast in the severest mould of the writer's thought; they have little of the sweetness and pathos that distinguishes his later work; their music is austere; their sound is calculated to go out, not through all lands, but throughout the land of the English. They chimed in, perhaps none the worse for all this, with the young man's reflections and observations. He had seen the whole world lying in wickedness, and how great that wickedness was. To this world of darkness Newman had opposed a world of light—the Christian Church, One Holy Catholic and Apostolic, with its sacramental aids. There were some who, in spite of Newman's secession, believed that the English Church embodied this conception as interpreted

---

[1] *Life*, i. 15.   [2] *Ibid.*, p. 24.

by, and adapted to, the needs and traditions of the English people. Cecil was among them.

The children of the Oxford Movement fell, and still fall, into two groups. There are those who look to it to undo the work of the Reformation, and there are those who see in it a regeneration of the Church of England on the lines of primitive Christianity. Salisbury must be placed in the latter school. He had no hatred of Rome, but he had no use for her. Catholic Theology and what is called Liberal Theology alike rationalised too much for him; [1] and his own theology, though it was satisfied by the doctrines and ceremonies of the English Church, rested in the last resort upon an individual and mystical basis— "upon a spiritual vision," to borrow his biographer's words, "which had an existence altogether apart from his intellectual processes and which was more compelling of conviction than any evidence which they could produce." [2]

This was not all. He was by instinct a rebel. "Criticism and revolt," we are told, "were prominent among his characteristics. Authoritative teaching, as such, was throughout his life and in all directions repugnant to him. He had what can only be described as an innate yearning after heterodoxy in all its forms." [3]

It followed that the Church which meant so much in his private life had no well-defined place in his political philosophy. He stood, indeed, firmly by the framework of society, both in Church and State, that he had inherited; but it is difficult to see how either the religious formularies of the one or the religious preferences of the other could have been hammered into shape by any so taciturn and tolerant an individualist as himself. He saw that Christianity was "incapable of co-existing permanently with a civilisation it did not inspire;" that it would admit of "no neutrality"; [4] that a fatal catastrophe lay in wait for a nation originally fashioned by Christian ideas and subsequently becoming faithless to them; that "disintegration" was the danger of the day. Yet there was little enough in his politics to suggest, as so constantly with Gladstone, the presence of ideals, enthusiasms, or even considerations derived from Christian sources. He was caustic and cynical, amusingly dry and gloomily sceptical.

It was these unreconciled proclivities that made Salisbury

[1] *Life*, i. 115, 116.　　[2] *Ibid.*, p. 114.　　[3] *Ibid.*, p. 101.　　[4] *Ibid.*, p. 108.

so puzzling to his countrymen. They did not know then that "while he had never known what it was to doubt the truth of Christian doctrine, he had all his life found a difficulty in accepting the moral teaching of the Gospels," [1] or otherwise they might have read the riddle. But, however that may be, it will at all events be found that in all his policy both at home and abroad he seldom if ever relied upon considerations to which a hardened 'man of the world' could take exception. In 1864, for example, he puts forward the view, in discussing the then dominant question of the franchise, that the State must be conceived, not as a spiritual but as a material entity, and proceeds to vindicate the analogy between it and a joint-stock company, arguing with great ingenuity that if we are going to distribute voting power in accordance with the principle of 'natural right,' the system which mankind adopt, when left to regulate their private business, affords the best criterion of what nature recommends. [2] And in foreign policy it is upon political interests, rather than upon political sentiments or causes, such as appealed to some of his other contemporaries like Gladstone or even Palmerston, that his eye fixes. "He is," argues Hatzfeldt, who knew him well, in a secret report of the year 1898, "a man who in general cherishes no sympathies for any other nation, and in the transaction of business is moved by purely English considerations." [3] And Wolff-Metternich repeats the judgment in different words, calling him "im Herzen ein stolzer Patriot"—a proud patriot at bottom, and, as the writer adds, "among living statesmen the one who above all embodies the prestige of England." [4] He was in reality not without care for the larger interests of Europe, but the pressure of circumstances, presently to be noticed, early taught him the hard truth that practical politics is one long 'second-best,' and his descent from more than one Lord Mayor in all probability supplied an instinct to treat international affairs as a branch of business.

It was no loss to him that the appearance of Alison's *Life of Castlereagh* drew him at the start to make a close study of Castlereagh's career. He found in that Minister, regarded in his public aspect, a character not unsympathetic to his own; and no figure

[1] *Life,* i. 102.   [2] *Quarterly Review,* April 1864, p. 26.
[3] *Die Grosse Politik der Europ. Kabinette,* xiv. p. 246.
[4] *Ibid.,* xvii. p. 3.

in English history—not even that of Pitt—probably influenced or interested him more. It is in his essay upon Castlereagh—as decisive a piece of work, one may guess, in determining the bent of his own life as any that he ever did—that he measures with cool discrimination and in words worth repeating the rewards and penalties of a diplomatic career. "There is nothing dramatic," he observes, "in the successes of a diplomatist. His victories are made up of a series of microscopic advantages : of a judicious suggestion here, of an opportune civility there, of a wise concession at one moment and a far-sighted persistence at another; of sleepless tact, immovable calmness, and patience that no folly, no provocation, no blunders can shake! But there is nothing exciting in the exercise of excellencies such as these. A list of such exploits lends no fascination to a narrative. Writers will not encumber their pages with a throng of minute circumstances . . . individually trivial, though in the aggregate they effect results of vast importance; and readers would not be found to read them if they did. The result is that, while the services of a commander are celebrated with almost undiminished enthusiasm from age to age, the services of a diplomatist fade rapidly away from a nation's memory." [1] Unadvertised, unostentatious work appealed to him, and, above all, work comparatively untrammelled by public and probably ignorant criticism; and he saw in Castlereagh one who had done such work excellently well. He speaks with an enthusiasm, rare in his writings, of Castlereagh's "courage, patience, and . . . faultless sagacity," [2] and, if he failed, as Professor Webster complains,[3] to detect the sanguine hope of European solidarity inaugurated by Castlereagh's policy at Chaumont, he remains none the less the foremost statesman to recognise the merit and lesson of Castlereagh's cool and practical intelligence. It is characteristic of him that his judgment challenges certain current conceptions of morality in treating of Castlereagh's corrupt practices to bring about the Irish Union and in his classic defence of the decision of the Eastern Powers to take their liberty from the Poles. A streak of realism, or

---

[1] *Essays by Robert, Marquess of Salisbury, Biographical*, p. 12.
[2] *Ibid.*, p. 69.
[3] " It is significant that one who was himself at a later date to place much trust in the ' Concert of Europe ' had no idea of the functions and objects of the European Alliance which Castlereagh had devised " (*Foreign Policy of Castlereagh*, p. 492).

something like it, runs from the first in his blood, and gathers and strengthens as the conduct of life proceeds. The year 1874, when he consents to serve under Disraeli, may be taken to mark its initial, the year 1878, when he adopts substantially his Leader's view of the Near Eastern imbroglio, its final triumph. He has by then definitely refused to sacrifice, as an idealist would have done, his chance of public service for an idea, and definitely decided, as a realist must do, to consider rather how the Queen's Government can best be carried on.

One might, perhaps, say, then, that the very profundity of his sense of the inherent obscurity of things—a sense, as we have seen, so profound as to make Christian dogma seem easy to him and Christian ethic difficult—tended to deprive his religion of that direct visible influence upon his politics, usually to be observed in men as firmly convinced of the truth of Christianity as he was himself; but that, if his creed lay covered—at any rate after his failure to recommend a Russophil policy to his colleagues in 1878—his character protected his policy from the charge of opportunism. The reserve and self-reliance of his nature appear in the isolation of his statesmanship, in that "splendid isolation" of Great Britain which one of his colleagues spoke of, and another supposed to have lasted all too long. He had the chance of coming to an understanding with Germany; his successor actually came to an understanding with France; but he himself preferred to leave his country as free to appropriate the famous lines of the old English diplomatist as he was himself.

> " How happy is he born and taught
>   That serveth not another's will,
> Whose armour is his honest thought,
>   And simple truth his utmost skill ! "

Salisbury's religious outlook affected his conduct of foreign policy in another way. It removed all haunting sense of responsibility. The very obscurity that hung about the decrees of Providence, the counsels of Christianity, even the moral value of any act or purpose of one's own, saved him from that anxious questioning about results which many men undergo. He recognised, indeed, a "burden of decision"—the actual trouble of making up his mind upon the facts at his disposal—

but, that trouble faced and dealt with to the best of his judgment, he suffered no further distress.[1] Only mysticism or callous indifference can provide this utter freedom from interior perturbation, and, as he was not guilty of the second, we must postulate the working of the first. For the rest—to put the matter, as his biographer does, quite plainly and simply, and relieve it of all those nebulous abstractions in which less really clever men delight, generation after generation, to clothe their convictions—"he worshipped Christ—not the Christ-type or the Christ-ideal or the 'Divine revealed in the human.'" [2]

Such then was the unusual man who, in the spring of 1878, during a grave international crisis, suddenly became Foreign Secretary. His career, both private and public, had so far been chequered. As a second son, and a second son who had married against his father's wishes, he had known the pains of poverty, had supported himself to some extent by high-class journalism, and, in the hope of substituting an assured for a precarious income, had been within an ace of sacrificing a parliamentary career and succeeding the ever-memorable Charles Greville in one of the two Clerkships to the Council. Then, through the death of his elder brother in 1865 and of his father in 1868, the wheel of fortune had come round full circle. He became, first, the heir to a great position and a great estate, then one of the chief magnates in the kingdom in an age when magnates still counted for much. His own political talent and the brilliancy and buoyancy of his wife,[3] once restricted by the narrow background of Duchess Street and Fitzroy Square, were thenceforward framed in the ample splendour of Hatfield.

A hundred years hence, when romantic mists have gathered thick enough round the nineteenth century, the home-circle of which he became the source and centre may conceivably seem as interesting and excite as much curiosity as the household of Sir Thomas More, or the community at Little Gidding, or the family of the Ferronays, or, to turn to something more secular for a comparison, the sodality that once gathered at Holland House. In that focus of late Conservatism, Church and State were held to be of even interest

---

[1] The basis of these observations will be found in the *Life*, i. 118, 119.
[2] *Ibid.*, p. 114.
[3] She was Miss Georgina Alderson, the daughter of Baron Alderson.

if not of equal honour; and all the problems they provided were
eagerly discussed.   A certain brilliancy and originality of treatment clothed old convictions with new ideas.   That which is
grave in life seemed to mingle without effort with what is gay.
The son of Sirach, it may be, would have paused to consider
whether he had not found here one of those famous men, rich in
virtue, that live at peace in their houses,[1] the wisest of men
have wondered if the mantle of his 'valiant,' or as some read
'virtuous,' woman [2] had not descended in this place.   And as
one drew an imaginary portrait of Cæcilia's household,[3] so may
another some day draw a portrait, not imaginary, of that of
Cæcilius.   There, at all events, it lies—a theme not yet ready for
the hand of the artist, but ripening to immortality as mortality
fails, and giving the lie to all Mill's talk about 'the stupid party'
—the picture of a great Conservative House in the last quarter
of the nineteenth century.   Disraeli looked at it and perhaps
loved it as he loved all things that gave colour to life, or savour
to conversation, or power to the head of the Conservative Party.

Salisbury had, with difficulty, reconciled himself to the Tory-
democratic leadership of that extraordinary man.   In 1867, over
the Reform Bill, he had resigned, together with General Peel and
Carnarvon, from a short-lived Government, in which he had
played the part of Secretary for India.   In his eyes, and not in
his eyes only, Disraeli had made—to borrow the title which stood
at the head of the most famous of all his articles for the *Quarterly
Review*—"the Conservative Surrender" of his time.   That which
had been done and the way in which it had been done offended
every instinct of his being—his faith in "squire Conservatism," [4]
and his sense of the need of a high standard of honour in working
a Constitution so lavish as ours is in pitfalls for a private conscience.[5]   "My opinions," he wrote to a friend, "belong to the
past; and it is better that the new principles in politics should
be worked by those who sympathise with them heartily." [6]

Achilles, therefore, retired into his tents, and for seven years
had neither part nor lot in the proceedings of Agamemnon.
He declined to take the leadership in the House of Lords; he
further resolved, after mature consideration, to decline all

---

[1] Ecclesiasticus, xliv. 6.   [2] Proverbs, xxxi.
[3] Marius the Epicurean, c. xxi.   [4] *Life*, i. 294.
[5] *Ibid.*, p. 273.   [6] *Ibid.*, p. 294.

co-operation with a man whom he utterly distrusted. Then, in 1874, there came a sudden dissolution and an unexpected victory for Conservatism at the polls. Through the channel of Lady Derby, his stepmother, he was approached by Disraeli and invited to take office. All his surest political friends—Heathcote, Carnarvon, Beresford-Hope, Northumberland—advised him affirmatively. With repulsion, with humiliation, with vast misgiving, he sacrificed his private inclination to the service of the State. He met his old enemy, took office as Indian Secretary in his Administration, gradually forgot the old antipathy, gradually acquired some sort of regard for the sardonic old Israelite. A mutual gift and appreciation of irony sweetened their intercourse. By the end of the elder man's life they were adaptable colleagues if not congenial friends.

It was the pressure of an international crisis that brought the two men together. Differing about democracy, disagreeing in Church matters, they found by degrees, though not immediately, a common ground in foreign affairs. They were at one in regarding British imperial interests as the true touchstone of foreign policy; at one in distrusting the perfervid idealism which poured in molten streams of eloquence from the golden-mouthed orators of the time—from Gladstone and from Liddon; at one in feeling the want of energy and initiative in Derby, whose conduct in revealing, as it happened inaccurately, the course of certain critical Cabinet discussions, Salisbury with a certain brutality in debate, curiously unlike, as people felt, his superb courtesy in private life, even compared to Titus Oates's proceedings in the matter of the Popish Plot.

And Derby at the Foreign Office was, no doubt, what is popularly known as a round peg in a square hole. Since Aberdeen died the Conservative Party had been greatly deficient in diplomatic ability. Malmesbury, indeed, had proved a much better Foreign Secretary than had been expected of him, but he came late to his business, and his terms of office were never more than short. But Derby, whom Disraeli had sent again to the Foreign Office, was admittedly a *pis aller*. His own father had originally appointed him, but with the frankest recognition that he was not really the man for the place.[1] As ill-luck would have it, the place in his time required diplomatic

---

[1] *Letters of Queen Victoria* (second series), i. 353.

talent above the ordinary. The trouble, as usual, was brewed in the Balkans. In Bosnia and Herzegovina the Christians had grown tired of Turkish misrule and were taking practical measures to be quit of it. Their rising raised again anxious questionings in the great European Chanceries, anxious hopes among their co-religionists in Turkey. The break-up of the Ottoman Empire once more seemed imminent, and it was not easy to foresee what that might not involve. Derby was a man of peace, and no doubt rendered doubly peaceful by memories of the diplomatic bungle that eventuated in the Crimean War. As certainly as Aberdeen he felt that the quarrels of Turkey were not worth an Englishman's bones; and his inactivity throughout the crisis, though partly temperamental, was doubtless based upon a determination at all costs not to fall into the mistake of 1854. History, however, has a Puckish ambition to repeat itself. At Constantinople, in Sir Henry Elliot, the British Government enjoyed the dubious advantage of a representative almost as self-willed and quite as Turcophil as Stratford de Redcliffe; and his conduct conveyed to the Turks the comfortable idea that all the resources of the British Empire were at their back. The Prime Minister was hardly less culpable. His mind was mysterious; his imagination receptive; his language was bellicose; his intentions were mild. "A study," observes a recent authority, "of the diplomatic despatches and conversations which passed between the Foreign Office and the Porte at that time, and of Lord Beaconsfield's concurrent correspondence with the Queen, his colleagues, and his friends, makes it impossible to resist the conclusion that all the admonitions, remonstrances, and veiled threats which were addressed to Russia on the subject of Constantinople were a gigantic piece of bluff." [1] The old Jew, in fact, never meant business, at any rate on the battlefield; but was as peaceful as the rest of his race. No one clearly understood that at the time—not the Queen, who was urgent for war; not Derby,[2] who resigned rather than see the Fleet moved up to the Dardanelles or Indian troops disembarked in Malta; not the Turks, who thought they had been unconscionably betrayed; not Salisbury, who supposed, what he doubted later, that the Prime

---

[1] *Camb. Hist. of British Foreign Policy*, iii. 126.
[2] Derby's remark in 1877 that " I don't think he (Beaconsfield) desires war ; he desires to place England in a commanding position," shows, however, that he had gauged Beaconsfield correctly (*Life of Disraeli*, vi. 139).

Minister was manœuvring England into a war in defence of Turkey;[1] not the Country, which fully expected that hostilities would follow the occupation of Constantinople by Russia, when in fact the Prime Minister, if it came to the point, was ready to swallow even that contingency rather than fight.[2]

Salisbury, it is essential to realise, had no love of the Turks either then or later. He recognised the greatness of the refusal that had been returned by John Russell to Nicholas's famous project of partition, deplored it, and worked always at the Near Eastern problem under the inherited load of a lost opportunity. So really was this the case that in September 1876, when the revolt in Bosnia had set all Europe by the ears, we find him writing to Lytton, then Viceroy of India, that 'he did not despair of being told to write to him for his best civilian to govern the new province of Egypt,'[3] and to Beaconsfield, in the same month, that 'the best chance of coming to a peaceful issue of these perplexities was—in his belief—to come to an early under-standing with Russia, and that ' the danger was that they should make that result impossible by hanging on to Austria.'[4] These aspirations were partly ideal, partly departmental. His sympathies, that is to say, were with the oppressed Christian nationalities of the Balkans rather than with their incompetent Turkish masters; and, also, in his capacity as Indian Secretary he was interested in coming to a good understanding with Russia in Asia and in safeguarding the route to India by the acquisition of Egypt. But these considerations were presently overborne by others.

During the course of the year 1876, two opportunities of getting the issue settled on satisfactory lines were lost, and for this the main responsibility lies with Elliot. The famous Andràssy Note, insisting upon the introduction of liberal and constitutional reforms under the ægis of a mixed commission in Bosnia and Herzegovina, was accepted by all the Great Powers of Europe, but, when it came to enforcing it, Great Britain, on no better pretext than that the rebellion in the revolted provinces ought

---

[1] *Life*, ii. 137.
[2] *Camb. Hist. of British Foreign Policy*, iii. 126. " . . . there is no justification for supposing that he was ever prepared to go to war on this issue alone, but every reason to conclude that he was ready, if the fortunes of diplomacy went against him, to accept accomplished facts and make the best of them."
[3] *Life*, ii. 83.
[4] *Ibid.*, p. 85.

to be crushed before the reforms were introduced, imposed her veto. It is a sufficient criticism of this performance that even Stratford de Redcliffe regarded it as the surrender of a great opportunity of doing civilisation service.[1]

Almost simultaneously with the British defection the Turks, to show how well they deserved that Britain should stand by them against the rest of Europe, initiated those famous atrocities in Bulgaria which evoked the thunders of a Gladstonian pamphlet. Beaconsfield, misled by Elliot, at first made light of the charges, but, eventually becoming more or less convinced of their justice, fell back upon the idea of a European Conference. It met at Constantinople, and Salisbury was sent out as British plenipotentiary. He passed through four of the five great capitals of the Continent on his way eastwards, made himself acquainted with Décazes, Bismarck, Andràssy, and the Powers that ruled in Rome, and with so much of their minds as he could discover. It was his baptism of diplomacy, if, that is to say, the diplomatists of that day can be reckoned among the regenerate.

Salisbury's was certainly one of the two great figures at Constantinople; out of the other, it is to be feared the old Adam had never been expelled. General Ignatieff, the Russian Ambassador, had charge, in virtue of his seniority, of the map where the conclusions reached were registered for reference. Salisbury noticed one morning that a frontier line agreed-upon had shifted its locality upon the atlas during the night. With every expectation of an unpleasant row he pointed out the change. But the Russians play diplomacy like a game of grab in which cheating is reckoned the finest tactics. Ignatieff acknowledged his defeat at once with bland, engaging charm. "Monsieur le Marquis," he said, "est si fin—on ne peut rien lui cacher." [2] It was consummate. No wonder Salisbury was convulsed with laughter.

Other consummation to the Conference there was little. Elliot saw to that.[3] He put his trust in the Young Turks of the time who were brought into power, whilst the Conference sat, with the obvious object of confusing counsel. To a project of local reform under Governors-general acceptable to the Great

[1] *Camb. Hist. of British Foreign Policy*, iii. 99.
[2] *Life*, ii. 110.
[3] For the evidence, see *Camb. Hist. of British Foreign Policy*, iii. 111, 112, especially the footnotes.

Powers in the revolted provinces of Bulgaria, Bosnia, and Herzegovina, Midhat, the new Grand Vizier, opposed a Liberal constitution for the whole of Turkey, which had every merit except an honest purpose on the part of the Sultan to put it into effect. On the strength of it the Turks rejected the recommendations of the Conference; then, as soon as the negotiators were gone, Midhat was shelved and his institutions with him. Abdul Hamid II., the last and subtlest of the successors of Othman thus established himself as one of the astutest rulers in Europe; against his masterly inactivity, principalities and powers —the Principalities of European Turkey and the Great Powers of Europe—were for thirty years to battle pretty nearly in vain. More deference is owing to him than he often gets. He was the faithful representative of his race. He professed and he practised the coarse creed of the False Prophet. He treated Christians as the dogs that ran about his streets. He slew the weaker of his opponents, and not least his mother's people, the Armenians, with whose blood he watered the highways and byways of Constantinople. But the stronger forces of Christianity he cheated, or jockeyed, or cajoled. If he sinned consciously, he sinned boldly—for the sake of his Empire and his Faith. Half the criticism of him should be in reality a criticism of Islam and not of its Caliph. To some of us there remains a memory of seeing this priest-king drive to Mosque in the latter days of his sovereignty. He looked no mean nor cringing despot, but rather a stern and pious Moslem upon whom all the ends of a low form of civilisation had descended, a prince of darkness, challenging the purity of the blue sky above and of the white city of the first Christian Emperor that lay gleaming across the Bosphorus.

Salisbury returned to England, worsted in the first encounter with this crafty diplomatist and yet with no loss of reputation. Beaconsfield who had criticised him severely during the course of the negotiations, declaring absurdly enough to Derby that he was "more Russian than Ignatieff" and did not seem aware that the object of his mission was "to keep the Russians out of Turkey, not to create an ideal existence for Turkish Christians," [1] now confided to Lady Chesterfield that Salisbury had "succeeded in everything as regards the Russians and much distinguished himself." [2] It was the absence of material sanctions in Derby's

[1] Buckle, *Life of Beaconsfield*, vi. 111.   [2] *Ibid.*, p. 112.

policy, as well as of rational incredulity in Elliot's Turcophilism which had weakened his hands in dealing with the Turks. He had been sensible of this at the time, and wrote urging that "the strongest means of pressure" should be brought to bear upon the Porte, and that the Ambassador should be put under instructions to leave Constantinople, if he did so himself,[1] although, upon his return, he inconsistently defended the Government's policy of confining pressure to moral suasion—a method long proved to be inapplicable to negotiations with Turks about Christians. That, however, was perhaps rather Derby's concern than his own. To the student of his career the important point to notice is that he emerged from the affair heir-apparent to the Foreign Office.

Derby's days, however, were not yet numbered, though all through 1877, as the Russo-Turkish War, which had followed the failure of the Conference, developed, power was slipping from his grasp and the Prime Minister pushing him from his place. How far this process had gone, even by August 1877, we may gather from the circumstance of Colonel Wellesley's mission to the Emperor of Russia. Accredited by the Queen and the Prime Minister, but without the knowledge of Derby or the Foreign Office, Wellesley was charged to inform Alexander that, if the Russo-Turkish War ran into a second campaign, Great Britain would be driven to join in the hostilities. This went beyond anything that the Cabinet had sanctioned, and was unmistakably Beaconsfield's boldest piece of bluff.

It required no longer any great subtlety to see that Derby was in the way to fall, if ever the minds of Salisbury and Beaconsfield should meet. Even with the Sovereign behind him, the Prime Minister, given his own antiquated conception of the place of magnates, both spiritual and temporal, in the Constitution, was perhaps not likely to have quarrelled at once with the masters of Hatfield and Knowsley; and for a long while Salisbury stood nearer to Derby in the Cabinet dissension over the Russo-Turkish War than he stood to Beaconsfield. He is indeed picked out, together with Derby and Carnarvon, by the warlike, indignant Queen, for special reprobation as a pacifist.[2] From these associates he became ultimately divorced. It is an interesting

---

[1] Cp. *Life of Salisbury*, ii. 115, with *Life of Beaconsfield*, vi. 113.
[2] Buckle, *Life of Beaconsfield*, vi. 149.

study in character and diplomacy to see how his mind gradually shifted under the pressure of thought and circumstance.

The progress of change proceeded somewhat in this manner. Recognising, as has been said already, more easily than some men that politics is one long second-best, he abandoned with the less difficulty that which seemed to him the better solution—the plan of Turkish partition. Not, however, without an effort! In the spring of 1877 he definitely urged the Cabinet to take the bolder course. His proposal was conclusively rejected by the majority of his colleagues, the Prime Minister even pronouncing it to be 'immoral.' [1] Thenceforward he felt himself free to deal with the situation in some less satisfactory but more practicable way. He took this decision with the less reluctance, no doubt, that, as his biographer tells us, "it was an axiom of his that, in foreign affairs, the choice of a policy is as a rule of less importance than the methods by which it is pursued." [2] And of all possible methods Derby's calculated, obstructive inertia—that quality in him which caused all controversy with him to seem like battling with a feather bed [3]—was to Salisbury the least acceptable. The Indian Secretary's clear and practical intelligence would have preferred a pro-Russian policy, could have endured a pro-Turkish policy, but found "the system of never making a plan beyond the next move" [4] utterly intolerable. This temperamental difference from Derby was accentuated by a difference of sentiment about the Eastern Christians. It was impossible but that their condition should appear to the Anglican churchman in the light of an appeal, to the agnostic Derby in the light of a nuisance.[5] All this—and also, as Carnarvon witnesses, the feeling that it was not for him and his best friend to play a second time 'the card' that they had played in 1867 and secede from the Government[6]— must be taken into account in estimating the circumstances that prepared the way for the *rapprochement* and *entente* of 1878 between Salisbury and Beaconsfield.

Not unaccompanied, so Carnarvon records,[7] by wild and ex-

---

[1] *Life of Salisbury*, ii. 134.
[2] *Ibid.*, p. 136.   [3] *Ibid.*, p. 115.   [4] *Ibid.*, p. 135.
[5] Cf. *The Life of the Fourth Earl of Carnarvon*, ii. 340, 355.
[6] Cf. *Ibid.*, p. 357.
[7] *Ibid.*, p. 360. "War," Salisbury is reported by Carnarvon to have said, " was necessary to blow up the whole unsound foreign policy of this country." Similar declarations, according to Carnarvon, were made on several occasions.

travagant statements indicative of great interior agitation, the diplomatic revolution in Salisbury's mind signified, when translated into practice, the substitution of an understanding with Austria, whose 'vocation in Europe' he had but lately declared to be 'gone,' [1] for an understanding with Russia.   The change was uncongenial, for he lacked the fear of Russia that lived in so many eminent persons of his period.   It is to this time that his famous advice to a noble lord to use large maps belongs. It was in this connection that he made characteristic mirth over Lytton's vice-regal panic, inspired as such panics are apt to be by the profession whose trade is courage, that Russia might be advancing upon India.   "You listen too much to the soldiers," he wrote.   "No lesson seems to be so deeply inculcated by the experience of life as that you should never trust experts.   If you believe the doctors, nothing is wholesome; if you believe the theologians, nothing is innocent; if you believe the soldiers, nothing is safe.   They all require to have their strong wine diluted by a very large admixture of common sense." [2]

It would consequently have meant but little to him if Russia had reached Constantinople, for he conceived her to be incapable of producing either the money or the seamen required to make that city into a formidable port.[3]   As Indian Secretary, however, he was concerned with the effect that its capture by Russia might have upon the Oriental mind, and for the sake of British prestige in Asia he was disposed to make its permanent occupation a *casus belli*.   According to a statement of Beaconsfield's to the Queen, the Cabinet did, indeed, at this time unanimously agree—"no one stronger and more decided than Lord Salisbury" [4]—to make war if Russia so much as laid hands on Constantinople.   But the Prime Minister had astutely left out the governing factor in the decision reached.   Salisbury, writing a day or two later, put Lytton in possession of the real facts of the case.   The Russians, he said, had given assurances that they did not intend to retain Constantinople.   Unless they broke this engagement there would be no cause for war.   Temporary occupation was doubtless an evil, but a lesser evil than the loss of Austria as an ally. Neutrality, based upon an Austro-British agreement to prevent any lasting transfer of Constantinople to Russia, had become, so

[1] *Life*, ii. 85.
[3] *Ibid.*, p. 142.
[2] *Ibid.*, p. 153.
[4] *Life of Beaconsfield*, vi. 155.

far as it could be defined, the British policy.   It involved war,
therefore, if Constantinople was permanently held by the Russians,
but, in Salisbury's eyes, not from fear of what Russia might do
with it, but for the sake of the inevitable blow to British prestige
unless the gain to Russia were compensated by some British
gain elsewhere.[1]   In other words, though the partition of Turkey
seemed to him a good policy, he would not allow Russia to
undertake it single-handed.

Salisbury's mind was now not far from Beaconsfield's, for they
both placed 'prestige' in the forefront of their thoughts, though
they appraised it with singularly different measures.   To Salisbury
it seemed one of those sentimental considerations that one had
to take into account in the management of inferior races; to
Beaconsfield it was the pure gold amidst the tinsel of politics—
the exceeding great reward that he sought as well for his country
as for himself, and for the love of which he still bore, at a time
when his colleagues were freely speculating [2] how long, with his
ghastly, corpse-like face, he could last, the burden and heat of the
day.   We become keenly conscious of this difference as we reach
the negotiations at Berlin.

The summer of 1877 wore into autumn, autumn into winter,
1877 into 1878, and still the Russians, notwithstanding reverses,
pushed on, and still the Turks, notwithstanding successes, were
driven back, and still the Cabinet debated, and still Derby
delayed.   The capitulation of Plevna had been followed by
the decisive defeat of the Turkish army at the Shipka Pass;
and from the capture of Adrianople the victors moved on to
the gates of Constantinople.   Peace, it was evident, would
have soon to be made—a peace dictated by Russia and accepted
by Turkey; a peace not influenced by England nor submitted
to Europe.   Derby's colleagues in the Government had long
felt desperate—how desperate we may judge from the fact that
an informal Committee of the Cabinet, consisting of Beaconsfield,
Salisbury, and Cairns, had been formed for the express purpose
of supervising the Foreign Secretary's administration of foreign
affairs.   At a certain date towards the end of January, when
the Cabinet had resolved to send the Fleet up to Constantinople,
Salisbury came at last to the parting of the ways—separated

---

[1] See his letter to Lytton, *Life*, ii. 149–50.
[2] *Life of the Fourth Earl of Carnarvon*, ii. 357.

from Carnarvon, his closest political friend, and Derby, under whose pacific, indolent standard he had hitherto fought—and joined Beaconsfield in the conviction that if Great Britain were to keep her diplomatic place in Europe something must be done, and done quickly, and that the Prime Minister, with all his faults, was a man of courage, ideas, and resource. To his friends the transition from the one camp to the other seemed sudden, to his critics cynical, but to himself the result of six months' search for strength and wisdom. He passed easily into that inner trinity of Ministers of which we have lately spoken, the best expert of the three in the knowledge of foreign affairs. Derby had indeed resigned the Foreign Office when the decision to send the Fleet into the Dardanelles was taken, but had returned there when some fresh information caused this decision (as Salisbury thought wrongly,[1] for he disapproved vacillation) to be reversed. For two months the exhausted, nerveless man struggled with a situation that he could not master; then at the end of March he definitely resigned. Without delay Beaconsfield transferred the direction of foreign affairs to the hands of Salisbury.

The effect was instantaneous, and has seemed to some critics the most memorable, as it was certainly the most dramatic, incident in Salisbury's career. He had to face the fact that, whilst Derby had dallied, the Russians had obliged the Turks to conclude a peace which violated, without the consent of Europe, the settlement of 1856. This was the only serious vice in the Treaty of San Stefano. In other respects it satisfied, well enough, the ideas of the modern world—far better, in fact, than the Treaty of Berlin, which, thanks to British diplomatic intervention, was soon to supersede it. If the truth be told, no fragment of British foreign policy has been more rapidly ridiculed by the event than the settlement which was so magniloquently described by its begetter as "peace with honour." The 'big Bulgaria,' sitting astride the Balkans, the thought of which so alarmed the statesmen of 1878, came into being actually under Salisbury's ægis in 1885. Serbia presently grew to the dimensions that the Treaty of San Stefano had assigned her, and beyond them. Bosnia and Herzegovina, which under that agreement would have enjoyed some measure of autonomy, passed under the control of Austria, to be transferred again,

[1] *Life,* ii. 193.

with much parade of speech, in our own time, to other hands. And the Turkish dominion in Europe was, just forty years later, gleefully reduced by British diplomacy to an acreage far more modest than Russia had assigned to it at San Stefano.

It is not, therefore, to the practical outcome of the international crisis of 1878 that a critic ought to turn to illustrate either the character or the consequences of Salisbury's diplomatic work. Though a high authority [1] has reckoned the drafting of his Circular at this critical juncture to be the high-water mark of his achievement, he rated it low himself. It sufficed, indeed, to give back to Britain her place in the counsels of Europe, but it was still no more—to use his own expressive language—than a "picking up" of "the china that Derby had broken," the sudden, violent effort of a falling man to recover his foothold.[2] Not thus does sound diplomacy make its way towards its goal.

The famous Circular, of which, with presumably accidental irony, the great Powers of Europe were apprised on All Fools Day, he wrote alone, behind locked doors, and between the hours of eleven and three on the night of 29th–30th March. The Cabinet to which it was subsequently submitted, made no more considerable alteration in it than the omission of a pronoun.[3] It voiced to perfection the mind of those who remained in the Government after Carnarvon and Derby were gone. It found an echo in the hearts of the great Chanceries of the neutral Powers—in France and Italy, where the distribution of strength in the Mediterranean was felt to be threatened; in Austria-Hungary, where Andràssy had despaired of peace; in Berlin, where Bismarck was waiting ready to play the rôle of 'honest broker.' It sufficed to convince Russia that the British Government was no longer divided and that the Great Powers of Europe stood ranged behind it.

The precise issue, upon which Derby had eventually resigned, sprang directly out of the question whether or not the whole Treaty of San Stefano was to be submitted to the proposed European Conference or not. Russia was claiming the power to keep certain parts of the settlement outside the purview of the Conference. Salisbury's Circular challenged this contention, not on the ground that any particular provision of the Treaty was indefensible, but that the Treaty as a whole violated at every

---

[1] Lord Rosebery's speech unveiling Salisbury's bust at the Oxford Union, 14th November 1904.   [2] *Life*, ii. 231, 232.   [3] *Ibid.*, p. 226.

turn the Peace of 1856 by extending Russian influence at the
Porte in a manner incompatible with the interests of a Power
concerned, as was Great Britain, in all that bore upon the road
to India.   The Circular, if luminously clear, was yet conciliatory,
and from the date of its appearance the diplomatic protagonists
drew towards a settlement.   Still, however, Russia refused to
submit the Treaty of San Stefano unreservedly to a congress;
still Great Britain stood out for the principle that any conference
must in all cases be the final court of appeal; and still Bismarck
refused to call the Powers of Europe together into counsel until
that step gave good promise of success.

It was in these circumstances that Salisbury resorted to a
series of secret treaties, by means of which concord between
the contending Powers might become reasonably certain before
the Congress met.   An Anglo-Russian Convention secured
agreement as to the Russo-Turkish boundaries both in Asia
and Europe, and incidentally extinguished for the time the
project of a 'big Bulgaria.'   An Anglo-Turkish Convention—
the 'Cyprus' Convention—a few days later in date, created an
Anglo-Turkish Alliance for the defence, against Russian aggression, of Turkish territory in Asia, according as its extent might
be determined at the forthcoming Congress, and afforded Great
Britain, in return, comfortable, if worthless, pledges of Turkish
reformation and tangible possession of the Island of Cyprus.
And, finally, an Anglo-Austrian Convention committed Austria
to the support of the British policy of a small Bulgaria and the
Balkan frontier in exchange for an undertaking to promote
Austrian designs in Bosnia and the Herzegovina.   This secret
diplomacy was not to pass uncriticised, and all the less that,
by the treachery of a copying-clerk in the Foreign Office, or
perhaps, as Salisbury suspected, by the action of the Russian
Government itself, the Anglo-Russian understanding was disclosed before its time.   Challenged in the House of Lords as to
its authenticity, Salisbury denied that the disclosure deserved
credence.   There was, in fact, a substantial error in the copy of
the Convention published in the *Globe*.   The denial, however,
went, and was intended to go,[1] further than this circumstance
justified.   It cannot be defended consistently with the tenet of
the Evangelical school of theology which makes of every lie

[1] *Life*, ii. 262, 263.

a sin. It must remain an offence to those who take the view that Parliament is a sovereign power with a right to full and accurate information on matters of public policy. But it presents no difficulties to such as hold with strict Constitutionalists that the Foreign Secretary owes fidelity to the Sovereign in the first resort, or with casuists that the obligation to speak truth is conditioned by a higher obligation of honour to preserve the secrets committed to us. Another, perhaps a weightier criticism was based upon the charge that by the Anglo-Turkish Convention Great Britain had seemed to be willing to sustain at the Congress a Turkish frontier-line in Asia which, by the Anglo-Russian Convention, she had already agreed to surrender. There was, however, no technical inconsistency between the two agreements. The British guarantee covered no more than the frontier to be fixed by the Congress, and there was nothing in the conduct of the Turks that gave them a title to any consideration in excess of the strict letter of the law.

Quarrel as men might with the secrecy of this diplomacy or the obscure interpenetration of its effects, it appears certain that without the Conventions the Congress could not have come into being. It is not less true that the Conventions half smothered their offspring. They had done their work so thoroughly that all the public activity at Berlin has seemed to some no better than a piece of play-acting. Be it so; for without the Congress a great actor must have been cheated of his finest part. Beaconsfield had no more detailed knowledge of European diplomacy than of high finance, but, as he had once carried off the part of Chancellor of the Exchequer, so now he studied the rôle of the Diplomatist. Time and Nature had given him the impenetrable face, the mysterious air, the grand manner, and the sardonic speech, that formed the paint and perruque of the diplomatic profession; and, sick and sorry as he was, he rose magnificently to his occasion. He went in great style to the Congress, made himself the cynosure of all eyes, delivered an oration, though not, happily, in French,[1] to his coadjutors, and returned with laurels wreathing

---

[1] Radowitz, *Aufzeichnungen und Erinnerungen* (ii. 37, 38), casts doubt upon the story of Lord Odo Russell's having dissuaded Beaconsfield from trying to address the Congress in French. It is worth while, therefore, to reaffirm it, which I am able to do on the authority of Isabelle, Lady Sligo, who heard the story from Lord Odo himself. Eckardstein (*Ten Years at the Court of St James*, p. 19) also has the story.

his brow and olive branches waving in his hands. The pose, the gestures, the fretting and strutting upon the stage had been admirable; but we have the best available evidence that the brilliant picture of his activities which has descended to us as a tradition and is enshrined in his biography was the work of Court painters. "What with deafness, ignorance of French, and Bismarck's extraordinary mode of speech," wrote Salisbury to his wife, "Beaconsfield has the dimmest idea of what is going on —understands everything crossways—and imagines a perpetual conspiracy." [1] Even the famous story that he overcame the opposition of the Russians by ordering an express train to be suddenly prepared for him, dissolves into a legend when the dates are checked ; for the Russian Emperor must have authorised surrender a day before the British Prime Minister began to work upon Bismarck's fears. [2] And like most persons who exaggerate the web of intrigue in which they have to work, Beaconsfield was 'done,' and 'done' by a man as old as, or older than himself. Gortchakoff contrived to wrest acute points of discussion out of the hands of the younger British representative who understood them, and thrust them into those of the elder, who emerged from the ordeal little better off than Isaac in face of the machinations of Israel and Rebecca. [3] Salisbury himself, however, as some recently published reminiscences [4] recall, did not escape at least one *mauvais quart d'heure*. He had indulged in some generous words about 'a valiant Mussulman nationality which rejected Russian domination.' He spoke, declares Radowitz, '*mit Rührung und Eifer*.' It was the more unfortunate that, when Schouvalov asked for the name of this deserving people, his memory proved to be defective and his notes to be lost.

It did not all very much matter. British interests had been sufficiently guarded by the Conventions and promoted by that 'labouring oar' which Beaconsfield, with pleasing gratitude, declared that his colleague had pulled at the Congress. For the rest the Prime Minister emphasised, with a familiar pomp of phrase and wealth of colour, the great consideration in which

[1] *Life*, ii. 287.
[2] Cf. *Life of Salisbury*, ii. 283, 284 (footnote), with *Life of Beaconsfield*, vi. 323, 326.
[3] See *Life*, ii. 292.
[4] Radowitz, *Aufzeichnungen und Erinnerungen*, ii. 56.

Britain and British diplomacy were now held by the nations of Europe. Salisbury disliked this part of the business and distrusted it as well. It was repellent to his private nature and out of keeping with his diplomatic sense. Boastfulness or self-congratulation in diplomacy was to him, not only an offence against good manners, but the very way to make the worsted negotiator recognise and resent his defeat. Even upon the prospects of his Party he distrusted, with, as it proved, reason enough, the effect of this *réclame*. The Party wire-pullers, he declared, would find out their mistake at the polls.

In the eighteen months or so of life that remained to the Conservative Government after the Congress was over Salisbury garnered the fruits of his diplomacy—some sweet, some sour. The juiciest apple, as it will seem to some, he left, indeed, to rot upon the tree. In 1879—and this was then the second time of asking—Bismarck, encouraged by the new vigour in British diplomacy and irritated by Gortchakoff's Francophil leanings,[1] preferred an Anglo-German Alliance, with Austria as a brilliant third. Beaconsfield was interested; Salisbury sceptical and unenthusiastic. It is hardly possible even to conjecture what might have happened, or might not have happened, if he had responded to these advances with more alacrity. As he saw things then—and in his own statement all the pregnancy of his decision appears—Germany, on "the sound rule that you love those most whom you compete with least," was "clearly cut out" to be Great Britain's ally.[2] As we see things now, the dominant factor in the history of Europe between the Congress of Berlin and the outbreak of the Great War in 1914 was the growing competition, naval and commercial, between Imperial Germany and the British Empire. Here, then, at this juncture, before ever they grew to rivalry, the two countries met, saluted, spoke, and parted, with no business done. Of all the 'might-have-beens' of the epoch this occasion surely furnishes the greatest. Less suspicion on Salisbury's part, more integrity on Bismarck's, and the British and German peoples might have been drawn together in an understanding such as Joseph Chamberlain is found urgently and eloquently advocating just twenty years later[3] as the most natural alliance

[1] Busch, *Bismarck*, ii. 393 (Eng. trans.).
[2] *Life*, ii. 373.
[3] Speech at Leicester, 30th November 1899.

in the world. No one can seriously pretend to say now whether the thing was feasible and or what consequences would have followed its success. For better or worse Salisbury let the opportunity slide; nor did he ever show any desire to go back upon that first decision. Four times during his period of power,[1] as well as once before,[2] did Germany make overtures more or less sincere for an Anglo-German Alliance; and four times without direct rejection did he allow matters to end in nothing. For this, besides his strong preference for isolation and perhaps some predilection for France, where first at Dieppe and then at Beaulieu he owned a villa, and for French literature, with which he was well acquainted, another personal reason may be alleged. If he was no more than cautious in his negotiations with Bismarck, he was profoundly distrustful of any dealings with William II. Of their historic meeting at Cowes in 1895 no certain record is available, but Salisbury's caustic criticism of the Emperor's account of the incident gives us the measure of its consequences. It showed, he observed, the importance of having a third party present at any interview with that monarch.[3] And, with rare sagacity, when Chamberlain took up the idea of an Anglo-German Alliance in 1899 with all the enthusiasm of an amateur diplomatist, he left the Colonial Secretary to discover for himself, by personal contact with the German Emperor and the Prussian Foreign Minister,[4] the value of German faith and the need for British circumspection.

The obstacles to an alternative understanding with France were of a different nature, and had their geographical centre in the region of the Nile, their psychological seat in the character of the French. Granville's treatment of the Egyptian question had proved as fatal to Liberal fortunes in 1885 as Beaconsfield's treatment of the larger question of Turkey to the Conservatives in 1880. The Country had at both Elections shown itself dissatisfied with the results of a foreign policy—in Granville's case too theoretical and ineffective, in Beaconsfield's too traditional and flamboyant. Salisbury, as has been seen, had, in 1878, consented, under protest, to act upon the view that commended itself to the Prime Minister and to the majority of his colleagues rather than to himself. He came back to office in 1885, and again, after

---

[1] In 1879; in 1889; in 1895; in 1899.   [2] In 1876.
[3] *Camb. Hist. of British Foreign Policy*, iii. 275.   [4] Bülow.

a short interval of Liberal Administration, in 1886, relieved of the incubus of Beaconsfield and in a position to pursue a diplomacy neither academic nor ambitious.   The tale of his Continental policy in the years that followed—the last years of Bismarck— has never yet been adequately told.   Whilst the magnitude of the African settlements that he negotiated attracts the eye, the fineness of his European diplomacy does not court observation in the same manner, nor is its detail fully available.   Yet his abilities were now at their prime; his position, now that the Premiership and the Foreign Office were both in his hands, was more absolute in foreign affairs than that of any of his predecessors; and the international situation, with Boulanger raising the wind in beaten France and Bismarck controlling the whirlwind in a Germany just made safe from a blow in the back by the secret treaty of 'reinsurance' with Russia, was tense enough to afford the utmost scope to diplomatic capacity.   Intent upon peace and convinced that Bismarck was a better friend to peace than Boulanger, he gave his policy a German orientation and even so far departed from his usual principle of avoiding alliances as to enter into a secret naval convention with Italy for the preservation of the *status quo* in the Mediterranean.[1] Further than this neither Italy with her wish for a compact directed against France nor Bismarck with his constant effort to bring England within the scope of the Triple Alliance could persuade him to go.   With Europe fast dividing into camps on the basis of a balance of power he remained faithful to Castlereagh's idea of a concert of the Great Powers pledged to preserve peace and treat one another with mutual consideration.

It had been Salisbury's complaint when he returned to the Foreign Office, that Granville had cut the thread of continuity in foreign affairs, and that with its disappearance the results of the Berlin Congress—notably in Asia Minor, where some ill-starred 'military consuls' had been set up to undertake the herculean task of reforming Turkish administration—had been lost.   He was not in the best position to bring the charge.   He himself in the growing conviction, which he owed perhaps to Sir William White, that the Balkan States might prove barriers and not outposts to the advance of Russia, almost immediately

---

[1] Feb. and March 1887. See Bourgeois, *Manuel Hist. de Politique Etrangère,* iv. pp. 45-6.

approved the formation of the Big Bulgaria against which he
had once strenuously fought. Not less in Egypt, after he had
made an ineffectual effort to get the Turkish Government to
work in with him, did his action, doubtless unavoidably, seem
to promote that decline of the Turkish Empire which at Berlin
he had helped to raise again. There is, indeed, no ground for
supposing, as the French do, that all the talk of a British evacuation of the valley of the Nile was from the outset moonshine and
that the British Government had no other thought but to remain
there. Yet it is certain, as both his own diplomatic instructions
and the abortive Convention of 1887 between Great Britain and
Turkey make plain, that Salisbury, in face of the hopeless
decadence of the Turks and the not less hopeless incompetence
of the Egyptians, would never have consented to a policy of
evacuation except on the condition of retaining a right of re-
entry in the event of internal or external trouble. This, doubtless, rendered the establishment of a British Protectorate in the
end inevitable. But that was not immediately plain.

The French, although they had accepted without a murmur
the suggestion to occupy Tunis, and were already building up a
vast African empire to counterbalance the loss of their eastern
provinces and counter their declining birth-rate, professed themselves greatly concerned at the progressive dispossession of the
Turks in Egypt and the growing dependence of the Egyptians
upon England. Their protests against the perfidy of Great
Britain were as usual vehement, but they softened them with
the gentle flatteries of imitation. Their whole African policy is
alleged to have been framed upon the principle of acquiring the
sources of the rivers that watered their neighbours' colonies;
and, however that may be, they adopted this plan in the case of
the Nile. As soon, therefore, as the British intention to recover
for Egypt the lost provinces of the Sudan became plain, the
French Government, whilst condemning the expropriation of the
Turks from an unsubstantial suzerainty, prepared to participate,
if convenient, in the division of the spoil. Before General
Kitchener had begun to prepare for the expedition which resulted
in the defeat of the Khalifa and the recapture of Khartoum,
Major Marchand had started upon his four years' march from
Senegal to Fashoda. It was in vain that Sir Edward Grey
issued in the spring of 1895 his memorable warning that the

advance of a French expedition into the valley of the Upper Nile would be treated—to use the restrained, but pregnant, language of diplomacy—as an "unfriendly act." The French Foreign Minister remained of opinion that the occupation by France of a hold upon the Bahr-el-Ghazal would prove a vantage-ground from which he might successfully negotiate the solution of all the conflicting issues arising out of French and British interests in Africa.[1]

The story of Salisbury's Egyptian diplomacy has of necessity run over into the brief but diplomatically as well as chronologically consecutive administration of Lord Rosebery [2]—himself an apostle of Imperialism in sympathy with his predecessor's African policy—and now runs on into Salisbury's third administration. On his return to the Foreign Office in 1895 his preoccupation was to prepare for a settlement of conclusions on the Upper Nile with the Dervishes and, if needs must, with the French as well. Not only his African but even his Asiatic policy must be considered in the light of that convergence of international interest upon the Southern Sudan, which has been pointed to as a kind of magnetic pole of the conflicting imperialisms of that period.[3] Conventions with Germany of the dates of 1890 and 1893—the latter the work of Lord Rosebery—had secured Great Britain from German interference in this region; and the limitation to no more than diplomatic protests of Salisbury's resentment at the annexation by France in 1896 of Madagascar, with the avowed object of suppressing British treaty-rights to preferential treatment in that island, had demonstrated both his pacific feelings and his excellent sense of proportion. A not less remarkable discretion was apparent in his avoidance of any quarrel in the Far East over the forced surrender to Germany and Russia of Kiaochow and Port Arthur. He accepted the inadequate compensation of the lease of Wei-hai-wei in the certainty that England could not afford to risk a war with either of those Powers in 1897 about affairs in China whilst she had still to face the

---

[1] " . . . L'idée maîtresse de la diplomatie française en 1894 fut que cette question du Nil, noeud de toutes les questions pendantes, pouvait devenir précisément le noeud d'un arrangement général" (G. Hanotaux, *Le Partage d'Afrique*, p. 69).

[2] Lord Rosebery was Foreign Secretary, 1892–94, and Prime Minister, 1894–95. Lord Kimberley succeeded him as Foreign Secretary in 1894. Sir Edward Grey was Parliamentary Under-Secretary during this time (1892–95).

[3] *Camb. Hist. of British Foreign Policy*, iii. 217.

possibility of a war with France in 1898 about affairs in the Soudan.
He hoped, indeed, that Kitchener might have outstripped March-
and in the race to the Bahr-el-Ghazal.   In fact, however, the
latter reached Fashoda some two months before the former had
recovered Khartoum.   The situation that thus arose could only
be adjusted by *force majeure*; and Salisbury did not scruple to
use it.   Duress was, however, applied with something like the
delicate formalities of an old-world duel.   The Englishman and
the Frenchman met and exchanged courtesies on the very
ground in dispute.   Kitchener then proceeded to claim the
region in the name of the English and Egyptian Governments;
Marchand, powerless to resist, volunteered to die at his post.
English common sense and French honour having thus been
satisfied, the representatives of two great nations, alien in mind
and will, but perpetually forced back into the semblance of
amity by larger interests, parted without personal friction.

It was too much to expect that the fine civility of gentlemen
or their ability to recognise facts without flinching should
characterise the Paris Press.   The French people were as furious
as the British Foreign Secretary was firm.   Except, however,
for this single cloud, the diplomatic sky was clear : Salisbury
had seen to that.   Neither Germany nor Russia wanted to be
drawn into war over Marchand's rebuff at Fashoda.   And, so
far as argumentation was concerned, Nemesis now overtook the
French.   Salisbury returned as good as he got in the affair of
Madagascar, and with a better case behind him.   Protests spent
their strength in vain against a purpose firm as rock.   The French
declare that to the eloquent speeches of M. de Courcel, the French
ambassador, in favour of French rights in the Bahr-el-Ghazal,
he opposed nothing but the inflexible, diplomatically invulnerable
observation: "Oui, oui, vous avez raison, mais il faut vous en
aller." [1]   If it was so, it would not have been out of keeping
with the instinctive operation of a mind always disposed to give
their full weight to practical necessities and accomplished facts.
It was plain to him, as it had been plain to Lord Rosebery and
Sir Edward Grey that, whatever the original rights and wrongs
of the business, Egypt, as things then were, could not afford to
relinquish the Soudan nor England the reward that was owed
her on account of her exertions for its recovery.   No lawyer's

[1] Mévil (André), *De la Paix de Francfort à la Conférence d'Algésiras*, p. 31.

argument about Turkish suzerainty or French priority could move him from this position. Boldly and publicly he treated conquest as the "most useful, simple, and salutary" of the two pleas for the Anglo-Egyptian condominium.[1]

After six months effervescence the fury of the French was spent. Their wisest statesmen began to take stock of the position and to realise that the diplomatic position of France left something to be desired. Certain recent diplomatic incidents taught them more than ever to distrust the proferred hand of Germany; and this latest crisis had enabled them to measure the value of Russian support. They concluded that even of perfidious Albion it might be possible to make a friend. Thus in the dark hour of Fashoda the seed of the future *entente* between France and England was sown. A diplomatic revolution, inseparably connected with the name of the memorable Delcassé, had that day begun.

Salisbury welcomed this development but with no open arms. "The French and German people both hate us," he had written to a correspondent in 1896; [2] and that strongly held opinion inevitably affected his policy. He distrusted, besides, the frequent changes of Government inherent in the democratic constitution of France, perceiving the discontinuity they engendered in foreign affairs. And neither he nor any Englishman had any reason to thank the French for their attitude towards Great Britain and the British Queen during the ensuing episode of the Boer War. He had come, as the years passed, to occupy a peculiar position in the counsels of Victoria. He was *par excellence* the Prime Minister of her latter days as Melbourne had been of her accession and Disraeli of her middle-age; he epitomised the massive wisdom of her stately and splendid reign; and, as chance would have it, he was in power both at the date of her first and of her second Jubilee when her Empire grew to self-consciousness. Some evidence even exists to show that she thought of him as the greatest of her Prime Ministers; [3] and it is certain, as his tribute to her discovers,[4] that he on his

[1] Speech in the House of Lords, 7th February 1899.
[2] Private information.
[3] Boyd Carpenter, *Some Pages of My Life*, p. 236.
[4] Speech in the House of Lords, 25th January 1901 : " She showed a wonderful power, on the one hand, of observing with the most absolute strictness the limits of her action which the Constitution draws, and, on the other hand, of maintaining a steady and persistent influence on the action of her Ministers in the course of legislation and government. . . . She left

side held not only her character but her judgment in high esteem.
He could not then have remained wholly indifferent to the filthy
insults that the French people permitted to be hurled at his aged
and honoured mistress. Beside them the attitude of the German
Emperor appeared friendly. He came to England, soon after
hostilities with the Boers had begun, and entered into negotiations, even though only abortive negotiations, for a closer understanding with Great Britain; and he came again, when the old
Queen died, and, by this judicious touch of nature at an hour
of high emotion, wiped out the memory of his much-abused
telegram, now five years old, congratulating President Kruger
upon the defeat of the Jameson Raid. A little more integrity
of purpose, a further manifestation of tact, and England might
have been drawn into the orbit of the Triple Alliance and France
have lain very much at the mercy of her ancient foe! For the
South African War had this importance in the history of diplomacy, that it put a term to the policy of splendid isolation with
which Salisbury had been so long associated. It was in truth an
oblique tribute to the dexterity of his diplomacy that England
had so long been able to avoid foreign commitments. Like
Bismarck, though not in Bismarck's way, he had known how to
keep five balls in motion with two at least always in the air.
There was no man after him who could do that trick, none who
would take the risk that he had taken and face a war in the
Colonies without a friend upon the Continent. Britain had thus
come perforce to the parting of the ways. In the first years of
the new century she had to make her choice between a close
relationship with the Triple or the Dual Alliance.

Salisbury did not remain in power to make the critical decision,
nor did he live to see it made. He left the Foreign Office in 1900,
when the Boer War was as good as won; he resigned the Premiership in 1902 after the long-delayed peace had been concluded;
and he died in the August of 1903, full of years and honours, so
that, as Lord Rosebery said, we are free in his case of that regret
for a career untimely finished or purpose imperfectly achieved
which often besets us in that of others. He had run his race and

upon my mind . . . the conviction that it was always a dangerous matter to
press on her any course of the expediency of which she was not thoroughly
convinced ; and I may say with confidence that no Minister in her long reign
ever disregarded her advice, or pressed her to disregard it without afterwards
feeling that he had incurred a dangerous responsibility."

finished his course. As we look back over his life we can see
that his figure dominated the last phase of a period and that his
policy preserved the last relics of a treaty. He was in fact the
residuary legatee of the system of Castlereagh and the settlement
of Vienna. His diplomacy began in a congress and ended in a
concert, but a congress whose work was provisional in character,
and a concert which was sharply divided into camps. It was
sufficient — maybe only just sufficient — for his time, and it
depended more than we may quickly recognise upon his own
prestige and sagacity and the presence of Victoria upon the
English throne. The storm which he had delayed in the 'seven-
ties was gathering again in the East—a storm destined, a decade
after his death, to grind Austria to powder, scatter Turkey to
the winds, and cause little to be left of the old Europe that he had
known. Meanwhile he had served his country well. His syn-
thetic outlook; his broad principle of maintaining things as they
were; his trust in time and patience to purge the diplomatic
air of passion; that "ability to see two sides of a question,"
which has caused one critic to say of him that "no Conservative
and few Liberal statesmen of modern times have brought to the
treatment of foreign affairs so much of 'the international mind';"[1]
even those "graceful concessions"—of Heligoland to Germany,
of British claims in Madagascar and on the Mekong to France,
and of British inhibitions at Panama to the United States—of
which his diplomacy was accused; all these in their several
ways contributed to give his country peace before the day of
decision arrived and the day of battle was forced upon them.
It would, indeed, be no idle flight of fancy to see in his work some
analogy to that which was accomplished by Elizabeth, if not
always with the sympathetic assent, at least with the practical
concurrence of his famous ancestor. As she nursed a distracted
kingdom into new and more abundant life by means of a tempor-
ising diplomacy based upon English character and island strength,
so did he foster and fortify the nascent energy of the great
Imperial movement of his day by doing nothing before the time,
keeping Britain free from entanglements, and maintaining the
old Europe of his youth with all its obvious defects and all its
less apparent but not less real merits. His death, as much as
that of any contemporary diplomatist at home or abroad, con-

[1] *Camb. Hist. of British Foreign Policy,* iii. 261.

stituted a sign that one age had passed away and that another was pressing on to take its place.

The Foreign Secretaryship of Lord Lansdowne, falling as it does between the administration of Salisbury and Lord Grey, may be treated either as the epilogue to the one or the prologue to the other. A Whig by family, a Conservative by force of circumstance, a man of much charm, a master of the two languages of diplomacy, and the descendant, if tradition is to be trusted,[1] of one author of the first *entente*—the illustrious Talleyrand— Lord Lansdowne had the best qualifications in the world for merging the foreign policy of a Conservative in that of a Liberal Government and bridging the gulf that separates the temperament of the French from that of the English. For the first year and a half of his administration he worked immediately under Salisbury's eye, but, even so, circumstances were drawing him away from the Salisbury tradition. The Anglo - Japanese alliance is of this date. The engagements of the contracting parties went, indeed, no further than a mutual pledge to sustain one another's interests in China and Korea by means of neutrality if either was assailed by a single Power or of hostilities if there were two assailants; nor did the "Agreement," originating as it did in the first instance with the German Government, and directed as it was, like the Anglo-German understanding of 1900, against the aggression in the Far East of Russia, foreshadow or even facilitate better relations with France. Germany was in fact still in 1902 endeavouring, though with indifferent skill, to attract Great Britain into the orbit of the Triple Alliance; and Lord Lansdowne, not uninfluenced by Joseph Chamberlain's fear of isolation, gave the project, as we may see from Eckardstein's vivid, personal narrative of the negotiation,[2] as full a countenance and as fair a chance as a foreign secretary, unable to count upon the Prime Minister's sympathy and assistance, was in a position to do. Not until 1903 was the crisis of the coming diplomatic revolution attained.

By that date the figures of Victoria and Salisbury had completely faded into the historic past and their places been fully taken by those of King Edward VII. and Lord Lansdowne, both

---

[1] Kerry, *Secret of the Coup d'Etat*, p. 29.
[2] Eckardstein, *Ten Years at the Court of St James*, c. xii.

of them good friends of France. Meanwhile at the Quai d'Orsay Delcassé continued to reign, still powerful, still urgent to bring about that closer union between the French and British peoples that Salisbury had benevolently declined. All this influence of personal sympathy, however, counted for less than that of national antipathy. Just as in 1899, when Bülow had actually agreed with Chamberlain upon the prolegomena of an Anglo-German understanding, the German nation caused the project to fail, so in 1902 the hostility of the British to the collaboration of Germany with England in the blockade of Venezuela rendered it impossible to accept the memorable offer of the German Government in the succeeding year. That offer will always stand to Germany's credit in any fair representation of events. German enterprise had just secured from the Turkish Government the handsome concession of the right to construct a railway to Bagdad and beyond it, with branch-lines in the parts adjoining. The Germans were not unwilling to share their spoil. British co-operation was invited; Koweit on the Persian Gulf was indicated as a possible terminus; the passage of the Indian mails by this quicker route put forward as an additional inducement. The offer was unequal so far as the control of the concern was concerned, but, nevertheless, in view of Germany's initiative in the project, not ungenerous. Mr Balfour's Government gave it consideration; but public agitation turned it down. Thus, for better or worse, Lord Lansdowne had made the great refusal. From that day, and ever more and more, Great Britain drew towards France.

Egypt, as it had long represented the crucial point in British foreign policy, so now supplied the crucial argument for an understanding between France and England. It was essential for the proper development of Egyptian resources to be quit of French obstruction on the Caisse de la Dette. The state of things in Morocco, together with other French interests in Africa, offered the basis of a deal. The two rivals decided to forswear their ancient jealousies and adjust their old disputes. England secured a free hand in Egypt, France in Morocco. The treaty of April 1904, which embodied the new understanding between them, was welcomed by the German Chancellor, but whether in good faith or guile we can speculate as we please. Unfortunately the published version of the Franco-British Convention did not contain the entire story. The independence of Morocco, affirmed and apparently safeguarded in the clauses that were made known, was threatened in certain eventualities by clauses that were kept secret. In these latter some provision was made for the division of Moorish territory contingently upon the termination of the Sultan's authority. The subsequent assent of Spain to the plans of the Entente Powers incorporated a similar, latent project of partition. These things were done in a corner, but not so much in a corner that Berlin got no wind of them.[1] They lay, detected or perhaps only suspected, but certainly inscribed, even if in invisible ink, upon the page of history, when the German Emperor, in a manner calculated to throw England only the more certainly into the arms of France, brought his yacht to Tangier in March 1905, and grandiloquently assured the German colony there that he intended to protect German trade in Morocco, and, in consequence, to preserve Moorish independence.

This dramatic intervention was not unproductive. It brought about the fall of M. Delcassé, who, with recklessness the more astonishing that it had no parallel in his dealings with Spain and Italy, had omitted to square the German Government before despatching a French mission to Fez; and it resulted in the summons of an international conference at Algeciras where Germany took her place among the other Powers interested in the fortunes of Morocco. But before that conference met, Lord Lansdowne, like M. Delcassé, had fallen from power. To some eyes Mr Balfour's Government had afforded a somewhat inglorious end to the long Conservative régime. But in foreign affairs, at least, it had left an indelible mark upon British history. Before he left office, Lord Lansdowne had reversed the old policy of splendid isolation, had renewed and extended the treaty with Japan, and caused his country to turn its back finally upon Germany and set its face firmly towards France. And in these decisive moves the Liberal leaders proved as ready to give him countenance and support, now that Lord Rosebery had retired, as the Conservative leaders, now that Lord Salisbury was dead.

[1] Valentin, *Deutschlands Aussenpolitik*, p. 54.

VII

LORD GREY OF FALLODON

[EDWARD GREY.—Born 1862. Succeeded to his baronetcy,
1882. *Under-Secretary for Foreign Affairs*, 1892–1895.
Foreign Secretary, 1905–1916. Created Viscount Grey of
Fallodon, 1916.]

LORD GREY OF FALLODON

In a letter addressed by Queen Victoria to Lord Aberdeen there will be found a pleasing allusion to a certain Sir George Grey, as a man "so very delicate in his feelings of honour" that especial care required to be taken, in making him the offer of a pension, to do this at an opportune moment when, should he accept it, no possible misconstruction could be placed upon his motives.[1] This sensitively honourable gentleman, in that on the whole sensitively honourable age, has an excellent title to remembrance for public services that included successive administrations of the Home Office and, incidentally, the removal of Botany Bay from the programme of convict life, but he is to us chiefly interesting as the progenitor and, by force of circumstances, foster-father of a grandson destined to occupy as large a place as any Englishman then living in the world-crisis of 1914.

The irony of circumstance—that infinite capacity in things for projecting the round peg into the square hole—is a commonplace upon which the historian becomes tired of insisting. Yet sometimes, even still, we marvel at it. "Nature," says a high authority of Louis XVI., "made him for a farmhouse. Fate tossed him into a revolution." Somewhat so, though certainly without the same tragic incapacity to rise to the greatness of his occasion, it was with Lord Grey. Nature made him for a country gentleman. Fate placed him, in a time of unexampled importance, at the head of the Foreign Office. Fate—or Providence! He preferred, and continued to prefer, country life, loving it with that illogical completeness that is the glory of the English squirearchy, rejoicing as well in the life of wood and field and river as in the destruction of that life. The poet who touched Nature most nearly and with the profoundest sense of its mystery became his poet. Just as some personalities seem to need for

[1] *Letters of Queen Victoria* (first series), iii. 121.

317

their rightful interpretation the voice, it may be, of Dante,
echoing sonorous down all the halls of time and out into the
eternities and infinities beyond ; or others, by reason of their pure
love of loveliness, Keats at hand to help them tell their tale ; or
some again, because they are born of the tribe of the children
of Nature, the music and sweet sounds of Shelley to bear them
company as they move across the stage of life, so is the charm of
Lord Grey's personality expressed in Wordsworth with a rare,
even extraordinary completeness.[1]

That mine, low-sunk, of simple faith and generous feeling, that
limpid, English well of high resolve and deep compassion, that
pure joy in the world of Nature, those brooding thoughts about
the world of Man—all these graces of the poet's soul are as a
mirror held up that catches and flashes wide the reflection of the
statesman's mind.   Wordsworth, to change the simile, fills all
the other's way with kindly light and grateful shade ; draws him
along the primrose path of spring; is his best guide and friend upon
that excursion into the forest of enigmas, which lurks, for all but
the Peter Bells of the world, beneath the petals of that lovely
flower; throws open before him the wicket-gate of civic duty with
the now well-worn but once novel exhortation to "plain living
and high thinking";[2] nor fails to follow him out into the dust and
din of battle with clarion notes, sounding forth against a tyranny
more gross and dreadful than any we have known.   This love of
the countryside—of the soil of England—broadening into and
blending with a love of the country itself, conceived as a noble
mistress worthy of all devotion and impatient of the least dis-
honour, is with Lord Grey as with Wordsworth a dominant
affection.   What other Foreign Secretary would have paused to
tell us, in the full flow of a political autobiography, how the
Austrian Ambassador had the misfortune to overturn a tall glass
of daffodils in the course of a sudden, anxious visit to discuss the
frontiers of Albania,[3] or have expended two pages of narrative
in describing the loveliness of beechwoods in May and lamenting,
some twenty years afterwards,[4] a lost opportunity of seeing them
in their first flush of verdant beauty owing to the procrastinating
diplomacy of the Sultan Abdul Hamid.

[1] Compare what he says of Wordsworth's place in his esteem and power of
intimacy in *Fallodon Papers*, pp. 12, 13.

[2] Wordsworth, Sonnet, 1802.

[3] *Twenty-five Years*, i. 208–9.   [4] *Ibid.*, ii. 127–9.

Nature can be an enchanting mistress, and politics a hard task-master. No one will probe the character of Lord Grey's administration who does not remember that he served the one with love, the other with duty. Politics claimed and kept the right to his first thoughts, but few who glance at his *Fallodon Papers* will doubt that he gave his best thoughts to the Northumbrian estate that had descended to him, to the birds that gathered there at his invitation and fed out of his hand, to the penetration of the mystery of all that sentient world around us which adds so much to our happiness and is yet held so remote from our communications. Not the extensive problems of international politics, but the intensive problems of natural history fascinate his imagination. And Fallodon is thus always the magnet that draws his mind. How far this kind of insularity went in him, and how deeply it impressed an acute observer, we may gather from an entry in Colonel House's *Intimate Papers*. "In speaking of Wordsworth," observes that observant American, "I asked him if he went often to the English Lake district. He replied that he had never been, that his country home was so much more attractive to him than any other place on earth that, when he had time, he always went there." [1]

A man who does not trouble to cross a county to visit the haunts of the poet that makes his pleasure can hardly be expected to cross a continent to become acquainted with the persons and problems that disturb his rest. And it is perhaps the first thing to be noticed about this Foreign Secretary that he is to a remarkable degree for his time an untravelled man, that he sees all things with English eyes, that both for better and worse he brings a purely English mind to the valuation and manipulation of forces that are not English at all.

This country squire, this great and kindly gentleman, with his Whig lineage and tradition—for the Greys more than any family in England are connected with the idea of political reform—enters Parliament at the age of twenty-two, from a characteristically generous, characteristically provincial motive. He feels it to be unfair that the rustic, and more particularly the Northumbrian rustic, should be at a disadvantage in comparison with the townsman in the matter of a vote; and he consents to come forward in support of the Reform Bill of 1884, the more readily

[1] *Intimate Papers of Colonel House*, i. 378.

that he reckons its author, Gladstone, to be the greatest man of his acquaintance.[1] He makes his mark in the House of Commons with high purpose, hard work, and straight speaking. He is appointed to be Under-Secretary for Foreign Affairs, when Lord Rosebery and subsequently Lord Kimberley are at the head of the Foreign Office. He follows his trade with so much diligence that when the Liberals return to office in 1905, he stands out as the obvious candidate for the Foreign Secretaryship. Had he been a Conservative his qualifications might have been less apparent. The great country houses and the great public schools were turning out, year by year, men of as fine integrity, as good sense, as grand a name as his own. But in the Liberal Party he was to some extent an anomaly. The Liberals had lost the most part of their Peers and were half afraid to make much of such as remained to them. The traditions of the Foreign Office desiderated an aristocrat, the development of the Party a commoner. Grey satisfied both requirements. He had the blood of the Greys in his veins, the feelings of the squirearchy in his bones, and Winchester and Balliol at his back. These were his *seize quartiers*. A Liberalism, farther reaching than all men guessed, and a seat in the House of Commons completed his claim to his appointment. For, so far at least as was generally known, his diplomatic studies were limited in extent; his knowledge of languages was of the slightest; and he had no facility in speaking French. Most of the foreign ambassadors at that time accredited to the Court of St James's were able to make good these deficiencies, but not the Ambassador of France. With M. Cambon, Lord Grey's diplomatic conversations were consequently bilingual, each man talking his own tongue and understanding that of the other. It was fortunate that this method met the situation, for no more pregnant conversations have taken place within the walls of the Foreign Office for half a century.

The Foreign Secretary, for all his old training under Lord Rosebery—as caustic a critic of the new line of development in foreign affairs as the country contained [2]—picked up the thread of the Anglo-French understanding to all intents and purposes where Lord Lansdowne had let it fall. He had, in truth, hardly

[1] *Twenty-five Years*, i. pp. xxv., xxvii.
[2] I assume that he is the critic indicated on p. 53 of *Twenty-five Years*, vol. i.

so much as time for hesitation. The Algeciras Conference, to which the issue between France and Germany in Morocco had been referred, was immediately pending. It might prove—as in fact it did prove, thanks to the secret influence of President Roosevelt upon the German Emperor—adequate to the situation; but also it might fail. If it failed, war between France and Germany was in sight; and, if war came, England, which King Edward, in conversation with the French Ambassador, was content to pledge to a diplomatic support of France "without restriction or reserves," [1] could hardly refuse to proceed to give warlike assistance also. Thus, at the very outset of his administration, Lord Grey was brought up against the fact, upon his insufficient appreciation of which Lord Loreburn has dwelt, [2] that any departure from the old diplomatic tradition of isolation and any acceptance of understandings or alliances upon a Continent, where conscription everywhere prevailed, might involve not merely a considerable diplomatic change, but a large military commitment.

It was in these circumstances that there began, with the Foreign Secretary's approval, those military conversations between representative General Staff officers belonging to the two countries, which have given rise to so much comment and so many subsequent heart-searchings. The matter seemed to him so urgent, the pre-occupation of many of his colleagues with the General Election of 1906 so great, that he authorised these meetings [3] without submitting the matter to the Cabinet. It was, consequently, no more than an inner circle of ministers together with the editor and military correspondent of the *Times* [4] who knew, until some years later, that French and British military experts had been discussing the mobilisation of a British force to meet the contingency of a German attack upon France across the Belgian frontier. Even the Lord Chancellor was kept in ignorance of what had taken place. [5] To

---

[1] *Camb. Hist. Brit. For. Policy*, iii. 348.

[2] *How the War Came*, pp. 10, 11.

[3] It is proper to say that some exchange of ideas had already taken place through an intermediary (Colonel Repington) in Lord Lansdowne's time; also there had been direct naval communications.

[4] *Camb. Hist. Brit. For. Policy*, iii. 347.

[5] See his remarks in *How the War Came*, pp. 80, 81. "There was no difficulty whatever," Lord Loreburn argues, "in summoning the Cabinet during the Election to consider so grave a matter."

Lord Grey, indeed, the conversations seemed, once the crisis at Algeciras was safely past, no great affair. But eventually he saw them in their true proportion and regretted the constitutional irregularity for which he had been responsible.[1]

All the protestations in the world that nothing more was in-tended than a hypothetical exchange of ideas, and that the British people remained free as air to fight, or not to fight on the merits of each occasion, could not prevent the growth of that subtle sense of obligation to see a friend through an emergency that affects most men in some degree and men of Lord Grey's public school and university education to a very great degree. His book bears witness at critical points to his rising loyalty to France and his constant fear lest England should be thought to have acted badly by her neighbour. But loyalties and senti-ments are not judicial qualities. As the Foreign Secretary drew closer to France in sympathy he lost insensibly and inevitably, though not entirely nor continuously, that detachment of mind which had been the best gift of the old policy of isolation and was the particular merit of one or more of his predecessors. This growth of partiality is a feature of his development of which the critic has to take account. By nature eminently just and dis-interested, he becomes, under the pressure of association, in-evitably biased. He takes one view of the German Emperor's calculated indiscretion at Tangier in 1905, another of Mr Lloyd George's parallel utterance at the Mansion House in 1911.[2] He has one law for the Italians when they seize Tripoli, which they had never before possessed, another for the Austrians, when they annex Bosnia and Herzegovina, which with the consent of Europe they had for a long while held. His attitude is hardly more consistent when it is a question of approving the appoint-ment in 1912 of a British admiral to train the Turkish Fleet, and in 1913, with Russia objecting, of a German marshal to train the Turkish Army. There is again a disposition apparent to view the political penetration both of Morocco by France and of Persia by Russia from a more favourable angle than is the case in regard to German aspirations on the Congo. All this, how-ever, was really inevitable enough, and another man might have

[1] *Twenty-five Years*, i. 86.
[2] The rebellious reader should consult Dr Gooch's article in the *Camb. Hist. Brit. For. Policy*, iii., chap. 6, *passim*, and especially p. 446.

accepted it with cynical resignation as the price of the Anglo-
French understanding. It was both the merit and defect of
Lord Grey's mind that he did not. Fairness was native to his
disposition, as his work on the Ambassadors' Conference, which
sat, without ultimate result, to discuss new frontiers in the
Balkans for six months in 1912–3, conspicuously showed. But
to be fair about the local boundaries of second- or third-rate
States was easy, and to be fair, when the elemental forces of
European politics were in play, as difficult a thing as could
well be.

An independent member, says the adage, is a member upon
whom nobody can depend. Lord Grey's attitude towards the
interests and relationships of the Great Powers seemed to them
to possess just such an incalculable character, even though he
probably himself enjoyed an interior, if never fully conscious
assurance that on really vital issues his judgment would tip
always a little to the side of France and Russia. It was an
attitude not out of keeping with the habits of his countrymen,
who like to feel free and independent to do what they
think proper and yet have no intention in any tight corner
of 'letting' their friends 'down.' It was, unfortunately, not
an attitude which gave equal satisfaction to the other parties
concerned. They understood the meaning of an alliance but
not of 'an understanding.' Germany became afraid that she
would be unawares encircled; France that in a crisis her new
friend might fail her; and Russia complained that in diplomatic transactions England gave her less than her proper share
of diplomatic support and pressed more and more urgently for
a bond that could not honourably be broken. For with Russia
also Lord Grey had by degrees become closely connected; and in
this especially his work constituted an advance upon that of his
predecessor who, even had he wished, could hardly for two reasons
have effected a *rapprochement* between Great Britain and her
old enemy of fifty years' standing. In the first place, the Anglo-
Japanese Alliance which he had himself concluded tied Lord
Lansdowne's hands until the issue in the Far East between
Russia and Japan had been determined by the Russo-Japanese
War. And, in the second place, the Dogger Bank incident—
the destruction of some harmless English trawlers by the Russian
Baltic Fleet as it sailed to its doom at Tsushima—had clouded

Anglo-Russian relations, until that "unspeakable outrage," as Lord Rosebery styled it at the time, had slipped from the political present to the historic past and could be spoken about quite unrhetorically because no one wanted any longer to speak about it at all. Lord Grey enjoyed another and rare advantage in seeking to reach a settlement with Russia. The Indian Secretary in the Liberal Government was a man of wide cultivation with an eye not bounded by India. Lord Morley's assistance was essential to a *rapprochement* in Europe inasmuch as a good understanding in the Middle East represented the condition precedent to anything of the sort. The path to the Triple Entente lay, in fact, in Lord Grey's time through Teheran, as in Lord Lansdowne's time it had lain through Cairo.

The Anglo-Russian Convention of 1907 delimiting the scope of British and Russian interests in Central Asia is the counterpart of the Anglo-French Convention of 1904, delimiting the scope of French and British interests in North Africa. In its local aspect the success of the Convention from the British standpoint is open to dispute. Lord Grey argued that we had got the best of the bargain, since we had given up influence over no part of Persia that we wished to penetrate,[1] while Russia had agreed to abandon her forward policy in that country. Lord Curzon, on the other hand, supposed that we had got the worst of the bargain, since Russian influence was left dominant in almost all the great cities of Persia and over the large majority of the trade-routes. And, finally, Lord Sanderson, an official of great experience and for some years Permanent Under-Secretary for Foreign Affairs, maintained that we had secured as good a bargain as could be got; and that was perhaps the real truth of the matter. It was not, however, primarily as a settlement of Asiatic differences, but as a pact of European amity that Lord Grey envisaged the Convention. A diplomatic achievement of first-class importance, it had drawn Russia finally beyond the fling of the net with which the German Emperor, under the affectionate style of "Willy," was continually casting to catch his imperial brother, the weak, well-meaning "Nicky." At Björko in 1905, when "Tsar" and "Kaiser" met, with the crowning catastrophe of the Russo-Japanese War fresh in mind and the prospects of a

---

[1] *Twenty-five Years*, i. 160.

broadened alliance between Great Britain and Japan full in view, Russia's treadings had wellnigh slipped. Only at the twelfth hour—for Nicolas had actually signed the proferred treaty—did she go back upon her decision to ally herself with Germany. The incident marks her growing consciousness of the insufficiency of the Dual Alliance to meet the full requirements of the international situation. Her weakness necessitated an understanding with Germany or with Great Britain, and, since the former proved to be impossible on account of the feeling of the French, the latter became inevitable.

The course of the Anglo-Russian *rapprochement* followed closely along the lines of the similar negotiation between France and England. King Edward VII., the best ambassador of the age, went to Russia as he had once been to France to cement the contract; and in due course, though not until early in 1914, naval conversations took place between British and Russian officers. To the British Foreign Secretary, a close understanding with France and Russia seemed no bar to a good understanding with Germany. Other important personages affected to think as he did, and perhaps really did so. During the seven critical years that went by between the signature of the Anglo-Russian Convention of 1907 and the outbreak of the Great War, many pretty amenities were consequently exchanged between the British and German Governments. The German Emperor came to England time and again, now as the guest at a Guildhall banquet, now as a mourner at King Edward's funeral, now as the grandson of the great English Queen, eager to do honour to her memory at the unveiling of her memorial, now as a private gentleman enjoying the pleasures of an English country-seat. He spoke of peace and goodwill, of an endeavour extending over nearly two decades to promote them, and of the good relations between Great Britain and Germany as the chief prop of international concord; and he tried to enforce the import of his words by two of those characteristically tactless indiscretions with which his career is so richly studded—by a private letter to the First Lord of Admiralty designed, or at any rate ostensibly designed to allay apprehensions as to German shipbuilding, and by an interview with a correspondent of the *Daily Telegraph*, in which he laid stress upon the recent friendly bearing of Germany towards England in international politics. The Crown-Prince followed in his father's wake, attended King George's coronation and travelled through British India.

These courtesies were not left unreturned. King Edward visited his nephew both privately and in state. Mr Lloyd George, who, once the War broke out, was to manifest a great horror of German duplicity, and then again, when the War was done, to declare that no Government had sincerely wanted war in 1914, produced on a British platform the double-frontier argument with which Germany had long been accustomed to apologise for her armaments, and returned from a trip to that country with the assurance that the Germans were a friendly people. And last, but not least, Lord Haldane paid that memorable, much-abused visit to Berlin, which was to cause all his good work as War Minister to be forgotten and all his high patriotism to be called in question, bearded the malevolent Tirpitz, the benevolent "Bethmann," and the Emperor with two faces, and returned with a possibly well-meant but certainly inadequate and unacceptable offer to barter a pause in German shipbuilding against a promise of British neutrality.

It was all to no purpose—of no more purpose than the Friendship Societies which had been manufactured both in England and Germany to bring the nations abreast of the nego-tiations between their Governments. These prodigious civilities, these polite conversations, these genial hospitalities were, in fact, but as froth and bubble upon the surface of a great deep, where the currents of hostility between Slav and Teuton were running ever stronger, and the latent, or, as some would say, patent chal-lenge to the time-honoured trident of Britannia must one day inevitably compel an answer. The German Michael, burnishing his shining armour and rattling his restless sword, was a formid-able but still tolerable figure. Endowed with ships and seamen by Tirpitz's brains and Bulow's pliability, he became a public peril, and none the less that a vain-glorious, bombastic Emperor, emulous of his English uncle's naval strength, announced himself with a sound and fury that indeed signified nothing to be none other than the "Admiral of the Atlantic." "Without a fleet," says a German critic who has made his name, "Germany could get on with England—with a fleet it was out of the question." [1] That elementary fact was beyond William II.'s capacity as a

[1] Ludwig, *Kaiser Wilhelm II.* (Eng. trans.), p. 247.

statesman to see, and beyond Bulow's tact as a courtier to state. Hence flowed a sea of tears upon which all the ships in Europe might have found space to sail.

In the seven years of crisis whilst the Great War was in the making there were two periods of acute alarm. In 1908 there occurred the Austrian *coup* in Bosnia, which coincided with a British naval scare; and in 1911 the German *Panther* made its famous pounce upon Agadir. It is not impossible that Lord Grey viewed the first of these occasions both in its terrestrial and maritime aspects with exaggerated apprehension. The Austrians had been long in Bosnia and Herzegovina—had gone there in fact in 1878 with Salisbury's full approbation. Kallay, who took the two provinces in hand and taught them what they knew of law and order, has, in fact, seemed to some a Bosnian Cromer. It was in the circumstances no more reasonable, perhaps, to expect the Austrian Government to evacuate the occupied territories than the English Egypt. And their indefinite tenure might have lasted indefinitely if it had not been for the success of the Young Turk Revolution, which, with its idle talk of self-government, threatened to raise awkward questions in these lost, but never formally surrendered provinces of Turkey. Aehrenthal, the Austro-Hungarian Foreign Minister, happened to be ambitious and energetic beyond the measure of officers of state in the Habsburg Monarchy. He decided to follow the time-honoured policy of Pepin *le bref* in regard to the Merovingian kings, to be quit of the *roi fainéant*, and to instal the *maire du palais* in his stead. Russia, as he knew, had no nice scruples in matters of this sort, and Isvolsky, the Russian Foreign Minister, was bidding for a deal. A meeting between the two statesmen was eventually arranged at Buchlau. The Russian proved as accommodating as the Austrian had hoped. In return for a consideration, which was to take the shape of the opening of the Dardanelles to Russian warships, Isvolsky discovered his willingness to see another provision of the ill-starred Treaty of Berlin set aside. Aehrenthal took him at his word, and then went on to take him unawares. What the one had regarded as a contingent possibility, the other translated into immediate action. Within three weeks of the meeting, Bosnia and Herzegovina were annexed, and Bulgaria, with Austrian consent, simultaneously declared her independence of Turkey.

The Russians had been jockeyed, but they had been known before this to jockey others. The Treaty of Berlin had been violated, but it was not for the first time. The power of Russia had been shaken, and the suzerainty of Turkey shaken off, but the territorial organisation of Europe remained for practical purposes exactly what it had been before. All that had happened was that a *fait accompli* had become a *chose jugée*; and there it might have been as well to let matters rest.

The Entente Powers had, however, suffered a loss of prestige in one of their members, and the Young Turks, in whose reforming virtue the Foreign Secretary was innocent enough to believe,[1] seemed to have received an ugly blow in the back just as they started upon their career of benevolent reform. Protests, reasonable enough in themselves, against the irregularity of Austrian procedure were therefore followed up by the despatch of a squadron to the Ægean and a demand for an international conference. These moves had no immediate or perhaps even ulterior relation to British interests, and were in fact from a merely British standpoint profoundly disinterested. But, though disinterested, they can hardly be styled impartial. They illustrate again that generous loyalty which was the virtue, if not the merit of Lord Grey in his public capacity. He had got mixed up, as ill-luck would have it, with a parcel of humbugs. The Russians cared little or nothing for international treaties; they had overridden them before, and, as he was presently to discover, they had been just as ready as Austria to override them again. The Serbs, who wept tears of rage and mortification at the annexation of the two provinces, wept, not because Turkey had been wronged, but because they had been intent upon annexing Bosnia and Herzegovina themselves. The Young Turks, who had the best occasion to complain, were, as the event was to show, the best disciples that Machiavelli has had even in our distracted century; their record of craft not unworthy of Cæsar Borgia, and their record of massacre, when all allowances have been made, well calculated to cast the little affair at Sinigaglia into the shade. "Que diable allait-il faire dans cette galère?" an observer of the Foreign Secretary's proceedings at this juncture might

---

[1] Lord Grey went so far as to say of the Turkish Revolution that "it had been one of the most wonderful and beneficent changes in history" (19th November 1908).

have inquired, not perhaps, if he knew his Molière, without reflecting that the remainder of Géronte's famous speech would have fitted the circumstances none too badly: "Ah! maudite galère! traître de Turc! à tous les diables!" Of what interest to England, indeed, was it that the Turks should receive, as they did receive, a financial compensation, or the Russians get quit of restrictions that so much British blood had once been shed to impose, or the Serbs break up the Empire of our ancient ally? And the only answer that can be returned is that the British Foreign Secretary was acting under the compelling influence of a new orientation and upon principles of loyalty to a new-found friend.

By principles of diplomatic fidelity Germany also directed her course, and with more energy and effect. Representations, not to call them an ultimatum, at Petersburg brought Russia to heel. A sop to the Turks, a sob and a surrender from Serbia —and the incident was over. Without a conference, without receiving any mark of Austrian contrition, the Entente Powers ratified the annexation. Lord Grey, as he had been in the first instance pushed forward by Russia, was now gradually pulled back, protesting not without occasion. He had spoken bravely but beyond his strength. It was a diplomatic weakness that he did not entirely succeed in avoiding.

This territorial rebuff to British diplomacy was, as has been said, coincident with a maritime scare. It was supposed by British naval authorities that Germany was accelerating her naval programme. The First Lord of the Admiralty made effective use of this opinion in proposing his estimates; and the Prime Minister gave it countenance. New ships to meet the contingency were immediately authorised by Parliament and ultimately built. Long before they had been constructed, it was generally recognised that the information upon which panic had been raised and action taken was incorrect.[1] The moral effect of the scare to public feeling both in Germany and Great Britain remained, however, to be reckoned with, for the tide of suspicion upon which jingoes float their craft had risen some degrees higher.

[1] Cp. W. S. Churchill, *The World Crisis*, i. 37. "The gloomy Admiralty anticipations were in no respect fulfilled in the year 1912. . . . There were no secret German Dreadnoughts, nor had Admiral von Tirpitz made any untrue statement in respect of major construction."

At Agadir two years later, over no graver matters than the fortunes of a half-barbarous African state, a new diplomatic contest between the Great Powers of Europe was joined. The French, in the process of assimilating African natives to European uses, had found it desirable to despatch a military expedition to Fez. This action, as Germany had previously warned them, threw the Moorish question once more into the witches' cauldron from which the Conference of Algeciras had extricated it; and Spain in alarm followed up the French lead by occupying the zone that the secret Treaty of 1904 had conditionally given her.

It was in these circumstances that the German warship, *Panther*, anchored off Agadir, ostensibly to defend the more or less imaginary interests of some more or less imaginary German subjects, but in reality to enforce a claim for compensation elsewhere. Impartiality might have hesitated to decide that the French were observing the spirit of the Act of Algeciras, or that the Germans were debarred from a course calculated, if Morocco became a French protectorate, to secure to them at least a *quid pro quo* elsewhere. Loyalty, however, dictated approval of the conduct of an ally; and Lord Grey gave the French Government his full support and met the German countermove with his strong reprobation. The French had, perhaps, a more intimate, if not more friendly comprehension of German manœuvres than himself. Negotiations for a settlement were quickly opened and slowly advanced between Paris and Berlin, but Lord Grey was made a party to the results only, and not to the proceedings. A new anxiety, which illustrates the innate delicacy of his diplomatic position, took hold of his mind. He became nervous lest Morocco might be partitioned and England be left without say in the matter; while the extent of the suggested compensation in the Congo alarmed him. German reassurances were slow in coming; and Mr Lloyd George was quick to speak. Before the situation had been fully elucidated, a strong but hasty warning that Great Britain would have to be considered and consulted before any bargain was struck had been trumpeted through Europe. The Foreign Secretary has taken the full responsibility for that memorable speech, which seemed perilously like a usurpation of his office.[1]   He approved its substance prior to its delivery.   It was, he says, "entirely Lloyd George's own idea,"

[1] *Twenty-five Years*, i. 224, 225.

welcome to him but not instigated by him and, in view of the speaker's cast of Liberalism and reputed Germanophilism, greater in its effect than could have been the case with any words of his own.   It had, he tells us, "much to do with preserving the peace in 1911." [1]   Yet something also, perhaps, to do with provoking the war in 1914.   It intensified of necessity the German feeling that at the bottom of the English mind there was one law for the Gaul and another for the Teuton, and the German fancy that the Central Powers were being 'encircled.'   Impartiality and loyalty, to repeat the theme with which the reader is by now familiar, are an ill-assorted pair of virtues to put together in harness, unless indeed that to which loyalty is owed be also itself impartial.   But this condition is seldom, if ever, fulfilled in the case of France, and too rarely, maybe, elsewhere.

The speech, whatever its merits or defects, did not immediately settle the issue of the Franco-German negotiations.   There were further difficulties and further agitations, and yet another panic before the two rival Powers came to a compromise.   Eventually, but only after M. Caillaux had taken the negotiations into his own hands, France secured that protectorate over Morocco which she coveted, and Germany the acknowledgment in a modified form of her ambitions in the region of the Congo.   M. Caillaux was not always to enjoy a high reputation for patriotism. It is the more curious to remember how at this time Lord Oxford invoked in his praise the great phrase of Disraeli and desired that he might be informed 'that he returned from Berlin, like Lord Beaconsfield, bringing peace with honour.' [2]   It is just possible that M. Caillaux's diplomacy had had more effect upon the German Government than Mr Lloyd George's oratory.

The *Panther* departed from Agadir; and the affair at Agadir itself dissolved into historical incident.   In the German Embassy in England there were changes calculated, as it was supposed, to make the relations between Great Britain and Germany better. Wolff-Metternich, stiff, exact and soldierly, gave way to Marschall von Bieberstein, whose statesmanlike realism, if Lord Oxford is right in his conjecture,[3] would have sufficed to prevent the Great War; and again Bieberstein, death taking him untimely, to

---

[1] *Twenty-five Years*, i. 226.
[2] Quoted in *Camb. Hist. Brit. For. Policy*, iii. 452.
[3] Asquith, *The Genesis of the War*, p. 104.

the amiable, pacific Lichnowsky.   In the Balkans there were wars, Turkey falling some steps further down the glacis of her fate under the impetuous onset of the Balkan League, and the Leaguers falling out amongst themselves, Serbia and Greece on the one part, Bulgaria on the other.   Out of this crisis in the Near East there sprang that "Ambassadors' Conference" in London, which caused Benckendorff, the Russian representative, to register the remarkable opinion "amounting," so he says, "to a conviction that of all the Powers represented there France was the only one that would envisage war without regret," [1] and at the same time showed Lord Grey's powers—his natural fairness, his love of peace, his transparent honesty of purpose—at their strongest.   If no diplomatic success crowned his efforts, the Foreign Secretary's action was at least effective in limiting hostilities to the Balkan peninsula.   It failed, however, to compel a settlement among the combatants on lasting lines. His warnings were despised, and his advice was flouted.   Turkey was reduced to a very small remnant;   and Bulgaria, docked of her conquests and denied access to the open sea, became no better than a besieged city.   It followed, as things worked out, that Russian influence rather gained ground in the Balkans, and Austrian lost.   But, for all that, the character of Lord Grey had made its mark in Europe.   No man who had seen him in council doubted any more his goodwill towards men or his strength of personality.

He remained, nevertheless, a dark horse—the darkest horse in the diplomatic stable.   This was partly due to the peculiar tradition of the British people and their long freedom from commitments, safe as they had been for centuries behind their wooden walls.   But it was also due to that, for him, recurring difficulty of reconciling the claims of impartiality with those of loyalty. His negotiations, so nearly successful, with Germany, in regard to the partition of Central Africa and the continuation on certain conditions of the Bagdad Railway to Basra, only excited apprehension in France and Russia.   Was he, these latter Powers wondered, a reliable comrade-in-arms as well as a well-intentioned friend?   Paul Cambon, accredited to the Court of St James, may have felt in his bones that France had no cause for fear; but Jules Cambon, accredited to the Court of Berlin, did not

---

[1] *Livre Noir*, ii. 303–6.

conceal the anxiety in his mind. And Sazonov, writing to Izvolsky—the new Russian Foreign Minister to the old—did not hesitate to declare that the time had come to convert the Triple Entente into a Triple Alliance. To that idea Lord Grey would give no countenance, but yet was ready to take another step significant of friendship, and, as Sazonov believed,[1] of something more.

Naval conversations with Russia, similar in principle to the defensive conversations already entered upon with France, were inaugurated early in 1914. For fear that they might seem incompatible with the cordiality that the Foreign Secretary continued to profess towards Germany, the very fact that they were being held was concealed. But an employé of the Russian Embassy in London betrayed their existence and their purport.[2] The German Government became aware that hypothetical plans for an invasion of Pomerania by means of co-operation between the Russian army and the British Fleet were being concocted, should occasion require. A kite was flown in the *Berliner Tageblatt*, and the conclusion of an Anglo-Russian Naval Convention alleged. The allegation drew from Lord Grey, both in conversation with Lichnowsky and in his place in Parliament, the kind of circumlocutory contradiction that merely confirms the idea that something is up. It was in vain that he assured Lichnowsky that he would give the other Entente Powers no point against Germany.[3] In Berlin they appreciated the diplomatic implications of naval conversations with a State like Russia better perhaps than he did. His impartiality had first compromised his loyalty with the Russians, and now his loyalty had compromised his impartiality with the Germans. He had tried to be all things to all men—both fair-minded and faithful—but the times were inordinately difficult. And whilst he strove to satisfy all parties without quite committing himself to any, the crisis of his diplomacy came upon him.

The storm, as everyone knows, blew up in the Balkans. Serbia had long assimilated, as it was her interest to do, the doctrine of nationality. In Austria-Hungary such doctrine was

---

[1] . . . " We attach special importance to the political aspect. We see in it an important step in associating England more closely with the Franco-Russian Alliance " (quoted in the *Camb. Hist. Brit. For. Policy*, iii. 484).

[2] Valentin, *Deutschlands Aussenpolitik*, p. 145.

[3] *Camb. Hist. Brit. For. Policy*, iii. 485.

calculated to split the Dual Monarchy into fragments.   There was, therefore, a conflict of principles about which we are likely to take sides according as Nature has cast us in a Liberal or a Conservative mould.   In practice, the contest between the old Empire of the Habsburgs and the nascent kingdom of the Jugo-Slavs was carried on with ugly weapons.   The Austrians fought with forged documents and judicial duress, the Serbs with savage propaganda, ruthless conspiracy, and, as the event showed, pitiless violence.   The heir to the Austro-Hungarian Monarchy did not seem to be unequal to the task of preserving it.   A temper at times bordering on and even perhaps initiating madness had not, so far as his life had gone, gravely impaired the value of a commanding will and a shrewd and statesmanlike judgment.   In international politics he stood for the "Drei-kaiserbund as far as possible in conjunction with England." [1] At home he saw that existing discontents could be alleviated, if not dispelled, by placing the Jugo-Slav section of his future subjects on an equality with the Magyars and the Germans; and he appears to have explored the political needs of his country with the generous thought of the American Federation in the back of his mind.   The analogy was not wholly fanciful.   Acton, a Liberal yet no doctrinaire, whose Continental education had strengthened his insight into Austrian affairs, has dwelt in one of his essays upon the intellectual richness of racially composite states, the intellectual poverty of single nationalities.   "The co-existence of several nations under the same State," he observes, "is a test as well as the best security of its freedom.   It is also one of the chief instruments of civilisation. . . ." [2]   He goes even further, repeating and strengthening his words, and picking out the British and Austrian Empires as "substantially the most perfect States." [3]   "That a nationality should produce a State," he asseverates, "is contrary to the nature of modern civilisation." [4] Such conceptions as these, more subtle as they are than those of the Jugo-Slavs and their supporters, were the Archduke's title-deeds and pregnant with peril to his Nationalist opponents. His policy of, "Trialism"—of the elevation, that is, of the Slavonic element in the Habsburg Monarchy to an equality with

---

[1] Unpublished military report of the Archduke's words from the German Military Attaché (quoted in Montgelas, *The Case for the Central Powers*, p. 72).
[2] Acton, *History of Freedom*, p. 290.
[3] *Ibid.*, p. 298.   [4] *Ibid.*, p. 292.

the German and the Magyar elements—must, if it had succeeded, have defeated the hopes of the Serbs, who desired to add Bosnia and Herzegovina to Serbia, and Croatia and Slavonia to Bosnia and Herzegovina.

Franz Ferdinand was due to visit these last-named provinces in the end of the fateful June of the year 1914; and Jugo-Slavs were not slow to take advantage of their occasion. They failed at the first attempt. His courage and contempt of danger gave them a second opportunity. Bullets achieved what bombs had failed to accomplish. The Archduke was killed, and with him perished the hope of Austria. The next heir to the throne—the ill-starred Karl—was but an amiable young man, cast only for a part in the fifth act of a dynasty.

The Austrians were nearly as angry as the English would have been if a Prince of Wales had been murdered in Ireland; and they addressed such an ultimatum to Serbia as their feelings prompted. It was judged at the time and not in interested quarters only to be overbearing and excessive, though, if we listen to von Jagow [1] and cast our eyes back to the case of Don Pacifico, or forwards to that of Sir Lee Stack, we are reminded that drastic ultimata have proceeded even from English minds. History at all events is compelled to judge it less severely than Lord Grey and his fellow-countrymen did at the time. As the origins of the War are unearthed, the benevolent complicity of the Serbian Government in the Archduke's assassination has become a plausible opinion. A Serbian statesman has inadvertently confessed it; [2] a Serbian professor [3] has reluctantly confirmed it; and, though Dr Seton-Watson retains his doubts and urges his objections, even judicious people, having in mind how low the reputation of Serbia stood after the murders of King Alexander and Queen Draga, may be of opinion that so grave a charge, ingenuously produced by a responsible member of the Government implicated, long undenied, and at long last irrelevantly dealt with [4] by the Prime Minister involved in

---

[1] G. von Jagow, *England und der Kriegsausbruch*, p. 13.
[2] The B.I.I.A. translation of M. Ljuba Jovanović's admission is published separately, and is also printed in Durham, *The Serajevo Crime*, pp. 127–47.
[3] Professor Stanojević.
[4] Pašić ultimately denied that he had told a Cabinet Meeting that he knew of the intended murder. This was not alleged. All that Jovanović had alleged was that Pašić had told his colleagues in the Government of the plot.

spite of Dr Seton-Watson's urgent appeal for a *démenti*, carries an admission in its trail. Pašić, indeed, is charitably supposed by Dr Watson to have had the vindication of his conduct all the while up his sleeve and to have refrained from producing it only lest it should damage his claim to a sympathetic appreciation of the subterranean activities of the less reputable of his countrymen.[1] It seems not to have occurred to the apologist to inquire whether a State, whose Prime Minister is afraid for fear of losing caste and influence to exculpate his administration from the charge of conniving at assassination, and whose citizens go so far as to "glorify"—to use Dr Watson's own phrase—the assassins by sweeping away the memorial shrine of the Archduke and building in its place a memorial sepulchre to his murderers, is—or ever was—deserving of the sympathy of English gentlemen. Civilisation, no doubt, except where it has been touched or turned by Christianity, is little but a veneer beneath which primæval human passions lurk and rankle, but at least we may ask that vice shall be forced, wherever nations claim to be civilised, to pay its proper tribute to virtue and a decent veil of hypocrisy be cast over the ugliness of the human heart.

The Archduke was murdered on 28th June, but, though the hand-grenades with which the first attempt was made proved to be such as the Serbian Arsenal contained,[2] the Serbian Government showed no alacrity to investigate the crime. Their apathy, whatever its import, played into Austrian hands. Berchtold, the Austrian Foreign Minister, was eager to settle conclusions once and for all with a perennially troublesome neighbour, and Conrad von Hötzendorf and the military party were in active sympathy with him. It is not easy, as we have seen, to condemn them off-hand. Serbia by all accounts, friendly and unfriendly, was the seat of a violent propaganda threatening the very existence of the Dual Monarchy; and Austria-Hungary had evidently as much right as any other constituted State to defend itself from destruction. The need of dealing in some way with the subversive elements in the Habsburg Empire had been indeed for some while obvious; the murder of the Archduke made it urgent.

[1] Seton-Watson, *Sarajevo*, p. 159.
[2] This was not, however, any proof of complicity on the part of the Government since arms had been freely supplied to Serbian guerillas during the Balkan War of 1912.

Berlin was first approached, and Berlin proved completely agreeable. The German Chancellor tells us that, at an informal consultation held at Potsdam on July 5th, the Emperor intimated that in his judgment Austria could not afford, without imperilling her existence, to let the Archduke's murder go unavenged, neither could Germany afford without endangering her own security to let her ally go unsupported. In these opinions Bethmann-Hollweg says that he concurred.[1] The answer returned to the Austrian Government was, therefore, that Germany would sustain her ally in any action Austria saw fit to take against Serbia, but that what that action should be it was for Austria herself to decide.

A blank cheque, or as in this case a cheque but partly filled in,[2] is a generous gift, and in politics too generous a gift. Austria had now not only the cash in hand to try conclusions with the Serbs, but credit sufficient to face the eventuality of a world war. The Germans knew what they were doing; they envisaged and accepted the possibilities of their reckless draft; and whilst some of them, like the Emperor, believed that diplomatic backing would, as in 1909, cause Russia to crumple up, there were highly-placed soldiers who, doubtless, hailed the occasion as "the day" when they might at length reap the reward of their profession, see service, and redden with the blood of the Slavs the sword of the Teutons. Some temperaments in all times and countries will find the romance of war engaging; some consciences be satisfied with the plea that, where a struggle seems ultimately unavoidable, the best occasion must be seized.

There can be no doubt that Berchtold, behind his exquisite manners and his enigmatic mask, worked with all his might for localised hostilities, regardless of ulterior consequences; nor any doubt either that Germany gave him countenance. The Austrian ultimatum—for by whatever name its author called it, it was in fact no less—was drastic, if not quite so drastic as was generally supposed. It insisted upon the collaboration of Austro-Hungarian officials in the suppression of the Jugo-Slav propaganda and of Austro-Hungarian delegates in the investigation of the crime, though it was subsequently explained to M.

---

[1] Bethmann-Hollweg, *Reflections on the World War*, p. 119.
[2] *Ibid.*, p. 122. "We did ascertain through Herr von Tschirschky the general lines of the demands that Austria was making on Serbia."

Sazonov, who does not seem to have thought it worth while to pass on the information, that, in regard to the former crucial requirement, no more was intended than the institution of a *bureau de sûreté*, similar to those which Russia herself had established in Paris and Berlin and consequently not open to the charge of infringing the sovereign independence of Serbia.[1] It seemed, however, to Lord Grey at the moment the most formidable note that one independent State had ever addressed to another. It seemed, even to the German Foreign Minister who knew well enough what sort of thing to expect, *reichlich scharf.*[2] It fulfilled all the better Count Berchtold's requirements. It hardly admitted of acceptance without delay and without reserve; and neither time nor modification was intended.

At this point of the proceedings when the Note had become the property of Europe, Lord Grey may be said to have stepped upon the stage. His concern, as at once he made plain, was not with the fate of Serbia but with the action of Russia. The sympathy of the Russians towards the Serbs was powerfully engaged; the prestige of the Russians in the protection of the Serbs deeply involved. Russian intervention seemed probable; its far-reaching consequences, if it occurred, were certain.

The Russian Government, though we sometimes forget it, was quite as inconsiderate of the fate of Europe as the German. The quarrel between the Austrians and the Serbs, whatever its precise rights and wrongs, was, as Lord Grey saw, no concern of the Entente Powers as such. The suppression of Jugo-Slav propaganda, so far as it threatened the integrity of the Austrian Empire, would have made for the peace of Europe; and the detection and destruction of assassins, under whatever auspices conducted, is never a loss to mankind. Russia, however, had her own reasons, good, bad, and indifferent, for interesting herself in the Serbian quarrel. Isvolsky had never forgotten his diplomatic defeat at Aehrenthal's hands. An open passage through the Straits for Russian warships remained the immediate, Constantinople, doubtless, the ultimate goal of his patriotic ambition; and all that we have since learnt of his communications both in Paris and Petersburg up to that final, triumphant cry

---

[1] Montgelas, *The Case for the Central Powers*, p. 159.
[2] G. von Jagow, *Ursachen und Ausbruch des Weltkrieges*, p. 110.

of his, reported by Bertie, "c'est ma guerre," [1] justifies a suspicion, though perhaps no more, that he did not eschew war amongst the means to gain his end. Nor have his activities alone to be considered in this connection. The fact that Sazonov had reported towards the close of 1913 that "the question of the Straits can hardly be advanced except through European complications," and that this opinion of the Foreign Minister was adopted in the ensuing February at a conference of the Russian military, naval, and diplomatic authorities,[2] gives, as the French say, furiously to think; and the discovery that both Sazonov's and Isvolsky's telegrams were garbled [3] is the best proof imaginable that all was not well with the conscience of the Russian Foreign Office at the outbreak of the war. Upon circumstances, indeed, no more telling than these the case against Germany has been built up; and Russia cannot hope to escape the counter-claim. Historians may well debate their rival merit for a long while to come.

Let the effective expectation of war in Russia and Germany respectively have been as it may, it is clear enough that whilst the localisation of the Austro-Serbian quarrel would have suited Austria perfectly, it did not suit the Russian book; and all the less because fear of domestic revolution, if the Serbs were worsted through Russian default, added its terrors.

It was the particular vice of the indeterminate character and uncertain aim of the Triple Entente that a complicated diplomatic situation might drive England to espouse a cause and even countenance a purpose of no interest or importance to herself. Lord Grey saw his peril and strove to avert it. To avoid the danger of Russian intervention he proposed European intervention. His proposal, in the final shape which it assumed on July 26th and in which it has become familiar, was that a Conference of the four Great Powers least concerned in the issue—England, France, Germany, and Italy—should mediate between the Three Powers—Austria, Serbia, and Russia—most concerned in it. The refusal of the German Government to co-operate in

---

[1] *Diary of Lord Bertie of Thame*, i. 66. " At the beginning of the war he claimed to be its author : ' C'est ma guerre.' Now he says : ' Si j'étais responsable . . . je ne me pardonnerais jamais.' "

[2] *German White Book concerning the responsibility of the authors of the War* (Carnegie Endow^nt. translation), Annex I, 133-143. (See also *Stieve Isvolsky and the World War*, pp. 189, 193.)

[3] Romberg, *The Falsifications of the Russian Orange Book* (Bridge).

this plan, ultimately if not immediately, determined his opinion of them, and in the retrospect, after full meditation, he took the day of their refusal to have been the fatal, decisive moment when the die was cast.[1] Their defence is now available. It has been given by Bethmann-Hollweg and more recently by Jagow, the two Ministers most responsible, and it amounts to this. They argue that, though Lord Grey allows them little or no credit for it, they accepted his original suggestion, for, in its first phase, on July 24th the project of intervention was confined to an attempt to mediate between Vienna and Petersburg. But, in its final aspect, the project had taken the form of a Conference of the Four Neutral Powers, authorised to mediate between Vienna and Belgrade as well, and thus in effect to impose a compulsory arbitration upon the two original parties to the quarrel, to one of whom Germany had already given the promise of a free hand. Jagow opposed the suggested development with the very sneer that the world had learnt from Canning. He wanted no "Areopagus," nor did he believe in its efficacy.[2] From the German standpoint, arbitration of the nature proposed seemed the more objectionable that the sympathies of the four arbitrators were likely to stand to one another in the relation of three to one, Italy, from jealousy of Austria, ranging herself with France and England on the side of the Slavs.

In other and simpler words, Germany was prepared to do her best to prevent a general war, but would do nothing to interfere with a local war, regarding, as she did, the suppression of the Jugo-Slavs as a necessary measure for the preservation of Austria. Lord Grey was driven to despair. From that moment, as it seemed to him,[3] Fate, after her manner in a Greek drama, struck blow upon blow, and Peace fought for her life against overwhelming odds. This was doubtless the poetry of the situation. In pale prose a mass of suspicions, ambitions, and entangling alliances had come between men and the things that belonged to their peace; and they do not, perhaps, greatly err who assert that each of the Great Powers acted, in the circumstances, exactly as might have been anticipated. When we reflect upon the German failure to restrain her ally, we have to

---

[1] House, *Intimate Papers*, ii. 54.
[2] *British Documents on the Origins of the War*, xi. p. 164.
[3] *Twenty-five Years*, i. 325.

remember also that Eyre Crowe in the secret minutes lately made public, was writing as early as 25th July that "the moment has passed when it might have been possible to enlist French support in an effort to hold back Russia." [1]

The tragedy now proceeded with quickened footsteps to its appalling end; the Austrians bent upon a local war, the Russians not shrinking from a general one, the Germans backing their ally, and the French theirs. Late on the 25th the Serbs, after taking counsel in Petersburg, put in a conciliatory reply to the Austrian Note, which, however, included a point-blank refusal to admit Austrian co-operation in the inquiry about the murder. By the 27th, Lord Grey had had time to consider this fresh development. His reflections induced him to put the strongest pressure upon his good friend, the German Ambassador, Lichnowsky, to promote a German gesture at the Ballplatz in favour of delaying hostilities; and his representations were so forcible and so menacing that Bethmann-Hollweg, anxious to avoid a general war, decided to take some sort of action upon them in spite of his continued reluctance to hamper Austria in her dealings with the Serbs. For a moment, therefore, German policy seemed to tack and falter. Bethmann's gesture, however, was weak,[2] while Berchtold's mind was already decided. The "Kaiser's" subsequent proposal that territorial annexation should be disclaimed by Austria, and Belgrade seized and held only until Serbia accepted the Austrian Note in its entirety, cut no ice. Berchtold was intent upon inflicting punishment, not upon taking hostages; and war was declared by Austria upon Serbia on July 28th—just a month after the Archduke's assassination —with no explicit reservations as to its scope or purpose.

It was war, but still a local and a little one. Russia raised the issue to a European plane and confounded the confused manœuvres of diplomacy with the counsels of soldiers, manœuvring for position. Mobilisation was decided upon on the 29th, and not a partial mobilisation only. It was indeed an idiosyncrasy of the Russian military machine that a partial mobilisation

---

[1] *British Documents on the Origins of the War*, xi. p. 81.
[2] I do not think the contents of Szögyény's famous telegram of the 27th July can be accepted without reserve in face of Bethmann-Hollweg's and Jagow's denials. (See Renouvin, *Les Origines Immédiates de la Guerre*, pp. 91–5, for a discussion of the affair; and Montgelas, *The Case for the Central Powers*, pp. 212, 213.)

presented practical disadvantages that were almost insuperable.[1]
Two decisions were therefore taken by the Council of State—one
for a partial mobilisation in public and the other for a general
mobilisation in secret.[2] The French Ambassador was forthwith
apprised of this and rendered a little uncomfortable in consequence.[3] He had at least the satisfaction of remembering that,
on the French Foreign Minister's instructions, he had warned
Sazonov, only a day or two before, how important it was to
avoid any precipitate military measures with a man like Grey
to deal with across the English Channel. "La moindre imprudence de votre part," he had urged, "nous coûterait le concours
de l'Angleterre." [4]

How much they divined in Berlin of what was going on behind
the scenes in Russia, it might be hazardous to say, but at least,
in these critical hours, "Willy" must have the credit of having
resumed those affectionate overtures to "Nicky" which the
world has so much derided. He warned his imperial cousin
that a general mobilisation of the Russian army would bring
Germany into the field. On the strength of his representations,
Nicholas overrode the wishes of his General Staff and rescinded
the general mobilisation order in the late evening of the 29th.
But, before the next afternoon was over, the arguments of the
military chiefs, assisted by pressure from Sazonov, had caused
him, pale, it is said, and torn by conscientious scruples, to go
back upon his resolve.

Not in Russia only, on that fateful 29th, were the soldiers
active. In Berlin, also, there was a struggle of which history
catches an echo; and in Berlin, too, the soldiers suffered at first
a rebuff and in the end secured their purpose. The Chancellor
beat them on the question of military mobilisation on that
afternoon, but the next day, just as in Russia with Nicholas, they
got the better of him. As he was in the very act of recommending at Vienna the "halt in Belgrade" policy [5] which Lord Grey
also was prepared to recommend in Petersburg, Moltke and the
German General Staff pressed once more the peril and urgency

---

[1] Dobrorolski, *Die Mobilmachung der russischen Armee*, 1914, pp. 18–20.
And see Renouvin, *Les Origines Immédiates de la Guerre*, pp. 101, 102.
[2] Paléologue, *La Russie des Tsars*, i. 36.
[3] *Ibid.*, p. 36. [4] *Ibid.*, p. 33.
[5] The policy—that is, of allowing Austria to occupy Belgrade pending
further negotiations under the auspices of the Great Powers.

of the military situation, with Russia armed and arming. A military argument at such a crisis has a prodigious plausibility. Every hour can be represented as precious, and the loss of an hour in the beginning as entailing the loss of a war in the end. To contradict is for a civilian impossible; to refuse assent may be to incur the reproach of having brought about the defeat of one's country. Bethmann-Hollweg yielded, as Nicholas yielded, to the arguments of his military advisers.

It was upon that same day—the 30th July—and in consequence of a communication from Lord Grey that the German Emperor's mind, to use a modern metaphor, ran completely off the rails. Essentially false and constitutionally vulgar, it had long been incapable of apprehending the character and purpose of intelligences of another order. Lord Grey and his countrymen had grown to be, above all, the target of its suspicions. That final, impressive appeal for co-operation and mediation, which the British Foreign Secretary addressed on the afternoon of the 29th to the German Ambassador, only confirmed the Emperor in his insane imaginations. We know that, as he read, this master of vanity and self-deception inscribed a comment to the effect that the English were hypocrites and scoundrels, and that, when he came to the passage in which Lord Grey had endeavoured in utter sincerity to avert the patent danger that Lichnowsky might be misled into mistaking personal friendliness for political consent, he exclaimed to himself, "Aha! the common cheat!" [1] This ebullition of imperial 'Billingsgate,' however, does not appear to have made any impression upon the course of events,[2] and is interesting chiefly as showing how the mentality of the British Foreign Secretary affected that of the German Monarch, and incidentally also at what hour precisely Bombastes became furioso. But to return!

Russia, in spite of her Sovereign's statement to the contrary to King George,[3] had thus the good or evil fortune to be first in the field with that order for a general mobilisation which French and Russian authorities alike—Boisdeffre in 1892 and Dobrorolski in reviewing the events of 1914—have explicitly declared to be

---

[1] Kautsky Documents, No. 368.

[2] Montgelas (*The Case for the Central Powers*, p. 149) points out that Bethmann-Hollweg had taken action on Lichnowsky's telegram containing Grey's appeal some nine hours before it was submitted to the Kaiser.

[3] *British Documents on the Origins of the War*, xi. 276.

the beginning of hostilities.[1]   Then came Austria.   Germany was last of the three.   Moltke, content at length [2] to urge upon the willing ears of Conrad von Hötzendorf the advice to mobi-lise all the Austrian forces in face of the growing menace of a Russian attack, had been careful to delay the mobilisation of the great German army until the decision to mobilise the Russian army was actually placed beyond a doubt.   To Lord Grey it seemed that the German Government was none the less re-sponsible for that.   In the last hour, before the clash of arms overtook and drowned the voices of diplomacy, Austria had seemed to show some disposition to treat afresh with Russia. Her action was by no means certainly sincere [3] and may in any case be attributed to pressure from Berlin.   But at the last moment that pressure was withdrawn.   Under the influence of military considerations, Bethmann-Hollweg recalled the telegram [4] in which he had "most emphatically" advised Austria to accept Lord Grey's suggestion of a military halt in Belgrade pending the mediation of the Powers.   The German General Staff had made up their minds that, since Russia was rapidly arming and speed was of the essence of their strategy, the situation permitted of no further hesitations.

Two challenges were then flung down simultaneously before the two Powers of the Dual Alliance.   Russia was required to cease from arming and France to signify her neutrality [5] in the event of a Russo-German war.   The limit of time accorded for accepting these ultimata was in the one case midday, in the other 1 p.m. on the 1st August; but in neither case was acceptance conceivable.

The eyes of all the world were now fixed upon Lord Grey.   As the menace of war increased, the study of his mind intensified in interest and importance for the statesmen of Europe.   To

[1] Dobrorolski, *Die Mobilmachung der russischen Armee*, p. 10.   Dobrorolski, as the reader is probably aware, was at the head of the mobilisation section of the Russian General Staff.

[2] In justice to Moltke and the German General Staff, the critic has to remember that on the 29th Moltke had told the Austrian Intelligence Officer in Berlin, who wired the opinion on to Conrad, that he did not regard the Russian mobilisation (presumably so far as it had then gone) as a reason for Austria to declare war on Russia, and hoped Austria would not do so (Conrad, *Aus meiner Dienstzeit*, iv. 152).

[3] See on this, Renouvin, *Les Origines Immédiates de la Guerre*, pp. 166–70.

[4] Kautsky Documents, No. 441 ; and see Nos. 395 and 451.

[5] A neutrality involving, as we now know, the temporary surrender to Germany of Toul and Verdun.

M. Poincaré, at that time President of the French Republic, it seemed—and the conviction must have been agonising—that the British Foreign Secretary had the issues of peace and war in his keeping, that a strong move on his part towards a closer association of England with France and Russia would have saved the outbreak of hostilities.[1] Yet he looked a darker horse than any of those now plainly visible upon the horizon—darker than the crimson charger of War, the sable mount of Famine, or the pale steed of Death. The French were terribly anxious. "Le gouvernement français," says one high French authority, "le 30 juillet et le 31 juillet, sent l'Angleterre lui échapper."[2] In Berlin they understood the British Foreign Secretary so little that on 29th July the Chancellor had the naïvety to ask for a pledge of neutrality from England in return for an undertaking from Germany that France should lose no foot of soil in Europe. Even in London Lichnowsky, as late as August 1st, was capable of so misunderstanding him as to report that, would Germany but leave France alone, England would answer for French neutrality; thus causing the Kaiser, to Moltke's utter dismay, to propose that the chief German battle-front be shifted from West to East.

This impression of obscurity, in the supreme hour of distress, was the nemesis of a policy which had sought to be in the counsels of a Continent divided against itself, and yet not really of them. Lord Grey, however, was but partly responsible. He himself knew well enough what loyalty required of him. He knew that, if France were involved and England would not help her, he must himself resign;[3] he had carried the *entente* as far as that. But he also knew that he had behind him a divided Cabinet, a party deeply pledged to peace, and a country still groping towards a judgment; and he guarded his lips the more carefully for the knowledge. To the French it became vital to force his hand, and eventually they found a way. The Naval Conversations with France had long ago led to a concerted distribution of the French and English Fleets which left the burden of defending the English Channel with Great Britain. It was now

---

[1] British Blue Book, No. 99.

[2] Renouvin, *Les Origines Immédiates de la Guerre*, p. 210. See Renouvin, pp. 185, 186. See also on this, *Twenty-five Years*, ii. App. F.; Molke, *Erinnerungen, Briefe, Documente*, p. 19.

[3] *Twenty-five Years*, i. 312.

too late to change the arrangement without grave prejudice to French defence. "Will you let Cherbourg and Brest be bombarded," inquired Cambon, "when it was in agreement with you and to suit your interest as much as ours that we concentrated our ships far away?"[1] The British Cabinet found themselves unable to resist the appeal. They gave an assurance that Great Britain would defend the coasts of France and the French Merchant Marine. Thus upon an honourable rather than a contractual obligation they committed themselves and took their side. It was not until the next morning that they found the fulness of their justification in the demand, addressed by the German to the Belgian Government, for a free passage of German troops through Belgium—through neutral country, that is, whose neutrality had been guaranteed as well by Prussia as Great Britain.

The Foreign Secretary, with this tremendous card[2] thrust into his hand by the German High Command, had no difficulty in carrying with him the large majority of his fellow-citizens and the most part of the world along the road that he had long been travelling. He spoke, as he tells us, on that memorable 3rd of August when Great Britain took her decision, without nervousness, short and inadequate as had been his time for preparation. The finger of Fate had pointed to him, a plain English gentleman and a great lover of peace and the pursuits of peace, as the spokesman of his countrymen in the greatest ordeal by battle that ever they suffered in all their history; and he did his duty, without show of oratory, or appeal to partiality,[3] or concession to hypocrisy. "In a great crisis," he says of this episode, giving us at the same time and as by accident the measure of his greatness and simplicity, "a man . . . has to do what is in him to do; just this is what he will and must do, and he can do no other."[4] The main consideration that he pressed upon the House of Commons was such as all his countrymen could at least understand. "The real reason . . ." he told them, to borrow his own brief paraphrase of his speech, "for going into the war was that,

---

[1] Quoted in Renouvin, *Les Origines, etc.*, p. 215.

[2] He did not receive the *official* intimation of the German ultimatum to Belgium until his speech in the House of Commons was over.

[3] Cf. *Twenty-five Years*, ii. 15, where he tells us how instinctively he excluded as inappropriate any emphasising of Bethmann-Hollweg's ignoble bid for British neutrality.

[4] *Twenty-five Years*, ii. 14.

if we did not stand by France and stand up for Belgium against this aggression, we should be isolated, discredited, and hated; and there would be before us nothing but a miserable and ignoble future."[1]

A cynic might urge that isolation had once seemed splendid, that discredit is soon lived down, and that hatred is our portion for ever, whether we stand by our neighbours as in 1914, or leave them to their fate as in 1870. A lawyer might question whether our guarantee of Belgian neutrality was, not merely joint, but also several. A historian might dwell upon the extreme complexity of the original issue, upon the mad fashion in which alliances and engagements and even conversations had dragged one great Power after another into the quarrel until all were involved, or upon the fact that, if Austria were responsible for a savage ultimatum, Russia was guilty of a too hasty mobilisation. Or, once more, a German statesman may complain that Lord Grey was ignorant of certain now familiar revelations, heedless of the fact that it was Germany that sought to localise the issue and Russia to Europeanise it, and indifferent to the consideration that with Austria the end was self-preservation, but with Russia prestige and power.[2] All this and more might be admitted, and yet Lord Grey's argument seem still compelling. Le cœur a ses raisons que la raison ne connait point. If cold reason falters fine feeling does not fail. Not all the publicists in Central Europe can make the violation of Belgian neutrality other than an ugly business; nor can any ravages of criticism tarnish the decent sympathy and generous instinct that drew England to the side of her neighbour, when a Power that held its plighted word for nothing better than a piece of paper threatened, with whatever promises of territorial restitution, to invade once more the pleasant land of France. If Lord Grey was "mere English" and his diplomacy so lacking in the fierce realism and lucid energy of the Continent that it could even seem to his official adversary "a staggering picture of insular misunderstanding and ignorance of continental conditions and circumstances,"[3] if, with his limited knowledge at the time, he made Germany seem too odious and let Russia off

---

[1] *Twenty-five Years*, ii. p. 15.
[2] Cp. Jagow, *England und der Kriegsausbruch*, pp. 47 and 58.
[3] *Ibid.*, p. 38.

too light, he did at the least represent his country at its best and bravest, rise grandly to his occasion, and rally his country-men, good, bad, and indifferent, almost to a man, behind him. Doubtless it will be difficult for future generations to envisage the causes of the War so simply as did the British Foreign Secretary upon that eventful August afternoon of 1914. Even his more recent treatment of the question whether or not the War might have been avoided [1] will seem to many minds superficial. He discovers the source and origin of the evil in the mere exis-tence of the great continental armies. But the armies were there only because there existed unsatisfied longings to be met or anxious fears to be repelled. The Dual Alliance and its satellites had the more obvious longings, the Central Powers or at any rate Austria, the more evident alarms. France would have liked to have back Alsace and Lorraine; Russia was wanting Constantinople and the Straits; and Serbia the break-up of the Habsburg Empire. But it is not obvious that Germany and Austria wanted anything substantial in Europe except to be left alone, or any concessions in Asia that could not have been arranged without a conflict. It was otherwise, perhaps, in the case of German ambitions in Africa and at sea; for the attempted bargain with England about neutrality at the beginning of the war immediately laid bare the former, just as the 'naval holiday' discussions had already discovered the latter. But it was a continental, not a colonial nor a naval issue that actually raised the whirlwind; and the historian, who gropes his way among origins, is consequently bound in fairness to remember that on the face of things the Central Powers had a greater interest in maintaining the territorial *status quo* than their Eastern adversaries. The war, it may be, could in the last resort only have been prevented by proscribing either the spirit of nationality or that of self-defence. But, if an English Liberal cannot very well condemn the one, neither can an Englishman the other.

Here, however, we stand upon the fringe of a wood where the native complexity of foreign affairs dissolves into the darker mazes of fatalism and free will. A biographical study may legitimately decline to be dragged farther into those primeval forests. It draws its best vigour, if not its actual being from a

---

[1] *Twenty-five Years*, c. 19.

belief that the pygmy hand of man can mix and wrestle, not altogether ineffectively, with the Titans in their contests—with just
such Time-spirits as we find here rushing into mortal conflict—
one of them a hoary Dynast, the other young and ruthless with
all the pride of Race.   On such a supposition there comes to each
leading actor in the diplomatic drama which inaugurated the
Great War, the ordeal of a particular judgment—to Berchtold,
most of all; to Tisza; to Jagow and Bethmann-Hollweg and their
master; to Sazonov and Isvolsky.   The heavier responsibilities
of these protagonists in the struggle we are not here required
to assess.   The question of Lord Grey's responsibility alone
concerns us.   Was it possible, the student of the British Foreign
Secretary's policy has to ask himself, for Britain in the days
and years before Armageddon, to have done anything, or to have
left anything undone, that would have caused the situation to
be saved ?   Free as this country is from any part or lot in crime,
if crime there was, is she also completely free from what we class
as blunder?   There are two questions here to be considered—
that of policy properly so-called and that of diplomacy; the one
more a matter of strategy and science, but the other of tactics
and art.   On the former point Lord Grey has been his own best
critic.   "The more I reflect on the past," he told a gathering of
supporters of the League of Nations in the autumn of 1926,[1]
"the more I am convinced that propaganda, and perhaps still
more counter-propaganda, to fix the war-guilt on any one nation
does not reveal, but, on the contrary, obscures the root-cause of
the last war, which was the condition of things which had been
growing up for generations in Europe.   It was the division of
Europe into groups of Powers, each with competing armaments." [2]
In so far as he had lent himself to that process of disintegration,
in so far as he had preferred it to the old policy of isolation,
which was not perhaps after all so bad a policy in times of such
distress, in so far, in a word, as he had allowed himself to be
drawn into the counsels of Europe, by way of the balance of
power and not by the 'Areopagus' way of congress and concert,
he had contributed something to accentuate even to encourage
the undesirable state of things in which he found in the end

---

[1] 2nd November 1926.
[2] Reported in the *Times* of 3rd November 1926.   I have transferred the
passage from *oratio obliqua* into *oratio recta*.

the source of the catastrophe. Those times were infinitely difficult; let him who supposes he would himself have managed matters better cast the first stone.

An answer to the other issue mentioned—the question of mere diplomacy—is easier than once it was to give and as easy, perhaps, as it will ever be. We have lately been made acquainted with all that is relevant in the diplomatic correspondence which passed through Lord Grey's hands in the critical month before the outbreak of hostilities;[1] we have precisely the facts and suppositions and advice before our eyes upon which his decisions were taken; and we can recover in imagination his exact standpoint at the time. The despatches and telegrams of the British Ambassadors, the minutes of the dominant Foreign-Office officials are become an open book. We know without reserves what opinion of the aims and action of the Central Powers Goschen was forming at Berlin and Sir Maurice de Bunsen at Vienna; in what manner Buchanan in Petersburg was dealing with a foreign minister whose diplomacy made Lord Carnock[2] declare that "one really does not know where one is with him";[3] and how the robust Bertie beheld the international situation through his French windows in Paris. Nor is this all. The veil of the Foreign Office itself is raised so that we catch glimpses of the mind of the powers that prevailed there —of Nicolson's pro-Russian tendencies—natural enough in one who had been noted for his admirable success as ambassador at the Court of St Petersburg—and of Crowe's anti-German leanings, so contrary to what the public suspected in a man unfairly circumstanced through German affinities. Only one figure, more influential, it may be, either than the Permanent or Assistant Under-Secretary of State, remains hidden still in obscurity —Lord Grey's official private secretary, Sir William Tyrrell.

It is not difficult to see upon what, if upon anything in his share of the negotiations, criticism of Lord Grey's diplomacy must ultimately fix. He had early disclaimed, in the most explicit

---

[1] *British Documents on the Origins of the War*, xi. 7.
[2] Sir Arthur Nicolson.
[3] *British Documents*, xi. 126. The then Prime Minister's tribute to Sir Edward Goschen, Sir Maurice de Bunsen, and Sir George Buchanan is an interesting one. "We were singularly fortunate . . . in having as our representatives at Berlin, Vienna, and St Petersburg, three diplomatists so qualified to handle a situation of almost unexampled difficulty by long experience, trained insight, and complete understanding" (*Genesis of the War*, p. 202).

manner and to the German Ambassador, any 'title' on the part of Great Britain 'to intervene' between Austria and Serbia.[1] He had no difference with Austria, as such, no brief for Serbia whilst she stood alone. The subject of their dispute was, as he told Sir Maurice de Bunsen,[2] no British concern. As late as July 29th, he would himself have been content that Austria should occupy Belgrade, pending complete satisfaction of her grievances, provided that she abstained from any further advance.[3] His personal attitude was thus scarcely distinguishable from the "halt in Belgrade" policy which "the Kaiser" at one moment advocated, and which Bethmann-Hollweg held to almost to the end; and, had it not been for Sazonov, there seems to be no obvious reason why he should have found the German proposal of July 30th [4] to guarantee Serbian integrity inacceptable. It is significant that actually on 27th July we find Bertie writing to him privately from Paris: "I am sure that the French Government do not want to fight, and they should be encouraged to put pressure on the Russian Government not to assume the absurd and obsolete attitude of Russia being the protectress of all Slav States whatever their conduct, for this will lead to war. . . . Isvolsky is expected back here to-day and he is not an element of peace." [5]

The loyalties, nevertheless, rather than the equities of the situation drove the Foreign Secretary continually forward. It was because Russia threatened to make the Serbian quarrel her own, and by so doing threatened also the peace of Europe that he had originally entered the field of negotiation, and it was because Petersburg like Vienna was resolved to suffer no moderating influences [6] that Great Britain found herself approaching continually nearer to the field of battle. Crowe had early reached the conclusion that any attempt to work upon the Russian Government was useless and that the cause of Triple Entente *versus* Triple Alliance was definitely joined. Two days

[1] *British Documents*, xi. 89 and 98.   [2] *Ibid.*, p. 73.
[3] *Ibid.*, p. 182.   [4] *Ibid.*, p. 191.   [5] *Ibid.*, p. 133.
[6] " S'il s'agit d'une action modératrice quelconque à St Pétersbourg, nous la déclinons à l'avance " (Sazonov to Isvolsky, 27th July). [See *British Documents*, xi. 143] : " Cette fois nous marcherons " (Soukhomlinoff at dinner on 25th July, reported as overheard by himself in Rosen's *Forty Years of Diplomacy*, ii. 163). It is interesting to notice that Rosen places Sazonov with Soukhomlinoff and Yanouchkevitch as the responsible authors of the Russian General Mobilisation (*ibid.*, p. 172).

before Bertie's letter, just quoted, in favour of the use of Franco-British pressure at Petersburg was written, he had minuted, Sir Arthur Nicolson not dissenting, the following sentences:— "It is clear that France and Russia are decided to accept the challenge thrown out to them. Whatever we may think of the merits of the Austrian charges against Serbia, France and Russia consider that . . . the bigger cause of Triple Alliance *versus* Triple Entente is definitely engaged. I think it would be impolitic, not to say dangerous, for England to attempt to controvert this opinion or to endeavour to obscure the plain issue by any representation at St Petersburg and Paris." [1] To Crowe, indeed, it seemed that his country stood at such a parting of the ways as Prussia had faced in 1805, and that to fail, as Prussia failed, to fight would be to fall, as Prussia fell, so soon as the enemy's hands were once more free. Lord Grey was not uninfluenced by these considerations.[2]

The doubt must, therefore, always remain for those who are not fully satisfied that the German Government was from the first contriving war, whether the British Foreign Secretary's record in regard to Russia was much better than that of the German Chancellor in regard to Austria. Neither one Minister nor the other succeeded in putting anything that can be called effective pressure on the associated Power. Lord Grey even tells us that he 'felt impatient at the suggestion that it was for him to influence or restrain Russia,' and that he 'could do nothing but express pious hopes in general terms to Sazonov.' [3] The Germans may, perhaps, be excused if they did not perceive the distinction between his obligation to exert influence upon his associate and their own obligation to exert influence upon theirs quite so clearly as he did. Even to less interested parties it may not seem obvious that circumstances had so entirely altered cases. For the British and German standpoints in regard to the Serbian issue were not, as we have seen, so widely different for us to be sure that a firmer word from the British Foreign Secretary at Petersburg recommending the proferred German guarantee of Serbian territorial integrity in return for the like from "the Kaiser" at Vienna insisting upon a "halt in Belgrade" would have been no better than an idle one.

[1] *British Documents*, xi. 81.   [2] *Twenty-five Years*, i. 337.
[3] *Ibid.*, p. 330.

Let such speculations be worth what they may: they form only the antechamber to another curious inquiry, also incon-clusive, yet not altogether unprofitable nor inappropriate as we draw towards the end of our journey. How, we may wonder, had they been confronted with it, would Lord Grey's pre-decessors have dealt with his problem—in the same manner or differently? Castlereagh, one might hazard, alert as he was to suppress every plague-spot of revolution, would not have waited for Russia to 'Europeanise' the issue, but would have used all the pressure in his power to place it at once upon a Congress rather than a Conference level. And about that we may say with confidence that an 'Areopagus' policy had more chance, if it had ever any chance at all, before Russia had taken the initiative than afterwards. Canning, on the other hand, we may suppose, would have turned his eyes forthwith towards the New World and have tried for such a solidarity between the Anglo-Saxon races as would have compelled Europe to maintain peace, or at worst to return to it ; and this policy, too, would not have been without possibilities and, had Roosevelt been sitting, when the quarrel occurred, in the place which Wilson occupied, might even have offered good promise of success. But to pass to another figure! Aberdeen, we may feel pretty certain, if left to himself, would not have thought the original[1] issue worth intervention ; would have felt all the talk about German world-domination too journalistically sensational to be politically probable; and might have translated "John Bull's" famous malediction "To hell with Serbia ! " into the milder adjuration "To heaven with your dispute ! " Palmerston, for his part, was not incapable of backing Serbia into hostilities, and then of backing Britain out of them. Salisbury, we may guess, if he had allowed himself to be drawn out of a policy of isolation in 1904, would not have let the Eastern situation develop so far by itself as Lord Grey did in 1914, nor have left his own ultimate intentions so long in doubt. A private letter to Berlin might have early indicated at what point Austrian polemics must encounter British opposition; a private letter to Petersburg have conveyed how long mobilisation must be restrained before he claims of Russian prestige could count upon British support; and a Circular terminating in a Congress, with the British Foreign

---

[1] The Serbian, that is, not the Belgian issue.

Secretary this time as honest broker, have sufficed to reconcile the claims of peace and honour for another quarter of a century. But then we have to remember that Salisbury would have had the Premiership in his pocket, the Conservative party at his back, and no Mr Lloyd George in his Cabinet—advantages in the conception and development of a strong diplomacy, one and all of them denied to Lord Grey.

It is rather, then, to Clarendon and Granville that we must look to find ministers who might have handled the negotiations of 1914 much as was actually done. There is latent in Liberalism a quality most creditable to its humanity, yet capable of producing in hours of crisis an element of delay and hesitation that slips almost imperceptibly into drift. Clarendon had betrayed this weakness in the negotiations of 1853-4, Derby (for Derby was, as the event showed, really a Liberal) in 1876-8, and Granville in his policy in Egypt. Each of these, from one cause or another, seemed unable to—so to speak—take hold of the situation. And this subtle defect it is not impossible that History may impute to Lord Grey. Long before matters came to a head, but as the Great Powers more and more ranged themselves in rival camps and it came to be a commonplace in military circles that Germany, in the event of war, would attack France through Belgium, he might well have taken occasion to remind his countrymen—publicly, yet in such a manner that the words should have seemed intended to be overheard not only in Germany but France—that the defence of Belgian neutrality was the paramount British interest in Europe, and that in this case only, saving that of Portugal, was Britain bound by treaty to engage in hostilities upon the Continent. Such a declaration might not have prevented the Austro-Serbian quarrel from engendering a general war, but it must at least have given the German Foreign Office ground for reflection in any subsequent treatment of Balkan problems and have made the British standpoint early familiar at home and inexorably plain abroad. For the rest it would be true to say that, if Lord Grey perhaps fell short of some of his predecessors in grasp and action, there were few if any who could have rallied the opinion of the world to the cause of the Allies so successfully as he did himself. Men perceived the integrity of his purpose, and perceiving it believed in the integrity of his judgment.

Diplomacy in time of war parts with its first innocence, is deposed from its high office of maintaining peace, and falls into a kind of servitude to the military departments. Lord Grey had shown what manner of diplomatist he made in peace time; he was now required to approve himself in the abnormal state of war. His pre-occupations, apart from the obvious business of contributing what he might to hold the three great Allied Powers of the Entente together, lay in the Near East and the Far West—in the Balkan Peninsula and the United States of America. It was of great importance to prevent the Turks from joining the Germans; to persuade the Bulgarians to join the Entente Powers; to induce the Americans to take a practical and not a platonic interest in European affairs. He had little to show on any of these counts at the close of his administration. The Turks entered the war on the wrong side in 1914; the Bulgars in 1915; and the Americans were still some months removed from giving the Entente their help when, on the fall of Mr Asquith's Coalition Government in the end of 1916, Lord Grey retired from office. It is not, however, in this way that his work can be judged. Diplomacy, as he pleads, was tightly tied to the lumbering waggon of war during his last years of power—as tightly tied as perhaps ever in history. All through that time the Germans gave continuous, arresting exhibitions of military strength, whilst the Allies had nothing better to bargain with than prophecies of ultimate victory. The Turks and the Bulgars had the misfortune to be pure realists in a world where idealism sometimes plays strange tricks and has always to be reckoned with; and their minds were powerfully and respectively affected by the failure of the British Navy to capture the *Goeben* and the *Breslau* at the outbreak of hostilities and of the Russian army to stand up to its opponents in the summer of 1915. All this, and more to the same effect, Lord Grey may fairly urge in his own excuse and that of his agents. Yet it must remain doubtful whether, before ever the war broke out, he had sufficiently perceived the supreme points of danger or in every case taken sufficient care to station the right man at each.

It may be that the British Foreign Secretary was not at the time so insensible as his memoirs suggest to some force in the criticism of his failure to save either Turk or Bulgar, recent and deadly foes to one another as they had been, from the long cast of the German net, or to compel the Serbs, however much Russia might complain, to make that surrender of Macedonia to the Bulgarians, which would in all probability have brought Bulgaria into line. A story which, if perhaps apocryphal, is yet not unworthy to be preserved among the fables that crystallise truth, tells how during the dark hours of the War he was caught explaining to a child with the aid of an atlas the grave anxieties of the military situation. The pupil's hand travelled across Eastern Europe, whilst the teacher unfolded the tale of disaster, and, as he did so, apportioned the blame. At last a little finger pointed to Bulgaria. "Ah!" said the teacher, "that was my mistake!"

If not a mistake, at least a supreme misfortune! With the Bulgarian surrender to German blandishments, and the British failure to force the Dardanelles, which Bulgarian assistance might have assured, there passed away all hope of finding a south-west passage into Russia or fixing a wall of partition between the Germans and the Turks. But, from a strictly diplomatic point of view, it was the seduction of the Porte that brought the greater consequence in its wake. Under the influence of this culminating proof of Turkish duplicity, and of the suspicion with which the Russian Government regarded the British landing at Gallipoli, Lord Grey reversed the immemorial policy of his predecessors and agreed to allow Russia to gratify her supreme ambition and possess herself of the city of Constantine. He came to this decision reluctantly, in the belief that the maintenance of the alliance of the Entente Powers intact must have precedence over all other considerations and with the approval of the Conservative Opposition whom he called into council.[1] As things turned out he was never required to honour his cheque. But for the Bolshevists, however, it would have been his doing that the age-long, mystic dream of Russia took its flight into the upper air, no longer through a delusive portal of shining ivory, but by the sober gate of horn.[2]

Lord Grey's diplomacy, rebuffed in Turkey and Bulgaria, sought with better success an ally in Italy and a base of military operations in Greece. Nothing is to be had for nothing, and least of all in war-time; but countries washed by the Medi-

---

[1] *Twenty-five Years*, ii. 181.   [2] *Aen*, vi. 893.

terranean Sea have as a rule their price, and perhaps a good
many other countries as well.   The Foreign Secretary came
to terms both with the Italians and the Greeks, but hardly
to the best of terms.   Italy coveted not only Trieste and the
Trentino, to which the nationality of the inhabitants gave her
a claim, but the South Tyrol, where the people were Germans,
and Dalmatia, where they were Slavs.   Lord Grey gave these
things secretly, 'reason of state' and Machiavelli, as it seemed
to some, prevailing in the urgent distress of the time against
Liberal doctrine and Mill.   The end—in this case the consolidation of a grand alliance against Germany—had once again been
held to justify the means, which here unfortunately signified
the sacrifice of some helpless populations to foreign domination,
quite in the old, much-abused style of the diplomacy of the
ancien régime.

In dealing with Greece, too, the Foreign Secretary, as he
admits,[1] put some strain upon his principles.   Serbia, thanks
not a little to her own obstinate determination not to cede
Macedonia to the Bulgars even if compensated elsewhere, had
seen the peril of her situation increased by the entry of Bulgaria
into the war.   The Allies desired to resolve the doubts of Greece
as to fulfilling her treaty-obligation to come to the aid of her
neighbours in face of a Bulgarian invasion by the presence of a
Franco-British army in the Balkans.   A military base was
essential, and Salonica fulfilled the requirement.   Salonica was
a Greek city, and Greece was neutral.   But the violation of
neutrality had been one of the chief counts against Germany;
and the Allies, in this respect above all, could ill afford to be
satisfied with a standard of conduct falling below that of Cæsar's
wife.   The Greek Prime Minister—the famed Venizelos—though
personally favourable to the landing of a Franco-British force,
could not be persuaded to refrain from a public protest against
so irregular a step.   The case was, therefore, one in which a
moralist was entitled to indulge in searchings of heart.

But, whilst M. Venizelos demurred and Lord Grey doubted,
the military authorities of France and England carried out the
projected occupation.   There are few minds so scrupulous that
they do not respond to the tonic of a *fait accompli*.   Though
M. Venizelos fell and Greece continued neutral, the armies of the

---

[1] *Twenty-five Years*, ii. 216.

Allies remained at Salonica and Lord Grey at the Foreign Office. "In war," as he observes in this connection, "many things are done that would not be done in peace." [1]   So had Bethmann-Hollweg argued, and many more besides both before and after him.

Not in his handling of Near Eastern but of Far Western problems was Lord Grey really in a position to show the faith and power that was in him. Just as upon the European Continent all was strange and uncongenial to his nature, so in compensation did he share with some leading Americans of his time a similarity of outlook and community of purpose that were pregnant with hope for humanity. Thus he found Whitelaw Reid particularly sympathetic, and of Roosevelt he made a sure friend and delightful correspondent. It was, however, preeminently upon the two men who represented during the War what was becoming day by day as Europe spent its strength more and more evidently the most powerful country in the world, that he exercised an influence of incalculable value to his country.

Ambassador Page—to use the quaint Americanism—has left behind him in his Letters as pleasing a tribute to Lord Grey as a foreign secretary could desire.   It is not merely that the transparent high-mindedness of the Englishman has plainly cast its spell over the American's earnest and generous soul, but that it has so fully broken down all the barriers set by alien nationality and neutral office as to produce an interchange of ideas and co-operation of effort beyond precedent in diplomatic history. There is no larger feather in Lord Grey's helmet than the fact that in the teeth of much ill-judged criticism at home, he contrived to keep America from active resistance to a European blockade of exceptional and increasing stringency—resistance that would probably have taken the form, necessarily fatal to the Allies, of cutting off the supply of munitions. Yet he could scarcely have accomplished so much unless Page had stood firmly beside him. The Ambassador, as we now know, admonished him how to avoid American susceptibilities; actually advised him to encourage the French Navy to rush in and capture contraband which the British, for fear of America, hesitated to seize; and even on one occasion placidly informed him that he disagreed with a despatch which, in accordance

[1] *Twenty-five Years*, ii. 216.

with his instructions, he had just read aloud, and went on to propose that they should put their heads together to defeat it.[1]

Hardly less attractive, hardly more conventional were Lord Grey's relations with the discreet and mouselike House, the missionary and other self of the American President. That remarkable man had come to Europe, in the late spring of 1914, charged to explore the possibilities of disarmament, arbitration, and peace—in short, of a League of Nations—both in England and Germany. He was a swallow that never made a summer, but he continued his activities during the War, flitting this way and that about the Continent, but homing back to England. His estimate of Lord Grey is a remarkable one: "the one sane, big figure" in British politics.[2]

It was to this foreigner that the Foreign Secretary, for the first time, perhaps, in modern English history, accorded a private code to facilitate rapid, informal correspondence.[3] Their communications were in truth not fitted for every ear. They were the secret depositaries of President Wilson's offer to the Allies in February 1916 to call a conference and compel Germany to accept peace on such terms as he thought just, and, should the German Government refuse, to enter the war on the side of the Allies.[4] The President's conditions, so House conveyed, would include the restoration of Belgium and the recovery of Alsace-Lorraine by France, but also the concession to Germany of some colonial compensation. The offer, after being communicated to the French Government, was left neglected. Its large humanity appealed to Lord Grey at the time more deeply than he has remembered to say in his memoirs. Precluded from confessing that, by the provisions of the Secret Treaties with Russia and Italy, he had committed himself to principles gravely at variance with Wilson's plan, he, nevertheless, told Colonel House, when he heard of it, that he was prepared to face the obloquy involved in its acceptance, even to the point of having his windows broken by a London mob [5]—so certain did he feel of its rectitude; so closely did he concur in regarding the consequent salvage of human life as worth more than a decisive victory at a year's remove.[6]

---

[1] *Twenty-five Years*, ii. 106.   [2] House, *Intimate Papers*, i. 388.
[3] *Ibid.*, p. 473.   [4] *Twenty-five Years*, ii. 123.
[5] House, *Intimate Papers*, ii. 183.   [6] *Ibid.*, p. 194.

The mood passed; or, perhaps, loyalty to France and Russia was too strong to give it play. He was not the only man who in that hour of desperate conflict lost faith in the counsels of peace, or who at the dawn of final victory forgot that he had been once disposed to favour a less triumphant and tremendous ending. But, during the long disillusionment that followed a fight fought to the finish and a peace imposed with all the advantages of dictation, doubt returned. We find him wondering in his memoirs whether true statesmanship did not miss its way with the rejection of that fateful offer. "If a Wilson peace in 1916 had brought real disillusionment about militarism," he tells us, "it would have been far better than what actually happened."[1] The condition seems incalculable, the conclusion platitudinous. In the light of the event we can see that in practice Europe was confronted in 1916–7 by a choice between leaving a military aristocracy still powerful in Prussia, or allowing a Bolshevist oligarchy to establish itself in Russia. A negotiated peace meant the one; a dictated peace involved the other. Each had its risks or terrors; we shall estimate them differently according as we hold civilisation to be in the greater peril from the presence in its midst of a State addicted to the manufacture of highly explosive arms or highly explosive ideas. The former seemed at the time the graver, because it was the more immediate danger; but there were men of mark who regarded the latter as no less formidable. Lord Morley was here in line with Lord Lansdowne; Dean Inge not so widely divided as usual from the Pope. History may well refuse to risk a judgment as to who was right. The policy that was followed had no success, but a policy untried has no credentials.

More countenance might, perhaps, have been given to peace negotiations in 1917 if Lord Grey had remained longer at the Foreign Office. But before the year of President Wilson's offer was out power had passed from his hands, and to a large extent from the hands of his Department. In their place there reigned, with a private, extra-departmental and hitherto unheard-of secretariate to help him, Mr Lloyd George, a pacifist turned warrior, and the less balanced for that. Whatever the military merits of the change, the diplomatic disadvantages can hardly be contested. The Foreign Office suffered an eclipse from

[1] *Twenty-five Years*, ii. 132.

which even Lord Balfour's presence there did not suffice to save it. At the Peace Conference the Prime Minister dominated the British Delegation; and the Peace, so far as Great Britain had any hand in it, must in justice be regarded as a reflection of his mind rather than of that of the wiser sort among his colleagues. It would, indeed, be as unreasonable to imagine that the subtle philosophic intelligence of Lord Balfour could have lent itself to the crude doctrine that the causation of the war rested with the Central Powers alone [1] as to credit his benignant and generous statesmanship with compelling a beaten foe to put his signature to that contentious opinion or supposing that any advantage could be drawn from a trial of the defeated and discredited Emperor by judges chosen by the victorious Powers.

Such passionate futilities merely served to throw into favourable relief the humane disposition and liberal education of Lord Grey; and there were some few who, as the mobile wizardry of the Prime Minister became more and more discredited and the conduct of the foreign business of the country, which was at that time its principal business, fell, through Curzon's complaisance, more and more into disrepute, looked to Lord Grey as the Englishman best qualified by disinterestedness of character, moderation of mind, and experience of foreign affairs to form the nucleus of a coalition party which might supersede the more or less obsolete division between Conservative and Liberal. To none of the old Party Leaders, however, was so brave a step acceptable; nor had Lord Grey, perhaps, the vigour to rise to this new occasion. Stricken with a failure of eyesight, which, as it was fatally accentuated by his work in the war, he had told Colonel House that he regarded as "the sacrifice he had to make for his country," [2] he fell gradually into the background of the stage, emerging from time to time rather as an apologist and advocate of the League of Nations, which he had done much to promote, than as a practical force in politics.

There may remain for some of us a lingering regret that one, whose foreign policy had, after its kind, contributed so much to a closer participation of Great Britain in the affairs of the Continent and of America in the affairs of the World, should

---

[1] Article 231 of the Peace of Versailles.
[2] House, *Intimate Papers*, i. 427.

have had neither part nor lot in the effort to restore to Europe
a sense of unity and to mankind a temple of peace.   But it is a
regret not without alleviation.   For he is returned to his first
and truest love.   He has exchanged the study of the law of
Nations for that of Nature—broken tables for an inviolable
code.   He can listen to the songs of English birds, different
and   distinguishable   as   human   voices   to   an   accustomed
ear.   And he is free to feel around him the presence of those
"beauteous forms" of which the Poet speaks—

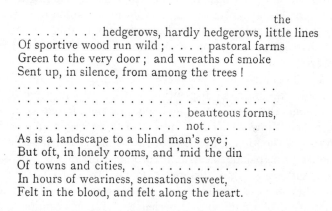

the

. . . . hedgerows, hardly hedgerows, little lines
Of sportive wood run wild ; . . . . pastoral farms
Green to the very door ; and wreaths of smoke
Sent up, in silence, from among the trees !
. . . .
. . . .
. . . . beauteous forms,
. . . . not . . . .
As is a landscape to a blind man's eye ;
But oft, in lonely rooms, and 'mid the din
Of towns and cities, ...
In hours of weariness, sensations sweet,
Felt in the blood, and felt along the heart.

Many things more might be said, and, doubtless, ought to be
said, about one who has played so great a part in public affairs,
whose character and abilities have fallen so much under discussion, and whose proper place in history is still so hard to
ascertain.   But, if one thing only be added, then it might well
be this—that, as Foreign Secretary, Lord Grey seems, in a singular manner, to have reflected characteristic features of British
diplomacy for a century past, to have reproduced them, or at
least some suggestion of them, in the face that he turned towards
the world, and thus in a measure to have served as the epitome
of his own predecessors.   This is not, of course, in itself surprising,
for upon him all the ends of British policy were come.   But, also,
unless this diagnosis be at fault, there ran in his veins a kind of
fatalism, such as appears sometimes in the last of a long line,
and the existence of which we may detect as well in his casual
observation that "there is in great affairs so much more, as a
rule, in the minds of the events (if such an expression may be

used) than in the minds of the actors" [1] as in his general comparison, already referred to, of the course of the negotiations
preceding the outbreak of the war with the inexorable march
forward of a Greek tragic drama.[2]

Here, then, we might say, as we look up at his portrait, was
one whose vision soared, like Castlereagh's, towards lasting
peace, and who, like Castlereagh, desired by means of common
counsel to bring Europe to a better mind, but yet was torn from
his course by adverse winds and weather. Here was one, too,
whose hand, like Canning's, was stretched out towards America
across the Western main, yet never freed himself from the
entangling meshes of the Old World nor stayed to feel the answer-
ing pressure of the New. Here was a minister who, as they
testify that marked his struggle to suppress atrocities along the
Congo and misrule in Macedonia, was richer than Palmerston in
that peculiar British instinct disinterestedly to champion the
cause of the under-dog, and who, like Aberdeen, put his hope
in an Anglo-French *entente*, strove hard for peace, yet closed
his course in battle. In him, the critic might pursue, there
lurked an insularity more alien than any man's from all connection with the Continent; yet in the event he was persuaded to
go full as far as Lansdowne in hand with France, and further
than ever Clarendon's or Salisbury's thoughts had travelled
along the road to Russia. A man, in short, of a most composite
lineage, yet withal of a great simplicity of nature and of a disposition less in keeping with latter-day diplomacy than Arthurian
legend! And, to conclude, a Foreign Secretary whose personal
character much more than the course of his diplomacy opened
the way to that participation of Great Britain in the affairs of the
world on the principle of 'Areopagus' rather than of alliance,
which British policy had, ever since Castlereagh's day, been
feeling after and even now, maybe, is finding!

---

[1] *Twenty-five Years*, i. 51.   [2] *Ibid.*, p. 325.

NOTE ON SERBIAN RESPONSIBILITY IN REGARD TO THE CRIME OF SARAJEVO

SINCE this book was first drafted there has occurred the death of M. Pašić. It may not, therefore, seem out of place to emphasise the necessarily provisional and tentative character of the observations on pp. 335, 336, respecting the nature and extent of Serbian responsibility in relation to the affair at Sarajevo. The strength of the case against the Serbian Government of 1914 has been shown in Miss M. E. Durham's book on the subject, and its weakness in that of Dr Seton-Watson. Whilst advocacy argues and judgment ripens, there would appear to be room to insist that no racial end nor patriotic purpose can absolve a Government and every member of it from using the utmost effort to avert assassination, or, if assassination has occurred, from showing by every possible means the utmost detestation of the crime. My remarks upon the event at Sarajevo will, I trust, be read in this light and not as if dictated by any hostility to the young Kingdom of Jugo-Slavia, to which it would be out of keeping with the so-called Locarno spirit to wish anything but the most prosperous future and the fullest partnership in European civilisation.

INDEX

Abd-ul-Mejid, 234.
Abdul Hamid II, 292, 318.
Abercorn, Duke of, 97.
Aberdeen, 4th Earl of, his interest in foreign affairs, 4.
  and Castlereagh at Basel in 1813, 18.
  mentioned, 20, 139, 156, 157, 160, 163 and *f*, 176, 179, 194, 195, 196, 197, 198, 199, 288, 289, 317, 353, 363.
  posterity and, 91.
  his character, 91–2.
  and Christian methods in diplomacy, 91.
  his Premiership, 92, 125–9, 235, 246.
  his appearance, 92.
  compared with Job, 92.
  Gladstone's estimate of, 92–3.
  and Napoleon, 93–4.
  Byron's " travelled Thane," 94.
  and his estates, 94.
  his religious nature, 95–6.
  death of his first wife and his second marriage, 96–7.
  effect of Napoleonic war on, 98–9, 102, 103, 128.
  accredited to Austrian Court in 1813, 99.
  and Metternich, 99–101.
  and Frankfort terms to Napoleon, 101–2.
  and Chaumont Treaty, 102.
  his tenderness of heart, 102–4.
  friendship with Wellington, 104.
  at the Foreign Office, 1828–30, 104–12.
  and Greek independence, 105–6, 107–8.
  his Near-Eastern policy, 106–8, 195.
  and Portugal, 108.
  and French Revolution of 1830, 108–11.
  and Catholic emancipation, 112.

Aberdeen, 4th Earl of:
  at the Admiralty and the Colonial office, 1834–5, 112.
  at the Foreign Office, 1841–6, 113–25.
  and France, 113–7.
  and Guizot, 116.
  and Nicholas I, 117.
  and the Spanish Marriages, 117–22, 159 and *f*.
  his description of Anglo-French *entente*, 120.
  and American boundary questions, 122–5.
  and Ecclesiastical Titles Bill, 125.
  his courage, 128.
  compared with Palmerston, 133, 134.
  an exponent of Castlereagh's international method, 134.
  and Clarendon, 236.
  and the Crimean War, 126–8, 236, 242, 244, 246, 247.
Aberdeen, Countess of, 96–7.
Aberdeen, Countess of (Lady Hamilton), 97–8.
Acton, Lord, 273 and *f*, 334.
Adams, J. Q., 72, 73.
Addington (Lord Sidmouth), 47, 61, 64.
Adrianople, capture of, 296.
Adrianople, Treaty of, 107.
Aehrenthal, Count, 327, 338.
Agadir, 327, 330–1.
Aix-la-Chapelle, Conference of, 36, 37.
Alabama case, 215 and *f*, 253, 259–60.
Albania, 318.
Alexander I of Russia, a dreamer, 17.
  his policy in 1814, 20, 22.
  at the Congress of Vienna, 25.
  and the Holy Alliance, 32, 33.
  contrasted with Castlereagh, 34.
  effect upon his mind of the events of 1819–20, 40, 41.